I Hear a Symphony

TRACKING POP

SERIES EDITORS: JOCELYN NEAL, JOHN COVACH, AND ALBIN ZAK

I Hear a Symphony

Motown and Crossover R&B

Andrew Flory

University of Michigan Press • *Ann Arbor*

Published in the United States of America by the
University of Michigan Press
Manufactured in the United States of America
⊗ Printed on acid-free paper

2020   2019   2018   2017   4   3   2   1

Library of Congress Cataloging-in-Publication Data

Names: Flory, Andrew.
Title: I hear a symphony : Motown and crossover R&B / Andrew Flory.
Description: Ann Arbor : University of Michigan Press, [2017] |
Series: Tracking pop | Includes bibliographical references and index.
Identifiers: LCCN 2017011934| ISBN 9780472036868 (pbk. : alk. paper) |
ISBN 9780472117413 (hardcover : alk. paper) | ISBN 9780472122875 (e-book)
Subjects: LCSH: Motown Record Corporation—History. | Rhythm and blues music—
    History and criticism.
Classification: LCC ML3792.M67 F56 2017 | DDC 781.64409774/34—dc23
LC record available at https://lccn.loc.gov/2017011934

Thank you to the Dragan Plamenac Endowment of the American Musicological Society,
funded in part by the National Endowment for the Humanities and the Andrew W.
Mellon Foundation.

Contents

Acknowledgments

IT SEEMS FITTING to begin by thanking the creative people at Motown. The musicians, songwriters, producers, arrangers, technologists, photographers, business people, and so many others. They made the music. They are the inspiration for the book.

So many people have helped me during my Motown research. I've been working on Motown projects for more than a decade and the debts add up. On the industry side, Harry Weinger was the greatest asset that any Motown scholar could want. Keith Hughes was constantly available with resources, time, and advice. Andy Skurow always seemed to get me out of a predicament by knowing something that I thought was unknowable. Others who generously gave me materials, provided advice, or shared their stories include Mick Patrick, Eric Charge, Jim Saphin, David Nathan, David Bell, Shelly Berger, Lindsay Farr, Mike McLean, Andrew Morris, George Troia, Mary Johnstone, Salaam Remi, Beatriz Staples, Mickey Gentille, David Ritz, Howard Manheimer, and Amy Gernon.

I studied in a lot of research facilities while writing this book. I cannot imagine undertaking this enterprise without the help of the librarians and staff at the Detroit Public Library, Eastern Michigan University, the Bentley Historical Library, Bowling Green State University, the British Library, Indiana University (Archives of African-American Music and Culture), UNC–Chapel Hill (Southern Folklife Collection), and the Rock and Roll Hall of Fame Library and Archives. I could fill a page with all of their names and write another book (or two) with the stories that they helped me to find.

I've been lucky to work at several fantastic institutions of higher education while working on Motown research projects. The Music Department at UNC–Chapel Hill was fantastically supportive of my work.

I am also thankful to Tracy Fitzsimmons, Bryon Grigsby, Larry Kaptain, and Michael Stepniak at Shenandoah University for giving me a lot of research support. I now work in an unbelievably encouraging environment at Carleton College. My Music Department colleagues deserve great thanks for their conversations, instigations, and advice. They include Larry Archbold, Justin London, Ron Rodman, Melinda Russell, Nikki Melville, Alex Freeman, Hector Valdivia, Lawrence Burnett, Andrea Mazzariello, Megan Sarno, Carole Engel, Diane Frederickson, Susan Shirk, and Holly Streekstra. The Interlibrary Loan specialists Carleton took a lot of extra time to help me track down rare sources. Thanks also to Carleton's Hewlett-Mellon Fellowship, Gilman Grant, and Humanities Center and to Dean Bev Nagel and President Steve Pozkanzer for their continued support of my research and teaching.

I've encountered thousands of students during the last fifteen years. I have been lucky to teach many classes about popular music, and during each my students have helped me to approach my ideas from different perspectives. It has been inspiring to work with a number of very talented and helpful assistants at both Shenandoah and Carleton, including Robbie Taylor, Alan Weiderman, Billy Barry, Miles Campbell, Jen Winshop, Julian Killough-Miller, Matt Jorizzo, Zhilu Zhang, Stella Fritzell, Sookin Lee, Josh Ruebeck, Ben Weiss, Elaine Rock, Lydia Hanson, Cyrus Deloye, Will Richards, and Molly Hildreth.

I am also thankful to a marvelous circle of people who work in academia, whose interests intersect in some way with mine. Whether I see them at conferences, on stage, or in the studio, I would not view music in the same way if it weren't for people like John Howland, Phil Ford, Travis Stimeling, Mark Burford, David Brackett, Annie Randall, Mark Clague, Bob Fink, Daniel Groll, Jason Decker, Mike Fuerstein, Joanna Love, Chris Reali, Mark Katz, John Brackett, Jon Hiam, Adam Olson, Walt Everett, Phil Gentry, Theo Cateforis, Mary Simonson, Will Fulton, Pat Rivers, and Brian Wright. Many of these friends provided feedback on portions of this manuscript, and I am very grateful for their time and willingness to help.

Chris Hebert has the calm presence that should be required of all editors. He helped me countless times using a supportive but firm style that is extremely difficult to achieve. John Covach has been my academic mentor for fifteen years. I cannot thank him enough. He encouraged me to pursue Motown studies and brought me to the Tracking Pop series in its earliest days. Albin Zak was also invaluable as a mentor. He guided me through the writing process from beginning to end, read numerous sections of the book multiple times, and always convinced me that I could make it better. Mary Francis, Susan Cronin, Mary Hashman, and Joy Margheim from the University of Michigan Press were extremely helpful at the end of the process.

The Flory and Billings families have been very understanding about my odd hours and seemingly endless amounts of work during vacations and holidays. My three children, Charlotte, Ben, and Alexander, are the loves of my life. I wouldn't get through many of my hardest days without their cheerfulness and energy, and they make the best days even better. I reserve the greatest thanks for my wife, Kate. Without her I would never have had the courage to enter academia and I certainly wouldn't have been able to envision or complete a project like this. I dedicate the book to her.

Introduction

> [Motown] did something that you would have to say on paper is impossible. They took black music and beamed it directly to the white American teenager.[1]
>
> —Jerry Wexler

MOTOWN RECORDS was launched in Detroit in 1959 by an African American man named Berry Gordy. It was one of several hundred record companies focused on rhythm and blues (R&B) that opened for business during a steady music industry expansion following the Second World War. R&B was defined by the race of its performers, whose records and live performances relied on outlets catering to a black clientele, such as "black appeal" radio stations, neighborhood record stores, and public spaces where jukeboxes provided entertainment. Most of the small, independent record companies (indies) that specialized in R&B were able to gain a foothold because they had little competition from major labels. But some of the more ambitious R&B firms reached even farther. Outfits like Atlantic, King, and Specialty were successful in the more lucrative mainstream pop market, which required not only going head to head with the majors but also winning over the larger pop-loving public with unfamiliar musical sounds. This phenomenon of commingling music markets that had once been mostly self-contained was known as crossover. It slowly became more common during the 1950s, setting the stage for a musical and cultural revolution in the years to come.

Motown's approach was calculated to transcend the R&B market, and before long its music was at the forefront of sweeping challenges to the record industry's longstanding practices of racial segregation. During the first years of the 1960s, Motown emerged as the most successful R&B

company specializing in crossover. Motown "beamed" its music far and wide. It led a musical tide out of the R&B market that crossed cultural borders and routinely delighted mainstream listeners, attaining a level of mainstream acceptance that was unprecedented for a company of its background. Motown then built on this crossover success in a number of ways. It established one of the industry's most important publishing houses, launched an extensive campaign to reach international audiences, moved into cabaret performance at elite venues, and expanded into mainstream television and film production. Crossover was at the heart of nearly all of Motown's most important initiatives during the 1960s and 1970s. It was the guiding principle that helped Motown to achieve the impossible.

Motown's history is well documented. David Morse published the first serious study of the company in 1971, followed by important works by Peter Benjaminson, Don Waller, Nelson George, Sharon Davis, Gerald Early, Suzanne Smith, Gerald Posner, and many others.[2] With only a few exceptions, however, these books do not contain detailed discussion of the most important aspect of the company's history: its music. Music was the point, after all. It was the focus of Motown's artists and creative staff, and the company's "sound" became a major selling point during the 1960s, when its executives developed marketing slogans like "The Motown Sound" and "The Sound of Young America." Much of the literature about Motown sidesteps this aural history, stripping the company of its soundtrack by telling stories and anecdotes, providing running commentary on record releases, or discussing the context surrounding the firm's musical activities. Although there are many valuable works of social history dealing with Motown, these studies offer little for readers interested in the history of musical style, the manner in which Motown forged sonic identity, or the company's musical relationship with the R&B market.

In this book I situate Motown's music within the larger history of R&B crossover by focusing on four interrelated phenomena: (1) interaction between R&B and other entertainment markets; (2) varying forms of African American identity that were highlighted or deemphasized during these interactions; (3) the different agents responsible for musical creation and identity formation at Motown; and (4) dialogue between musical works that helped to situate Motown's music within both domestic and international markets.

My focus is on Motown and R&B crossover after about 1960, but issues of market interaction, black identity, agency, and dialogue had become central to the work of black performers much earlier in the twentieth century. In the 1880s and 1890s, when African Americans created their first significant body of musical recordings, there was no segregated category for African American musicians.[3] Black recording artists explored a variety of popular musical styles during this time, including vocal ensemble music, jubilee singing, opera and art song, band-oriented dance music, and various other forms of instrumental music. Tim Brooks has suggested that the early recording industry was even liberating to some black performers. The mostly white businessmen who ventured into this new field, he writes, "did not have the luxury of enforcing 'the color line,'" recruiting "any performer who could induce people to buy their records and drop nickels into their automatic music machines."[4] But during the next several decades, systemic racial oppression created a growing chasm between performers of African and European descent. David Suisman's sobering account of this time recalls that African Americans faced "formidable, complex challenges" working in popular music at the turn of the twentieth century, a time when song theft, intimidation, difficulty working with large publishers, and stylistic appropriation plagued many African American entertainment professionals.[5] Segregation and demographic stereotypes eventually led record companies to develop a separate marketing category for African American music during the early 1920s. Following a national craze for urban blues, the industry established a full-fledged "race" market that featured recordings of blues, theatrical songs, religious music, string bands, and jubilee singing.[6]

Race music, which was later recast as R&B, was a demographic-based market within the music business of the United States. As conventionally conceived, it comprised music made by black performers for black audiences. But it was never this simple. From the dawn of the race category, initiated primarily by the mainstream popularity of Mamie Smith's "Crazy Blues" in 1920 and 1921, white buyers purchased race records and white performers created music that used elements gleaned from blues and earlier ragtime. Similarly, black buyers were never limited to purchasing music marketed under the race rubric, nor were black performers restricted to performing in stereotypically "black" styles. The process of detaching markets for race and folk (which was later called country and western) from the American mainstream gained traction nevertheless. These divisions continued to drive demographic markets during the decades following the Second World War and remain at the bedrock of the music industry to the present day.

Writers such as Philip Ennis, Albin Zak, and John Broven have all contributed to our understanding of market interaction during the fascinating period before Motown's arrival on the scene, setting the stage for the story I tell in this book.[7] But apart from trade books that profile companies by discussing artists and their most popular records or studies that focus on styles within R&B, few authors have considered R&B after the 1950s as a market or discussed interaction with the mainstream in a holistic way.[8] The relationship between R&B and the mainstream was complicated, to say the least, and without a larger perspective on the history of R&B it is easy to view Motown as a company that created music by black performers for the purpose of reaching the ears (and wallets) of white audiences. To the contrary, there was a far more intricate web of connections between music that was popular in both the R&B market and the mainstream. Songs, recordings, performers, and styles crossed between markets in often unpredictable and fascinating ways.

Throughout this book I treat R&B as a category that included many different kinds of music created by black performers, and similarly, I use the term *R&B market* as something of a catchall. Swing, blues, doo-wop, girl group, and soul were only some of the musical styles closely associated with R&B during the 1950s and 1960s. As a black-owned company with mostly black performers, Motown formed within and was initially supported by black audiences and was known best for musical styles closely aligned with R&B. Yet Motown's acts were never limited to musical stereotypes. Its artists and executives explored a range of musical styles that are not usually associated with R&B, material that helps to broaden our assessment of African American culture during this period.

Motown asserted cultural identity through its music in many ways, and the company's rhetorical strategies varied markedly. Some of Motown's music connected to social issues and politics, such as the Supremes' "Love Child" or Edwin Starr's "War," revealing perspectives on black consciousness and the long civil rights movement. Themes of place were important, often relating to large-scale African American migration patterns during the first half of the twentieth century.[9] Each of the cities named in Martha and the Vandellas' "Dancing in the Street," for example, had a significant influx of African American residents following World War II, and records like Stevie Wonder's "I Was Made To Love Her" depicted tales of growing up in the South.[10] Compounding aspects of race were a variety of gender perspectives.[11] The countertenor voice of the Temptations' Eddie Kendricks, the Supremes' girl-group naiveté, assertive soul-oriented female vocalists like Gladys Knight, and the gruff vocal style of Four Tops vocalist Levi Stubbs all projected wildly different gender roles. With all of these viewpoints and experiences, Motown's music helped to convey an extremely diverse postwar African American experience in the United States.[12]

As the most successful black-owned company of its time, Motown worked with many powerful and outspoken figures in the African American community during the 1960s and 1970s. It released recordings and produced television and film programs featuring Reverend Martin Luther King Jr., Huey Newton, Jesse Jackson, Bill Cosby, Richard Pryor, Sammy Davis Jr., Margaret Danner, Langston Hughes, Amiri Baraka, and many others. Suzanne Smith has written extensively about Motown's complex relationship with Detroit's black communities, which was evident in the ways the company navigated the political unrest associated with the city's 1967 riots and interacted with political figures and grassroots organizers while simultaneously leading a new form of postwar black capitalism.[13] In local, national, and international campaigns, Motown's promotional efforts often magnified issues of class and region in contradictory and perverse ways. At one point in the mid-1960s, the company advertised the Supremes as glamorous stars who had risen from the poverty of Detroit's Brewster Projects to the highest echelon of the entertainment business while simultaneously leading a new soul style that exploited a simple, rural, "authentic" southern identity. There are countless other examples of seemingly contradictory practices in Motown's history, many of which reflect the complex reality of black society at the time.

Motown often asserted black identity to serve its crossover agenda. Most obviously, the company's artists used comportment, choreography, and image fabrication to depict an idealized black middle class.[14] Against the backdrop of the rising soul movement, Motown groups like the Supremes and the Temptations were visibly "uptown" performers during the last half of the 1960s, performing on prime-time television programs like *The Ed Sullivan Show* and their own specials and working in high-class cabaret nightclubs. These groups used musical style in pointed ways in these mainstream venues, recording standards and interpreting their hits in interesting hybrid forms. In research relating more generally to African American studies, authors such as Wahneema Lubiano, Valerie Smith, and Martin Favor have discussed issues of economics and identity that are especially relevant to these practices. They write about a paradox associated with African American class mobility during the postwar era: as modern members of the black middle class struggled for uplift, their success was often equated with distance from authentic blackness.[15] As my study unfolds, it will become apparent how this double standard followed Motown through its most successful years during the 1960s and 1970s.

Within Motown's ranks there were many people who held important creative roles. Motown was well known during the mid-1960s for its musical "assembly line," a metaphor drawn from the company's proximity to the center of the U.S. automobile industry. In addition to well-known performing artists like Marvin Gaye and the Supremes, Motown employed songwriters, arrangers, backing musicians, technicians, audio engineers, background vocalists, personal managers, publishers, evaluative personnel, and many other agents responsible for shaping its music. The manner in which these people interacted to create a record is often unclear, and their collaborative work makes authorial attribution a difficult and murky task.

Of the many actors who contributed to Motown's creative process, I am especially interested in the role of the record producer. Like a project manager, they oversaw and participated in the entire record-making process, from songwriting and arranging to recording and mixing. In many cases a single producer worked closely with a particular artist for a lengthy period, helping to craft sonic and musical continuity. There were dozens of important producers at Motown during the three decades that the company was independently owned and operated. Throughout the book, I profile the work of several of the most prolific and successful, including Berry Gordy, William "Mickey" Stevenson, Smokey Robinson, the team of Holland-Dozier-Holland, Norman Whitfield, Lionel Richie, and Rick James.[16]

Collaborative agency often leads me to consider Motown itself as a historical agent. While one of our most eminent music historians, Richard Taruskin, cautions that "no historical event or change can be meaningfully asserted unless agents can be specified, and *agents can only be people*," this mandate is too limiting when studying American popular music, which is so often entangled in institutional commercial forces.[17] People were always at Motown's helm, and together they formed a corporate body. What we observe as corporate strategy is often the result of collective agency. It is not always easy to know who was at the center of Motown's decisions, what debate took place, and why policies were enacted. It is sometimes necessary, then, to broaden our conception of agency when dealing with the commercial music industry, allowing a corporation to represent a group of individual participants.

Motown's songs and records were often connected to other releases in interesting ways. Throughout the book I refer to these associations between musical works as *dialogue*.[18] The most commonly cited instances of dialogue in postwar popular music historiography are mid-1950s white cover versions of R&B hits. These notorious records by singers like Pat Boone and Georgia Gibbs used strikingly similar arrangements and the power of the mainstream to overshadow original R&B recordings. More accurately termed "copy" records, releases like these were widely condemned by critics from Langston Hughes to Alan Freed and had a relatively brief heyday.[19]

Far more common in the history of Motown were myriad other forms of dialogue.[20] Both white and black artists recorded Motown songs during the 1960s and 1970s, and this large body of recordings was oriented toward audiences of various ages, regions, and social backgrounds. Some white artists targeted the pop market, but their records were rarely released in temporal proximity to Motown's original versions, and few actually competed with Motown's tracks. Many black acts also recorded Motown songs, making an effort to emulate the company's crossover success, and R&B-oriented companies like Cameo and Chess made popular singles that that sounded a lot like Motown's well-known hits.[21] By the mid-1960s, dialogue of this sort extended far past the borders of the United States. A variety of performers from other countries recorded famous (and some not-so-famous) Motown songs to sell in their own regions; these international versions often used translated texts and adapted the musical features of Motown recordings in interesting ways.

Conversely, Motown artists also recorded non-Motown songs, connecting to different styles, genres, artists, and companies. Beginning early in Motown's history, its artists participated in a tradition of "answer songs" that commented on current hits by creating textual and musical responses. Most of the sources for these songs were originally associated with the R&B market and had already achieved significant crossover success, such as the Silhouettes' "Get a Job" and the Shirelles' "Will You Love Me Tomorrow." Connections like these revealed glimpses of Motown's corporate goals. In later instances, material for album tracks and popular singles was taken from a variety of historic and contemporary sources, connecting Motown's artists to other markets, styles, and epochs. During their most popular period, for example, the Supremes recorded albums of country standards, British Invasion songs, Rodgers and Hart material, selections from the musical *Funny Girl*, and music associated with Sam Cooke. There was also significant dialogue within the Motown catalog. The technique of self-answering (or intracompany answer songs) helped to establish stylistic continuity and fostered public perception of a Motown Sound. Most of Motown's most famous songs were recorded multiple times by a variety of Motown artists, Motown acts created foreign-language versions of their hits for the international market, and the larger Motown catalog had many musical and textual answers within its own ranks.[22] This often led to further instances of allusion, quotation, and contrafact by non-Motown artists.[23]

With these themes in mind, *I Hear a Symphony* focuses on music to consider Motown in the context of postwar R&B crossover. I do not offer a play-by-play account of Motown's output, but musical evidence is at the center of each chapter and fundamental to the book's overall argument. I am especially indebted to a handful of sources that made it possible for me to write this type of book. One of the most important is the ongoing discography by Keith Hughes, *Don't Forget the Motor City*.[24] I have also benefited from the spate of reissued Motown material during the last two decades, particularly the large-scale *Complete Motown Singles* project masterminded by Harry Weinger at Universal Music, Motown's current parent company, with assistance from Motown experts like Hughes and Bill Dahl. In addition to normal commercial releases, through my work as a consultant with Universal Music I have had the privilege to hear many vault recordings, which allowed for more detailed study of Motown's creative processes. This material is at the bedrock of my musical understanding of Motown, especially the sonic attributes often associated with the Motown Sound. Because music is the book's primary topic, I have created about two dozen transcribed musical examples to better illustrate connections between simple musical aspects like formal structure, melody, harmonic content, and instrumentation. None of these examples includes intricate music analysis, and for those who do not read music most are explained in the accompanying text. I also use musical terminology from time to time. This may be off-putting to some readers, but in each case it is the most efficient way to convey the point at hand.

During the long process of writing this book I have conducted a number of very useful interviews with people who worked for Motown. But in contrast to a lengthy tradition of historical scholarship about popular music, I have not used this interview material to derive the majority of my factual material. In the context of a book about subjects who (in some cases) are still living, some may view this as a shortcoming. I found early in my work, however, that after fifty years of questions being asked on the same topics it was often difficult to derive noteworthy material from a Motown artist or employee that was not already available in published form or in an archive.[25] I use these types of interviews, but also broadened my scope to include primary print, audio, and video sources. Industry publications like *Billboard* and *Cash Box* were especially useful for the manner in which they portray R&B as a market, crossover as a business phenomenon, and the changing relationship between R&B and mainstream markets during Motown's most important three decades.

This study was aided by the use of proprietary archival material, the most important of which were the Motown tape filing cards and session logs from the company's Detroit years. Other archival materials were important to my understanding of Motown's inner workings, including collections at the University of Michigan's Bentley Historical Library, Eastern Michigan University, the Detroit Public Library's E. Azalia Hackley Collection, Indiana University's Archives of African American Music and Culture, the British Library, the Library of Congress, the Music Library and Sound Recordings Archives at Bowling Green State University, and the Rock and Roll Hall of Fame Library and Archive, which offered letters, press releases, newspaper clippings, fan club materials, interview transcripts, telegrams, handwritten notes, in-house newsletters, publishing records, photographs, and a wide variety of other ephemera. Several private collectors, most notably Eric Charge, Keith Hughes, and Jim Saphin, provided source items that were not possible to locate in research libraries. George Troia, Mary Johnstone, and Andrew Morris also helped to provide difficult to obtain union documentation.[26]

The book's six chapters follow a general narrative timeline (with some significant overlap), and each considers some aspect of Motown's history with crossover. Chapter 1 begins by discussing the rise of the R&B market in the 1940s and the importance of independent companies in this history. First, I consider instances of crossover before 1960 that were antecedents to Motown's crossover strategy. The story then turns to Detroit, focusing on the creative activities of four Gordy siblings who worked together during the late 1950s and early 1960s in various areas of the music business. Motown had a wide stylistic range as it emerged out of this family group between 1958 and 1962. Gordy's new company used musical attributes, performer type, and answer records to connect with both local communities and proven crossover acts. During a wave of R&B crossover in 1960, several Motown artists became national stars, providing the foundation for the company's future success in the crossover field.

Chapter 2 focuses on the Motown Sound. I argue that the company's vertical integration and fast production pace helped to create stylistic consistency beginning in about 1963. In part, the style that came to be associated with Motown at this time, often called the Motown Sound, was the result of recurrent collaborations between producers, writers, and artists. Among the many important agents during Motown's early years, Smokey Robinson worked as writer and producer for Mary Wells, and the team of Brian Holland, Lamont Dozier, and Eddie Holland collaborated closely with artists like Martha and the Vandellas, the Supremes, and the Four Tops. I define the Motown Sound as a construct incorporating five intertwining elements of composition, arranging, performance, and production: the "Motown Beat," a distinct style of backing vocals, active electric bass lines, adventurous orchestration choices, and targeted uses of reverb. The company began to market the Motown Sound in 1965, which furthered a sense of stylistic unity, and music exhibiting the Motown Sound was extremely popular during the middle of the decade, comprising dozens of the most successful singles released by African American performers in the United States.

Chapter 3 considers Motown's role in the significant strain of R&B called "soul music" that became popular during the 1960s. Elements of the soul style, including musical similarities to gospel and lyrical references to rural life and the South, were present in some of Motown's earliest successful singles. Motown started an imprint called Soul in 1964, and many Motown artists incorporated elements of soul into their most popular records. As soul became more popular with mainstream audiences in the middle of the decade, this segment of the Motown catalog helped to further the company's crossover agenda using a style that sometimes contrasted with the Motown Sound. Soul became the dominant form of crossover R&B during the second half of the 1960s, which radically changed the relationship between R&B and the mainstream. Soul-oriented companies like Atlantic and Stax often used coded elements of class and region to market their music as an alternative to the Motown Sound, creating conflict within the reception of Motown's music. All the while, Motown producers like Norman Whitfield specialized in soul. Whitfield worked with artists like Gladys Knight and the Pips, Marvin Gaye, and the Temptations during the mid-1960s to further soul at Motown and was a pioneer in a later hybrid style called psychedelic soul, which drew equally on elements of R&B and psychedelic rock but was still connected to the Motown Sound in fascinating ways.

The premise of reaching multiple markets extended into international sales for many independent R&B companies during the early 1960s. Motown's connection with listeners outside of the United States is the subject of chapter 4. Britain was an especially important site for American R&B. After Motown established distribution agreements to sell records in the UK, many British musicians became Motown fans and recorded versions of the company's songs, creating instances of transatlantic dialogue. The British music press reported extensively on this practice and some artists, like Brian Poole and the Tremeloes, were heavily criticized, while the motives of groups like the Beatles went mostly unquestioned. British audiences campaigned for Motown's music and, for several years during the mid-1960s, a fan club called the Tamla Motown Appreciation Society served as a de facto overseas promotion arm. Working closely with this society, Motown intensified efforts to reach British audiences beginning in late 1964 by sending artists to the UK, establishing a new imprint, and mounting a large-scale British tour. Continued British interest in soul was evident in Northern Soul, an underground dance-oriented movement centered in northern cities like Manchester and Blackpool that developed during the late 1960s and had its peak activity during the following decade. In addition to the UK, Motown's music was popular in a lot of other countries around the world during the 1960s and 1970s. The company established many local distribution agreements to sell recordings and sent artists on international tours, and some acts even created foreign-language versions of their hits. Local reception of Motown varied in these places, which was evident in the dozens of non-American artists who recorded new versions of Motown material in wide-ranging locales like Australia, Germany, Sweden, Jamaica, Yugoslavia, and many others.

Motown's work in television and film is the subject of chapter 5. Music was an important aspect of early African American crossover in both of these media, and Motown executives showed a heightened interest in pursuing links to both television and film during the mid-1960s. Motown formed a dedicated visual media arm called Motown Productions in 1968, which was active in film and television production for the next two decades, producing television specials for Motown artists, feature films, made-for-television movies, and even cartoon programming. The company also began to record music in California after opening a Los Angeles office in 1963. A slow drift westward accelerated during the late 1960s and early 1970s, and the official Motown headquarters relocated to Los Angeles in June 1972. Two film projects from the time—*Lady Sings the Blues* and *Trouble Man*—asserted the company's new focus on visual media, showing how Diana Ross and Marvin Gaye adapted to their new environs. Throughout the 1970s, Motown continued to release important crossover R&B and myriad other styles of music, its artists appeared on television programs targeted to a variety of audiences, and its record division released soundtracks in conjunction with film and television projects.

Chapter 6 follows the Motown story through the 1980s and beyond. The company remained successful at the beginning of the 1980s in music, television, and film, but the distribution network that supported independent companies collapsed during the early part of the decade. This led to Motown's alignment with the "major" MCA distribution network in 1983. Several years later, Berry Gordy sold the company and his additional Motown holdings, effectively ending Motown's creative life under his leadership. In later years several larger corporations absorbed Motown, and the company's past became an increasingly important element of the Motown brand. Artists, executives, and other agents exploited and celebrated Motown's history in a number of ways, establishing museums and landmarks, writing books, and producing musical reissues, television programs, documentaries, musicals, and new recordings of Motown-like material by former Motown artists. Motown's identity became increasingly diluted during the 1980s, leading to a nonspecific genre that I call *motown*, examples of which popped up regularly in television advertising and on records in various non-Motown settings. From the "You Can't Hurry Love" bass line, which was the basis for many rock songs in the 1980s, to the California Raisins singing "I Heard It through the Grapevine," motown was a powerful force in popular culture. While sometimes detrimental to public perception of the company's history, Motown's ubiquity was the realization of a longtime strategy aimed at reaching the widest possible audience.

Crossover is the binding element of this history, but I use the term in different ways throughout the book. In the first half of the study (chapters 1–3), I use crossover to discuss the manner in which Motown's music navigated record markets within the United States. In these chapters, Motown's crossover success helps to illustrate the changing relationship between R&B and the mainstream, as different styles representing the "black division" of the American record business become popular outside of segregated R&B outlets. In the second half of the book (chapters 4–6), crossover becomes a concept that invokes a broader strategy of reaching audiences beyond U.S. mainstream record buyers. International sales, television and film production, and advertising are all aspects of Motown's history discussed in this part of the book that connect to the crossover principle.

The Supremes' "I Hear a Symphony" is the source of this book's title. Released in October 1965, this record was the group's fifth single in an eighteen-month period to reach the top of the mainstream charts. In contrast with earlier hits by the Supremes—records like "Where Did Our Love Go," "Baby Love," and "Come See about Me—"I Hear a Symphony" displayed a fascinating conflict of representation that embodied Motown's crossover agenda. The lyrics express a young woman's first love, and the manner in which the protagonist describes this feeling—hearing a symphony whenever her boyfriend is near—offers a specific image to accompany her teenage crush. The metaphor extends to the musical arrangement. Unlike the simple harmonic language and primitive foot stomping at the heart of earlier Supremes records like "Where Did Our Love Go," "I Hear a Symphony" has numerous key changes and incorporates sweeping strings that use cartoonish tremolos.

These obvious allusions to "classical music" evoked the learned genre of the symphony, which was historically associated with adult white males, not African Americans, and especially not young, African American women. On the one hand, these references to classical music were tongue in cheek. But in the context of Berry Gordy's larger project—taken together with Motown's emphasis on glamour, intricate choreography, and refined record production—"I Hear a Symphony" served as a symbol. Evoking high art to describe teen romance, the record suggested the scope of Gordy's and Motown's ambition. Crossover, for Motown, meant not only transcending the societal and musical stylistic boundaries shaping record markets but also seeking broad, international legitimation for a body of work and a corporate institution made by black Americans. With this in mind, I adopt the title to encapsulate the themes and topics examined in this book, a story of black musicians in the 1960s and 1970s who animated mainstream music markets with sounds and images associated with blackness. Motown represented the possibility that a commercial music enterprise aimed at teenagers (and comprising some as well) might aspire—in its songwriting, musical performances, arranging, recording, and marketing—to the cultural significance a symphony suggests. As it grew into one of the twentieth century's most successful music and entertainment enterprises, Motown attained a cultural relevance few could have foreseen in its meager beginnings.

ONE | Searching for Motown

A New R&B Market

During the first decades of the twentieth century a new industry centered on sales of commercial recordings transformed music into a mechanical and portable object that could be enjoyed by anyone with the means to purchase a player and some records. The mass-marketed products of inventors like Alexander Graham Bell, Emile Berliner, and Thomas Edison formed the bedrock of a recording-oriented wing of the music business that dramatically changed the manner in which music was consumed. Foundational companies like Victor, Columbia, and Edison created new interest in recordings, quickly becoming major firms with steadily growing sales. Many of their hit records, like Sophie Tucker's "Some of These Days" and the Heidelberg Quintette's "By The Beautiful Sea," were by white performers who had emerged from nineteenth-century performance traditions like minstrelsy, burlesque, and vaudeville. Although audiences had a healthy interest in art music, popular song sold in great numbers and became the engine behind a new mainstream market.[1] Recordings, sheet music, movie and theater tie-ins, and the emerging medium of commercial radio were all intertwined in this new enterprise, forming a web of businesses that worked together to sell American popular music.

Entertainment companies used music to represent cultural difference in a variety of ways. Ethnic music and coon songs, which were among the most popular strains that didn't adhere to white Anglo-Saxon traditions, were often sold to mainstream listeners as cartoonish depictions of life outside of the white middle class. As the industry expanded during the early 1920s one of its biggest growth areas was the "race" market, which focused on records created by black musicians. African Americans had recorded music in a variety of styles since the late nineteenth century, but the popularity of blues records during this time by female singers like Mamie Smith, Mary Stafford, Daisy Martin, and Ethel Waters created an industry stir that put black artists in the sights of many businessmen.[2] Newer record companies like Okeh, Vocalion, Gennett, and Paramount explored various forms of music associated with the black vernacular, including different forms of blues, jazz, and ragtime, helping to align the record business with a long performance history of minstrelsy while giving voice to a new generation of African American musicians.[3]

Records were novelty entertainment and the business surrounding them was built on shaky ground. When the American economy collapsed at the end of the 1920s and recording sales plummeted, race music and black artists were disproportionately affected.[4] Companies like Gennett and Paramount went out of business and other labels that had once recorded black musicians aligned with larger companies, stopped production, or moved away from the race market.[5] It took a long time for the record business to recover, with a number of factors hampering its resurgence. Radio became wildly popular during the 1930s, shellac rations relating to America's involvement in World War II made it difficult to get the supplies needed to mass produce 78 RPM discs, and a union strike in the early 1940s prevented instrumentalists from recording for a period of more than two years.[6]

When sales eventually began to increase after the war, the record business entered a new era in which music by black performers played a large role.[7] The industry decline of the 1930s had created space for firms that focused on race records, and during this period new methods for promoting music to a black demographic had emerged. The growth of radio led to a new "black appeal" format that featured shows targeting African American listeners and black personalities on air.[8] The dance band movement that had been popular before the war established national touring routes for black musicians, a loose network often called the Chitlin' Circuit, which blossomed during the 1940s.[9] Performance spaces catering to black clientele, in addition to related lodging, restaurants, and promotional opportunities, were all part of this live environment. The demand for coin-operated record machines, later called jukeboxes, also rose steadily. A new group of industry salesmen placed these devices in diners, barbershops, and other public spaces, offering music to many patrons who could not afford to own actual records.[10] Other retailers served the "black demographic" by opening stores located in African American neighborhoods, selling race records and other popular hits to patrons who were not permitted to shop alongside white customers in mainstream outlets.[11]

Unlike the initial race record craze of the late 1920s, during and after World War II the music industry began to view the infrastructure that supported black popular music as a distinct, self-contained market. An indication of this occurred in October 1942, when the trade magazine *Billboard* started to cover sales of records by African American performers in a separate category. As a publication developed to support advertisers in the carnival and variety businesses during the late nineteenth century, *Billboard* was not originally a music-oriented enterprise, and the magazine's growing coverage of popular music reflected the resurgence of the recording industry and a heightened importance of the black market. (*Billboard* began to follow the sheet music business in the 1910s, added commentary on radio in the 1920s, and moved into coverage of recorded music with the rise of coin-operated machines in the 1930s.) The first *Billboard* charts to follow the African American market were titled "Harlem Hit Parade" and listed the most popular records of the week as reported by a handful of shops in this well-known African American neighborhood of New York City.[12] In February 1945 the magazine began to use the nonregional term *race records* to describe this category of releases and altered its tracking of black music from sales to jukebox statistics, further reflecting the growing importance of this device in black communities.[13]

The *Billboard* editors renamed the black market yet again in June 1949, this time labeling it with the euphemistic term "Rhythm and Blues" (R&B).[14] This new designation was reflective of changing attitudes toward racial nomenclature, but it also helped to indicate stylistic shifts within black pop at the time. Between the first "Harlem Hit Parade" listing in 1942 and the name change to "Rhythm and Blues" in 1949 there was a curious transformation in the sources for many records listed on these *Billboard* charts. The most popular "Harlem Hit Parade" records during the war—by artists like Louis Jordan, Earl "Fatha" Hines, and Billie Holiday—had been released by large record companies like Decca, Bluebird (RCA-Victor), and the newly formed Capitol. These firms were often called majors; they were well financed and frequently were divisions of larger corporations that had ties to other aspects of the entertainment business. But by the end of the 1940s the new R&B charts were mostly populated with music released by independently owned firms with no larger show-business ties or corporate parentage. The independent companies responsible for releasing the most popular records in the R&B market during this period ranged in size but mostly specialized in music for the black market and had limited financial backing. To be sure, majors continued to support black artists during the late 1940s and early 1950s: Columbia revived the Okeh imprint, Decca released music by Louis Jordan and Ella Fitzgerald (among many others), and Chicago's Mercury records made R&B one of its many priorities after forming in 1945.[15] Yet there was an unmistakable shift in corporate agency over the most popular R&B records during the late 1940s. Majors released only three of the fifteen records that appeared on the first R&B chart in July 1949, and none of these were even in the chart's top ten.

Hundreds of independent firms emerged in the R&B field as the record business started to boom in the 1940s, a handful of which became responsible for the lion's share of hits in the black market. Savoy, King, Specialty, Atlantic, Chess, Modern, and Duke all opened for business in the decade between 1942 and 1952 and were among the most prominent indies of the time.[16] These companies had a lot in common.[17] They were led by hands-on owners and often entrusted creative work to dedicated artists and repertoire (A&R) directors. All but one of the firms listed above were led by white men—most of whom were Jewish. Many of these figureheads had been involved in other areas of the music business before starting labels; some had owned nightclubs and others had run record retail outlets. Most of these companies also maintained a tape-based recording studio, giving them the freedom to control their own recording processes and adding to the consistency and uniqueness of their output.[18] And each was associated with a particular region, interacting closely with local R&B scenes by employing musicians and creative staff and working with clubs, radio, and shops. Home to millions of new migrants during the late 1940s, large metropolitan areas like New York, Chicago, and Los Angeles were important centers for R&B. But so were smaller cities in the American Midwest and South, such as Cincinnati, Houston, and Memphis. In a booming postwar business environment, with innovations in recording technology, accessible record pressing and distribution, and the rise of black appeal radio, these independent firms helped to establish a business model for companies specializing in R&B that would remain viable until the mid-1970s.

Although R&B was becoming more popular at the time, the music business positioned it as a secondary market in a number of ways. R&B signified a performer's race rather than a musical style, aligning with the laws and cultural norms of the United States that limited the ability of black performers to work in the mainstream market.[19] Black musicians belonged to different unions, record companies often used alternate labels to release R&B material, jukebox operators stocked their devices differently in public spaces coded as African American, and stores located in black neighborhoods were usually the best places to find R&B records. Performing on mainstream touring circuits was nearly impossible for black performers due to the need for race-based accommodations, and advertisers were wary of using African Americans to appeal to white buyers, limiting promotional appearances on radio (and later television).[20] These differences were meaningful to an artists' career. Some of the most successful African American artists of the time had little or no success outside of the R&B market, people like Erskine Hawkins, Johnny Moore's Three Blazers, Ruth Brown, the Clovers, and Dinah Washington.

Within this segregated world, there were a variety of styles that were consistently popular on the R&B charts. Some records connected to mainstream trends, including releases by vocal groups like the Ink Spots, young harmony groups like the Orioles, crooners like Billie Holiday, and instrumental dance musicians in the vein of Duke Ellington.[21] Yet, a number of R&B styles had no mainstream representation. Some of this music was adult-oriented, which was evident in the sexual double entendre invoked by records like "My Ding-a-Ling," "Long John Blues," and "Big Ten-Inch Record" or records that celebrated the "high life," such as "Drinkin' Wine Spo-Dee-O-Dee" and "One Scotch, One Bourbon, One Beer." Another popular group of R&B-oriented records featured electric versions of country blues performed by small groups with a single vocalist (who was also often an instrumentalist) backed with drums, guitar, acoustic bass, and sometimes piano and harmonica. This "electric blues" style was especially popular in Chicago, where companies like Chess and Vee-Jay released records performed by artists like Muddy Waters, Howlin' Wolf, and Jimmy Reed.[22] Also popular was a strain of dance-oriented "blues shouting," or jump blues, performed by vocalists like Louis Jordan (Decca), Wynonie Harris and Bull Moose Jackson (King), Eddie "Cleanhead" Vinson (Mercury), and Amos Milburn (Aladdin). These recordings featured accompaniment derived from boogie-woogie and swing, featuring prominent horns and reeds and a standard jazz rhythm section of acoustic bass, piano, and drums.

Multiple versions of a single song were common within the R&B market during the late 1940s, which helped to create a common repertoire among artists and listeners. Jordan and Erskine Hawkins both released successful versions of "Caldonia," for example, and there were four nota-

ble recordings of Cecil Gant's song "I Wonder." "Good Rockin' Tonight"
became popular in versions by both Wynonie Harris and Roy Brown,
and multiple R&B artists had hits with "Corn Bread" and "Cole Slaw."
Songs that were popular with black listeners often elicited responses and
"answer songs" from within the R&B field, creating further dialogue.[23]
Jackie Brenston's "Rocket 88" was a reworked version of Jimmy Liggins's
"Cadillac Boogie." "Drinkin' Wine Spo-Dee-O-Dee" inspired several response songs, including "No Wine, No Women," recorded by Mr. Google
Eyes with Billy Ford and His Musical V-8's. Hank Ballard's "Work with
Me Annie," a song ostensibly about encouraging a woman to dance, was
transformed by Etta James and Johnny Otis into "The Wallflower" (also
called "Roll with Me Henry"), an answer song that took to task the male
character in "Work with Me Annie" by asking him onto the dance floor.
Some R&B artists answered their own hits, creating assemblages of dialogic singles. Roy Brown followed "Good Rockin' Tonight" with "Rockin'
at Midnight" and "Boogie at Midnight"; after their success with "Corn
Bread" the Hal Singer Sextette released "Beef Stew"; and Hank Ballard
continued the narrative of "Work with Me Annie" with "Annie Had a
Baby" and "Annie's Aunt Fannie."

Only a handful of black artists broke out of the R&B mold at the
time. Before 1950, Louis Armstrong, Nat Cole, Ella Fitzgerald, the
Mills Brothers, the Ink Spots, and Louis Jordan were the most popular African Americans in the mainstream market.[24] Armstrong was an
anomaly, whose unique vocal style, virtuosic performance abilities, and
comedic appeal led to massive success that was not shared by many of
his contemporaries. Cole and Fitzgerald recorded mostly jazz-oriented
standards, aligning with other crooners who became popular after the
decline of instrumental big bands during the war. The Ink Spots and
the Mills Brothers were emblematic of a vocal harmony style that had
become popular during the AFM strike of the early 1940s.[25]

Louis Jordan pointed in a new direction. Recording for the major
Decca, he achieved mainstream success with jump blues, a style that had
previously been limited mostly to the R&B market. His crossover hits like
"Is You Is or Is You Ain't (Ma' Baby)" and "Caldonia" freely discussed
black life using a jive vernacular. Like many R&B artists of the time,
Jordan's repertoire came from varied sources and included many interesting examples of how musical dialogue helped to bind the R&B market
during the postwar years. He often performed contemporaneously popular songs, such as "Keep-a-Knockin'" and "Honeysuckle Rose." He also
recorded the last in a series of five popular crossover versions of "Open

the Door Richard," a novelty number that stemmed from a black vaudeville comedy routine.[26] His overall popularity also elicited dialogue from
a variety of mainstream musicians. Jordan's version of "Caldonia," for
example, inspired a recording by Woody Herman that recast the song's
stylized minstrel humor into a mainstream swing setting.

There was a dramatic increase in dialogue like this, which occurred
among markets, during the years immediately following the war. At first,
songs crossed over rather than original recordings. These songs moved
in multiple directions.[27] Louis Prima's "Oh Babe!" started as a pop song
but later found popularity with R&B audiences.[28] "The Hucklebuck,"
which was an adaptation of a Charlie Parker jazz track, was first popular in R&B records by Paul Williams, Roy Milton, and Lionel Hampton
before being interpreted by mainstream artists like Tommy Dorsey and
Frank Sinatra.[29] "Rag Mop" crossed between the country and western,
R&B, and pop markets. It was first successful on the country charts in a
version by Johnnie Lee Wills, the western swing artist who helped to write
the song. It then achieved popularity in the R&B market with recordings
by Joe Liggins, Lionel Hampton, and Doc Sausage and broke into the
pop market with *seven* different recorded versions, the most popular of
which was by the Ames Brothers.

The commercial paths of these songs helps to illustrate how the musical and cultural boundaries between pop, R&B, and country were beginning to slowly erode during the late 1940s and early 1950s. Companies
that supported black artists faced continuing challenges, but market
overlap began to provide new opportunities for independent firms that
specialized in R&B.[30] Before long, R&B records themselves began to
cross over much more frequently, projecting both the songs and sounds
of black America into mainstream outlets. White artists and listeners
showed great interest in R&B-oriented styles and black artists who recorded teen-oriented records for independent companies emerged on
the mainstream radar for the first time.

Record crossover from R&B to the mainstream occurred in four distinct stylistic areas during the 1950s. Teen-oriented male vocal harmony
groups, who were mostly aligned with small independent companies, saw
their records achieve popularity with mainstream listeners beginning in
1953; artists associated with high-energy rock and roll such as Chuck
Berry, Fats Domino, and Little Richard first found success in the mainstream during 1956 and 1957; a cadre of African American male song
stylists, some of whom emerged from vocal group settings, also became
popular in the mainstream in the middle of the decade; and toward the

end of the 1950s African American female harmony groups started to achieve crossover success for the first time. There had been crossover before, but the scope of interaction between R&B and the mainstream during this time was unparalleled in the young history of the recording business.

From Shopkeeper to Record Man

Berry Gordy Jr. was born in Detroit on November 28, 1929, into a tightly knit family that had only recently fled the South.[31] Unlike many accounts of the Great Migration, the mass movement of millions of African Americans to urban areas in the North and West that occurred during this period, the Gordy family's move did not conform to stereotypes of poor southerners leaving home in search of jobs.[32] In 1922 Gordy's father, also named Berry (but called Pops), had left a 168-acre tract of land in Georgia after he received a particularly large payment in his business dealings. His newfound financial stature violated racial codes and challenged societal norms so he and his wife, Bertha, moved the family moved to Detroit, where it was more acceptable to own property and operate small businesses. Pops Gordy was a rural southerner who struggled to conform to the cutthroat dealings of a major metropolitan area, but his financial holdings, business experience, and goals of ownership set him apart from most migrants seeking manual labor on the city's automobile assembly lines.

The Gordy family operated several small businesses in Detroit, including a print shop, a construction firm, and an insurance company—all of which catered to black clientele. By the late 1940s, twenty-five years after their northward move, they had grown into an enterprising, driven, and savvy group of ten (including parents and children) who had a wide range of successful endeavors. Their status was documented in a 1949 profile in *Color*, a glossy magazine that catered to the black middle class. It called the Gordys "America's Most Amazing Family," mentioning Pops Gordy's Georgia sawmill and his more recent contracting business, his brother-in-law Barton's insurance business, and his daughter Esther's employment in the War Department and position as head of the family printing firm (figure 1.1).[33] It also commented on the family's leisure activities, noting that they were expert bowlers and horseback riders and that Berry Jr. had been an avid boxer who played boogie-woogie piano for family entertainment. The article portrayed the Gordys as close knit. "Whenever a Gordy appears in a program, or in any event, whether a

Fig 1.1. A *Color* magazine article from the late 1940s featuring the Gordy family

boogie-woogie contest, boxing match, riding exhibition, bowling tournament, or speech," the article read, "the entire family always finds time to be present and cheer its member to victory or success."[34]

The photograph accompanying this article depicted the family in a parlor scene, dressed in their finest clothes and gathered around a grand piano. They are making music as a form of family entertainment. One Gordy male appears to be singing while the rest of the family listens. The name of the nineteenth-century Norwegian composer Edvard Grieg is visible on the cover of the vocalist's sheet music, but it is doubtful that the sounds of refined art song permeated the room, because Berry Jr. could not perform from a written score. During the shoot, it was more likely that he was entertaining the family with boogie-woogie, creating a conflict between respectable image and vernacular sound that was emblematic of the period.

Berry Gordy Jr.'s interest in music began as the record business was on the rebound.[35] After a stint in Korea from 1951 to 1953, he opened a record store called the 3D Record Mart, a shop where he hoped to "educate customers about the beauty of jazz."[36] Gordy ran the store with his brother, George, and it was located on the same block as the family's print shop and grocery. Record retail was a common route to owning a record company, but Gordy did not really fit the profile of a record man at the time. He was black and from a respectable, tight-knit family who saw business as a form of service to his local community.[37] He didn't run in the same circles as the dominant Jewish businessmen who ran King, Specialty, and Chess or the rough African American restaurateur Don Robey who owned Duke and Peacock. In the end, Gordy wasn't very successful in the record retail business and the 3D Record Shop closed not long after it opened.

Gordy took different jobs after this, working as a cookware salesman and an autoworker for Lincoln-Mercury (a division of Ford). A lifelong musical amateur, his interest in music turned to songwriting. He frequented Detroit's downtown clubs, like the Flame Show Bar, where four of his siblings—Gwen, Anna, Robert, and George—ran the photo concession, giving him entrée to the local music business. The bar manager at the Flame Show was a man named Al Green (no relation to the singer), who owned a music publishing company called Pearl Music and represented several artists, including a Detroit-based singer named Jackie Wilson. Green introduced Gordy to a local musician named Roquel "Billy" Davis, also known as Tyran Carlo. Before long, Gordy, Davis, and Berry's sister Gwen began to write songs together with Wilson in mind.[38]

Wilson had just left the Dominoes, a vocal harmony group that recorded for Federal (a King subsidiary) with a long history as a successful R&B act. Their 1951 record "Sixty Minute Man" had been a crossover hit despite its decidedly adult-oriented lyrics. The group had recorded seven successful R&B records in the two years following, a period when lead vocalist Clyde McPhatter became its featured member. McPhatter then departed the Dominoes in mid-1953 to form the Drifters (on Atlantic) and went on to a successful solo career. Wilson, a native Detroiter, stepped in as his replacement, performing lead vocals on records like "You Can't Keep a Good Man Down" and "Rags to Riches." The group declined in popularity after McPhatter's departure, however, and Wilson left the Dominoes in mid-1957 after recording mostly as a backing vocalist on more than a dozen singles that did not appear on either the R&B or pop charts. When he began working with the Gordys and Davis, Wilson had just returned Detroit to regroup. He connected with Green, who died shortly thereafter, and Nat Tarnopol, who helped him sign with Decca's Brunswick subsidiary, jump-starting a new solo career.[39]

It was an auspicious time for African American male vocalists. Against the backdrop of rock and roll singers and vocal harmony groups, recordings by black men performing as song stylists began to achieve mainstream popularity with considerable regularity during the late 1950s. Some of these vocalists, such as Al Hibbler, Johnny Mathis, and Harry Belafonte, had significant support from mainstream markets, in large part because they were signed to major labels. These singers were mostly "album artists," a growing area for artists of color who sought to simultaneously navigate the ephemeral world of single releases in addition to a more adult-oriented album market.[40] As their fortunes grew during the 1950s, independent companies that specialized in R&B began to cultivate this type of vocalist, eventually achieving success with records by pop-oriented male African American balladeers like Johnny Ace, McPhatter, Chuck Willis, Thurston Harris, and Sam Cooke.

Wilson joined this new cadre of crossover song stylists with material written by Gordy's new team. His first record, "Reet Petite," appeared on the record charts in November 1957, and during the next eighteen months Gordy helped to write six more Wilson A-sides.[41] The most popular of these was "Lonely Teardrops," which peaked in popularity during December 1958. This record mixes a Latin-based groove with square backing vocals and mildly suggestive lyrics. The most prominent aspect of the recording is Wilson's vocal performance, which combines learned head voice with melismatic runs emblematic of African American performance traditions, all while creating a sense of urgency because of the vocal line's remarkably high range. This mélange of ethnic and class references in "Reet Petite" foreshadowed many of Gordy's later productions.[42]

Success with Wilson helped Gordy and Davis place songs with other artists. They wrote or produced more than a hundred sides in 1957 and 1958 with Gordy's siblings Anna, Gwen, and Robert and other collaborators in varying combinations. These records appeared on a wide range of labels, including Federal, Aladdin, End, Mercury, Chess (and its Argo subsidiary), and Back Beat (a Duke subsidiary). Apart from Wilson's records, this group's most popular release was "It's So Fine," a song written for LaVern Baker that was a stylistic continuation of her previous hits "Jim Dandy" and "Jim Dandy Got Married."

As his own writing progressed, Berry Gordy also began to work with other collaborators, most notably a young performer that he managed named William "Smokey" Robinson. Robinson was seventeen when he met Gordy in late 1957; he was little more than a local kid who fronted a young vocal harmony group called the Matadors. But he fancied himself a writer and had a lot to learn from Gordy, who was more than ten years his senior. Moreover, Robinson's brand of teen-oriented vocal harmony, often called doo-wop, was one of the new styles that Gordy was starting to embrace.

Gordy began to produce many of his own recordings during 1958 and 1959, which allowed him to further explore arranging and technological embellishment. Despite national hits with singers like Jackie Wilson, Etta James, and LaVern Baker, Gordy's productions often used local performers. Most of his music appeared on independent labels controlled by other people.[43] Working closely with his new wife Raynoma, Gordy leased records to larger companies based outside of Detroit, a common arrangement at the time in which a small-time producer made a record and then turned to a more-established company to finance printing and distribution. In 1958, Gordy released a single called "Got a Job" in this manner through New York–based End Records. It was the first single by Robinson's group, now called the Miracles. A commentary on the travails of having to perform menial labor, Robinson, Davis, and Gordy had crafted the text of "Got a Job" as a response to the current Silhouettes crossover hit "Get a Job."

Gordy recorded a number of other records that appeared on End, and he forged similar arrangements with imprints like Coral, Mercury, and Aladdin. His most significant partnership was with United Artists, a label that leased recordings of Wyatt "Big Boy" Shepherd, Eddie Holland, and Marv Johnson. Working under the auspices of this United Artists agreement, in late 1958 Gordy wrote and produced the record "Come to Me" for Johnson at a local studio called United Sound Systems. The vocal delivery on this recording was unmistakably similar to Jackie Wilson's. The group-harmony backing vocals, obbligato saxophone, and heavy backbeat of the arrangement similarly drew upon styles explored by Wilson, the Miracles, and other groups for which the Gordy collective had written and produced recordings. Incorporating elements that had recently proven successful for African American artists in multiple markets, "Come to Me" had great crossover potential. Gordy leased it to United Artists for national distribution but also released it locally on his own new startup imprint.

Needing $800 to cover his end of this deal, Gordy approached his family with the hopes of borrowing from a cooperative family savings account. This money was not easy to get. The Gordy family was serious about its finances and wary of Berry's potential for success. The savings co-op was administered by a board and it required a contract to complete the loan, a level of fiscal conservatism that was indicative of the manner in which the family approached its business endeavors.[44] After some debate, the agreement eventually was ratified, and in January 1959 "Come to Me" was released regionally on Berry Gordy's new Tamla label.

"Come to Me" was remarkably successful in light of the other releases created by people in Gordy's orbit at the time, appearing in prominent positions on the national record charts in both the R&B and pop markets. (In early April 1959 "Come to Me" literally surpassed Jackie Wilson's "Lonely Teardrops" on the *Billboard* "Hot R&B Sides" chart.)[45] But the fact that "Come to Me" was a United Artists single was a reminder that Gordy still did not have the wherewithal to release music on a national scale. Because of contractual obligations established during this period, he continued to work as a songwriter and producer for music released on labels he did not control until 1963, several years after forming his own record firm. His recordings with Johnson, who was signed to United Artists, were the most significant of these outside projects. Gordy and his team wrote or produced more than a dozen Johnson singles between 1959 and early 1963, several of which rose to the top ten of the national R&B and pop charts. These singles were sonically interchangeable with Gordy's other productions, but their affiliation with United Artists was a relic of Gordy's industry status in early 1959.

Berry Gordy's interaction with Chicago-based Chess Records during these early years was also significant. In 1960 Chess recorded Etta James's "All I Could Do Was Cry," one of the Gordy collective's most popular songs, and released it on the jazz-oriented subsidiary Argo. During the same period Chess also leased several of Gordy's records for national distribution, including Ron and Bill's "It" and the Miracles' "Bad Girl" and "All I Want (Is You)." (In the Detroit region "Bad Girl" appeared on a new Gordy-owned imprint called Motown, which marked the first time this name appeared in print.) Chess similarly distributed releases on Anna Records, a company formed by Gwen Gordy and Billy Davis in April 1959. About two dozen singles appeared on Anna during 1959 and 1960, the most popular of which was Barrett Strong's "Money (That's What I Want)," a track written by Berry Gordy and a Motown secretary named Janie Bradford and produced by Gordy. It was one of the few records not produced by Davis to appear on Anna.

In a convoluted, family-oriented business deal, "Money" was released in August 1959 on Berry Gordy's Tamla imprint then leased to Anna later in the year to receive national distribution through Chess. It became a runaway hit, rising to number two on the "Hot R&B Sides" and nearly reaching the top twenty of the "Hot 100" during the early months of 1960. "Money" was unlike anything Gordy had ever released. The song used a twelve-bar blues form, Strong's vocal performance incorporated a grainy baritone that also evoked the blues, and the record's backing vocals were raw and amateurish. The lyrics were similarly crude and direct, drawing on African American vernacular tropes in a manner that Gordy's writing usually avoided.

Gordy's relationship with Chess fostered closer dealings with a performer, songwriter, and producer named Harvey Fuqua. Fuqua was the nephew of Charlie Fuqua, an original member of the Ink Spots, and he had also been a member of the Moonglows, whose 1954 recording of "Sincerely" was one of the first significant doo-wop crossover records. During his time at Chess, Fuqua recorded several songs written with Gordy and his frequent collaborators, including "See Saw," "Soda Pop," and "Don't Be Afraid to Love," a song Fuqua wrote with Davis and Gordy and recorded as a solo act to support a performance included in the 1959 Alan Freed jukebox film *Go Johnny Go!*[46] As the Moonglows declined in popularity, Fuqua was employed for a short time as a Chess executive and then began to focus more closely on creative work at Anna Records. Fuqua's interest in building a label, along with his friendship with Davis, led him to move from Chicago to Detroit.[47] After relocating, Fuqua collaborated regularly with the creative group loosely surrounding the Gordy family, writing songs for Anna artists and working tirelessly to develop artists' costumes, choreography, and comportment.

The line between Anna and Tamla grew increasingly sharp during 1959, with Fuqua, Davis, and Gwen running their label and Berry working on his various projects. Fuqua's connection to the Gordy family intensified when he and Gwen Gordy married in 1961. Anna Records ceased production at this time, and Davis moved to Chicago to form the Chess subsidiary Check-Mate.[48] "I would see [Berry Gordy] practically every weekend," Fuqua later remembered, but "I was on one side and I said, 'I ain't going on the other.'"[49] Despite this distance, Fuqua's working methods and professional experience made a huge impact on Berry Gordy during a period in which he was quickly becoming a formidable "record man."

Motown

Berry Gordy's first significant step toward creative self-sufficiency was to establish a publishing firm, which he called Jobete.[50] Working with his second wife and creative partner Raynoma, he applied for his first copyrights under the auspices of Jobete in November 1958 and incorporated the company in the state of Michigan in June 1959. His first batch of copyright applications included material used for Miracles and Frances Burnett records that were leased to Chess and Coral ("All I Want [Is You]" and "How I Miss You So"); a vocal jazz song recorded later by Marvin Gaye for Tamla ("Let Your Conscience Be Your Guide"); demos written for his related companies called Ray Music and Rayber Music ("Crying Alone" and "Patty Cake"); and Johnson's "Come to Me."[51] Gordy applied for copyrights on more than seventy songs before the end of 1959, nearly three times the number that he released officially on disc.

Gordy was becoming a well-known record man in Detroit. A profile published in city's major black newspaper, the *Michigan Chronicle*, showed how the local African American community perceived his place in the music business at the time (figure 1.2).[52] The piece called him an "independent producer of records," noting specifically his work with United Artists and Chess, and cited three businesses that Gordy led as president: Jobete, Tamla, and Rayber, which was a music writing company. The article also pointed out that Berry was "born into a family which was to produce its share of contributions to the benefit of a great city."

Writing and publishing music was relatively inexpensive, but recording demonstration material and full-fledged productions for release was more financially taxing. Gordy worked in various Detroit-based studios during this period to produce recordings and demos of his songs. The most prominent of these was United Sound Systems, which was the best studio in town. It had been in operation since the 1930s, and it offered modern technological amenities and a large space for live recording. Gordy recorded there many times, producing tracks for the Miracles, his brother Robert, Barrett Strong, and Marv Johnson.[53] But United wasn't appropriate for every job. The Rayber portion of his business was designed to write material and demonstrate it using documentary recordings.[54] United was expensive, and given Rayber's small scale it was more cost effective for Gordy to maintain his own facility.

After working out of his sister Gwen's house and an apartment at 1719 Gladstone that he shared Raynoma, in mid-1959 Gordy purchased

From Boxing to Music

★ ★ ★ ★ ★ ★ ★

Berry Gordy Jr. Finds Fame in Composing

Turn on your radio today and chances are excellent the song you hear will have been written by a young Detroiter who hung up boxing gloves for the tools of the composer.

At 28, Berry Gordy, Jr., is winning nation-wide recognition for his songwriting talents on the basis of several tunes which have satapulted many of today's vocalists to the top in their profession.

Born into a family which was to produce its share of contributions to the benefit of a great city, young Berry soon acquired a natural talent for music.

This was evinced in his ability to play the piano at the age of five.

With his sister Gwendolyn, also a songwriter, Berry developed a creative style of his own, style evident in such songs as "Reet Petite", "To Be Loved", "Lonely Teardrops" and "I'll Be Satisfied".

Everything had its beginning and with Berry it started following his graduation from Northeastern high school in 1948.

After a stint with the army during the Korean conflict, Berry returned to his native Detroit and worked in an automobile factory.

But under the influence of Gwendolyn, young Gordy took

BERRY GORDY, JR.

the plunge into the myriad field of music.

The choice has been gratifying.

The first years were typical: writing, rewriting, hoping and writing.

But Berry had one ace —a rising young singer who often tried out his songs.

Then came the moment and the song: "Reet Petite" which made a national figure of Jackie Wilson and gave that essential lift to Gordy.

Other successes followed and Berry was on his way.

He wrote "Come To Me" which is bringing laurels to vocalist Marv Johnson and followed it with "I'm Coming Home".

Singer Eddie Holland is riding toward prominence with Gordy's "Merry-Go-Round".

Other stars — LaVerne Baker, Bob Kayli, Nick Noble and Frances Burnette — have attained wide popularity with songs written by young Gordy.

In addition to composing, Berry functions in the business facet of music as president of the Jobete Music Publishing Company, Inc., the Tamla Recording Company and the Rayber Music Writing Company, all with headquarters in Detroit.

He is an independent producer of records, United Artists and Chess records.

During his recording sessions, Berry provides a vocal group, the Rayber Voices; and a band, the Swinging Tigers.

Many young entertainers have found contact with Berry to be a stepping stone to fame through his managerial talents and compositions.

Primarily among these are The Miracles, the first group with whom Berry worked, and the same group which received acclaim for their performance of Gordy's composition "Bad Girl".

In retrospect, the music world has profited immensely since Gordy decided to quit the boxing profession several years ago to make the fateful decision to enter music.

Fig 1.2. A 1959 profile of Berry Gordy Jr. in the *Michigan Chronicle*

a rudimentary setup of recording apparatus from local studio owner Bristoe Bryant and moved his operations to a former photography studio at 2648 West Grand Boulevard.[55] The Gordy contracting business converted the main floor of the house into a recording studio and office space. There were only a handful of Tamla releases at the time, and the name Motown had yet to appear in print, but with an established project studio at his disposal Gordy was now able to record music for his own imprints, a function that quickly became the facility's main focus. Housed in an odd space that was once a garage, the 2648 West Grand Boulevard studio became a sonic laboratory for Gordy's audio experimentation. He worked closely with performer and producer Robert Bateman to operate and maintain his new equipment and took great interest in the technological and creative aspects of recording. In this space, Gordy slowly developed the devices, personnel, and experience required to use recordings in a manner that far surpassed simple documentation, instead imbuing his recorded works with indelible layers of electronic mediation.

Rather than shopping his songs to other artists or leasing his recordings to outside companies, Gordy began to use the Tamla and Motown imprints to release the recordings that he wrote and recorded. Still identifying mostly as a songwriter, he worked under the auspices of Rayber and Jobete for about fifteen months before incorporating Motown Records in April 1960.[56] With Billy Davis, Harvey Fuqua, and Gwen Gordy focused on their own endeavors, Robinson and Raynoma helped to lead a new cast of characters in this emerging Motown venture, including Bateman, Brian Holland, Janie Bradford, and a host of other creative and technical support staff. Several people assumed foundational business roles at this time, including sales director Barney Ales, billing director and later head of Jobete publishing Loucye Gordy Wakefield, publicist Al Abrams, A&R head William "Mickey" Stevenson, and head of Motown's International Talent Management managerial arm (ITMI) Esther Gordy Edwards.[57] Gordy's early success gave him inroads with many of the regional firms that made up a well-trodden distribution network for independent companies, including Schwartz Brothers in the Washington, D.C., area and Mainline Distribution in Philadelphia.[58]

The songs and recordings flowed freely. He released about 125 singles between 1959 and 1962, far more than the various ventures of his sister Gwen.[59] About a quarter of these singles appeared on the national *Billboard* charts, which was a remarkably favorable success rate (table 1.1).[60] But Motown's musical character was still far from established, and many of the people and styles represented in this body of work were fleeting. Most of the popular Motown acts at the time, including the Marvelettes, the Contours, and Mary Wells, did not have successful careers past the mid-1960s. Others who emerged later as the most important artists at the company—acts like the Supremes, the Temptations, Marvin Gaye, and the Martha and the Vandellas—made Motown recordings in this period with little success.

Motown experimented with many different styles during the late 1950s and early 1960s. Many of the company's records reflected a close relationship with the black community of Detroit and had little potential for national crossover. Gordy released a lot of gospel music during this

Table 1.1. Motown records released before January 1963 that appeared on the *Billboard* charts

Release	Artist	Title	Pop	R&B
1/59	Marv Johnson	Come to Me	30	6
8/59	Barrett Strong	Money (That's What I Want)	23	2
9/59	The Miracles	Bad Girl	93	
9/60	Mary Wells	Bye Bye Baby	45	8
9/60	Singin' Sammy Ward	Who's the Fool		23
10/60	The Miracles	Shop Around	2	1
2/61	The Miracles	Ain't It Baby	49	15
6/61	The Marvelettes	Please Mr. Postman	1	1
6/61	Mary Wells	I Don't Want to Take a Chance	33	9
6/61	The Miracles	Broken Hearted	97	
6/61	The Miracles	Mighty Good Lovin'	51	21
9/61	The Miracles	Everybody's Gotta Pay Some Dues	52	11
10/61	Eddie Holland	Jamie	30	6
10/61	The Valadiers	Greetings (This Is Uncle Sam)	89	
12/61	The Marvelettes	Twistin' Postman	34	13
12/61	The Miracles	What's So Good about Good-by	35	16
2/62	Mary Wells	The One Who Really Loves You	8	2
3/62	The Temptations	(You're My) Dream Come True		22
4/62	The Marvelettes	Playboy	7	4
4/62	The Miracles	I'll Try Something New	39	11
5/62	The Supremes	Your Heart Belongs to Me	95	
6/62	The Contours	Do You Love Me	3	1
7/62	Marvin Gaye	Stubborn Kind of Fellow	46	8
7/62	Mary Wells	You Beat Me to the Punch	9	1
7/62	The Marvelettes	Beechwood 4–5789	17	7
7/62	The Marvelettes	Someday, Someway		8
7/62	The Miracles	Way over There	94	
10/62	Mary Wells	Two Lovers	7	1
10/62	The Marvelettes	Strange I Know	49	10
11/62	The Miracles	You've Really Got a Hold on Me	8	1
11/62	The Supremes	Let Me Go the Right Way	90	26
12/62	Marvin Gaye	Hitch Hike	30	12

time—eight singles and two full-length albums—and even created a dedicated gospel imprint called Divinity.[61] He worked on spoken-word projects by African American poets and preachers, including a prominent release called *The Great March to Freedom*, which featured a recording of Martin Luther King Jr. performing his "I Have a Dream" speech during a visit to Detroit in mid-1963.[62] After the March on Washington that summer and a series of lawsuits with King, who was involved in disputes with several record companies that wanted to capitalize on his growing national popularity, Motown released another King album that commemorated his more famous Washington speech called *The Great March on Washington*. Several jazz-oriented releases also appeared on Motown imprints.[63] Marvin Gaye released an album and several singles containing middle-of-the-road standards and the company initiated a short-lived imprint called Workshop Jazz in 1962, through which it released six singles and nearly a dozen LPs.

Not all of Motown's music from the time aligned with stereotypes of black culture. The first solo female act to release a single on the Motown imprint was Debbie Dean, a white woman who recorded about a dozen songs in a style that resembled the music of Brenda Lee and Connie Francis. Motown also released a number of records that aligned with the country market during this period.[64] White rockabilly performer Johnny Powers worked at Motown in various capacities (as songwriter, producer, and singer), although little of his music was released at the time. Andre Williams, a black performer who played rockabilly, contributed similarly to many Motown singles in the early 1960s. Robert Gordy's "Small Sad Sam" was a parody of Jimmy Dean's contemporaneous hit "Big Bad John," a record that had recently reached the top of both the country and western and pop charts.[65] Mickey Woods's "They Rode through the Valley" was a western-themed response to Larry Verne's historical novelty hit "Mr. Custer."[66] About a dozen other country-oriented records appeared on Motown imprints between 1963 and 1965, many of which were produced by Al Klein and released on the company's new Mel-O-Dy label.[67]

Most of Motown's records connected with trends in R&B, however, especially those that had a proven history of pop crossover. The company's handful of answer songs from the period were in dialogue with hits by vocal harmony groups like Jerry Butler and the Impressions and The Four Seasons, girl groups like the Shirelles, and Chubby Checker's various Twist releases (table 1.2).[68] Other Motown records similarly reflected popular R&B styles of the time. The first singles by the Contours connected to the emerging soul movement, especially the 1962 hit "Do

You Love Me." Elements of doo-wop were present in the backing vocals of many arrangements, and the company released more than a dozen singles by vocal harmony groups like the Satintones and the Contours.[69] The Miracles were Motown's most successful male-oriented vocal group, scoring a half-dozen singles on the national pop charts before the end of 1962. Their most popular record was "Shop Around," which straddled old and new styles by beginning with an old-fashioned Tin Pan Alley verse ("When I became of age") before launching into a more contemporary section in which Robinson used vocal range and melisma to propel his performance.

Motown's records explored a variety of musical identities common in the R&B market, depicting a range of class representation within African American communities. Music by Amos Milburn, Singin' Sammy Ward, Gino Parks, and Barrett Strong aligned with the blues tradition, while singers like Chico Leverett, Eugene Remus, and Henry Lumpkin emulated the traditional song stylists of the late 1950s. Motown had much more success with lighter song stylists. One of the company's hits in this style was "Jamie," performed by Eddie Holland, a singer who had once sung on Gordy's song demos for Jackie Wilson.[70] "Jamie" connected to Wilson's style in a number of ways, including Holland's enunciation throughout the record, the high range of his vocal performance, the Latin groove under the verse, and the track's soaring string arrangement. Marvin Gaye was another popular Motown song stylist during this

Table 1.2. Selected Motown answer songs, 1957–62

Original release	Motown answer
The Silhouettes, "Get a Job"	The Miracles, "Got a Job"
Jerry Butler and the Impressions, "For Your Precious Love"	The Temptations, "Your Wonderful Love"
Chubby Checker, "The Twist"	The Twistin' Kings, *Twistin' the World Around*
Gene Chandler, "Duke of Earl"	Little Otis, "I Out-Duked the Duke"
The Shirelles, "Will You Love Me Tomorrow"	The Satintones, "Tomorrow and Always"
The Four Seasons, "Sherry"	The Temptations, "Paradise"
Jimmy Dean, "Big Bad John"	Bob Kayli, "Small Sad Sam"
Larry Verne, "Mr. Custer"	Popcorn and the Mohawks, "Custer's Last Man" Mickey Woods, "They Rode through the Valley" The Valadiers, "Please Mr. Kennedy"

period. After recording a number of unsuccessful records in an adult-oriented standards style, Gaye released a series of upbeat pop singles that achieved moderate crossover, culminating with "Pride and Joy" in mid-1963. Unlike his middle-of-the-road pop, Gaye's newer singles pointed to a new direction for crossover R&B that would flower mid-decade, in which pop-oriented vocalists used vernacular language, musical accompaniment related to blues, and grainier singing styles.

Motown's female artists were equally as varied in the early 1960s. Mary Wells released her first Motown single in late 1960 and emerged as a national star in 1962, joining a group of solo female vocalists in the larger R&B market who used a similar youth-oriented style, such as Ketty Lester, Barbara George, and Barbara Lynn.[71] The popularity of Wells's tracks like "The One Who Really Loves You" and "You Beat Me to the Punch" made her one of Motown's most popular acts. Motown also released music by two new girl groups in 1961, who used "choirgirl diction" and "focused, ringing timbres of their upper vocal registers" to sublimate their age and sexual character.[72] One of these groups was the Supremes, who struggled for several years before releasing a successful single. The other, the Marvelettes, was immediately popular. The debut Marvelettes single, "Please Mr. Postman," became the first Motown release to reach the top of both the pop and R&B *Billboard* charts.

Motown's music embodied a tension between older, segregated forms of R&B and the emerging styles of black pop positioned for crossover success. On one hand, the use of adult-oriented themes and double entendre revealed the company's roots in a segregated postwar R&B market. Chico Leverett bragged about his "long Cadillac Fleetwood" in "Solid Sender" and Barrett Strong's "You Knows What to Do," Eugene Remus's "Gotta Have Your Lovin'," the Contours' "Whole Lotta Woman," and the early Supremes single "Buttered Popcorn" all used overtly sexual texts.[73] Other tracks explored newer views on sex and dating. The Miracles' track "Bad Girl" portrayed a female who had engaged in sexual behavior but wanted "to be free" of commitment. Similarly, LaBrenda Ben's "The Chaperone" was written from the perspective of a young female who feels constrained by a conservative overseer. Like other teen-oriented companies at the time Motown regularly employed older women in this manner, including members of the Gordy family, to serve as models of personal and professional behavior and keep its young female artists "respectable" when representing the company on live performance tours.[74]

Several instrumental Motown releases further connected to R&B

market trends. One of these was "Snake Walk" by the Swinging Tigers, which explored a style similar to crossover hits by King Curtis, the Mar-Keys, and Booker T. and the MGs.[75] Amid the national fad surrounding "The Twist" that began in late 1960, the company also released an LP called *Twistin' the World Around*, which contained tracks that set the twist in a series of different settings. The collection had an erudite twist ("The White House Twist"), a yuletide interpretation ("The Xmas Twist"), a slower twist for geriatric audiences ("The Old Folks Twist"), and two "ethnic" versions of the twist that used musical tropes and spoken elements to connect to the twist theme. The first, the "Mexican Twist," begins with someone in a feigned accent asking, "Eh, Manuel, why go to the bullfight when you can do the twist?" The other, the "Congo Twist," was also released as a two-part single. It mentions the recently executed Congolese leader Patrice Lumumba before launching into a tom-tom-fueled percussion groove with little relation to the twelve-bar dance forms that dominate the other tracks on the album.

Many features of the early Motown catalog served as harbingers of the company's style and approach later in the 1960s. One was the inclusion of orchestral instruments on selected tracks to "sweeten" their sonic character. The company had several guitarists in its emerging backing band, but early Motown records often deemphasized this instrument's role, echoing instead a larger trend toward elaborate string arrangements in the R&B market. Early singles like "Everybody's Got to Pay Some Dues" and "What's So Good about Good-By" were arranged by Riley Hampton and recorded in Chicago.[76] The contrast between strings and guitar, and the manner in which they represented "high" and "low" culture, were significant for Motown and other R&B firms at the time. During a period in which African American acts hoped to achieve mainstream success, foregrounding string arrangements was one manner of sonically aligning with an integrationist black middle class. Musicologist Robert Fink has written about class tensions like this in Motown's music, citing a gap between the image projected in the Gordy *Color* profile and the raucous gospel style of the Miracles' "Way over There." Likening the message of "Way over There" to a statement on Berry Gordy's class aspirations within the early Motown enterprise, he argues that the company's early music exhibited both social and musical teleology and that the increasing use of strings helps to further this "move" toward the mainstream.[77]

Underpinning a handful of hits that are still well known fifty years later, Motown released more than a hundred mostly forgotten singles (and a few long-play albums) during the first years of the 1960s that revealed a company searching for an artistic center. One single portrayed naïve pop appropriate for teenagers, while the next offered suggestive adult-oriented R&B. Gospel music was complemented by insolent recollections of Custer's Last Stand, and comedic doo-wop appeared alongside distorted instrumental dance music. Some releases showed strong connections to the local African American community and the work of other independent labels based in Detroit, and other records did not fit neatly into African American stereotypes at all, revealing connections to other regions and styles. "One of the most striking features of Motown's early output," writes R&B historian Brian Ward, "was not its homogeneity, but its diversity."[78]

From R&B to Mainstream

In 1960, the year that Berry Gordy incorporated Motown, a rash of African American artists crossed into the mainstream. In November, African American singers or groups performed six of the top-ten records in the United States (and half of the top twenty). Crossover was so common that the industry publication *Cash Box* stopped tracking a separate R&B chart for most of the year.[79] In contrast with recordings by black vocal harmony groups and rock and roll outfits that had crossed over so regularly after the mid-1950s, many of the records that achieved mainstream popularity that year were by male song stylists. Unchanged from the 1950s was the fact that most of the African American artists represented in the upper reaches of the *Billboard* and *Cash Box* pop charts recorded for independent companies, although a few acts had recently made the move to a more stable major. Harkening back to the success of artists like Nat "King" Cole and the Ink Spots in the 1940s, the material featured in these crossover recordings was usually tailored to a wide audience, and some black artists even found more success in the pop market than the R&B field. The new decade had brought new potential for crossover, and independent companies like Motown benefited greatly from the mainstream market taking notice of popular black artists.

Only a year removed from his last collaboration with Gordy and Davis, Jackie Wilson enjoyed a double-sided hit with "Night" and "Doggin' Around" and released several more crossover hits before the end of the year. Marv Johnson's "You Got What It Takes" reached the pop top ten in February 1960 and he released four more singles that year, all written and produced by Gordy and released on United Artists.[80] A spate of other African American male vocalists followed. In March and May, respectively, Jimmy Jones nearly topped the pop charts with "Handy Man" and "Good Timin'" (both on MGM's Cub imprint); Billy Bland's "Let the Little Girl Dance" (Old Town) rose to peak popularity in May; Ron Holden's "Love You So" (Donna) entered the pop top ten in June; "A Million to One" (Promo) by Jimmy Charles became a crossover hit in October; and Joe Jones's recording of "You Talk Too Much" (Ric) peaked in November. Most of these men recorded for indies, but only Holden's record betrayed a sense of amateurishness. The others were all professionally produced, incorporating crafty arrangements, interesting orchestration, skilled backing vocalists, audio enhancement (especially reverb), and an approachable vocality that hinted at stereotypical African American aspects of melisma and slurred pronunciation while focusing mostly on singing in a style redolent of Western vocal training.

Several figures who had been important in 1950s R&B continued to release popular crossover singles in 1960. Ray Charles left a successful career at Atlantic to sign with ABC-Paramount, where his first successful ABC single, "Georgia on My Mind," was a massive hit. Brook Benton released two hits on Mercury, "It's Just a Matter of Time" and "Endlessly," and several popular duets with Dinah Washington. Fats Domino's "Walking to New Orleans" featured a prominent string section performing in call-and-response with his vocal part, showing how his musical arrangements had changed since the peak of rock and roll. Sam Cooke also had multiple singles on the charts after making the shift from an independent (Keen) to a major (RCA-Victor). "Wonderful World" (Keen) peaked in popularity during the summer and "Chain Gang," Cooke's RCA debut, was released in the fall. Less weighty than Cooke's album material at the time, these singles were similar in style and production quality and both included Cooke performing in a multivalent manner that suggested his gospel abilities within a pop context.

The popularity of vocal harmony groups was winding down in 1960, but there were still some notable crossover examples in this style. Records by white groups performing in the doo-wop harmony style, such as the Hollywood Argyles, the Safaris, the Ivy Three, the Capris, and the Four Seasons, regularly appeared on the pop and R&B charts, and there were also many important African American vocal harmony groups. Hank Ballard appeared several times on the pop charts in 1960 as a performer and songwriter. His two most popular singles of the year with the Midnighters, "Finger Poppin' Time" and "Let's Go, Let's Go, Let's Go," were reminiscent of mid-1950s rock crossover, with fast shuffle rhythms, saxophone solos, and stylized lyrics.[81] The Drifters had a notable crossover hit with new vocalist Ben E. King, "There Goes My Baby," and followed in short order with "Save the Last Dance for Me." The popularity of this record led King to focus on his solo career, and Atlantic released his singles "Spanish Harlem" and "Stand by Me" not long after. Amid this sea of male vocalists and male-oriented vocal harmony groups, the success of the Shirelles represented the onset of girl-group popularity in mainstream markets. Their single "Will You Love Me Tomorrow" was released in November 1960 on Scepter and peaked in popularity in February of the next year.

There was a remarkable streak of African American representation in the coveted peak positions of the "Hot 100" beginning in September 1960. Chubby Checker's version of "The Twist" (#1) was followed by Cooke's "Chain Gang" (#2), "Save the Last Dance for Me" by the Drifters (#1), Charles's "Georgia on My Mind" (#1), and the Maurice Williams and the Zodiacs recording of "Stay" (#1). This crossover stretch continued well into 1961, when a *Billboard* cover story in June cited a whopping sixty-one different labels represented in the "Hot 100," which had been hit by a "surge of R&B type performances and material [that had never] been so pronounced."[82] The conduit was wide at the time for African American artists who purveyed styles popular within the R&B market to gain equal or greater success with mainstream listeners, an audience that just ten years before had been on a different cultural planet.

Motown joined this wave in early 1961, mirroring the success of other crossover-minded independent companies. "Shop Around" by the Miracles slowly ascended the charts at the end of 1960, peaking in popularity during February of the next year. The Marvelettes' "Please Mr. Postman" rose to prominence at the end of 1961. The following year Motown placed four hits in the top-ten of the "Hot 100."[83] Mary Wells released two of these records, "The One Who Really Loves You" and "You Beat Me to the Punch," the Marvelettes followed their "Postman" success with "Playboy," and the Contours scored a hit with their recording of "Do You Love Me." Motown's popularity with mainstream audiences only intensified during the coming years. By the end of 1963 the company had released more than a dozen bona fide crossover hits.

After a wide exploration of styles, Motown increasingly focused on making records that had the ability to cross between multiple markets. All of the company's popular singles during this time, records like "Shop Around," "Please Mr. Postman," and "The One Who Really Loves You," explored strains of R&B that had a proven track record of achieving mainstream popularity. These records represented the old and the new. They were products of the R&B market of the past, which had been largely segregated, but they also explored stylistic areas that Motown would use in later years to become one of the most consistently successful crossover-oriented companies in the record business. The achievements of Motown and Berry Gordy Jr. were remarkable during the early 1960s, but the journey was far from over. This period marked the beginning of a cultural and musical voyage that lasted for decades. The searching was complete, but the real journey was still to come.

TWO | The Rise of the Motown Sound

> Motown has come to stand for a distinctive kind of R&B. It is so
> distinctive that it is known the world over as the Motown sound or
> the Detroit sound.[1]
>
> —Richard R. Lingeman, *New York Times*

Assembly Line

Motown was a well-oiled machine in the mid-1960s.[2] The company expanded exponentially after its early success, hiring dozens of songwriters, arrangers, backing musicians, and producers. It had offices and departments for sales, marketing, and finance, and Berry Gordy owned the company's music publishing, managed its artists, and even employed personal development specialists and a "quality control" board.[3] All of this activity occurred within a newly acquired row of buildings in downtown Detroit immediately adjacent to the West Grand Boulevard recording studio. Motown occupied eight houses on the block that accommodated a wide variety of activities and businesses, controlling all of the components needed to create and sell its own music.[4] Economists call this "vertical integration," but Berry Gordy used more blue-collar terminology to describe his company's methods. He called it an "assembly line."

Artist management was a cornerstone of Motown's business model. In late 1960 Gordy formed a company called International Talent Management (ITMI), which represented most of the artists under contract to record with Motown.[5] This arrangement was rare because it created the potential for conflict of interest. Most managers negotiated fiercely with record companies, and controlling both of these things gave Motown more power over its acts. As the central agent of their artists' careers, Motown coordinated far more than recordings, managing appearances on television and film, live performances, press and promotion, and other public events.[6] Gordy's oldest sister, Esther Edwards, ran ITMI, and in the early days she and Berry were the company's main agents.[7] During the second half of the 1960s people like Shelly Berger, Charles Graziano, Taylor Cox, and Phil Wooldridge also worked closely with ITMI to manage various acts within the company.[8]

Motown exerted influence over its artists in unconventional ways. In 1963 the company formed a division called Artist Development, which focused on choreography, vocal rehearsal, and etiquette. It was run initially by Harvey Fuqua and Gwen Gordy, who came to work for Motown in mid-1963 after selling their record labels and artist contracts to Berry Gordy.[9] In his Artist Development role, Fuqua worked with local bandleader Maurice King to supervise vocal rehearsals and live performances.[10] He greatly increased the visual appeal of Motown acts, using his experience creating polished live performances to assist Motown groups with their choreography and stage presence. Artist Development employed many other well-established entertainment professionals to work with artists, including Cholly Atkins, a choreographer with nearly two decades of experience on the Chitlin' Circuit and Broadway, and Maxine Powell, a well-known finishing instructor in Detroit, who coached Motown acts in etiquette, manners, and style.[11]

Many record companies specializing in R&B dabbled in song publishing, but Motown's work in this area was among the most successful of the time. The company ran two publishing houses during the mid-1960s, Jobete and Stein and Van Stock. Loucye Gordy Wakefield was the head of Motown's publishing holdings during the first half of the decade. After she died tragically in 1965 Robert Gordy moved into this role. Like many publishers associated with rock and roll and R&B, Motown's Jobete publishing house was aligned with the Broadcast Music Incorporated (BMI) performance rights organization. Stein and Van Stock was formed in 1964 to focus on Broadway-oriented songwriting and was associated with the more prestigious American Society of Composers, Authors and Publishers (ASCAP).[12] Jobete was always the more successful house, and Motown's stable of staff songwriters built it into one of the most lucrative publishing organizations in popular music during the mid-1960s. By the end of the decade Motown's copyright holdings included thousands of songs, written by hundreds of different authors.[13] The company published an extensive array of sheet music and Jobete was awarded many BMI Awards, a citation given to the organization's "most performed" songs.[14] In 1966 *Billboard* reflected Motown's extraordinary track record in this field by calling Jobete "the most successful [contemporary] publishing entity affiliated with a recording operation."[15]

By the middle of the decade, Motown had established a large creative network that developed songs from basic ideas into polished recordings. It employed a stable of arrangers who created original parts for orchestral instruments, usually horns and strings, and also wrote lead sheets for backing musicians, a process they called arranging "rhythm."[16] These rhythm parts were not usually written verbatim. They combined notated elements with ad-lib sections, allowing session musicians to flesh out their own performances.[17] "They know their instruments so well," arranger Paul Riser once said of studio musicians, "why should I try to teach them?"[18] The company also employed a backing band, a group that called itself the Funk Brothers.[19] There were between fifteen and twenty core members of this group during the mid-1960s, and scores of other, less frequent contributors. The instrumental forces of the Motown band usually included electric bass, two or three electric guitars, one to three keyboard instruments, one or two drum kits, and a battery of auxiliary percussion that ranged from hand drums to mallet instruments and tambourine.

There are no available company records that provide documentation of arrangers and musicians on individual sessions, but biographies, interviews, films, and union contracts contain a lot of information about these individuals and their performances.[20] The most active Detroit-based arrangers during Motown's peak years were Henry "Hank" Cosby, David Van DePitte, Willie Shorter, Wade Marcus, Johnny Allen, Jerry Long, and Paul Riser. An early version of the backing band consisted of drummer Benny Benjamin, pianist Joe Hunter, bassist James Jamerson, and guitarists Eddie Willis, Joe Messina, and Robert White. Other musicians joined the group during the mid-1960s, including drummers Richard "Pistol" Allen and Uriel Jones, percussionists Jack Ashford and Eddie "Bongo" Brown, and keyboardists Johnny Griffith and Earl Van Dyke.[21] Saxophonists Thomas "Beans" Bowles, Andrew "Mike" Terry, and Kasuka Mafia (a.k.a. Norris Patterson) also performed frequently during the mid-1960s, and bassist Bob Babbitt and rock-oriented guitarists Dennis Coffey and Melvin "Wah Wah Watson" Ragin played on many sessions in the second half of the decade. The Rayber Voices, the Love-Tones, and the Spinners provided backing vocals on many early Motown sessions, and the Andantes eventually became the company's most important background ensemble.[22] Most of the capable session musicians working in Detroit complemented the company's full-time band at one time or another, establishing a rotating cast of creative talent that was brimming with musical ability.

Producers were responsible for shepherding music through the assembly line.[23] They paired performers with material, commissioned arrangements, ran recording sessions for backing tracks and overdubs, and supervised postproduction. Many of Motown's most successful producers also worked as songwriters, mixing these two important creative roles. "The producer was present at every session," remembers onetime studio manager Ralph Terrana. "The project was his 'baby,' so to speak."[24] Berry Gordy led nearly all of Motown's recording sessions during 1959 and 1960, tinkering with the soundboard, directing musicians, altering arrangements, and helping to organize the instrumental mix to fit onto the two audio tracks available on Motown's early tape machine.[25] He also asserted his creative ideas during the final mixing process, famously experimenting with levels and effects to create many different versions of some recordings. "I was the tape librarian so I saw the reels of tape that were used," remembers Motown's in-house archivist Frances Maclin (née Heard). "There were times that he mixed a song hundreds of times."[26] Gordy showed great interest in technology and sound, and he established a manner of record production that many later Motown producers emulated.

In early 1961, as Gordy started to focus more of his energy on business tasks, a cohort of younger collaborators emerged to produce the company's recordings.[27] William "Mickey" Stevenson ran sessions for singer Eddie Holland, Smokey Robinson for Mary Wells and the Miracles, and Brian Holland and Robert Bateman for the Marvelettes.[28] Norman Whitfield produced his first hit in the summer of 1964 and continued to work in this role to record songs written with Eddie Holland and Barrett Strong through the early 1970s.[29] Eddie and Brian Holland later joined with Lamont Dozier to form the Holland, Dozier, and Holland writing and production team.[30] Many other producers worked in various combinations at Motown during the 1960s, the most successful of which were Clarence Paul, Ivy Jo Hunter, Hank Cosby, Johnny Bristol, Harvey Fuqua, Sylvia Moy, Richard Morris, Al Cleveland, Nick Ashford, and Valerie Simpson.[31]

Recording at Hitsville

During the first two years in his West Grand Boulevard space, Berry Gordy ran recording sessions using a two-track machine purchased from a local DJ named Bristoe Bryant. Early hits like "Shop Around" and "Bye Bye Baby" were created with this setup, in which one track held instrumental performances and the other lead vocals. In mid-1961 engineer Mike McLean built the company's first three-track recorder, which made it possible to capture lead vocals on one track and use the two remaining tracks to record instrumental performances.[32] Three-track capability inspired changes to Motown's production style, and as new producers became more experienced they experimented with recording and arranging techniques, revealing the new sonic possibilities of the 2648 West Grand Boulevard studio. McLean went on to convert the studio to eight-track capability in December 1964, years before most of the recording industry. The ability of this technology to record elements like bass, drums, and backing vocals on separate tracks helped to forge a standard Motown style.

Motown's engineers and technicians were an indispensable part of the creative team. Working in departments called Recording Engineering and Technical Engineering, people like McLean, Bob Olhsson, Cal Harris, Russ Terrana, and Lawrence Horn established many of the systems that were integral to the company's creative process.[33] Recording engineers placed microphones, monitored levels, administered audio effects, and helped to plan the use of multitrack tape by deciding which instruments to combine onto a defined number of available tracks. They also created final mixes, sometimes in collaboration with the producer, and cut demonstration discs (called acetates) to be considered for release by the Motown Quality Control department. Technical engineers built and serviced many of the recording devices used in Motown's studios, including multitrack machines, mixing desks, preamplification units, reverb chambers, tape-to-disc machines, and in-office hi-fi systems.[34]

There was recording activity nearly every day at West Grand Boulevard.[35] In 1962 alone, the company's logbook tracked about 250 sessions, which produced recordings of nearly 500 songs. These figures did not include unlogged sessions for editing, mixing, and tape transfers. Guitarist Dennis Coffey, who began to work regularly for Motown later in the decade, recalled that the house band often worked in two three-hour sessions each day, one beginning in the late morning and the other in the late afternoon, completing "about one song every hour or about six songs a day."[36] Productions were more intricate after 1964, when overdub sessions became the common method of adding auxiliary instrumental and vocal performances. Motown started to contract union sting players from the Detroit Symphony at this time, whose recording work often began late at night, after the orchestra had completed an evening concert.[37] "Many times as we were leaving, the horns and, or [sic] strings would be waiting to do their overdubs on the tracks that we just cut," remembers guitarist Ray Monette.[38]

In addition to the main Hitsville facility, Motown's recordings occurred in a variety of spaces in Detroit. A number of early large sessions were conducted at the Graystone Ballroom, a local theater that Berry Gordy bought in 1963. Gordy later acquired a second proper recording facility, located at 3246 West Davidson, from one-time competitor Ed Wingate through the purchase of the Golden World label in 1966.[39] It was immediately upgraded to eight-track capability and usually called "studio B." (Hitsville was often called "studio A" after this time.) Motown also built recording facilities at "Motown Center" (also called the Donovan Building) at 2457 Woodward, a large tower where the company moved many of its offices in 1968. According to Ralph Terrana, during the late 1960s producers mostly used studio A (Hitsville) for basic tracks and vocal overdubs, studio B (Golden World) for horn and string overdubs, and the Donovan Building facilities for mixing.[40]

These sessions produced a lot of material, which was organized using an intricate system designed to conserve tape and catalog music and songs in various creative stages. Rhythm sessions with multiple takes were initially recorded using temporary reels. The producer then collated overdubs onto one of these performances, and a multitrack version of the completed take was copied onto a safety reel with nine or ten others (by various artists).[41] The temporary reel was recycled after this, eliminating all of the unused performances from the initial tracking session. Multitracks were later mixed to mono or stereo masters, which were assembled onto a series of "duplicate master" reels. Unlike the different multitrack takes from the initial tracking sessions, multiple versions of mixes were saved.

The company established various paper-based systems to document this recording activity. It started a detailed log in mid-1961 that registered individual sessions, using discrete numbers for later reference.[42] Tape librarian Fran Heard also assigned each tape a number according to an intricate system that indicated the number of tracks on the tape and used separate classification codes for temporary reels, safety reels, duplicate masters, and various other kinds of tape. Heard and her coworker Pat Cosby affixed typewritten sheets to each duplicate master box and created "tracking sheets" for the company's eight-track safety reels, which listed the recordings on each tape and accounted for the content of the tracks within each performance.[43] The company used a "tape filing card" system to organize much of this information. Tape file cards were created for every song recorded by a Motown artist. They listed the song's author and publishing information and compiled production credit, session numbers, and tape sources for each recording of the song.

Examining the documentation for one release, the Four Tops' version of "Reach Out I'll Be There," helps to illustrate Motown's typical creative process during the mid-1960s. The tape file card for "Reach Out" shows that the record's rhythm track was taped during session number 2723 onto temporary reel 8020 (figure 2.1). The studio logs tell us that this session occurred on July 8, 1966.[44] The eleventh take of this track was transferred to safety reel labeled "8S096" two days later and notated onto the tape file card in the "S series" column. The temporary reel was then recycled, which was indicated by a line drawn through the number 8020 in the "TS" column. Three overdub sessions, numbered 2775, 2785, and 2790, added backing vocals and two lead vocal performances to the rhythm track. These overdub sessions occurred on July 21, 26, and 27. The tracking sheet affixed to the tape box of reel 8S096 shows the organization of its completed multitrack tape (figure 2.2).

Five mixes of "Reach Out" were created from the 8S096 reel, four in

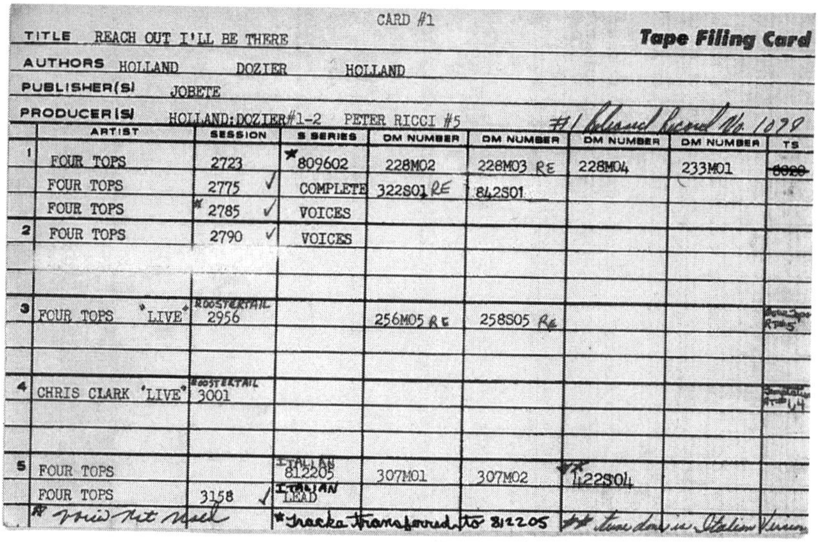

CARD #1

Tape Filing Card

TITLE REACH OUT I'LL BE THERE
AUTHORS HOLLAND DOZIER HOLLAND
PUBLISHER(S) JOBETE
PRODUCER(S) HOLLAND:DOZIER#1-2 PETER RICCI #5

	ARTIST	SESSION	S SERIES	DM NUMBER	DM NUMBER	DM NUMBER	DM NUMBER	TS
1	FOUR TOPS	2723	*809602	228M02	228M03 RE	228M04	233M01	~~8020~~
	FOUR TOPS	2775 ✓	COMPLETE	322S01 RE	842S01			
	FOUR TOPS	# 2785 ✓	VOICES					
2	FOUR TOPS	2790 ✓	VOICES					
3	FOUR TOPS "LIVE"	ROOSTERTAIL 2956		256M05 RE	258S05 RE			
4	CHRIS CLARK "LIVE"	ROOSTERTAIL 3001						
5	FOUR TOPS		ITALIAN 812205	307M01	307M02	422S04		
	FOUR TOPS	3158 ✓	ITALIAN LEAD					

*Tracks transferred to 812205

Fig 2.1. The tape filing card for "Reach Out I'll Be There." (Courtesy of Universal Music Enterprises.)

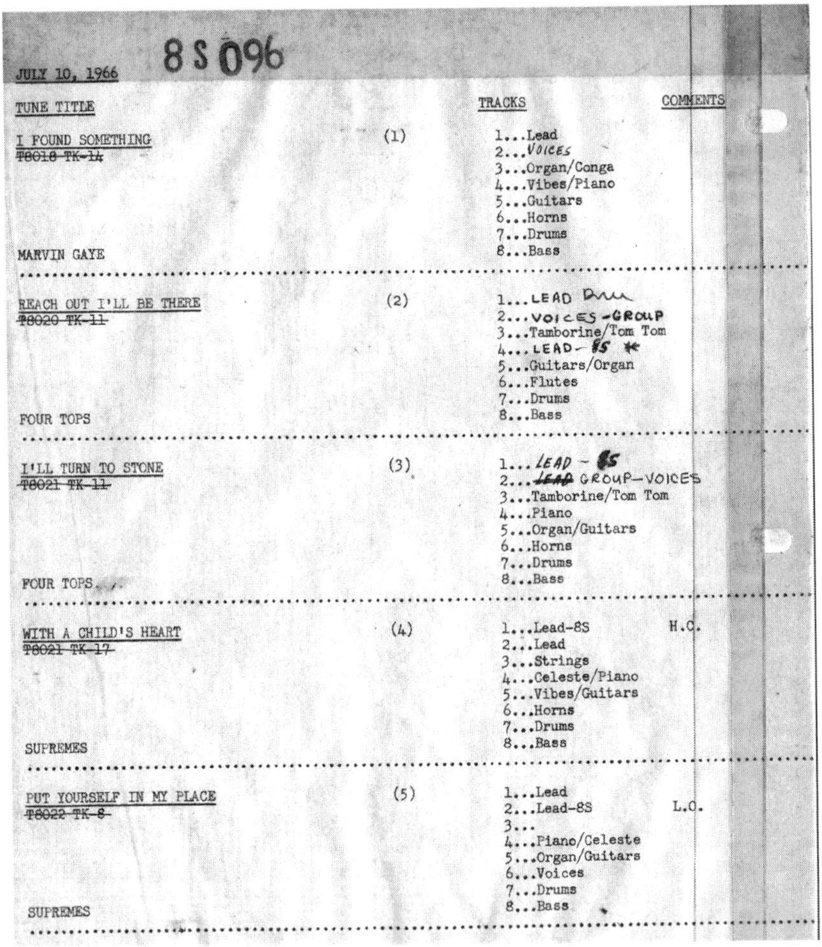

8S096

JULY 10, 1966

TUNE TITLE		TRACKS	COMMENTS
I FOUND SOMETHING ~~T8018 TK-14~~ MARVIN GAYE	(1)	1...Lead 2...VOICES 3...Organ/Conga 4...Vibes/Piano 5...Guitars 6...Horns 7...Drums 8...Bass	
REACH OUT I'LL BE THERE ~~T8020 TK-11~~ FOUR TOPS	(2)	1...LEAD Dru 2...VOICES-GROUP 3...Tamborine/Tom Tom 4...LEAD-8S * 5...Guitars/Organ 6...Flutes 7...Drums 8...Bass	
I'LL TURN TO STONE ~~T8021 TK-11~~ FOUR TOPS	(3)	1...LEAD - 8S 2...~~LEAD~~ GROUP-VOICES 3...Tamborine/Tom Tom 4...Piano 5...Organ/Guitars 6...Horns 7...Drums 8...Bass	
WITH A CHILD'S HEART ~~T8021 TK-17~~ SUPREMES	(4)	1...Lead-8S 2...Lead 3...Strings 4...Celeste/Piano 5...Vibes/Guitars 6...Horns 7...Drums 8...Bass	H.C.
PUT YOURSELF IN MY PLACE ~~T8022 TK-8~~ SUPREMES	(5)	1...Lead 2...Lead-8S 3... 4...Piano/Celeste 5...Organ/Guitars 6...Voices 7...Drums 8...Bass	L.C.

Fig 2.2. A tracking sheet for Motown Reel 8S096. (Courtesy of Universal Music Enterprises.)

mono and one in stereo. Three of these were collated as performances 2, 3, and 4 on duplicate master reel 228 (figure 2.3).[45] Using the handwritten abbreviation "RE," the tape filing card indicates that third cut on this tape was the mix used for the single release. Many of Motown's intricate codes were even printed on officially released record labels. In the case of "Reach Out," the duplicate master (DM) number appears on the left-hand side of its label along with the three-letter code "HSJ" (figure 2.4). This letter code contains producer and engineer information: "H" refers to Brian Holland and Lamont Dozier as producers, but exact

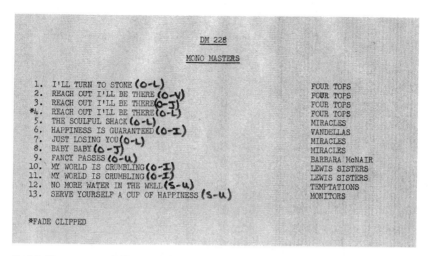

DM 228

MONO MASTERS

1.	I'LL TURN TO STONE (O-L)	FOUR TOPS
2.	REACH OUT I'LL BE THERE (O-V)	FOUR TOPS
3.	REACH OUT I'LL BE THERE (O-J)	FOUR TOPS
*4.	REACH OUT I'LL BE THERE (O-L)	FOUR TOPS
5.	THE SOULFUL SHACK (O-L)	MIRACLES
6.	HAPPINESS IS GUARANTEED (O-I)	VANDELLAS
7.	JUST LOSING YOU (O-L)	MIRACLES
8.	BABY BABY (O-J)	MIRACLES
9.	FANCY PASSES (O-U)	BARBARA McNAIR
10.	MY WORLD IS CRUMBLING (O-I)	LEWIS SISTERS
11.	MY WORLD IS CRUMBLING (O-I)	LEWIS SISTERS
12.	NO MORE WATER IN THE WELL (S-U)	TEMPTATIONS
13.	SERVE YOURSELF A CUP OF HAPPINESS (S-U)	MONITORS

*FADE CLIPPED

Fig 2.3. The contents of duplicate master tape 228. (Courtesy of Universal Music Enterprises.)

attribution of the other two letters (S and J), in addition to the letters used on the DM sheet (O and J), is not clear.

Early Self-Dialogue

Motown recorded more music than it was possible to release. It was common for an artist to record two or three different songs to be considered as the A-side for each of their singles. A department called Quality Control, run by Billie Jean Brown, gathered on Friday mornings to decide which of the company's records had the greatest potential for success.[46] "Careers depended on the choices made those Friday mornings," Gordy remembers. "Everybody wanted to be there."[47] The politics of these meetings were often intense, with Gordy intentionally breeding competition among his creative staff. If a producer failed to provide a hit for an artist, Gordy was prone to choose a different creative team for the act's next single. But when a songwriter or producer was able to create a successful record, as many producers did regularly in the mid-1960s, he or she usually had the opportunity to write and record a follow-up single for the same artist.[48]

Ongoing collaboration between producers and artists was crucial to Motown's emerging sonic identity. In light of the manner in which Motown writers and producers had participated in the answer song tradition, it was a logical next step to create self-dialogue, in which aspects of a successful single were reused in an artist's later work. Motown's most

Fig 2.4. The Four Tops' "Reach Out I'll Be There" single label

successful producers during the first half of the 1960s used this technique of compositional discourse. Self-dialogue was central to Motown's
creative model. It created a level of consistency and helped to form what
would later come to be known as the "Motown Sound."

An early example of this occurred in a series of records produced
by Smokey Robinson for Mary Wells. After two hits produced by Berry
Gordy ("Bye Bye Baby" and "I Don't Want to Take a Chance") and a
disappointing follow-up release ("Strange Love"), Wells and Robinson
worked together to create six singles during a two-year period, all but
one of her remaining Motown A-sides.[49] The first five releases that
emerged from this Wells-Robinson collaboration—from "The One
Who Really Loves You" (February 1962) to "Your Old Stand By" (April
1963)—shared many musical characteristics. They had similar tempos
(from 100 to 115 beats per minute), used conga drumming, incorporated call-and-response between the lead and background vocals, and
featured a Latin-tinged backing band. Wells's vocal work was clearly a
vital element of these singles, but their stylistic consistency was more a
result of Robinson's influence. Other singles written and produced by
Robinson during 1962 used a similar formula, including recordings by
the Supremes ("Your Heart Belongs to Me"), Mickey McCullers ("Same
Old Story"), and the Temptations ("Slow Down Heart").[50]

Operating under the name Brianbert, the production team of

Brian Holland and Robert Bateman also created successful examples of self-dialogue during this period.[51] One of their first singles was the Marvelettes' "Please Mr. Postman," which became a crossover hit and served as the template for the next two Marvelettes releases, "Twistin' Postman" and "Playboy."[52] "Twistin' Postman" continued the "Postman" story and also connected to "The Twist," which had reentered the pop charts during the fall of 1961 for the second time in two years. "Playboy" returned to the musical style of "Please Mr. Postman," beginning with a solo vocal line singing a refrain over a backbeat pattern articulated by the snare drum and hand claps. It also recycled a subtle descending chromatic pattern of four notes in octaves on the piano at the end of its chorus section.

The Brianbert team parted ways in early 1962 when Bateman left Motown to work at a rival start-up called Correc-Tone Records.[53] This led Brian Holland to form a new partnership with his older brother Eddie and Lamont Dozier, a team that came to be known as Holland, Dozier, Holland (or HDH). The members of this team were all particularly skilled at navigating the Motown assembly line.[54] As both songwriters and producers, they often took liberties with the initial tracking session for a piece of music. Their creative ideas were disseminated through a combination of aural and written forms, allowing for both premeditated arranging by the composers and dedicated arrangers and on-the-spot decisions made by the producers and performers. In many instances they created a backing track before they had written a melody or lyrics, which is evident in the dozens of recordings produced by them in the Motown vaults with no overdubs or vocal tracks, to which no known melody or lyrics exist. Tracking sheets and tape cards also reveal that song titles by HDH and others were often changed after the overdub process was complete, which was the result of completing or changing a song's lyrics and vocal melody while recording. "Ninety percent of the time, we never knew who the session was for and the songs had no titles," studio guitarist Eddie Willis once claimed. "They just threw a chord chart at us and said 'just play and make us a hit.' We never knew where our music would wind up."[55]

In January 1963 HDH wrote and produced "Come and Get These Memories" for Martha and the Vandellas. This record was only moderately successful on the "Hot 100," but it became the template for the group's next release, "Heat Wave," the first significantly popular HDH production. HDH continued to use elements of both of these songs in the next two Martha and the Vandellas releases, "Quicksand" and "Live

Wire." There is clear stylistic continuity among these four records, showing the manner in which the earliest HDH productions participated
heavily in techniques of self-dialogue. They share a heavy shuffle rhythm
in the drums; bass emphasizing each quarter note of the common time
measure; a piano groove that hits on the downbeat and the syncopated
space between beats two and three; a prominent baritone saxophone
part; handclaps, tambourines, and other percussion instruments often
emphasized with reverb; and recycled harmonic progressions, most notably a stepwise pattern rising from ii to V (through either iii or I^6, followed by IV). It is no wonder that many fans referred to "Quicksand" as
the "Son of Heat Wave."

HDH and The Supremes

Beginning in 1964 HDH used self-dialogue to create some of Motown's
most successful music of the period with the Supremes. Their first important collaboration was "Where Did Our Love Go," which was released in June 1964.[56] After this breakthrough record, the Supremes
achieved a level of crossover unthinkable for an African American girl
group at the time. They opened as headliners at the Copacabana, appeared on the cover of *Time*, and performed on the *Ed Sullivan Show*,
all bolstered by their consistently popular musical releases. Motown
released sixteen Supremes hits during the four years after "Where Did
Our Love Go," forming one of the most successful sequences of singles by any artist in popular music during the 1960s. In less than three
years ten Supremes records reached the number-one position on the
Billboard pop chart, and most of their other releases appeared in the
top twenty of both the pop and R&B listings.[57] Each of these singles was
written and produced by HDH, who also grew in stature from unknown
members of the assembly line to international celebrities.[58]

The Supremes' roster changed several times during the 1960s, but
Diana Ross, Florence Ballard, and Mary Wilson were the group's three
singers for the majority of these peak years. Ballard and Ross shared the
role of lead singer early in the decade, but Ross took over this position
permanently in 1964. The disparity between the vocal approaches of
these two singers was pronounced: Ballard was known for her strong
alto and Ross had a breathy, cooing approach.[59] Based in part on Ross's
vocal type, the Supremes and HDH forged an aural style that was musically simple and straightforward, contrasting at times with an increasing sense of visual glamour among the group. According to musicologist

Jacqueline Warwick, this type of mixture was at the center of the girl group genre, projecting from a teenage perspective "fantasies of a far-off adulthood, a life that seemed impossibly distant from the mundane realities of parents, homework, and drippy boys."[60]

A number of Supremes records released during the next eighteen months contained tropes relating to "Where Did Our Love Go." In the beginning, young girls were an important target audience for their music. "It was mostly females that were buying records," Eddie Holland once commented, recalling the impulse behind his lyrics for the group. "I felt that females in that teenage group were always in love with some guy; a high-school guy or someone in the neighborhood. It's just a common feeling—young girls have crushes."[61] Including the repetitive lyrical phrase "baby, baby" was one method that he used to infuse the group's songs with a young female perspective.[62] It figured prominently into each of the four Supremes singles immediately following "Where Did Our Love Go" and grew to become an important element of the Supremes' mid-1960s identity.[63] The Supremes' gender and age were often projected in songs about a powerless woman in an unhappy relationship with a man. There was begging in "Where Did Our Love Go," confession of mistreatment in "Baby Love," and romantic depression in "Come See about Me." "Stop! In the Name of Love" portrayed Ross as confrontational, providing a sense of development in this record-to-record narrative. Nevertheless, depictions of mercurial teenage relationships continued in the group's later singles, such as "Back in My Arms Again," "Nothing but Heartaches," and "I Hear a Symphony," which were all about the fluctuating state of young relationships.

The musical features of these records contained many dialogic connections. The light quality of Ross's voice established a nonthreatening vocal style throughout much of the group's output.[64] Later singles also incorporated the vibes, piano, obbligato saxophone, and striking quarter note pulse that had appeared in the opening measures of "Where Did Our Love Go," which had been achieved by stomping on boards and accentuated through dense reverb.[65] Key and tempo were also similar. Each of the Supremes' singles released in 1964 and 1965 (except for "Come See about Me") was set in the key of C major and proceeded at a tempo of between 115 and 135 beats per minute.

Under the sheen of these common features, HDH slowly changed aspects of harmonic language in their writing for the Supremes, providing a sense of character development in the group's output over time. While many of the lyrical tropes stayed the same, the music behind the group's recordings became much more complex. "Where Did Our Love Go" used a single diatonic progression, but "Baby Love" began with a misleading introduction (incorporating VII) and used a chain of applied chords ($V^2/V^7/ii$), and "Come See about Me" incorporated a minor subdominant. "Stop!" employed an even more complex harmonic vocabulary, using inversions, modal mixture, and a chorus in the parallel minor. There were similar developments in the songs' formal structures. "Where Did Our Love Go" repeated predictable eight-measure units with no contrasting chorus or bridge, but later singles explored new formal features in a seemingly cumulative manner.[66] "Baby Love" was based on a twelve-bar cycle that included three discrete phrase sections—a four-bar refrain, a six-bar static verse, and a two-bar turnaround. "Come See about Me" used a three-part structure that spanned twenty-two measures, in which an eight-bar static verse was followed by a short four-measure bridge leading to a ten-measure chorus.[67] The form of "Stop! In the Name of Love" had an even more intricate phrase structure, in which a single refrain ("think it over . . .") was used in both the verse and chorus sections.

In September 1965 the Supremes and HDH recorded the single "I Hear a Symphony." This record included many of the musical and textual features of earlier Supremes hits. It was also in dialogue with the non-Motown record "A Lover's Concerto," a recent release by the New York-based girl group the Toys that was itself based on the melody of J. S. Bach's G-major minuet from the "Notebook for Anna Magdalena Bach." "A Lover's Concerto" used a vocal style extremely reminiscent of Motown girl groups and it had an instrumental track that shared many sonic characteristics with Motown's most popular hits from the time, including a tambourine and saxophone figure taken directly from "Stop! In the Name of Love."[68] In response, the Supremes completed "I Hear a Symphony" over the course of several days immediately after the Toys' record first appeared on the national charts.

Rushed into stores less than two weeks later, "I Hear a Symphony" was the Supremes' fifteenth Motown single. Musicologist Michael Long has discussed the manner in which the full piano chords performed at strategic moments during the second half of this record evoke a "symphony's rhetorical or expressive range," generating a "broader musicopoetical process that tilts the interpretation of the song's lyrics in a particular direction."[69] In light of the group's preceding singles and the sonic identity created through consistent work with HDH, several other features tilt the piece in a similar manner. The harmonic progression of the song's introduction, which reappears in the bridge, prepares the standard Supremes key of C major in a learned manner that evokes Western harmony, using a III chord and a surprising Picardy third resolution, and later in the song several "truck driver" key changes move the key upward by a semitone through D♭ and D, resting finally on E♭.[70] "I Hear a Symphony" was the first Supremes single to incorporate strings, an instrumental choice that reflected the song's lyrics and signified on the classical style. (The string ensemble enters at the beginning of the chorus to accompany the first iteration of the words "I hear a symphony.") Rather than the sweeping arco style used in other Motown arrangements from the time, this arrangement uses a cartoonish tremolo, shimmering in a manner that briefly commands the recording's sonic space. In the context of the Supremes' naïve identity, allusions to classical music in "I Hear a Symphony" provide an aural snapshot of how the Supremes were supposed to understand the symphony through the lens of simplistic teenage love, as music with complex harmonic motion, dramatic tremolo string sections, and endless modulations of key.

In 1966 HDH went on to write and produce several more singles for the Supremes that referred to the stylistic tropes of "Where Did Our Love Go." Records such as "My World Is Empty without You," "Love Is Like an Itching in My Heart," "You Can't Hurry Love," and "You Keep Me Hangin' On" used similar instrumentation, percussive patterns, reverb, active backing vocals, and textual themes relating to teenage relationships. At the same time, newer aspects of production, such as the vocal double tracking used in "You Keep Me Hangin' On" and the opening signal generator sound of "Reflections," distanced later Supremes singles from the "Where Did Our Love Go" template. Vestiges of early work by the Supremes continued within records like "Love Is Here and Now You're Gone" and "The Happening," but cumulative elements of experimentation with subject matter, instrumentation, form, and harmony eventually created a significant stylistic distance between the Supremes' style forged in mid-1964 and the group's work later in the decade.

HDH and The Four Tops

HDH also created a number of hit records for the Four Tops. A quartet that included singers Renaldo "Obie" Benson, Abdul "Duke" Fakir, Lawrence Payton, and Levi Stubbs, the Four Tops met in Detroit while still in high school. They first called themselves the Four Aims but changed their name while working as background vocalists for Detroit's

Chateau Records in 1956. They released a few early records on Chess and Columbia, singing mostly complex vocal jazz arrangements, but had little success as recording artists before signing to Motown in 1963 at the urging of their friend William Stevenson. The Four Tops entered the mainstream pop market for the first time during the summer of 1964, at the same time as the Supremes, and the period of collaboration and success between HDH and these two groups was virtually identical.[71] Between 1964 and 1968 they scored fifteen consecutive top-twenty hits on the R&B charts, five of which reached the top-ten on the pop listings. Nearly all of these records were written and produced by HDH.[72]

The Four Tops were an average of seven years older than the Supremes. Before working with HDH they had hoped to record standards at Motown.[73] The group's age and gender did not support naïve simplicity in the same manner as the Supremes' girl-group identity. Instead, the lyrics of many Four Tops songs discussed issues relating to masculinity. Many of the songs that HDH wrote for the group during this period mentioned weeping. The protagonist often sang about his own crying and considered it a weakness.[74] Writing and production that accentuated the upper register of lead vocalist Levi Stubbs's dark baritone vocals supported this perspective, helping to create a vocal timbre that enhanced lyrical themes of loneliness and obsession. In contrast to the low, sultry character HDH created for Diana Ross, Eddie Holland once remarked that HDH, "emphasize[d] the power and strength in [Levi's] voice, even to the point that sometimes we cut in keys a little high for him, to force him to reach for the notes."[75]

The first collaboration between HDH and the Four Tops was "Baby I Need Your Loving," which was released in August 1964.[76] It was the first of a dialogic pair, and the group's next single, "Without the One You Love," shared many of its musical features. These records used similar string and horn arrangements, background vocals, percussive accents using snaps and cymbals, and key structures.[77] The opening line of "Without the One You Love" even recited the words "baby I need your loving" in a clear reference to the earlier work. Released within a three-month span during mid-1965, "I Can't Help Myself" and "It's the Same Old Song" formed another dialogic group. Each of these records was in the key of C major, began with a vernacular catchphrase, proceeded at virtually the same tempo, and was based on a similar bass ostinato (example 2.1).[78] The harmonic patterns used in these songs were nearly identical, and comparable saxophone solos performed by Mike Terry occurred in both recordings.[79]

A:

B:

Example 2.1. The ostinatos in "I Can't Help Myself" (A) and "It's the Same Old Song" (B)

Unlike other dialogic connections in Motown material from the time, "I Can't Help Myself" was the subject of "It's the Same Old Song." After the success of "I Can't Help Myself," Columbia Records had reissued a five-year-old Four Tops record called "Ain't That Love" as a single in an effort to capitalize on the quartet's newfound popularity. "Berry was pissed," Dozier remembers. "He said we had to get out something right away. I just turned the bass figure around from 'I Can't Help Myself' and started yelling out 'It's the same old song, but with a different meaning since you been gone.' The titling of the song was very conscious on our part."[80] Anecdotes recall HDH and the Four Tops working through the night to compose and record "It's the Same Old Song," which was released only eight days later in an effort to combat sales of the Columbia single.[81] Motown corporate records reveal a slightly different story. HDH had actually created the backing track for "It's the Same Old Song" two months before, intending to record it with the Supremes. It was still a reactionary record, but part of the composition was originally intended for a different group.

Melding a Supremes-oriented track with a melody and lyrics created for Stubbs, "It's the Same Old Song" exemplified the HDH style during the summer of 1965. It was in the key of C, featured a rhythmic character emphasizing quarter notes, used an obbligato saxophone with a solo by Terry, employed a commonly used style of vibes performance, and proceeded at a tempo comparable to records like "Where Did Our Love Go" and "Baby Love." HDH had certainly created connections within the catalog of a single artist, but the history of "It's the Same Old Song" also helps to demonstrate the growing overlap between many compositional features shared among HDH records during this time. As producers and writers, their "sound" became as recognizable as the voice of a singer.

HDH continued to work with the Four Tops throughout 1966 and 1967. The most significant dialogue created during this time occurred between "Reach Out I'll Be There," "Standing in the Shadows of Love," and "Bernadette."[82] These records were bound together by both lyrics and musical similarities. The intensity portrayed in their texts increased in a cumulative manner, extending the emotional, masculine perspective of the group's earlier "weeping" songs. The protagonist of "Reach Out" proclaimed that he would "be there to love and comfort" his female lover during a series of challenging scenarios; "Standing in the Shadows of Love" confessed "you've taken away all my reasons for living"; and "Bernadette" verged on obsession, with Stubbs performing lines like, "I want you because I need you to live."

HDH used a variety of compositional and production techniques to create musical continuity among these three records. Their arrangements all featured a rhythmic pattern that emphasized quarter notes in common time, prominent backing vocals, and a dominant independent bass and the recordings used reverb, equalization, and compression to create a similar sonic environment. All three records featured woodwinds: there were two flutes in "Reach Out," doubled flutes and oboes in "Standing in the Shadows," and a four-part ensemble with two flutes, a French horn, and an obbligato oboe in "Bernadette." There were also harmonic and motivic connections between these songs. The flute passages in "Reach Out" and "Standing in the Shadows" outlined the minor subdominant and a time-stopping diminished chord (examples 2.2–2.4); "Standing in the Shadows" and "Bernadette" used descending minor tetrachord patterns in their choruses; and the verse progressions of all three songs used the same three chords—G♭ major, A♭ minor, and D♭ major—in a different order.[83]

The Motown Sound

Holland, Dozier, and Holland were not the only Motown producers who were successful mid-decade. Smokey Robinson, Mickey Stevenson, and Hank Cosby were among a growing group of producers who created dozens of hit records at the time.[84] In 1965 alone, Robinson contributed to eleven singles that reached the top ten of the *Billboard* or *Cash Box* R&B charts. After writing and producing "My Girl" for the Temptations with Miracles bandmate Ronald White (released in December 1964), Robinson's iconic tracks that year included "Ooo, Baby Baby" (the Miracles), "Ain't That Peculiar" (Marvin Gaye), and "Don't Mess with Bill" (the Marvelettes). Stevenson directed hits by Eddie Holland and the Marvelettes and helped to create a popular string of dialogic records for Marvin Gaye beginning in mid-1962, starting with "Stubborn Kind of

Example 2.2. The flute melody in the introduction to "Reach Out I'll Be There" (0:00–0:08)

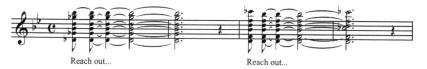

Example 2.3. The diminished chord in "Reach Out I'll Be There" (0:37–0:43)

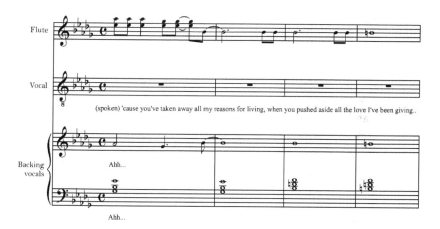

Example 2.4. The diminished chord and flute melody in "Standing in the Shadows of Love" (0:33–0:42)

Fellow" and extending to "Hitch Hike" and "Pride and Joy." Stevenson also teamed with Hank Cosby to produce Stevie Wonder's "Uptight (Everything's Alright)" and "Nothing's Too Good for My Baby."[85] There were many others. Norman Whitfield, Clarence Paul, Harvey Fuqua, and Johnny Bristol were only a few of the other Motown producers who had important crossover hits in 1965 and 1966.

Regardless of the producer or artist, a lot of Motown's most popular singles from the mid-1960s had common elements.[86] While producers often helped to create a style for an artist, and some successful producers like HDH also had a creative voice, there were now elements that began to reflect a larger Motown Sound. Many of the company's musical arrangements emphasized each quarter note within an up-tempo common-time measure, for example. In "Where Did Our Love Go" this pulse was articulated by boards banging together; in the Four Tops' "I Can't Help Myself" the kit drummer used the snare drum to perform the pattern; other records used tambourines and bongos to weave this feature into the band's arrangement. Records like Marvin Gaye's "Hitch Hike" and Martha and the Vandellas' "Heat Wave" featured this figure, and it became a hallmark of the earliest popular singles by the Supremes. Motown used this rhythmic pattern so commonly that some journalists began to call it a "Motown Beat."[87]

Backing vocals were another element that was common in Motown arrangements during the mid-1960s. Dedicated support singers like the Andantes often sang these parts, but others did as well, including members of groups like the Supremes or various mixtures of group members and extra vocalists. Motown's style of vocal backgrounds drew equally from male vocal harmony and girl group traditions; it alternated between call-and-response, homophonic, and heterophonic textures, often making backing singers an active part of the record's vocal composite. Far from simple accompaniment, the male vocals behind a record like "You Beat Me to the Punch" by Mary Wells were a featured element of the record's arrangement, and many of Motown's male and female vocal groups incorporated backing vocals in a similar manner. The Vandellas' "Come and Get These Memories" used call-and-response; the Supremes' "Baby Love" employed a complex heterophonic texture between the lead and backing vocals; and the doo-wop backgrounds created by the Temptations on a track like "My Girl" surrounded the tenor lead of David Ruffin with dense group harmonies that harkened back to the styles popularized by black vocal groups during the 1950s.

Motown's arrangers often melded these backing vocals with sophisticated instrumental textures. In the company's early years, organ performances lent a sense of gospel texture while auxiliary percussion and mallet instruments accentuated both melodic and rhythmic elements of band tracks. The vibraphone performance on the 1965 Miracles ballad "Ooo Baby Baby," for example, featured percussionist Jack Ashford performing spacious dotted quarter notes over a 12/8 time during the chorus, adding tremendous depth to the aural field.

Overdubbed strings were used sparingly on early Motown releases because of the expenses involved in contracting and recording. The addition of strings to early tracks by the Miracles ("Way over There"), the Satintones ("My Beloved"), and Mable John ("No Love") showed a heightened level of commitment to these productions. As the company became more successful, hired staff arrangers, and employed union players from the Detroit Symphony, string and horn arrangements became much more common on Motown recordings. Strings were used in a variety of ways. They were purely supportive in many instances, sweetening the sound of a track with a bit of timbral flare. Strings commanded a more prominent voice in other records, such as the Supremes' "I Hear a Symphony," the Temptations' "My Girl," and Jimmy Ruffin's "What Becomes of the Brokenhearted."

The role of horns varied greatly in Motown arrangements. Early tracks often used group brass and reed parts, ranging from the blues-oriented "Pride and Joy" (Marvin Gaye) to the more sophisticated "Two Lovers" (Mary Wells). HDH were particularly fond of the baritone saxophone, and many of their popular records included solos performed by Mike Terry, Beans Bowles, or Norris Patterson. Later records exploited the expressive characteristics of low brass, such as "Ain't Too Proud to Beg," which featured exposed trombones in each verse, and Marvin Gaye's "I Heard It through the Grapevine," which used dramatic octaves and flutter-tongue effects performed by French horns. A lot of Motown recordings after 1965 also took on the characteristics of the "chamber pop" movement that emerged in popular music during the time. The Four Tops' recording of "Bernadette" had an oboe part, bassoon was prominent in the lower line of the Miracles' "The Tears of a Clown," harpsichord was central to the Supremes' "The Happening," and the introduction of Stevie Wonder's "Signed, Sealed, Delivered I'm Yours" featured an electric sitar.

James Jamerson quickly became very comfortable in his role as a session bassist during the early 1960s, and he helped to make the bass another vital element of Motown records. Jamerson created active lines that often used syncopation across the bar and downward leaps followed by ascending passing tones to create linear passages that evoked gospel harmonization.[88] Rather than using a microphone to capture the sound of an amplifier, Jamerson's performances were recorded through a direct input, which helped to shape his sound. After late 1964, Motown's eight-track apparatus recorded bass performances on a separate track, which allowed for further enhancement and placement in final mixes.[89] Jamerson's playing was revolutionary in popular music at the time, and others who performed at Motown, such as Bob Babbitt and Tony Newton, emulated his style. Before the early 1960s the bass had been relegated to a purely supportive role in most popular music, but Jamerson helped to change this. His performances inspired many other bassists in the R&B and rock communities to command a new sense of freedom.[90]

Motown's releases had a technological sheen that was unlike other pop records at the time. Engineers used compression, limiting, and equalization to tailor the sonic elements of the company's recordings. These effects changed a recording's sound in a manner that was often difficult for listeners to articulate, but the sonic environment they helped to create nevertheless branded a song as a Motown production. Reverb was more obvious, and it was often exaggerated and used in creative ways on Motown recordings.[91] Engineers had many options for reverb at Motown. There were reverb chambers built into three different West Grand Boulevard houses (2644, 2648, and 2652), the company owned several EMT plate reverb units that were housed behind the West Grand Boulevard studio, and by the end of the 1960s there were also options for spring reverb and tape delay.[92]

These effects were used widely during the recording and mixing processes. Reverb was sometimes recorded directly to individual safety reel tracks before mixing, making it inseparable from the performances themselves.[93] When used on a particular performance, it had the effect of either distancing or highlighting the contents of the track. Motown producers often used reverb to feature percussion instruments, vocals, guitars, and even strings, although it was rarely employed in this expressive manner on more than one track within a single multitrack performance. The Motown Beat board-whacking on "Where Did Our Love Go" and the backbeat percussion performance on "Dancing in the Street" were both emphasized with dense reverb, as were the lead vocal performances of "Baby Love" and "What Becomes of the Brokenhearted," the guitars in "Nowhere to Run" and "It's the Same Old Song," and the strings in "Ain't Too Proud to Beg." Reverb was also an essential tool during the final mixing process, when it was often used on an entire master to enhance the overall sound of the record. Motown engineers and producers experimented with reverb extensively during mixing, which is evident when comparing multiple mixes of a record.

The Four Tops' "Reach Out I'll Be There" demonstrates in a single record many elements of the Motown Sound during the mid-1960s (example 2.5).[94] During the first verse of "Reach Out" the snare drum emphasizes quarter notes in each measure, creating a Motown Beat. There is a prominent flute duet in the introduction and chorus, showing evidence of Motown's adventurous orchestration. An active bass is prevalent throughout the record, using anticipatory tones and synco-

Example 2.5. The Motown Sound in "Reach Out I'll Be There" (0:16–0:23)

pation across the bar line. The bass is also featured for a single measure before each chorus during a tension-building diminished chord.
There are prominent backing vocals, performed by the Four Tops and
the Andantes, which include nonmelodic percussive parts, melody lines,
and dense homophonic chords.[95] Reverb also appears in multiple layers
on the track. The guitar parts were enhanced with this effect during the
tracking session, and the overall mix has a generous sheen of reverb
throughout, which is audible in the spacious quality of the flutes and
percussion during the introduction.

The Motown Sound was more than a musical phenomenon. Motown's
promotions and advertising departments worked diligently to create a
wider public perception of commonalities within the Motown catalog.
Motown branded its sonic consistency as a "sound" in advertisements,
press releases, and album art, which helped to codify the company's
sonic character for many listeners.[96] The slogan "The Sound of Young
America" appeared in various advertisements, describing the company's
youthful locus in relationship to all fans of youth-oriented American

pop, not just African American listeners. The "Detroit Sound" was another important early marketing term, which Motown executives used as synecdoche, asserting authority over the musical output of their entire hometown.[97] In one 1965 memo, press agent Alan Abrams advocated to legal counsel Ralph Seltzer that Motown should protect the term, writing, "In view of the national publicity being received by the Detroit sound—may I again request that we register 'The Detroit Sound' as a trademark before some 2 bit label does this and humiliates us."[98]

In late 1965 Motown started to favor the more specific "Motown Sound" in its marketing efforts.[99] The company printed "The Motown Sound" conspicuously on the rear, upper corner of its LP jackets, urging customers and retailers to think of it as a genre label.[100] It was discussed in liner notes for releases like the 1965 Choker Campbell collection *Hits of the Sixties* and an Earl Van Dyke album from the same year called *That Motown Sound*. Tour books from the company's "Motortown Revue" were also billed as "An Evening with the Motown Sound." The concerted effort to use this term was also evident in an internal white paper for the sales department from the period that described the assembly line process in detail and attributed Motown's success to the slogans "The Motown Sound" and "The Sound of Young America."[101]

Marketing efforts and musical similarities between many Motown records inspired a number of journalists to begin using "Motown Sound" as a genre label during the mid-1960s. A 1965 article in *Life* discussed a number of popular "sounds" from the period, including the "Detroit Sound (or Motown Sound)," which was described as having "a heavy, rocking beat and a strong gospel flavor, plus some control-booth tricks that others have tried but have failed to copy."[102] Dozens of other print sources also used the term, including a large profile published in the *Chicago Daily News* called "That Motown Sound" and a prominent 1966 *New York Times* article by Richard Lingeman.[103] Although Motown never protected the mark "Detroit Sound," it did officially register "Motown Sound" with the U.S. Trademark and Patent Office in August 1966, revealing the company's active interest in marketing and trademark and the extent to which the term had both monetary and intellectual value (figure 2.5).[104]

Motown's Other Sounds

In July 1965, at the same time that the Motown Sound was in full swing, the Supremes performed for the first time at the Copacabana in New

Fig 2.5. A "Motown Sound" advertisement printed in the August 27, 1966, issue of *Billboard*. (Courtesy of Universal Music Enterprises.)

York. This was an important marker of crossover for Motown, but of a different variety than HDH was simultaneously achieving with the group. The Copa was no Motown Sound venue. It was an upscale supper club that catered to adult audiences. This series of performances helped Motown to "cross" into a different direction. From publishing to live performances and recordings, the type of middle-of-the-road pop (MOR) featured at the Copa was quickly becoming an important area of interest for Motown.

Berry Gordy responded to the stature of the Supremes' first shows at the Copa by putting a lot of resources into planning the opening. As per

Motown's business model, he was in a powerful position to coordinate aspects of the group's affairs like publicity, live performance preparation, and recording.[105] A later LP called *At the Copa* contained a selection of Supremes' performances from these evenings, only a few of which used stylistic characteristics associated with the Motown Sound. Instead, the trio performed mostly in a cabaret style, singing standards like "Put on a Happy Face" and "Rock-a-By Your Baby with a Dixie Melody" along with newly arranged versions of many of their hits. This record was clear evidence that Motown's creative borders extended far past the confines of a single style or approach.

The Supremes were not the only Motown act to move into this stylistic and economic area of the music business at this time. A sizeable number of Motown LPs from the period—by artists like Paula Greer, Marvin Gaye, and Billy Eckstine—were released for the MOR pop market.[106] Similarly, a number of Motown groups, including Gaye, the Temptations, the Miracles, and Stevie Wonder, performed in elite supper clubs, places like New Jersey's Latin Casino, the Fairmont Hotel in San Francisco, and Bermuda's Clay House Inn. Like the Supremes at the Copa, many of these performances included "floor shows," which incorporated musical styles far removed from the Motown Sound.[107]

Other records from this period betrayed Motown's continued interest in music outside of R&B and MOR.[108] Motown released a lot of this music on the V. I. P. imprint, which began in December 1963. About sixty singles and eight albums were released on V. I. P. before it was discontinued in late 1971. The styles featured on these records ranged from the British invasion and European sounds of the Hornets ("Give Me a Kiss"), Oma Heard ("Lifetime Man"), and Richard Anthony ("I Don't Know What to Do") to the country music of Ray Oddis ("Randy, the Newspaper Boy"), the bubblegum rock of the Headliners ("We Call It Fun"), the Irish folk music of the Abbey Tavern Singers, and the early psychedelia of the Underdogs ("Love's Gone Bad"). Motown had no breakthrough success with these V. I. P. releases. The only records on the imprint that made any impact on the sales charts were soul releases by the Elgins and the Spinners. Nevertheless, these releases help to disavow the notion that all of Motown's recorded output sounded alike.

Connections to MOR existed throughout the Motown catalog, but "For Once in My Life" is perhaps the best-known song from the time to emerge from the company's work in this market. It was written in 1965 by Ron Miller and Orlando Murden for the company's Stein and Van Stock publishing wing. Connie Haines first recorded it for Motown, and

Tony Bennett released a version on a 1967 Columbia LP. Several other Motown artists interpreted it during the following years, including the Temptations, who recorded it for their studio album of standards called *In a Mellow Mood.*[109] It first became popular when Stevie Wonder retrofitted it with an uptempo Motown Sound performance in 1968. A crossover hit, Wonder's "For Once in My Life" blended perfectly Motown's interest in cabaret standards and groove-oriented R&B.

The End of a Sound

The Motown Sound was always in flux. This was especially apparent in the last years of the 1960s, when elements of the company's mid-1960s style became increasingly less common. These changes were sometimes the result of choices within the traditional assembly line. In other instances, new trends were the result of alterations to the assembly line itself. The company increasingly used different spaces, like the Golden World recording facility and various studios in Los Angeles, and upgraded to sixteen-track recording equipment in its facilities during late 1969.[110] Many of the producers and songwriters who had helped to establish Motown's signature style became less active during the late 1960s. In early 1967 Mickey Stevenson and Kim Weston, who were married, both left Motown to work for MGM Records.[111] At virtually the same time, Smokey Robinson's production work became much less active and the HDH team enacted a self-imposed work slowdown before departing in early 1968.[112] New people filled Motown's most important creative roles after this, including producers and songwriters like Richard Morris, Frank Wilson, Nick Ashford and Valerie Simpson, and Norman Whitfield.

Without many of the central proponents of the mid-1960s Motown Sound in the creative background, the character of Motown's releases slowly transformed after 1967. The Four Tops worked with various producers and writers after the departure of HDH but never recorded another top-ten pop hit at Motown.[113] HDH were behind the first three singles released by the newly christened "Diana Ross and the Supremes," but much of this work was completed as the team's production efforts for Motown were slowing. To ensure the Supremes' success, which was key to the company's future, Gordy formed a new writing partnership called "The Clan," which included R. Dean Taylor, Frank Wilson, Pamela Sawyer, and Deke Richards. This newer collective immediately wrote two hits for Diana Ross and the Supremes, "Love Child" and "I'm Livin' in Shame," but neither of these connected very closely to the Motown Sound.

In the eyes of the pop market, the character of R&B crossover was much different in the late 1960s. By the end of the decade the Motown Sound was an old-fashioned style associated with an earlier outlook. Smokey Robinson reflected on these changes in a 1970 interview printed in Britain's *Record Retailer*. "I don't think you can talk about music formulas anymore," he said.

> In the sixties all music forms fused together. . . . The walls came down, and for the first time on a large scale young, average people got into music. The kid next door could write a song and be in the charts the next day. Because of this, music has become more earthy.[114]

Robinson and Gordy had once been those "kids next door," but the pop market was no longer the same as it had been in the late 1950s. Now, more than ten years later, they were at the helm of the most successful black-owned company in the United States, leading an assembly line model that was quickly becoming outdated.

Societal attitudes toward the Motown Sound had also changed. Earlier in the decade there was a civil-rights-oriented optimism that drove the market for crossover R&B, aligning Motown's sounds and images with a highly visible black middle class. Perceptions of racial authenticity valued Motown's class alignment much differently at the end of the 1960s. From Robinson's perspective, the "walls came down" and the Motown Sound no longer fit into the trend of "earthy" R&B that was currently popular with mainstream listeners. Motown's reactions to these trends in the R&B market formed another fascinating chapter in the company's history.

THREE | Motown and Soul

Soul Music

The Motown Sound was not the only popular style of crossover R&B during the 1960s. At the same time that Motown's music became synonymous with mechanization, urbanity, and refinement, another significant strain of R&B slowly emerged that featured different signifiers of African American identity. Audiences, musicians, and critics increasingly called this newer style "soul" music. Musically, soul incorporated vocal techniques, instrumentation, and harmonic progressions derived from gospel music. It also used texts that focused on rural or southern themes, some of which had overt connections to the Black Freedom movement. To be sure, the Motown Sound had always been connected to this strain of R&B, but after 1965 there were increasing differences between the crossover pop of groups like the Supremes and the Four Tops and the rising tide of soul. In a manner similar to the Motown Sound, soul became very popular among listeners outside of black communities during the 1960s. By the end of the decade it was a national phenomenon.[1]

The rise of soul was closely related to the popularity of commercial gospel music, which grew dramatically during in the period immediately after World War II. A number of significant hits on the R&B charts during this time helped to bring gospel into the national spotlight. Mahalia Jackson's "Move On up a Little Higher" and Sister Rosetta Tharpe's spirituals like "Strange Things Happening Every Day," "Up above My Head, I Hear Music in the Air," and "Silent Night (Christmas Hymn)" were among the most important of these records. These tracks helped to make gospel a lucrative area of the music business during the early 1950s. Industry magazines listed "spiritual" music alongside R&B, and many R&B independents moved into the gospel field. Major labels also showed interest in gospel during this time by signing several of the movement's biggest stars. For the majority of the 1940s and 1950s Tharpe was signed to Decca, and Jackson signed to Columbia Records in 1954. Jackson also hosted a national radio show on CBS and appeared as a guest on Ed Sullivan's *Talk of the Town*, which was a major coup for an African American religious singer.

Since the 1930s "soul" had been an important part of the ethos surrounding black pop music.[2] One of the most successful groups on the black gospel circuit in the 1930s and 1940s was called the Soul Stirrers, and many R&B records from the time referred to soul in their texts, including B. B. King's "Story from My Heart and Soul," LaVern Baker's "Soul on Fire," Eddie Boyd's "Tortured Soul," and Sonny Parker's "She Sets My Soul on Fire." Later jazz artists participated in a related strain of hard bop often called "soul jazz," which became popular in the mid-1950s and featured what scholar John Gennari has described as a collection of "tuneful blues voicings, song titles displaying the speech inflections of vernacular black speech," and "a general ambience redolent of the down-home rhythms and spirit of the sanctified church."[3] Soul jazz records from the 1960s like Mongo Santamaria's version of "Watermelon Man" (1962), Lee Morgan's "The Sidewinder" (1963), and Ramsey Lewis's "The 'In' Crowd" (1966) even charted on the *Billboard* "Hot 100," revealing a heightened mainstream interest in instrumental, soul-oriented music. As ethnomusicologist Ingrid Monson has written in her work about cultural attitudes in jazz during this time, stylistic labels such as "hard bop" and "cool jazz" were drenched with racial connotations. The titles of these records and their groove-oriented rhythms and reliance on solo organ and aggressive tenor saxophone signified a deeper connection to what audiences often perceived as "black sounds."[4]

There were never prescriptive attributes for a soul style in the R&B market. Soul music adhered loosely to a set of characteristics in the realms of text, instrumentation, harmony, live and recorded performance practice, and visual image. Soul songs commonly discussed rural life or the South and evoked black culture using vernacularisms, references to food, and messages of uplift. Many R&B singers who had earlier experience with church music integrated gospel songs into their otherwise secular album releases. Soul records often avoided large-scale arrangements featuring strings, varied orchestration drawing from Western classical traditions, overt use of reverberation, and signs of overdubbing in favor of an approach that valued earthiness and spontaneity. A lot of nonreligious soul records incorporated tropes relating to sanctified gospel, including the use of organ (sometimes with a rotating speaker), harmonic patterns such as the alternating I–vi cycle or progressions moving from I through I^6 (with a descending bass) to IV, and vocal styles with heavy grain, distortion, and melisma. Musicians performing in the soul style often showed signs of physical exertion, danced ecstatically, and loosened formal clothing as performances escalated and energy levels rose.

Records released in the first years of the 1960s on Vee-Jay and Fury by Gladys Knight and the Pips ("Every Beat of My Heart") and Lee Dorsey ("Ya Ya") were among the first important crossover soul records.[5] Both of these companies were independent, which was common in the soul field. A new crop of companies based in southern locales became especially significant, including Dial (New Orleans), Stax (Memphis), and Fame (Muscle Shoals).[6] Each of these firms navigated the rise of soul differently, but by the middle of the 1960s they were all invested heavily in a very similar style of soul that was imbued with southern character.[7] Later hits followed suit. The Isley Brothers had a crossover hit with "Twist and Shout" and the Inez Foxx recording of the lullaby "Mockingbird" reached the pop top ten.[8] Stroll-oriented instrumental dance records by King Curtis ("Soul Twist") and Booker T. and the MGs ("Green Onions") were particularly popular, featuring saxophone and organ in a manner that connected to soul jazz. As with Harry Belafonte's hit records from the late 1950s, Caribbean dialects and calypso tropes expressed racial identity in records like Jimmy Soul's "If You Wanna Be Happy" and Millie Small's popular "My Boy Lollipop," while gospel themes in the texts of Esther Phillips's "Release Me" and "Steal Away" by Jimmy Hughes made strong connections to the black church.[9] The Garnet Mimms and the Enchanters hit "Cry Baby" and Joe Tex's "Hold What You've Got" even included recited sections that resembled sanctified preaching.

These early soul records were often politically charged, incorporating themes of social uplift that connected to the emerging Black Freedom movement. The lyrics of songs like "It's All Right" and "Keep On Pushing," both by the Impressions, cited soul as an element of personal strength in the context of the civil rights movement, and Sam Cooke's "A Change Is Gonna Come" reflected the movement's struggle and optimism, becoming an anthem in the African American community after his tragic death in 1964. A number of popular records also referred to soul in their titles, such as "Soul Twist," the Impressions' "Woman's Got Soul," Sugar Pie DeSanto's "Soulful Dress," Gene Chandler's "Soul

Hootenanny," Fontella Bass's "The Soul of a Man," and the Dixie Drifter's "Soul Heaven." The term *soul* began to appear widely in black culture at the time. This was increasingly reflected in music business nomenclature, when radio and retail outlets used soul as a metonym for the R&B market. In 1966, for example, a new local record store called the "Soul Shack" opened for business in Washington, D.C. and the prominent "black interest" AM radio station WOL rebranded itself "soul radio."[10] Stations and shops in other regions used the term similarly.

Soul was very appealing to mainstream record buyers, and its rise to popularity furthered a dynamic relationship between the R&B and mainstream markets. There was a lot of crossover between R&B and pop at the time. Like the short stretch during 1960 when *Cash Box* stopped tracking R&B as a distinct entity, *Billboard* suspended its R&B charts between November 1963 and January 1965, presumably because the markets had become so interchangeable.[11] Rather than using numerical charts, *Billboard* coverage continued in an ad-hoc manner during this interstitial period. In July 1964 the magazine introduced a new corresponding editor, Kal Rudman, who profiled regional radio professionals and organized several special "market analysis" sections about R&B in places like Philadelphia, Atlanta, Baltimore, North Carolina, and Cleveland.[12]

Editorials and articles in industry magazines reflected the ubiquity of soul-oriented R&B in the mainstream and the music business trying to come to grips with the style. "For the trade," read a May 1964 editorial in *Cash Box*, "'soul' music has evolved into one of the staple sounds of the pop singles market."[13] Bill Gavin, compiler of the well-known radio publication *The Gavin Report*, argued that despite the persistence of race-oriented market divisions in the business there was more of an opaque "musical color line," because "negroes buy and enjoy many different kinds of music, while many rhythm and blues records are well received by whites."[14] Rudman also viewed soul as a subset of R&B that appealed to older African American listeners. "When it is said of a record that it has 'soul,'" Gavin wrote, "the reference is to a deeply felt expression of a mature emotion, as opposed to a typical teenage preoccupation with 'first love' and its attendant frustrations."

Soul was extremely popular in mainstream outlets during 1965. Motown and Atlantic were the most important soul-oriented companies, but there were many other players in the field, such as Chess and Vee-Jay. Artists like James Brown and Solomon Burke, who had worked on the R&B circuit for years with little outside attention, achieved success in the pop market for the first time. White artists from both Britain and the

United States also released music that industry publications called "blue-eyed soul." British acts who performed in this style, such as the Animals, Dusty Springfield, Manfred Mann, the Rolling Stones, and the Spencer Davis Group, received little attention from the U.S. R&B market, but white American artists like the Reflections, the Righteous Brothers, and the Rascals had significant success in R&B outlets.[15]

During the first half of the 1960s the most important soul-oriented companies were located in large urban areas in the northern and western United States. Atlantic, Fury, and Scepter were all based in New York, Lenox and Imperial operated out of Los Angeles, and Chess and Vee-Jay were headquartered in Chicago. The soul scene in Motown's home of Detroit was also significant, with companies like Fortune, Lu Pine, and Anna all releasing crossover records in the late 1950s and early 1960s, and larger outfits like United Artists, Chess, and ABC-Paramount leasing records that were created in Detroit. Detroit-oriented soul hits from the time included Andre Williams's "Bacon Fat" and "Village of Love" by Nathaniel Mayer and the Fabulous Twilights (Fortune) and several records by the Detroit-based vocal group the Falcons, including "You're So Fine" (Lu Pine/Unart) and "Just for Your Love" (Anna/Chess).[16]

When *Billboard* reinstated its numerical R&B chart in January 1965 soul music was a significant part of the R&B and pop fields. Motown had three of the top-ten R&B singles at the time: the Temptations' "My Girl," which featured the soul-oriented vocals of David Ruffin, and the Supremes' "Come See about Me" and Marvin Gaye's "How Sweet It Is (To Be Loved by You)," neither of which connected very strongly to the soul movement. Alongside these tracks was a large group of records that invoked soul characteristics much more freely, such as Sam and Dave's "Hold What You've Got," "You've Lost That Lovin' Feelin'" by the Righteous Brothers, "Twine Time" by Alvin Cash and the Crawlers, and the posthumous Sam Cooke single that included "Shake" and "A Change Is Gonna Come." All of these records achieved significant crossover success, showing a new penchant for soul-oriented R&B to achieve wider popularity.

Motown's Early Soul

Motown participated heavily in the soul movement during the early 1960s. Early hits like "Money (That's What I Want)," "Way over There," and "Bye Bye Baby" had significant soul attributes, and several Motown artists became known for their soul-oriented releases. The Contours established a strong soul identity in a series of early singles produced by Berry Gordy. Their early B-side "Come On and Be Mine" featured a particularly growling vocal performance and "Do You Love Me" used a similar style. (After the success of this song the group released several self-answer songs, including "Shake Sherry" and "Can You Do It.") Many of Marvin Gaye's collaborations with Mickey Stevenson beginning in mid-1962 also incorporated soul elements. The vocal performances on "Stubborn Kind of Fellow" and "Hitch Hike" explored the upper reaches of his voice, creating grainy vocal textures, while the lyrics of both songs reflected an assertive form of black masculinity commonly found in soul. Gaye's 1963 single "Can I Get a Witness," written and produced by HDH, featured a similar vocal style in addition to lyrical and titular references to gospel over a pulsating, ecstatic instrumental track.

The first singles by Little Stevie Wonder, created mostly in collaboration with producers Berry Gordy and Clarence Paul, were strongly aligned with soul. The text of Wonder's first single, "I Call It Pretty Music but the Old People Call It the Blues," was a commentary on historical listening practices, genre naming, and generational divides within African American communities of the time. His next single was a duet with Paul called "Little Water Boy," in which Wonder played the role of a water-fetching youngster within a dialogue that drew upon a southern work song trope.[17]

Wonder's first hit, the live "Fingertips (Part 2)," had a complex history that connected him even more deeply to the soul movement. A studio recording of the song, featuring a lengthy flute solo by Motown backing musician and tour manager Thomas "Beans" Bowles, had first appeared on the 1962 album *The Jazz Soul of Little Stevie*. The "Fingertips" that achieved popularity was quite different, however. Recorded live at the Regal Theater in Chicago later that year, it features Wonder on harmonica and bongos, exemplifying soul in a number of ways. His vocals incorporate melismatic vocal improvisation redolent of gospel, and there is a series of call-and-response segments with the audience that highlight a style of communal singing commonly found in black churches. In the same manner that seasoned R&B performers like James Brown created dramatic tension by staging false endings to their concerts, a central element of the record is a chaotic instance in which the song seems to end, the band starts to play transition music, and Wonder refuses to stop playing.[18] This live version of "Fingertips" was later released as a single and it also appeared on the album *The 12 Year Old Genius*. Both records rose to the top of the *Billboard* charts in the summer of 1963.[19]

There were also a lot of unsuccessful Motown releases that evoked soul, through both text and musical references. Henry Lumpkin's "Mo Jo Hannah" told the tale of a voodoo woman; the Creations' "You're My Inspiration" transferred religious imagery into a love song; and the Miracles' "I Gotta Dance to Keep from Crying" took its title from a well-known southern work song.[20] The Miracles single "Way over There" featured a I–vi progression and an emphatic gospel-oriented vocal performance by Smokey Robinson.[21] The Temptations' B-side "Isn't She Pretty" featured a fast backbeat texture emphasized by clapping, a I–vi progression, and melismatic solo vocals along with dense vocal harmony. The early Holland and Dozier instrumental "Come on Home" used gospel-oriented piano, a prominent organ, and cyclical harmonic movement between I and IV.[22]

Soul was often the subject of discussions about R&B and pop at the time. In a 1965 issue of *Life*, Berry Gordy and producer Phil Spector both commented on the role of soul in mainstream pop. Spector was a white writer and producer, who had helped to create a number of popular girl group records, including the Crystals' "He's a Rebel" and "Da Doo Ron Ron" and the Ronettes' "Be My Baby." He was at the height of his popularity at the time and in the midst of a successful run of singles with the blue-eyed soul group the Righteous Brothers that included "You've Lost That Lovin' Feelin'" and "Unchained Melody." In the article, Spector uses the lens of soul to describe his work, defining the essence of the term as a "yearning to be free, to be needed, to be loved." Gordy aligned his music with the African American experience: "We've had the rats and the roaches—and the problems," he said. "Our sound was never calculated technically. It is something we just feel. We've never stopped to think about it."[23]

Gordy's reasoning—that Motown emerged from the black community and maintained an authentic sense of spontaneity—stood in direct opposition to the company's attempts to promote its music as the product of an assembly line. Motown's most popular records of the period, like those created by HDH for the Supremes, were certainly not known for features like heavy vocal timbres, improvised arrangements that eschewed instruments associated with Western classical music (especially strings), antagonistic attitudes toward mechanism and audible recording studio "trickery," or texts that connected with rural areas and the South. Positioned against Spector, Gordy's remarks depicted Motown through the lens of class and "natural" ability, a position that might not have been as tenable in comparisons with R&B producers from the South.

Interviews like this revealed how Motown's music and branding some-times used the soul aesthetic to represent a black perspective at the same time that it was constructing a "Motown Sound" brand.

There was another fascinating exchange in print that year between LeRoi Jones (later Amiri Baraka) and Charles Keil, which revealed how cultural critics perceived Motown and soul in a binary relationship. In a review published in *Down Beat*, Jones recommended that avant-garde jazz musicians might avoid becoming the music of "another emerging middle class" by listening to the "nasty ideas" of a variety of contempo-rary crossover R&B acts, including Motown groups like the Supremes, Mary Wells, Marvin Gaye, and the Four Tops. Keil questioned this advice in his book *Urban Blues*, expressing how he viewed Motown as the antith-esis of soul music. He wrote,

> Are "all the really nasty ideas" really there? Diana Ross, lead vocal-ist with the Supremes, contends: "It's less wild than most of the big beat music you hear today, but it still has feeling to it. We call it sweet music." "Sweet" and "nasty" are not necessarily contradictory terms, as used by Negros, and most Negros would agree that all these per-formers have "soul," that is, the ability to communicate something of a negro experience . . . but the Detroit sound is a soft-spoken, refined, polished soul music for the most part; the lyrics are usually pleasant, sometimes innocuous; the supporting beat is firm, simple, four to the bar, and highly danceable. Ironically, the Detroit sound is the one Negro-produced style that comes closest to being "the music of another emerging middle class," and a culturally integrated middle class at that, at least to the extent that white teenagers are committed to it.[24]

Even though they both consider it to be an undesirable affiliation, Jones and Keil do not view the alignment of popular music and the black middle class in the same way. Jones is concerned with the decline of the proletarian aspects of jazz; Keil is turned off by Motown's penchant for widespread cultural integration, arguing that it lessens the company's ability to reflect the "negro experience" at the heart of the soul style. Despite Motown's wide range of stylistic exploration, Keil's perspective was pervasive in the reception of Motown during the last half of the 1960s, a period when listeners commonly conflated Motown with the lighter side of the Motown Sound.

The Soul Imprint and Other Soul

Motown invested heavily in the soul market. In March 1964 the company started a dedicated imprint called Soul, which made an immediate impact on the record charts.[25] Among the two dozen singles released during the label's first two years, nine made the top twenty of the *Billboard* R&B charts and four appeared on the top twenty of the "Hot 100." Jr. Walker and the All Stars, a group that came to Motown from the Harvey imprint, was the first Soul act to have mainstream success. Released in January 1965, their record "Shotgun" was the first hit on the Soul label. They followed with several like-minded singles, including "Do the Boomerang," "Shake and Fingerpop," and "(I'm a) Road Runner," and also released a sequence of albums that explored soul characteristics in their titles and artwork, including *Shotgun* (1965), *Soul Session* (1966), and *Road Runner* (1966). Using specific forms of album iconography, references to rural life, aggressive saxophone melodies, and distant vocals with vernacular language and accent, Walker's records were part and parcel with the soul aesthetic of the time.

The next wave of popular Soul artists included Gladys Knight and the Pips, Jimmy Ruffin, and Shorty Long. These acts released a number of major crossover hits that trafficked heavily in the soul aesthetic, such as Ruffin's "What Becomes of the Brokenhearted" and Long's "Devil with the Blue Dress" and "Function at the Junction." While they were released on an imprint called Soul, and featured many common stylistic aspects of the soul movement, these records also incorporated elements of the Motown Sound. Long's "Night Fo' Last" used soul tropes like a Memphis-style guitar, dense organ, and gospel-oriented backing vocals but also featured a prominent Motown Beat. Walker's soul-oriented versions of "How Sweet It Is (To Be Loved by You)" and "Come See about Me" translated iconic Motown Sound tracks into a soul style.[26]

The music on Soul was only part of Motown's soul output in the mid-1960s. In addition to his duets and a continuing interest in cabaret music, many of Marvin Gaye's most popular solo records of the time furthered the soul orientation of his early work. "I'll Be Doggone" and "Ain't That Peculiar" used vernacular catchphrases and the minor key of "One More Heartache" was supported by a relentless shaker percussion track, providing dark text painting and a characteristic Motown Beat in support of a passionate lead vocal performance.

Stevie Wonder also continued to pursue soul. His singles "Hey

Harmonica Man," "Happy Street," and "Kiss Me Baby" were similar to "Fingertips," featuring soul-oriented elements like virtuosic harmonica performances, backbeat clapping, repetitive blues structures, and colloquial dialogue. His version of the Tommy Tucker hit "High Heel Sneakers," which was recorded live in Paris, used a similar approach. It called for audience participation and featured wailing soulful vocals and a text with blues tropes and vernacular musings. There were two B-sides to "High Heel Sneakers," and both connected differently to the soul movement. One was a live version of the Willie Nelson song "Funny How Time Slips Away," performed in a duet with Clarence Paul, which revealed commonalities between the evocations of rural life in both country and soul music.[27] An original song called "Music Talk" accompanied "High Heel Sneakers" in other printings. It followed a common soul formula in which the singer lists all of the instruments in the band, noting, "Everybody seems to be playing with a lot of soul." Later that year Wonder released "Uptight (Everything's Alright)." This single mixed Motown Sound elements like a strong Motown Beat, an active bass, and backing vocals by the Andantes with soul-oriented characteristics like heavy melismatic vocals, an arrangement featuring prominent horns in a southern soul style, and consistent modal motion between I and VII. The song's text, which describes a "poor man's son from across the railroad tracks," evokes rural, low-class stereotypes that were endemic to soul.[28]

Many other soul-inflected acts released music on Motown's Tamla, Gordy, and V. I. P. imprints during the mid-1960s, including the Elgins, Chris Clark, the Monitors, the Vows, Edwin Starr, Martha and the Vandellas, and the Isley Brothers. The Elgins' best-known singles, "Darling Baby" and "Heaven Must Have Sent You," were created with HDH in 1965 and 1966, during the height of the team's work with the Four Tops and the Supremes.[29] Starr was known best for his Ric-Tic single "Agent Double-O Soul," which was rereleased on the 1968 Gordy album *Soul Master*.[30] Reeves turned more closely to the soul style after the departure of HDH, which was evident in her last single of note, "Honey Chile," a track that contained a fascinating mix of soul-oriented lyrical images relating to rural life and a dense lead vocal performance. The Isley Brothers had a long history of crossover success that further signaled the company's interest in connecting to the soul market. The cover of their 1966 album *This Old Heart of Mine* depicts a white couple, but the notes on the back comment on this element of their music, recalling the group's earlier non-Motown hits and informing listeners that "their gospel-like warmth springs from their childhood experience singing in Sunday schools."[31]

Despite these releases, Motown still struggled to receive recognition as a soul-oriented company. A ninety-page *Billboard* special report published in June 1967, called "The World of Soul," was a clear reaction to the popularity of the soul aesthetic at the time.[32] Among profiles of Atlantic, Chess, and Stax, the article on Motown, which was called "The Best Ears in the Business," focused on the Supremes and mainstream crossover. There was no mention of successful releases on the Soul imprint or soulful singles by Stevie Wonder, Marvin Gaye, or Martha and the Vandellas.[33] Conversely, Atlantic was depicted as "paving the way" for the rise of R&B into the mainstream and Stax founder Jim Stewart was called the "voice from Soulsville" in a short piece that featured a photo of Rufus Thomas in a virtual minstrel pose with rising arms and bulging eyes.[34] With its Fordist models, technology-laden recordings, frenetic rhythmic patterns, and adventurous arranging techniques, the sonic and marketing elements of the Motown Sound seemed antithetical to the established character of soul.

Southern Soul and Motown

Atlantic Records was Motown's biggest competitor in the soul field. Atlantic artists had been vital to the formation of soul since the mid-1950s, when a series of releases by Ray Charles—"I Got a Woman" (1955), "This Little Girl of Mine" (1955), and "Hallelujah, I Love Her So" (1956)—fused gospel-oriented musical elements with secular themes, a formula at the foundation of an impressive string of R&B hits between 1953 and 1960.[35] Charles never had pop success during this period, but other Atlantic artists explored crossover using a variety of styles during the late 1950s, especially under the leadership of vice president and producer Jerry Wexler. Atlantic released novelty tunes by the Coasters, vocal harmony music by the Drifters, records like "Mr. Lee" by the girl group the Bobbettes, and song stylist performances such as "C. C. Rider" and "What Am I Living For" by Chuck Willis.

Atlantic continued to release a variety of successful soul-oriented music during the mid-1960s. Some of the formative blue-eyed soul artists of the time recorded for Atlantic and its Atco subsidiary, including Sonny and Cher and the Young Rascals (later simply the Rascals), a white rock group whose "Good Lovin'" rose to the top of the *Billboard* "Hot 100" in mid-1966.[36] Atlantic's African American soul acts were also extremely popular in the middle of the decade.[37] The company's most notable artist at the time was Aretha Franklin, whose background, performance ability, and history in the music business helped to create an archetype within the soul movement. The daughter of a celebrity preacher from Detroit, Franklin was well heeled in gospel from an early age. She signed to Columbia records while still in her teens and released several popular R&B singles in 1960 and 1961, including "Today I Sing the Blues" and "Won't Be Long."[38] After a decline in popularity and a general stylistic departure from the soul aesthetic, Franklin signed to Atlantic in early 1967 and returned to her soul roots. She recorded initially in Alabama and then New York with the group later called Swampers, the well-known backing band from Muscle Shoals. Her arrangements were stripped to bare essentials in these early Atlantic recordings and she was more involved in the creative process than she had been at Columbia, performing on piano, writing some songs, and providing extraordinary lead vocal performances.

Similar to the success of the Supremes earlier in the decade, Franklin's singles during this period often rose to the top of the pop charts, and records like "Respect" and "Chain of Fools" were among the best-known R&B releases of the time.[39] After her initial popularity on Atlantic, some of her arrangements used a more sophisticated pop sheen, such as "A Natural Woman (You Make Me Feel Like)," but she always maintained strong connections to the soul aesthetic. Her album repertoire included versions of songs by canonic soul figures like Sam Cooke, Curtis Mayfield, Otis Redding, and Don Covay. The notes accompanying these LPs connected her to Atlantic figures like Ray Charles and discussed her supernatural vocal abilities and gospel roots.[40] "1967 saw the greatest emergence of the blues in recent pop music history," wrote rock critic Jon Landau in his essay included on the back of Franklin's *Lady Soul.* "It was the year in which . . . 'soul' became the popular music of America. And in the vanguard of this sweeping restyling of popular music was the remarkable Aretha Franklin."[41] By the middle of 1968, when her image appeared on the cover of *Time* under the simple headline "The Sound of Soul," a half dozen of Franklin's records had reached the top ten of the "Hot 100."[42]

During a time when black communities saw the beginnings of a large-scale "return migration" back to the southern locales from which many families had originated earlier in the century, Franklin's alignment with Atlantic exemplified a wider music business trend in which southern-based companies and recording studios were increasingly attractive for northern artists.[43] The 1965 Arthur Alexander single "Detroit City," a remake of a country song made popular in recordings by Billy Grammer and Bobby Bare, echoes this perspective in song, presenting the perspective of a migrant living in Detroit who "wants to go home." (Alexander, a black performer, changed the song's words in several places, taking out references to "cotton fields" and other elements that were unseemly to African American migrants.)

Detroit was a wellspring of talent for southern companies during this time. Mable John, who had recorded for Motown early in the company's history and later performed behind Ray Charles as a Raelette, started recording for Stax in 1966. Darrell Banks signed with Atlantic's Atco subsidiary in 1967 and later moved to the Stax-owned Volt imprint, although he still recorded much of his work at United Sound in Detroit.[44] Eddie Floyd and Wilson Pickett, who sang together in the Detroit-based Falcons in 1961 and 1962, had similar trajectories.[45] Floyd signed to Stax records as a songwriter in 1965, and he later found fame singing his own songs. Pickett continued to work in the North for a short time after departing the Falcons, recording songs like "It's Too Late" with former Motown producer Robert Bateman (released on the Double-L imprint). He then signed with Atlantic in 1965 and released his first substantial hit, "In the Midnight Hour."[46]

For both performers and listeners, small firms from the South evoked an air of freedom because of their distance from the bustling centers of the music business. Yet large northern companies like Atlantic maintained an often-opaque connection with many of these small R&B independents, helping to create and distribute their soul music. In the same way that Chess and United Artists had once leased records from the smaller Gordy collective, a lot of the records that Atlantic acquired in this manner were produced outside the creative purview of Jerry Wexler or company founder Ahmet Ertegun. Some of these recordings appeared on the Atlantic or Atco imprints and others retained their label identity despite their Atlantic affiliation. Atlantic released a lot of soul music during the mid-1960s through agreements like these, especially records that came from the South.[47]

Atlantic's most important southern partner in the middle of the decade was Stax Records, a company based in Memphis owned by Jim Stewart and Estelle Axton.[48] After a 1960 licensing agreement for "'Cause I Love You," performed by the father-daughter duet Carla and Rufus, Atlantic and Stax developed a significant relationship that lasted until late 1967. Stax released a number of popular crossover records during this period. The company's first hit, the mostly instrumental single "Last Night," was recorded by the Mar-Keys and released on the Satellite imprint in mid-1961. It became a crossover smash at the end of the summer.[49] Another instrumental record, "Green Onions" by Booker T. and the MGs, crossed into the mainstream during the fall of 1962. In the mid-1960s Rufus Thomas scored several pop and R&B hits for Stax, including "Walking the Dog," and Otis Redding slowly emerged as an R&B star.[50] Jerry Wexler even sent one of his own acts, Sam and Dave, to record at Stax on a full-time basis during the period that Atlantic distributed the Stax catalog.

Like Motown, Stax used marketing techniques to support its musical identity.[51] In 1965 Jim Stewart petitioned Atlantic to add a dedicated promotions director, and Jerry Wexler agreed to pay half of the proposed salary. Stewart hired a former Washington, D.C., disc jockey named Al Bell, who recognized that in the growing soul music market the regional character of Stax was paramount.[52] According to Stax historian Rob Bowman, when Bell came to Tennessee in 1965 he "insisted that 'The Memphis Sound' be inscribed on virtually every piece of paper that emanated from the company."[53] As a result, this slogan appeared widely in industry publications, the popular press, and advertisements. The campaign was clearly modeled on Motown's simultaneous efforts to publicize both the "Detroit Sound" and the "Motown Sound."[54]

In forging a southern identity, Bell positioned Stax against the backdrop of Motown's market dominance, helping to construct the southern soul aesthetic as an alternative to the Motown Sound.[55] The company released singles like "Boot-Leg" by Booker T. and the MGs, Otis Redding's "Respect," and Sam and Dave's "Hold On! I'm Coming." In response to the mechanization of Motown's creative process, discussions of recording procedures at Stax became an important part of the way these records were marketed. Stax artists and executives condemned manufacturing and assembly line metaphors, forming a coordinated effort to establish a lack of technological mediation as an aspect of authenticity in their music. This was apparent as early as 1965, in an article about the "Memphis Sound" in *Billboard*, a piece that profiled four record company owners, including Stewart, who all agreed that Memphis-based music was created through "spontaneity" and "casualness" achieved through the use of head arrangements, or not using lead sheets during recording sessions, which created an "intangible feel" that "cannot be taught."[56] Well-known label owner and producer Sam Phillips also provided his perspective in the article, viewing music from Memphis as "derived from the influence of the uninhibited nature of the Negro in the South."

Another statement on the topic stemmed from an August 1967 Otis Redding interview originally printed in *Hit Parader* and later quoted in a January 1968 article in *Rolling Stone*. When asked about the differences between Stax and Motown, Redding explained that Motown's music was "mechanically done," and provided a romanticized view of creating music at Stax that fit perfectly into the soul aesthetic.[57] "At Stax the rule is: whatever you feel, play it," Redding said. "We cut everything together—horns, rhythm, and vocal. We'll do it three or four times, go back and listen to the results and pick the best one. If somebody doesn't like a line in the song, we'll go back and cut the whole song over. Until last year, we didn't even have a four-track tape recorder."

Depicting Stax as a homegrown, spontaneous, egalitarian environment was important for its emerging identity, and statements like these promoted the crude nature of the company's recording sessions as a mark of authenticity.[58] Despite the documented efforts of Atlantic engineer Tom Dowd to use "East coast technology" to modernize the Stax facilities early in the relationship between the two companies, commentary like this fabricated a sense that recordings created in Memphis were unmediated by industry forces.[59] Brian Ward has written about the manner in which this depiction defied the reality of the record business. "Critics have tended to privilege the recordings of Stax, Fame and their southern brethren over those of Motown, largely because the musicians who played on those southern sessions have been viewed as genuine artists, not artisans," he writes. "Southern players, so the legend goes, improvised amazing riffs and spontaneously wove together sublime rhythmic and harmonic patterns from the very warp and weft of their souls. Those protean moments were then instantly committed to tape and transferred, unsullied, onto vinyl."[60]

Stax executives expressed their soul identity in a variety of other ways. In 1964 the company created a response to the famous sign outside of Motown's Detroit headquarters, emblazoning the marquee of the Stax theater-turned-studio on McLemore Avenue in Memphis with the moniker "Soulsville U.S.A" (figures 3.1a–b). Similarly, the 1966 Mar-Keys album *The Great Memphis Sound* featured on its cover a swirling circular pattern leading directly to a map of Memphis, signifying on the well-known Motown "map" label that had been used on both long-play records and singles as far back as 1961 (figures 3.2a–b).[61]

One of the people who helped to establish marketing strategies at Stax during this time was Alan Abrams, who had worked as Motown's publicist between 1959 and 1966. Abrams went to work for Stax after leaving Motown, assisting Bell in his promotional efforts for a little more than a year, from April 1967 to May 1968.[62] While working for Motown,

Fig 3.1a. The façade of 2648 West Grand Boulevard in Detroit. (Courtesy of Al Abrams, Motown Black and White Collection.)

Abrams had been the author of many "Detroit Sound" and "Motown Sound" press releases, and it was no coincidence that nearly all of his publicity for Stax used the phrase "The Memphis Sound." Employing a formula similar to the one he had used to associate Motown with Detroit, many Abrams-authored Stax press releases from the time connected the music of Stax with the city of Memphis. He used the "Memphis Sound" campaign as the basis for several large-scale projects designed to facilitate crossover.[63] In one example, he solicited Tennessee senator Howard Baker to write the liner notes for the album *King and Queen*, which featured duets by Otis Redding and Carla Thomas. Referencing people like Tennessee Ernie Ford, W. C. Handy, and Elvis Presley, Baker's short essay emphasized the place of the new "Memphis Sound" within Tennessee's storied musical history.[64] Abrams then sent promotional copies of the record to various senators and reported their congratulations in a press release, announcing, "U. S. Senate Leaders Unite in Support and Praise of 'The Memphis Sound.'"[65] Stax later presented Baker with a plaque of appreciation from the company, which became another press opportunity for both parties.[66]

In another instance, Abrams participated in a series of articles and

Fig 3.1b. The façade of the Stax studio in Memphis. (Courtesy of Al Abrams, Motown Black and White Collection.)

letters printed in Detroit's black daily, the *Michigan Chronicle*, during early 1967, which targeted Detroit audiences with the Memphis Sound campaign. The initial piece was a routine announcement citing the recent arrival of Abrams at Stax, which laid the following claim: "The Stax-Volt people are contending that the Memphis Sound will replace the Detroit or Motown Sound, just as the folks from Hitsville USA, paced

Fig 3.2a. Motown's "Map" label. (Courtesy of Universal Music Enterprises.)

Fig 3.2b. The album
cover of the Mar-Keys,
The Great Memphis Sound

by The Supremes, replaced the Liverpool Sound of The Beatles."[67] Two
weeks later the paper published a response from Abrams in which he
used soul as a barometer to differentiate between the music of Motown
and Stax (table 3.1).[68] The letter appeared with several words in bold
that highlighted soulful descriptors of Stax in the text. (These emphatic
terms may have been the creative work of an editor.) Amid clear language referring to the elements of soul in Stax's music, the negative
connotation of the term *computerized* was especially pointed in Detroit,
a place where thousands of autoworkers were constantly wary of work-
place mechanization.[69]

Despite the perceived differences between working methods at Motown
and Stax there were a number of interesting musical connections between
records released by these two companies at the time. Stax musicians and
writers listened closely to Motown's music and often recorded Motown
songs. Booker T. Jones remembers using the Satellite Record Shop, located in the front of the Stax building on McLemore Avenue, as a "library"
to learn about popular music of the time, specifically citing his interest in

listening to Motown records.[70] Songwriter David Porter, who wrote many of the most popular Stax songs from the company's Atlantic era with Isaac Hayes, once recalled that he used the Temptations record "Don't Look Back," written by Smokey Robinson and Ronnie White, as a model for many of Sam and Dave's hits from 1966 and 1967, records like "Hold On! I'm Comin'" and "Soul Man."[71] Stax also released lighter music by vocal harmony groups like the Astors and singers like Carla Thomas, such as the pop-oriented record "B-A-B-Y."

Attentiveness to the Motown catalog sometimes translated into instances of quotation. Perhaps the best example of this occured in the Otis Redding and Carla Thomas song "Tramp," which was the first single from the album *King and Queen*.[72] (This was the release promoted so heavily by Al Abrams.) In the song's first verse, underneath a spoken dialogue between Redding and Thomas, the backing band quotes the main riff of the Temptations' single "(I Know) I'm Losing You," a Motown record that was rising up the charts at the time (table 3.2, example 3.1).[73] This

Table 3.1. A letter written by Alan Abrams published in the *Michigan Chronicle*

Dear Sir:

Many thanks for your kind words about "The Memphis Sound" and especially about Miss Carla Thomas in this week's issue of the Michigan Chronicle.

However, I must take issue with your comment (however intriguing the possibilities may be) that the "Memphis Sound" is out to replace the "Detroit Sound" as the dominant sound in today's music.

First of all, I am a firm believer in the principle of co-existence.

There is room enough in the world of popular music for both the "Memphis Sound" **and** the "Detroit Sound" . . . and there's still room for more, including the **other** "Detroit Sound" of Lebaron Taylor's Solid Hitbound Productions.

However, I firmly feel the "Memphis Sound" is the major **soul** sound today. A leading British musical publication recently pointed out the comparison by saying that the "Detroit Sound" has become like computerized music in that everything is worked out before a session takes place and that a lot of overdubbing is used.

The article went on to say that the "Memphis Sound" recording artists are **"live"** on a session, and that they are thus able to **"feel"** a session, which results in an overall sound with more **"heart"** and more **"soul"** than the music that Motown produces. An interesting argument when you come to think about it.

Lately I've noticed that the Stax-Volt artists are rapidly gaining a beachhead in this area. Some of our local DJ's are even using the "Memphis Sound" phrase to introduce Stax-Volt records on the air.

Listen to Sam and Dave now at the 20 Grand and really capture Detroit for the "Memphis Sound."

Best regards,

Al Abrams

Example 3.1. The guitar riff in "(I Know) I'm Losing You" and "Tramp"

Table 3.2. A conversation between Otis Redding and Carla Thomas in "Tramp"

(00:35)
CARLA: You know what Otis?
OTIS: What?
C: You're country.
O: That's all right.
C: You're straight from the Georgia woods.
O: That's good.
C: You know what? You wear overalls, big old Brogan shoes, and you need a haircut, tramp.
O: Haircut? Woman, you (goofin'?).

created a striking aural portrait of the complex relationship between Stax and Motown at the time. Within an overt display of the Memphis Sound, which was cited by a local politician as essentially Memphian, the Stax band had playfully included a reference to a current soul-oriented Motown hit.

Whitfield and "Grapevine"

Motown artists continued to embrace soul during the late 1960s. In 1967 alone the company released singles like "Ain't No Mountain High Enough" by Marvin Gaye and Tammi Terrell, Stevie Wonder's "I Was Made to Love Her," and the Gladys Knight and the Pips recording of "I Heard It through the Grapevine." A series of nominal soul albums on Motown imprints also appeared that year, including the Temptations' *With a Lot O' Soul*, the Isley Brothers' *Soul on the Rocks*, and Chris Clark's *Soul Sounds*. The importance of soul was evident in a Detroit speech delivered that summer by Motown vice president Esther Gordy Edwards. Addressing a group of teens about the "role of youth in a changing society," Edwards remarked, "Motown Record Corporation takes great pride in producing the Motown sound known throughout the world as the 'Sound of Young America,' but most recently hailed as the 'Soul of Young America.'"[74] Even the Supremes were pitched using soul vocabulary. In the liner notes to the 1967 album *The Supremes Sing Holland Dozier Holland*, Detroit radio DJ Scott Regan wrote, "All the songs in this album are real, they have feeling, depth and soul."

Norman Whitfield rose to prominence during this period as Motown's most important producer and songwriter in the soul style.[75] He had only dabbled in production before coming to Motown during the early 1960s, creating small-time records for the Detroit-based Thelma and K. O. imprints. At Motown, Whitfield's first writing and production credit was "Wherever I Lay My Hat" for Marvin Gaye in September 1962. He also helped to write Gaye's "Pride and Joy," which was released the next year. Whitfield produced his first hit in mid-1964, the Temptations' "Girl (Why You Wanna Make Me Blue)," which he had written with Eddie Holland.

Whitfield often wrote songs with collaborators, mostly Eddie Holland and Barrett Strong, but acted as sole producer during the recording process. As producer, he worked as a musical auteur, taking substantial creative liberties with arrangements, technical choices, and songwriting. As his stature grew, he stretched the musical and conceptual bounds of the Motown producer role. Whitfield often rerecorded his songs with multiple Motown artists, changing the style and arrangement in different versions. It had been common for Motown acts to revisit the company's previous hits and include them as B-sides or album filler to beef up publishing royalties for Jobete. Whitfield took this a step further. He produced contrasting versions of his songs that were often released as singles, revisiting works like "(I Know) I'm Losing You" (the Temptations and Rare Earth), "I Wish It Would Rain" (the Temptations and Gladys Knight and the Pips), and "Papa Was a Rolling Stone" (Undisputed Truth and the the Temptations).

The most successful multiple-version Whitfield and Strong hit was "I Heard It through the Grapevine." Whitfield produced seven versions of "Grapevine" during a four-year period, including recordings by Bobby Taylor, Gladys Knight and the Pips, Marvin Gaye, the Temptations, the Undisputed Truth, and the Miracles (who recorded it twice) (table 3.3).[76] Strong recalls that he developed a preliminary draft of "Grapevine" in 1966, and Smokey Robinson and the Miracles first recorded it not long after.[77] The Miracles often used material written and produced by Robinson himself for single releases (sometimes in collaboration with other members of the group), so Whitfield's production didn't get much traction with Motown Quality Control. Undaunted, Whitfield made several more recordings of "Grapevine" the next year. In February 1967 Gaye performed vocal duties on a new recording that replicated many aspects of the Miracles' version but used a much slower tempo. Gaye's rendition was also not issued as a single. Instead, the company released a version of the song "Your Unchanging Love," which hit stores in June 1967.

Less than a week after Quality Control rejected Gaye's "Grapevine," Whitfield revamped the song with a different set of rhythm section charts and started the process of recording a third version. This new attempt featured Gladys Knight and the Pips, a group that had achieved cross-over success with soul styles earlier in the decade while recording for R&B-oriented independents such as Vee-Jay, Fury, and Maxx. Knight and the Pips had recently signed to Soul and were marketed heavily as a soul-oriented group. A glossy tour program produced during the group's early years at Motown introduced them as "Messengers of Soul," containing quotes from Knight about the meaning of soul. Similarly, the liner notes to Knight's first LP, *Everybody Needs Love*, called the group "soulful exponents of the Motown Sound."[78]

Knight's "Grapevine" exhibits many musical connections to the soul aesthetic (example 3.2). The rhythm section uses a relatively austere set of instrumental forces that includes drums, bass, guitar, two pianos, and tambourine. There is a squealing six-bar saxophone solo during its instrumental bridge, but, like most Stax productions from the time, this version of "Grapevine" has no arranged orchestral instruments. The featured drum part that begins the track evokes a polyrhythmic pan-African percussion line, and two closely voiced pianos perform in a distinct gospel style with slurred notes and blues-inflected seventh chords. Knight's

Table 3.3. Multiple versions of "I Heard It through the Grapevine" produced by Norman Whitfield, 1966–70

Artist	Recording initiated	Release date	First release
The Miracles	August 2, 1966	September 1998	*Motown Sings Motown Treasures*
Marvin Gaye	February 8, 1967	August 1968 November 1968	*In the Groove* Single
Gladys Knight and the Pips	June 15, 1967	September 1967 September 1967	*Everybody Needs Love* Single
Bobby Taylor	December 13, 1967	September 1968	*Bobby Taylor and the Vancouvers*
The Temptations	May 18, 1968	February 1969	*Cloud Nine*
The Miracles	May 21, 1968*	August 1968	*Special Occasion*
The Undisputed Truth	January 14, 1970	July 1971	*The Undisputed Truth*

Note: *New vocals were created on this date over the Miracles' 1966 version

Example 3.2. Gladys Knight and the Pips, "I Heard It through the Grapevine" (0:07–0:18)

dark, melismatic vocals conjure a church setting while delivering the song's text, which uses the metaphor of a grapevine to discuss a rumor gone awry, a reference to gossip within the African American community.[79] The arrangement is in C major, and she plays with the intonation of blue notes in her vocal line, especially in her approach to the tone E. Depending on harmonic function (generally over I or IV) and melodic direction, Knight alternates between E and E♭ when she approaches the tone during the verse and chorus sections.[80] (In the second line, she even sings the word *blue* while performing a lengthy blue-note slur.) She also slides around the tone G, most prominently in the vocal entrance at the beginning of the record.

Instrumentally, the performance of Motown studio bassist James Jamerson helps to create a strong sense of soul in "Grapevine." In light of perceptions that Motown's music was manufactured and preplanned, it is instructive to understand the extent to which Jamerson improvised his performance. In the original band chart, the arranger wrote out the feel for the first verse but left the line blank for Jamerson to ad lib at the beginning of the first chorus section.[81] At this point in the recording (0:30), Jamerson's performance changes tack by including a syncopated downward leap to a first-inversion subdominant followed by a chromatic ascent back to the tonic, an alteration that clearly invokes gospel harmonization.

While Jamerson's performance was mostly constructed on the spot, the multitrack masters of Knight's "Grapevine" show that Whitfield used advanced studio technology to carefully craft the final amalgamation of performances. Several noticeable overdubs are apparent when listening to the eight tracks in isolation, including the omission of a guitar part from the original tracking session, a reworked piano performance that omitted a four-bar electric piano solo, added drum accents, and an overdubbed tambourine and saxophone solo. In addition, there is evidence that Knight's final vocal performance was created from several takes rather than a single, continuous performance. But none of this "trickery" was audible, and "Grapevine" fit perfectly within the rising tide of soul. After its release in September, the record climbed steadily up the national record charts and by the end of the year it rose to the top of the *Billboard* "R&B" chart and to number two on the "Hot 100," propelling Gladys Knight and the Pips into a soul craze on the "Hot 100" during late 1967.

Like many of Whitfield's most popular songs, "I Heard It through the Grapevine" had a life beyond Knight's popular recording. Motown revisited Gaye's version less than a year later when, as Berry Gordy recalls, "the DJs played it so much off the album that we had to release it as a single."[82] This older-but-newer version debuted on the "Hot 100" in November 1968 and four weeks later it reached the number-one position, a spot that it held for seven weeks.[83] In contrast to the dense piano, African drum line, and prominent saxophone of Knight's version, Gaye's record approaches soul in a different manner (example 3.3). The tempo is a bit faster than Knight's, but its quarter-note pulse and lack of syncopation make it seem slower and more brooding.[84] It features an electric piano (probably a Wurlitzer), a pulsing low organ, a lavish French horn and string arrangement by Paul Riser, and a serpent-like tambourine and primitive toms, both used to connote exotic, nonurban symbols.[85] The backing vocal parts, performed in Gaye's version by the Andantes, focus on crisp homophonic harmonies and produce an affect quite different from the vocals performed by the Pips.[86]

The vocal approaches of Knight and Gaye provide an interesting perspective on the gendered nature of soul singing. Gaye's performance evokes a distressed male outlook, connecting to the weeping trope exhibited by Levi Stubbs in many Four Tops singles from the mid-1960s. His strained voice nearly cracks several times as he reveals the manner in which he learned of his lost partner. Knight, on the other hand, uses a confident, full voice throughout her performance, belting the entire piece in an open-throated manner. In contrast to Gaye's vulnerability,

Example 3.3. Marvin Gaye, "I Heard It through the Grapevine" (0:17–0:25)

Knight engages in a finger-wagging, aggressive threat when she sings lines like "I'm just about to lose my mind." The mood of her performance—with its rhythmic drive, melodic language, and range—is far more self-assured than Gaye's approach, shading the text as confrontational instead of tragic.

Whitfield and the Temptations

Whitfield developed an especially important creative relationship with the Temptations in the late 1960s. The first Temptations ensemble had formed in 1960, several years before Whitfield came to Motown, and included five members: Melvin Franklin, Eddie Kendricks, Elbridge "Al"

Bryant, Otis Williams, and Paul Williams. After releasing six singles that were not very popular on the national record charts, the group entered a series of successful collaborations with Smokey Robinson as writer and producer in 1964.[87] The most important product of Robinson's work with the group was "My Girl," which featured lead vocals by new member David Ruffin (who replaced Bryant).[88]

Whitfield's first sessions with the Temptations were in November 1962, when he produced the B-side "May I Have This Dance." He recorded several other Temptations B-sides and album tracks during the next three years in addition to one moderately successful single, "Girl (Why You Wanna Make Me Blue)." His first standout production for the group was "Ain't Too Proud to Beg," released in May 1966. This track was an interesting example of hybridity between soul and the Motown Sound. It incorporated elements like a Motown Beat, a typical Motown solo saxophone, a subtle string arrangement, and a strong independent bass line, but it also used soul-oriented slang and vernacularisms, gruff lead vocals performed by Ruffin, gospel-oriented backing vocals, brassy horn arrangements, and prominent bongos. Whitfield's success with "Ain't Too Proud to Beg" allowed him to replace Smokey Robinson as the Temptations' de facto producer. His productions for the group during the next several years included other successful records records like "(I Know) I'm Losing You," "I Wish It Would Rain," and "You're My Everything."

In mid-1968 the Temptations experienced a major lineup change after Ruffin developed a rift with his bandmates and was voted out of the group.[89] New vocalist Dennis Edwards led the vocal element of the next Temptations single, "Cloud Nine." This release marked the group's departure into psychedelic soul, a style that had became popular in 1967 and 1968 when a group of artists including Jimi Hendrix, Sly and the Family Stone, and the 5th Dimension began to fuse elements of soul and rock. "Cloud Nine" departed from Motown Sound stereotypes in a number of ways.[90] The track was pieced together out of a D-minor jam and dwelled on a single riff, creating an especially static harmonic language. "Primitive" hand percussion evoking the soul aesthetic and a repetitive sixteenth-note hi-hat motive complimented this figure. Wah-wah, distortion, and other guitar effects aligned the track with rock and funk. Lyrically, the song discussed issues of poverty, abuse, depression, social and personal responsibility, and violence.[91] It also indirectly invoked the use of recreational drugs, which was uncharacteristic for Motown.

"Cloud Nine" was revelatory for Whitfield. In the six years between its release and his exodus from Motown in December 1974 he used the record's psychedelic soul template to create dozens of other tracks (table 3.4). Like the music created by HDH, Robinson, and Stevenson earlier in the decade, Whitfield's work with the Temptations in the late 1960s and early 1970s established a clear dialogic identity. He retained elements of the Motown Sound like eclectic orchestral instrumentation, prominent idiomatic string and horn arrangements, characteristic independent bass, and intricate backing vocals, while simultaneously stretching the limits of acceptable subject matter and musical ideas

Table 3.4: Psychedelic soul records written and produced by Norman Whitfield for the Temptations

Title	Debut date
Cloud Nine	October 1968
Runaway Child, Running Wild	January 1969
Don't Let the Joneses Get You Down	May 1969
I Can't Get Next to You	July 1969
Message from a Black Man	September 1969
Slave	September 1969
Psychedelic Shack	December 1969
Friendship Train	March 1970
Hum Along and Dance	March 1970
Take a Stroll Thru Your Mind	March 1970
War	March 1970
You Make Your Own Heaven and Hell Right Here on Earth	March 1970
Ball of Confusion (That's What the World Is Today)	May 1970
Ungena Za Ulimwengu (Unite the World)	September 1970
Love Can Be Anything (Can't Nothing Be Love but Love)	April 1971
Smiling Faces Sometimes	April 1971
Superstar (Remember How You Got Where You Are)	October 1971
Stop the War Now	January 1972
Take a Look Around	January 1972
What It Is	January 1972
Mother Nature	June 1972
Funky Music Sho' Nuff Turns Me On	August 1972
Papa Was a Rolling Stone	August 1972
Run Charlie Run	August 1972
Hurry Tomorrow	February 1973
Law of the Land	February 1973
Ma	February 1973
Masterpiece	February 1973
Plastic Man	February 1973
Let Your Hair Down	November 1973
1990	December 1973
You've Got My Soul on Fire	December 1973
Zoom	December 1973

Note: Bold indicates that the track was released as an A-side single

at Motown. He also experimented with song length. In opposition to Motown singles from the early 1960s, which rarely spanned more than three minutes, Temptations albums after 1968 frequently contained tracks that were six minutes or longer.[92] These extended tracks were often the result of a different approach to song form that used soul cinematically by fusing symphonic musical gestures with funk riffs and texts about inner-city black life.

Like other psychedelic soul records, Whitfield's productions for the Temptations juxtaposed musical elements of rock and pan-African culture.[93] They incorporated rock guitar effects like distortion, delay, and frequency modulation, often performed by newer Motown guitarists Melvin "Wah-Wah" Ragin and Dennis Coffey. The wah-wah, in particular, appeared on nearly every Whitfield-produced record in this style, changing the timbre of individual guitar tones and chords and heightening the presence of strummed or muted eighth- and sixteenth-note patterns.[94] Musical allusions to "Africa" occurred in many forms in these records, such as the opening of "You Make Your Own Heaven and Hell Right Here on Earth," which featured a unison chant on the words "kumba ya ya."[95] Hand drums assumed a nationalistic perspective and black viewpoints were reflected in the texts of songs like "Ball of Confusion (That's What the World Is Today)," which recited a list of things wrong with the ghetto due to white flight and urban renewal.[96] Similarly, songs like "Slave," "Run Charlie Run," and "Ain't No Justice" addressed themes pertaining to black history, and "Message from a Black Man" repeated during a lengthy chorus section the pro-black phrase, "no matter how hard you try you can't stop me now."[97]

Short, repetitive riffs were an important musical component of Whitfield's psychedelic soul style.[98] Many of his productions used a repeating melodic pattern in the bass that lasted for two to four measures and contained only a handful of pitches (usually a minor pentatonic collection). Once established, these riffs often continued throughout the entire song. Temptations tracks like "Papa Was a Rolling Stone," "Masterpiece," "Smiling Faces Sometimes," and "Take a Stroll Thru Your Mind" were based on slow riffs of this type, changing chords very slowly and deemphasizing harmonic progression as a method of providing forward motion through the form.[99] In the album version of "Papa Was a Rolling Stone," for example, the song's riff plays throughout the record accompanied by a closed hi-hat performing eighth notes and stressing each beat. Over the course of the twelve-minute piece, rhythmic elements enter and exit in a modular fashion, in logical accordance

Example 3.4. The groove in "Papa Was a Rolling Stone" (8:40)

with the four-measure riff cycle and the overall song structure.[100] The densest groove occurs before the final verse, from 8:43 to 9:30, a section that includes the drum kit's eighth-note hi-hat pattern, a kick drum on beat two, a snare on beat four, the bass riff, off-beat quarter-note hand claps, and a wah-wah guitar performing a sixteenth-note pattern (example 3.4). The groove in this climactic section of the record miraculously floats above the sparse riff for forty-five seconds, superimposing features of the Motown Beat and a laid-back half-time feel.[101]

After the Soul Explosion

The popularity of soul changed the trajectory of R&B crossover in a number of systematic ways. Discussion about soul became widespread in mainstream outlets during the last years of the 1960s, displaying the manner in which R&B had become further entrenched into larger conversations about music and popular culture. *Esquire* published an "Introduction to Soul" for its mostly white and male readership, Aretha Franklin appeared on the cover of *Time*, and a spate of soul-oriented publications sprang out of the woodwork, including a newspaper created by Los Angeles radio station KGFJ called *Soul,* a California-based glossy magazine called *Soul Illustrated,* and nearly a dozen other international publications that used the term *soul* in their titles.[102] New York's PBS affiliate began airing a weekly television series called *Soul!* and several years later Don Cornelius started the black-oriented dance program *Soul Train.*[103] After publishing "The World of Soul" for several years, in 1969 *Billboard* even changed the name of its black pop charts from "Rhythm and Blues" to "Soul."

Economically, the success of soul music changed the nature of R&B crossover. For one, it made independent companies specializing in R&B attractive targets for corporate acquisition. Atlantic was an example of a high-profile firm that changed ownership during this period, when Warner Brothers–Seven Arts purchased it in late 1967. This sale reshaped Atlantic's modus operandi and altered the future of the company's many smaller partners, such as Stax, which elected to dissolve its distribution agreement and lost the rights to its master recordings.[104] After the sudden death of Otis Redding and the departure of Sam and Dave because of the Atlantic sale, Stax was forced to completely redefine its image, roster, and sound. Ironically, Stax had a particularly strong connection to Detroit during its post-Atlantic period, which diluted the sense of regional dualism created by the Memphis Sound campaign. Al Bell hired a number of non-Memphians to work for Stax, including Detroit-based songwriter and producer Don Davis, whose arrival was announced with a press release written by Al Abrams titled "Do Mixed Marriages Work?"[105] A number of Davis's Stax tracks were recorded in Michigan, and Isaac Hayes, whose music helped to define the new direction of Stax, even produced a portion of his 1969 album *Hot Buttered Soul* in Detroit.[106]

The rise of a soul aesthetic helped to foster large-scale changes in public attitudes toward African American corporate leadership. In line with the growing popularity of nationalist thought, many black listeners began to question Motown's economic commitment to the black community. "During the height of the black power and black pride movement," observes historian Gerald Early, "many younger blacks thought Motown sounded too 'white,' too crossover, and not authentically 'black' enough." According to Early, this was "not actually a realization that grew from Motown's 'sound' as much as from its marketing success."[107] A striking example of these newer attitudes occurred in late-1967, when African American journalist Lee Ivory held a press conference to speak about Motown's penchant for mistreating artists, managing news, and snubbing black disc jockeys. "Sooner or later the wraps will be pulled from the entire set-up," Ivory told reporters, "and the world will know that it is not 'love' that keeps entertainers recording for Motown."[108]

Motown's economic perspective prompted some listeners and critics to improperly discount the company's role in the soul movement. Involvement in soul music was seen as an example of Motown opportunistically and disingenuously pursuing a sector of the R&B market, exploiting its connection to African American culture after having accepted the fruits of white society. Changing conceptions of blackness in the corporate arena and pressure on black-owned businesses to become involved in African American communities inspired a well-publicized set of expansion plans at Motown in October 1967. The company hired several important black executives during the next year, such as former Vee-Jay president Ewart Abner and one-time Southern Christian Leadership Conference public relations director Junius Griffin.[109] Motown also started a spoken word imprint called Black Forum several years later, through which it released a handful of socially conscious recordings by activists and intellectuals like Stokely Carmichael, Ossie Davis, Amiri Baraka, and Elaine Brown.[110]

Economics and civic involvement helped to put a public face on Motown's commitment to the black community during the late 1960s, but the content and breadth of Motown's releases during this time were just as revealing. These records help to tell a story about Motown and soul that is uncommon in histories of R&B. Just as Ray Charles, Curtis Mayfield, Aretha Franklin, and Otis Redding were widely considered to be central characters in the emergence and popularity of soul during the 1960s, Motown artists like Stevie Wonder, Jr. Walker and the All Stars, Gladys Knight and the Pips, Marvin Gaye, and the Temptations were also among soul's most important stars. Motown made a huge impact on the soul field, and the manner in which these artists' sonic depictions of blackness interacted with contested aspects of American identity is a reminder of Motown's historical alignment with the R&B market and the continuing tensions surrounding race that existed in pop music during the late 1960s.

FOUR | Motown International

The International Market

Many record companies that were aligned with the R&B market in the 1960s pursued audiences in foreign countries. A lot of these firms were simultaneously navigating a move into the American mainstream, and attempts to enter a vast international marketplace became another form of crossover. But there were differences between crossover at home and foreign sales. There were no market divisions for R&B and country and western in other countries, governments often ran radio, musicians faced regulations concerning foreign work permits, and there were usually different distribution systems. The long history of slavery at the bedrock of American segregation was also not echoed in many countries around the world, causing African American identity to be perceived differently. Nonetheless, a number of firms were immensely successful in the quest to court non-American listeners, and by the end of the decade black pop from the United States was a fixture on top-ten lists all over the world.

The popularity of R&B extended a long reception history of pop music by African American performers in many international sites. Ragtime and swing had become especially popular in Europe after World War I, when jazz musicians and their recordings first left the United States and vibrant scenes emerged in places like France, Denmark, and Italy. Shared language, wartime alliances, and cultural similarity helped to make England one of the most important outposts for American popular music during this time. The Fisk Jubilee Singers had become the "biggest black music sensation of the Victorian period" during two important tours of the UK.[1] Minstrelsy and dance band music led by African American musicians and bandleaders had also gained popularity in the

1880s, and big band jazz made its mark on British society in the late 1910s with the arrival of the Southern Syncopated Orchestra.[2] Some of this music was performed by white locals, in spite of the diverse populations within the UK at the time. Most of the nonwhite musicians were from other countries.[3] "By far," writes blues historian Paul Oliver, "the majority of black artists who performed on the public stage in Britain were from the USA."[4]

Work permits for foreign musicians became extremely hard to obtain between 1934 and 1955, which made it difficult for Americans to perform in Britain.[5] Adherents of blues and jazz helped to promote performances by American musicians like Big Bill Broonzy and Josh White during the early 1950s, both of whom performed as "variety musicians." Most pop performers were simply unable to work in Britain during those two decades.[6] There was a dramatic resurgence of British interest in American popular music when these regulations loosened. Rock and roll, jazz, and blues performers from the United States toured the UK, often in large revue packages. Bill Haley visited in 1957 after several highly publicized screenings of the film *Rock around the Clock*, helping to further a teen-oriented craze for American rock and roll that had started several years earlier with the release of his recordings.[7] Other important rock acts followed, including a popular tour featuring the Everly Brothers in 1959.

Many pop-oriented black artists visited the UK during the late 1950s. Johnny Mathis toured in February 1957, and the Platters completed several extended tours. Frankie Lymon and the Teenagers traveled extensively in the British Isles, headlining one package that had lengthy residencies in Liverpool, Birmingham, London, Manchester, and Glasgow. Dozens of other artists who had crossed from the R&B charts to mainstream success in the United States made trips to Britain during the first years of the 1960s, including Clyde McPhatter (1960), Chubby Checker (1962), Little Richard and Sam Cooke (1962), Bo Diddley and Little Richard (with the Everly Brothers) (1963), Ray Charles (1963), and Chuck Berry (1964).[8] These artists' performances were often received with great anticipation, which was evident in coverage within a well-established group of weekly music-oriented papers that catered to young British fans, including *New Musical Express, Melody Maker,* and *Record Mirror.*[9]

In addition to live performances, recordings were vital to the popularity of American artists abroad.[10] The London American label, an imprint of (British) Decca records, was one of the most important firms to release records created by independent companies in the United States for British audiences during the postwar period.[11] Beginning in the mid-1950s, London American issued recordings from the catalogs of Imperial (Fats Domino, T-Bone Walker), Atlantic (Ruth Brown, Clyde McPhatter, the Drifters), Sun (Carl Perkins), Chess (Willie Dixon, the Moonglows, Chuck Berry), Specialty (Little Richard), Keen (Sam Cooke), and many others.[12] These records appeared in the UK and other places on the London American imprint, but their printed labels included references to original American record company sources. This provided vital information for foreign listeners.

Widespread interest in establishing connections with international markets prompted U.S. industry magazines to print foreign contact information during the late 1950s. *Billboard* began coverage of the international jukebox market in late 1959 and added a more robust "International Music" section early the next year.[13] In December 1963 it published its first "International Talent Directory," a sixty-page supplement that listed artists, booking agents, impresarios, music critics, and record companies. Throughout the 1960s this coverage intensified, with talent directories, "international market reports," a news-oriented section called "From the Music Capitals," and listings of international charts labeled "Hits of the World." *Cash Box* focused similarly on foreign markets in the early 1960s, with a substantial semiannual "International Directory" and heavy weekly coverage.[14]

Like other crossover acts from the United States, Motown artists were poised perfectly to engage with international audiences through recordings.[15] Because of its association with United Artists, the first Tamla single, "Come to Me," was released in the UK on London American in May 1959. The Miracles' "Shop Around" and "Ain't It Baby" and Barrett Strong's "Money" also appeared on London American in the following months.[16] Motown used three other distributors in the UK in later years, illustrating both the company's resolve to release music in Britain and the unstable nature of international distribution for an independently owned company from the United States. Fontana released four Motown singles in late 1961 and early 1962, including the Marvelettes' "Please Mr. Postman" and "Twistin' Postman," the Miracles' "What's So Good about Good-By," and Eddie Holland's "Jamie."[17] Later that year Motown's distribution moved to Oriole, one of the most prominent independently owned companies in Britain.[18] Oriole issued nearly twenty Motown singles during 1962 and 1963, establishing the first important body of Motown records in Britain on a single imprint.[19] Motown entered a new distribution agreement with EMI in mid-1963. The first Motown release on the EMI Stateside imprint was Martha and the Vandellas' "Heat Wave" in October 1963, and several dozen singles followed in the UK and Australia during the next eighteen months.[20] This was the beginning of a relationship between Motown and EMI that lasted for decades, helping Motown to establish a strong sales presence in the UK for years to come.

British Youth Culture and the Emergence of R&B

British music historians often write about an "Americanization" of British popular culture that began after World War II and continued throughout most of the 1960s.[21] Many of the popular styles in the UK during these years, including rock and roll, trad jazz, skiffle, high school, and beat music, were related to styles first introduced in the United States.[22] African American pop was especially important to several subcultural groups that formed in Britain after World War II.[23] The earliest of these was the Teds, which emerged during the early 1950s. Teds (or Teddy Boys) had a collective sense of fashion and were enamored with first-wave rock and roll. Often wearing drape jackets and coiffing their hair in a distinctive manner, Teds aligned with a new post–World War II British youth market whose interests were based on images and sounds of American youth filtered through the lens of popular media.[24] Teds were not accepted by older Britains. Cultural historian Paul Gilroy has written that the rise of the Ted subculture incited controversies surrounding racial mixing similar to the reception of early rock and roll in the United States. There was "not only fear of the degeneration of the white 'race' in general and defilement of its womanhood in particular," he writes, "but also the creation of a youth sub-culture in which black style and expertise were absolutely central."[25] A related group known as the Rockers formed later in the 1950s with a similar working-class bent. They were also interested in rock and roll, but they wore trademark leather jackets and greased-back hair and used motorcycles for transportation.[26]

British listeners discovered American R&B in a variety of different ways during the early 1960s.[27] Many older fans became interested in R&B after a decline in the popularity of trad jazz. Black pop found its "early audiences on the fringes of the folk and, more importantly, jazz club world," recalls British pop music historian Iain Chambers, and "these musical interests were often intersected by an art school bohemia."[28] During the 1940s and 1950s, a large group of British blues aficionados had collected American records, attended and organized live performances, and formed fan clubs called "appreciation societies." A leading blues enthusiast in the UK was historian Paul Oliver, who published his first book on the subject in 1959 (a biography of Bessie Smith), followed by many other seminal works.[29] A number of serial publications, often in the form of appreciation society newsletters, helped to connect British fans of American blues. Simon Napier's *Blues Unlimited*, the journal of the Blues Appreciation Society, was first published in April 1963; Roger Eagle's *R&B Scene* began in June 1964; and Bob Groom's *Blues World* published its first issue in March 1965. Blues fans created an important network of reception that often showed interest in related forms of black pop like R&B and soul music.

In 1963 a movement emerged around a group of young Britains who called themselves Mods. Known for a striking clean-cut sense of fashion, Mods often wore smart suits and thin ties and had a frenetic lifestyle in which they worked all day, danced all night, and buzzed through London on Lambretta scooters.[30] Mods became the most noteworthy group to appropriate R&B during Motown's early years in the UK.[31] The importance of R&B to Mods was evident in many ways, including record collecting habits, music played at social events, and the repertoire and performance styles of British rock bands closely associated with Mod subculture at the time, groups like the Small Faces and the Who.

London's gay community was another significant audience.[32] A large number of young gay men in the UK became fascinated with Motown's music at this time. As early enthusiast David Nathan remembers, "many of the leading lights in the Motown movement in the UK were gay."[33] Some fans were closeted or too young to understand the nature of their sexual identity, but others were better known and more open to the gay community, such as John Stephen, the fashion designer and shop owner known as the "king of Carnaby Street," who spearheaded Mod fashion and participated in the underground network of men who frequented clubs like Le Duce, one of London's early gay nightclubs.[34] Another gay pioneer from the time was Peter Burton, who worked as a journalist and managed Le Duce during the mid-1960s. In his memoirs Burton depicts an emerging dance club culture that enjoyed fast-paced American R&B, recalling the ways in which black music from America aligned with the heightened, drug-induced emotions of his circle.[35] "Blues [pills] gave you energy," he once wrote. "they kept you awake for the all-night sessions—if straight at the Scene; if gay at Le Duce."

> . . . dancing was important. As was the music that was popular with the Mods and the young gays who frequented Le Duce. The two groups

shared the same music. The mid Sixties saw the slow beginnings of acceptance of black music—soul, blue beat, ska (which subsequently transmuted into reggae) and Tamla Motown. . . . Early Motown was "gay music" every bit as much as Hi-Energy [*sic*] is now.[36]

Connections like this, between queer British culture and American R&B, have been chronicled in Annie Randall's work on transatlantic dialogue in the music of Dusty Springfield and Madeline Bell.[37] Still, homosexuality was mostly closeted in London at the time, leaving a disproportionately small amount of evidence about the manner in which gay fans contributed to R&B reception.

Most African American performers had been reared in a segregated society and they found different attitudes toward racial difference in the UK. After World War II there had been massive immigration to England from colonies like Trinidad, Barbados, Jamaica, Pakistan, and India, which created communities of Caribbean and South Asian descendants in many English cities.[38] An influx of citizens of color spurred several notable race riots and led to a lot of public debate about this new sector of the British public.[39] In one 1966 study, Norman Pannell and Fenner Brockway claimed that immigration had become "one of the most controversial issues of the day"; Peter Griffiths's 1966 book *A Question of Colour* connected these immigration issues directly to race, opening with the evocative passage "Britain has a racial problem"; another contemporaneous writer, Lord (Godfrey) Elton, called this "unarmed invasion" a "social crisis."[40]

Motown's "invasion" of the UK took on pointed cultural meaning. Even though most UK fans were white listeners from the middle and working classes, they consumed Motown's music against a backdrop of long-standing British attitudes toward race and ethnicity imbued with a complex history of colonialism. As African Americans, Motown artists emerged into British society at the same time that this immigration problem reached a tipping point. When British fans of Motown reveled in the new sounds of American R&B created by these groups from Detroit they were exhibiting a controversial form of racial acceptance in the face of a national "crisis."

Transatlantic Dialogue

With few American records available to the public and little knowledge of Motown as an institution, interpretations of Motown songs became

common in the UK during the early 1960s. These records and performances were both controversial and important.[41] Because most audience members were unaware of Motown's records, or didn't feel strongly
about records as primary texts, racial power dynamics of "copy covering"
that had been largely abandoned in the United States were still prevalent
in the UK.[42] New British versions often obfuscated their sources and prevented Motown's original recordings from achieving popularity, but they
also disseminated the company's songs to a wider international public
and provided impetus for listeners to look for records by Motown acts.

British musicians used Motown's catalog as a wellspring of source material. Many British fans were first exposed to Motown's music through
live performances or recorded covers by British artists. British groups
and singers interpreted a range of different Motown songs during the
early 1960s.[43] Female song stylists like Cilla Black, Lulu, Helen Shapiro,
and Dusty Springfield recorded a lot of Motown's music. They used songs
recorded by Motown girl and guy groups as well as male and female
solo performers, and the styles of their sources ranged from Motown's
middle-of-the-road material to its early experiments with soul.

Motown's music was also very popular with rock-oriented bands active in both London and Merseyside, including groups like the Beatles,
the Rolling Stones, the Searchers, and Bern Elliott and the Fenmen.
"Money" was the most popular Motown song among these groups. It was
released as the A-side on at least five singles in 1963 and 1964 and became
standard repertoire for British rock bands of the period.[44] These records
were stylistically similar, and their collective treatment of "Money" provides some evidence of how Motown's music was treated among British
rock bands of the time. Each of these records was performed in D major
or E major, easy keys for guitarists, rather than the F major of the original
Barrett Strong recording. Several groups also increased the song's tempo dramatically, such as Freddie and the Dreamers and Buddy Britton
and the Regents, or interpreted the song in a surf style, which further
emphasized a faster tempo and the role of the guitar.

British rock musicians often struggled to interpret the modal language of "Money." The song is in a major key but includes flatted (blue)
third and sixth scale degrees in its vocal melody and instrumental riffs
(example 4.1). This created the need for performers who learned the
song aurally to choose between minor or major modes in several key
spots, which were sometimes interpreted differently. The song's IV
chord, for example, was most commonly played in the major mode, but
one Merseybeat group, the Undertakers, interpreted it consistently as a

Example 4.1. The introduction to Barrett Strong, "Money (That's What I Want)" (0:04-0:10)

Example 4.2. The introduction to the Beatles, "Money (That's What I Want)" performed during their Decca Records audition on New Year's Day 1962 (0:00-0:06)

minor triad.[45] Likewise, in an early Beatles recording from their Decca Records audition in January 1962 the group avoided the natural third scale degree by altering the chromatic climb in the main riff—which moves $\hat{1}$–$\flat\hat{3}$–$\hat{3}$–$\hat{4}$—by inserting a return to scale degree 1, resulting in a more menacing minor pattern of $\hat{1}$–$\flat\hat{3}$–$\hat{1}$–$\hat{4}$ (example 4.2).[46]

Only a few Motown songs released by British groups became popular on the UK charts, and all of these records were by male rock bands. The first was Brian Poole and the Tremeloes' version of "Do You Love Me," which reached the top of the Britsh *Record Retailer* listing in October 1963,

Example 4.3. The beginning of the chorus in the Contours, "Do You Love Me" (Gordy 7005)

Example 4.4. The beginning of the chorus in Brian Poole and the Tremeloes, "Do You Love Me"

about a year after the Contours' version hit in America.[47] There were some interesting musical differences in this new version. Rhythmically, it smoothed the consistent syncopation of the Contours' arrangement by deemphasizing the subdivision on beat 2 that had appeared in the snare drum throughout the Motown record (examples 4.3 and 4.4). There were also melodic changes. The Tremeloes' version was arranged a minor third lower than the original, in D major rather than F major, which led to a much different vocal style by allowing the melody to sit in a more comfortable area of the average male range. This was evident in a contrasting approach to the melody in the chorus, particularly the tone accompanying the rhythmically emphasized word *love* in each phrase. Contours lead singer Billy Gordon consistently sang this pitch between the notes, emphasizing its blue quality. Poole normalized it.[48]

Brian Poole and the Tremeloes' live performances also showed evidence of cultural translation. "Do You Love Me" depicts a protagonist who tries to regain the affection of a significant other by demonstrating various individual dances. Bodily movement is central to its lyrics. A clip

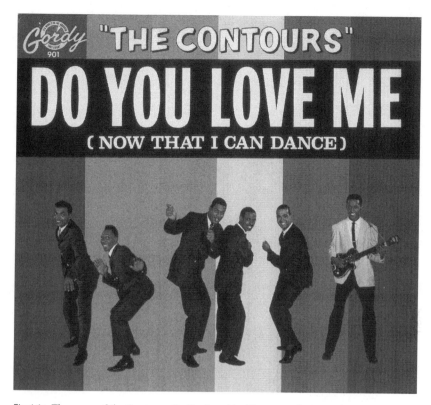

Fig 4.1a. The cover of the Contours, *Do You Love Me*. (Courtesy of Universal Music Enterprises.)

of the Contours performing at the Apollo Theater with the Motortown Revue in 1963 documents the manner in which the group's wild choreography echoed this textual narrative, featuring fast, seemingly uncontrolled and chaotic group movement punctuated by twisting, turning, and splitting.[49] This approach to dance was reflected on the cover of the Contours' first Motown LP, *Do You Love Me*, released in the United States in October 1962 (figure 4.1a–b). In contrast, the rigid choreography used in an early promotional video for the Tremeloes' recording was deeply ironic. Poole remained stationary throughout most of the performance, hardly moving his lower body, while the group's three guitarists were arranged in a regimented line and moved only in unison.[50]

The Tremeloes were criticized for their success with "Do You Love Me" within a series of articles in the British music weeklies that were part of a growing conversation about native interpretations of American

Fig 4.1b. A screen capture of the Tremeloes performing "Do You Love Me" from a 1963 promotional video

R&B.[51] Despite the differences between their version and the original Contours record, the sense that they had appropriated material from an African American source prompted readers and columnists to call the group's interpretive strategy "copying." Poole responded in a November 1963 article, claiming that the band was hurt by these accusations.[52] His reply seemed to call more attention to the origins of "Do You Love Me," eliciting many letters to the editor during the next several months.[53]

The Tremeloes next single, "I Can Dance," was an answer song to "Do You Love Me." It included a text that commented on the original song and also used many its musical features.[54] Poole defended the originality of "I Can Dance" to *Record Mirror* columnist Peter Jones, saying, "They can't complain about 'I Can Dance,' because it was written specially for us."[55] He spoke to Jones again a month later, the results of which were published in an article called "Brian Poole Answers His Critics: 'I Can Dance' Is No Copy of 'Do You Love Me.'"[56] Many listeners were clearly dubious, however, which led Poole to acquiesce during a February 1964 interview. "We genuinely believed in 'I Can Dance' at the time," he told

Record Mirror columnist Langley Johnson. "Now we know we were wrong. It failed to make the grade in the charts and we realised the fans thought it was a mistake."[57]

There were other popular covers. One was a version of "Baby I Need Your Loving" by the Merseybeat band the Fourmost, which entered the British charts during the summer of 1964.[58] This group was aligned professionally with the Beatles in several ways. The two bands had played on the same bills, Brian Epstein managed both groups, the Fourmost had recorded several songs written by Lennon and McCartney (like other Epstein clients), and they had also worked closely with George Martin, the producer who was integral to the Beatles' recording process.[59]

Like Poole's interpretation, the rigid delivery of vocalist Brian O'Hara was one of the biggest differences between the Fourmost recording of "Baby I Need Your Loving" and the Four Tops original.[60] But this new version was more notable for its striking similarities to Motown's HDH production. The key, tempo, instrumentation, and backing vocal arrangements were nearly identical to the Motown record, creating a version so similar that undiscerning listeners might mistake one for the other. Like "Do You Love Me," this record elicited charges of "copying" in the press. Fourmost bassist Billy Hatten commented on these negative views in a public response published in *Record Mirror*. "The situation quite simply is this," he stated.

> The Four Tops disc came out weeks ago and despite a heck of a lot of plugging it just didn't do much on sales. We waited, deliberately, to give the Americans a chance to make it—or not to make it. We liked the song. In fact, it was easily the best we'd heard in a long time. If John and Paul had come up with a better one . . . O.K. we'd have done that. But it IS a big song and it needs a big backing. That's where the "copying" allegation comes in. We used a big orchestra and choir. Our recording manager **George Martin**, said we needed this sort of sound—and we accepted his word. After all, he's had a lot of hits.[61]

Hatten's strategy in this passage was clear. He sought to align the Fourmost with the Beatles, a group whose interpretations of American music had not been questioned by the British press.

The Beatles had been fans of Motown for years and their interest was crucial to British reception of the company's music during 1963 and 1964. They had played songs like "Money" during their early years in Liverpool and went on to record a batch of Motown songs in 1963, during the height of Beatlemania in the United Kingdom, which significantly aided Motown's rising popularity in the UK.[62] A version of "You've Really Got a Hold on Me" was recorded in July 1963, six months after the Miracles track had been released in the United Kingdom on Oriole. It was set a minor third lower than the original, with John Lennon singing lead and George Harrison performing Motown's horn arrangements on guitar. They also recorded a new version of "Money" during the same session. Echoing the ambiguity between minor and major found in other British rock group recordings, the piano arrangement used parallel thirds in the introduction and solo that emphasized the song's modal mixture. An interpretation of "Please Mr. Postman" was recorded two weeks later, using the new four-track machine at Abbey Road Studios to overdub two performances of Lennon's lead vocals.[63]

As lead vocalist on all three of these Beatles Motown recordings, Lennon was especially dedicated to pursuing the music of Motown. During the mid-1960s he owned a portable jukebox for personal entertainment while traveling, which contained a number of Motown releases, including three Miracles singles ("The Tracks of My Tears," "Shop Around," "What's So Good about Good-By"), the Contours' "First I Look at the Purse," and Barrett Strong's "Money."[64] His familiarity with current Motown music was on display during a playful section of the band's 1965 Christmas fan club album, when he spontaneously burst into a rendition of "It's the Same Old Song."

Unlike reactions to the Tremeloes and the Fourmost, critics and fans widely considered the Beatles to be anointed disseminators of American R&B. Their markedly different reception was based on personal and professional connections with American artists, relationships that were often depicted in the music weeklies.[65] Mary Wells performed with the Beatles during a tour of the United Kingdom in the fall of 1964, and told *Melody Maker* that Motown groups had "a lot to thank the Beatles for."[66] Brenda Holloway joined the group for their U.S. tour the next year. There were even rumors in the press at the time, started by Motown's press agents, that the Beatles were interested in commissioning songs from HDH and recording at Hitsville. The UK music papers connected the Beatles to Motown so frequently that John Lennon once bristled at a Motown reference by a reporter, remarking that the press made it seem as if they indiscriminately liked all Motown music.[67]

Motown executives and artists relished the Beatles' interest in their music. The company publicized significant instances in which the Beatles mentioned Motown, such as Lennon's fan club recording quotation and the group's interest in recording with HDH.[68] One notice informed the news media that Berry Gordy was lobbying to bring the Beatles to Detroit as a way of saying "thank you" to the city's teenagers.[69] Motown artists also recorded interpretations of British music. The 1964 Supremes album *A Bit of Liverpool*—retitled *With Love (From Us to You)* in Britain—contained a collection of songs originally recorded by the Beatles and other British Invasion groups along with rerecorded versions of Motown songs popular among British audiences, including "You've Really Got a Hold on Me" and "Do You Love Me."[70] In another instance, an obscure record by a Motown group named the Hornets called "Give Me a Kiss" revealed the extent to which Beatlemania was present at Hitsville. Recorded on the same day the Beatles first landed on American soil, it was a contrafact of "I Want to Hold Your Hand" that featured the same harmonic progression and a melody that was strikingly similar to the well-known Beatles song.[71]

British Mediators

British listeners were exposed to Motown records in a variety of other ways. The government-owned BBC played little popular music, but water-based pirate stations like Radio Caroline and Radio London were at their peak during this time, often playing new records from America.[72] Independent companies from the United States also sponsored shows on Radio Luxembourg, a station that undermined the BBC stronghold by broadcasting from outside the UK's borders.[73] These stations helped to establish new on-air personalities, such as Tony Blackburn and Mike Raven, who gained authority with British youth. (Both Raven and Blackburn went on to work for the new pop-oriented BBC 1 in 1967 after the passage of the Marine Offenses Act, which effectively ended the pirate movement.)[74] Television appearances also helped to popularize R&B. Many American performers appeared on *Thank Your Lucky Stars* and *Top of the Pops*, and the youth-oriented *Ready Steady Go!* was especially important for American R&B acts after premiering in mid-1963.[75]

Like Blackburn and Raven, journalists writing for the music weeklies helped to spread knowledge about Motown. Reporters like Norman Jopling, Tony Hall, and Peter Jones doggedly promoted original American recordings in *New Record Mirror* (later called *Record Mirror*).[76] Jopling first singled out the music of Motown in March 1963. In the first installment of a lengthy series called The Great Unknowns, he made hyperbolic claims about the popularity of the Miracles in America that helped to underscore his excitement for Motown's music:

Currently in the U. S. top ten is a disc called "You Really Got a Hold On Me." It's by a group called the Miracles, and it's on the Tamla label. What's so peculiar about that, you may well think, just another of those American groups that don't mean a thing here. That's the point. They **should** mean something. For the Miracles have had more hits than almost any other U.S. group—and threequarters of them haven't been issued in Britain. . . . there are still many hits from this label that haven't been issued here. Hits by artists who have suffered considerably from a lack of a steady British outlet.[77]

Environments that catered to dancing were also central to Motown's growing popularity. An important group of nightclubs in and around London provided venues for groups performing covers of American R&B and blues.[78] Many of the venues that had featured trad jazz during the late 1950s slowly shifted their focus to accommodate this interest. In March 1963 Bob Dawbarn reported in *Melody Maker* that several of London's largest clubs, including the Marquee and the Flamingo, were now focusing on R&B, and the 100 Club made a similar transformation during this time.[79] The growth of black pop in the UK rapidly changed the character of many performance venues. Instead of thought-provoking trad jazz performances, a number of clubs began to use records and live performances by local R&B outfits to elicit dancing.[80] As a result, the London-based Scene and the Twisted Wheel in Manchester, and various disk jockeys who worked at these establishments, like Roger Eagle and Guy Stevens, became especially important arbiters of R&B in the UK.[81]

British-based appreciation societies fulfilled another promotional role.[82] Many organizations of this type had formed around an interest in blues and jazz early in the decade and as interest in pop-oriented R&B grew a variety of new groups emerged. The most important for Motown fans was the Tamla-Motown Appreciation Society (TMAS).[83] This group was founded at the end of 1963 by Dave Godin, who became the main conduit between Motown's corporate offices in Detroit and the British public.[84] The TMAS focused on record collecting, disseminating information, and discussing issues pertinent to UK fans of Motown. It maintained the appearance of a self-sufficient fan club, but Godin's activities were financed in part by Motown, showing the company's adroitness for understanding and exploiting postwar social networks of British youth.[85]

Membership was probably between five hundred and one thousand during the organization's peak years of 1965 and 1966.[86] Most members resided in and around London, but the society kept a watchful eye on other locales.[87] In January 1964 the group published its first newsletter, *Mary Wells and Motown News*, which spanned five issues over the next six months.[88] About a year later, the TMAS began to reflect a broader interest in Motown artists and its newsletter was renamed *Hitsville U.S.A.* This publication comprised thirteen issues published throughout 1965 and early 1966. Godin's voice was dominant throughout the newsletters, and he was often quick to offer ideas and opinions. Each edition began with a letter from Godin, initially addressed "Dear Friend" and later changed to "Dear Swinger and Friend" (figure 4.2). The remaining pages were filled with news, single and album reviews, feature articles, charts of readers' top singles, and facsimiles of American and British articles from the popular press.

The TMAS was a finicky lot that preferred original recordings and exhibited a visceral reaction toward interpretations of American black music by British groups. Group members felt that deep, knowledgeable consumption elicited a fuller understanding of African American culture, while imitation and uninformed appropriation was unethical and showed an unforgivable level of cultural ignorance. In one letter to the editor, reader Mike Carlyle suggested that American publishers impose restrictions on cover versions. "Why on earth doesn't Motown Publishing Dept. [*sic*] follow Dionne Warwick's lead and have all their songs insured by legal means against being covered," he wrote. "This would mercifully stop the murdering of great Motown originals by third-rate British groups."[89] Carlyle didn't realize that Motown executives and songwriters promoted these versions and profited greatly from their existence.

Like writers for the music weeklies, Godin and other members of the TMAS were comfortable with R&B interpretations by artists like the Beatles and Dusty Springfield but held scorn for a number of other British acts who recorded and performed American songs. Godin singled out the Rolling Stones as particularly guilty of co-opting blues and soul.[90] The Rolling Stones "have been a source of controversy amongst the R&B. [*sic*] fraternity since they first appeared," he wrote.

> But regardless of if you think they play R&B. [*sic*] or not, the fact remains that they do deliberately exploit their role of [*sic*] walking symbols against parents, etc. . . . Is it too much to ask the promoters for an all American Rhythm & Blues show without having to endure the exhibitionism of neurotics and phonies, who are more intent on projecting a sexual image than in making music.[91]

HITSVILLE USA ✳ Vol.1 No.2

Contents: FEBRUARY 1965

Dear Swinger & Friend ✳

WOW! The response to the "new wave" magazine was simply overwhelming and I would sincerely like to thank all of you who wrote letters of congratulations. As you will observe more improvements are operative, and I hope that this will continue. Certainly our next step forward will be to increase the number of pages. All this of course is a far cry from just one year ago, and it is all due to the loyal support we have in our club, that unites us into being the most friendly club in the country. Soon we will be sending out another questionaire to feel the pulse of the club so to speak, but in the meantime I can answer one or two points that have cropped up in the mail. Firstly, I welcome all articles that readers care to submit - this is your club and your magazine. Secondly you can send up to 20 titles for the Hot 20 poll each month. Finally I hope I will meet many of you personally during March. **Dave**

Photos by courtesy of MOTOWN RECORD CORPORATION, MRS.
CLAUDETTE ROBINSON and SUE RECORDS - - - - - - - - -
★★
Published by the Tamla-Motown Appreciation Society,
139 Church Road, Bexleyheath, Kent, England.
Copyright 1965 by Tamla-Motown Appreciation Society.

Fig 4.2. The table of contents and "Dear Swinger and Friend" column from *Hitsville U.S.A.* 1, no. 2 (February 1965). (Courtesy of the Mick Patrick Collection.)

Godin may have been biased because he had a personal history with Mick Jagger. Both men went to Dartford Grammar School and Godin often claimed to have exposed Jagger to R&B during the 1950s.[92]

References in TMAS newsletters revealed members' attitudes toward politics, race, and subcultural membership. Advertisements were printed for organizations supporting muscular dystrophy and Oxfam, a member's campaign to collect guide dogs for the blind, and Godin's later efforts against cruelty to animals in filmmaking.[93] The clear racial divide between TMAS members and their subjects was apparent in a small advertisement in the first issue of *Hitsville U.S.A.* for *Black like Me*, an experiential nonfiction book that recalled a white author's experiences in the South after purposefully altering his skin color.[94] "I was recently asked by a journalist if the members of The Tamla-Motown Appreciation Society were mostly 'mods or Rockers,'" Godin wrote during the summer of 1964, just after a series of public riots in Brighton between Mods and Rockers at a beachside resort. "I replied that we were neither, but were all 'swingers and friends.'"[95]

Society membership was decidedly male, and there was a strong connection between the group's work and the growing interest in pop-oriented R&B within London's young gay community. One veiled example of this appeared in a special issue published around September 1965 that memorialized Mick Page, an active TMAS member who had recently committed suicide. While it is not made explicit that Page was gay, there were strong indications in what seems to be coded language within the tribute issue, which repeatedly described him as "sensitive." One passage by Godin alludes to the fact that bouts of depression ultimately contributed to Page's self-inflicted death.

> Maybe from Mick's point of view it was inevitable and beyond his control that he had to do what he did; almost as a symptom of his sensitive character that he knew the pain of too much tender feeling in a world that is only too happy to be harsh, brutal and unloving. This same tenderness of heart that is so well reflected in the music we loved.
>
> I liked Mick though <u>exactly</u> as he was, and though I wish with all my heart this had not happened, I wouldn't have wanted <u>him</u> to be different. So if the sorrow of the past few weeks is the inevitable price that must be paid for knowing him <u>just</u> as he was, <u>exactly</u> as he was, then I can pay it by abiding his decision and be grateful for the good times we did have together, and the good fortune that brought him into the Society to begin with.[96]

Just as Peter Burton's memoirs reflected connections between Motown's message and a sense of "sentiment and emotion" within London's gay community, Godin's eulogy for the "sensitive" Page highlighted a "tenderness of heart" in Motown's music that made it especially meaningful for some British fans.

The TMAS interacted directly with artists in a number of ways. The group congratulated Motown acts publicly for their British success by placing an advertisement in *Record Mirror* to draw attention to the results of the magazine's annual R&B poll. Motown lavishly hosted several members of the Society at its Detroit headquarters during the period, including Godin and Clive Stone. *Hitsville U.S.A.* printed accounts of these trips, depicting them in vivid detail. The TMAS threw receptions and sent welcoming parties to the airport when Motown artists arrived in London. Godin remarked prior to a Supremes visit in October 1964 that he hoped to "give at least the semblance of an Apollo audience reaction."[97] The society often published photographs of events like this in its newsletters, documenting receptions for and interaction with artists (figure 4.3).[98] Motown artists and employees reciprocated by submitting letters and providing industry photographs for reprinting.[99] The most fascinating example of this was a recording called "Greetings to Tamla Motown Appreciation Society," a special two-sided single produced and printed by Motown.[100] The first side began with Berry Gordy offering "greetings to all you swingers and friends," and the remainder of the recording included spoken messages from about dozen artists, who thanked Godin and the society and expressed their interest in coming to Britain.

TMAS members were ultimately focused on supporting an intense culture of fandom surrounding American black pop. They were active listeners with an interest in making direct contact with artists. They had a thirst for rigorous factual knowledge about artists and recordings and a commitment to promoting their chosen music to peers.[101] Extensive discographies were printed in most newsletters, and reviews often carried manufacturer numbers for both British and U.S. releases, which helped to clarify the availability of Motown records for non-American buyers.[102] In the inaugural issue of *Hitsville U.S.A.*, Godin discussed the overriding importance of taste to the society's goals. "We know what we like, the type of music we like, and the stars we like," he wrote. "Last year we earnt [*sic*] the compliment that we were more than just a fan club but more a way of life."[103]

Fig 4.3. Personal snapshots documenting the activities of the Tamla Motown Appreciation Society. The Supremes performing during a promotional event at EMI in London, October 1964 (top); The Marvelettes arriving in London, June 1965 (bottom). (Courtesy of the E. Azalia Hackley Collection of African Americans in the Performing Arts, Detroit Public Library.)

Tamla-Motown in the UK

In December 1963 and January 1964 Stevie Wonder performed live concerts in France and appeared on *Ready Steady Go!* and *Thank Your Lucky Stars* in Britain.[104] These were the first of many transatlantic performances by Motown acts during the mid-1960s, a series of visits that showed an increasing interest in courting British listeners. In June 1964 Mary Wells's recording of "My Guy" became the first Motown recording to break into the British mainstream.[105] The Supremes' "Where Did Our Love Go" and "Baby Love" became popular not long after, and the group traveled to Britain for three weeks in October, performing on *Thank Your Lucky Stars* and *Top of the Pops.* Their various appearances during this trip were well publicized in the music weeklies and British trades.[106]

In the middle of November "Baby Love" reached the top of charts in the UK, which prompted Bob Dawbarn to report in *Melody Maker* that the Detroit sound had formed a "beach-head."[107] "Britain exported the Liverpool sound to America," he wrote, "now America is sending us back the Detroit sound in the shape of Tamla-Motown artists." A Motown press release at the time similarly cast these Supremes' appearances in light of the British Invasion, noting, "Their appearances on British television shows caused crowd scenes reminiscent of the Beatles [*sic*] reception in America."[108] Before the end of the year there was a quick succession of visits by other Motown acts—Martha and the Vandellas, Marvin Gaye, the Miracles, Kim Weston, and Earl Van Dyke—who mostly spoke with reporters, greeted the TMAS, and recorded performances for television.[109]

The culmination of Motown's promotional activity during this period was a large-scale tour that traveled to the UK in early 1965. Motown press releases made it clear that the company was, in fact, hoping to create a "reverse" invasion with this package, countering the Beatles' first three visits to the United States. The revue was organized in collaboration with Arthur Howes and Harold Davidson, British promoters who organized many popular traveling shows during the 1960s. It included the Supremes, Martha and the Vandellas, the Miracles, Stevie Wonder, the "Earl Van Dyke Six," and British singer Georgie Fame and completed a four-week run of live shows between March 9 and April 12. In January 1965 *Melody Maker* proclaimed, "The first British tour by the Tamla-Motown American pop package has been set. The Supremes top the bill, and chart-topper Georgie Fame will be special guest star." A multitude of other articles and advertisements about Motown appeared in print during the weeks before the trip, updating readers regularly about performance dates and television appearances.[110]

Package tours featuring American rock and R&B artists had been common in the UK since the late 1950s, but it was rare for a single company to promote a tour in this manner.[111] Initial reactions indicated that the visit had strong potential for success. Norman Jopling wrote an article called "America Hits Back with Tamla Motown Attack" and *Melody Maker* printed a feature by Bob Dawbarn that called Tamla-Motown "Not So Much a Pop Sound, More a Way of Life."[112] But there were also indications that the revue might encounter difficulties, and many of these fears came to light. A negative editorial was published in *Record Mirror* in mid-February by Tony Hall, who worked as a promoter for British Decca in the UK, the same company that ran the London American imprint and housed releases by a variety of American imprints.[113] Hall criticized Motown's style, claiming that the "the most important reason for the Detroit failure to monopolise our charts is . . . the material," which he thought was "too samey," "too rhythmic and not melodic enough for the masses here."[114] Two weeks later, only months before his death, TMAS member Mick Page replied in a letter to the editor:

> Tony Hall asks how much a way of life is **Tamla Motown** over here. If he wants to find out, he should join the **Tamla-Motown Appreciation Society** which is streets ahead of any other fan-club in the country and is not only a way of life but the firmest and strongest link between R and B fans. Tamla may not have broken through in the way we'd like, but then neither have American records in general. What breakthrough there has been in this respect is proportionately more Motown's than anyone else.[115]

There was also an apologetic interview with Godin, "Tamla-Motown's 'biggest fan,'" printed in *New Musical Express* in the middle of March. He spoke about the great potential for disappointment and publicly warned Motown artists that British audiences were "much tamer" than those in America.[116] On the whole, the crowds were both small and tame, and the tour was a major disappointment for Motown.[117] After it was over, Alan Smith's review in *New Musical Express* called it the "much-vaunted, ill-fated Tamla-Motown road show." "When it ended its first British tour last week," he wrote, "[the Tamla-Motown show] left behind a trail of near-empty theatres halfway across the country."[118]

But all was not lost. The tour coincided with the launch of a new EMI-distributed label call Tamla-Motown, which was a major development in the company's brand identity in the UK.[119] In the weeks before the Tamla-Motown launch, *Record Retailer* was swarmed with advertisements announcing the grand scope of Motown's formal entrance into the British market.[120] The first Tamla-Motown singles were mostly by the artists featured on the British tour, and a selection of EPs and albums—including the Supremes' *With Love from Us to You*—were also released concurrently.[121]

Numerous television appearances by Motown acts were broadcast in Britain during the period immediately surrounding the tour, which made a big impact on the company's reception. The most important was a special called *The Sound of Motown*, created by producer Vicki Wickham and the team that produced *Ready Steady Go!*[122] The program highlighted the artists featured in the touring review along with the Temptations, who had traveled to England to tape their performance. It used prerecorded music by the Funk Brothers, and Motown's acts danced and performed their vocals live in the studio.[123] In quick succession, Motown stars positioned in different places within a large thrust stage configuration performed more than a dozen of the company's hits, both old and new. Short medleys of songs allowed Motown performers to connect their identities to works already known well by British audiences. Fast tempos and frenetic energy were evident throughout the special, often contradicting Motown's usual style of comportment. This was especially evident in the version of "Mickey's Monkey" by the Miracles that closed the show, in which members of the group performed the song's wild signature dance, lowering to the ground, whipping their hair, and eliciting screams from the audience.[124]

Georgie Fame did not perform on the program. Instead, Dusty Springfield served as host. She opened the special by performing several of her hits with Martha and the Vandellas, including "Wishin' and Hopin'" and "I Can't Hear You."[125] In spite of Springfield's close relationship to American R&B artists, her performance style on *The Sound of Motown* contrasted in many ways with the choreography of Motown's acts.[126] During "Wishin' and Hopin'," for example, Martha Reeves focused almost completely on the act of singing, while Springfield mimed objects discussed in the lyrics, laughed and giggled freely, and even patted Reeves on the head in one awkward moment (figure 4.4).[127] Springfield introduced all of the acts during the show and in one extended passage during the middle of the program she briefly introduced Motown itself

Fig 4.4. A screen capture of Martha and the Vandellas and Dusty Springfield performing "Wishin' and Hopin'" during *The Sound of Motown* television special

to a new British audience, explaining that a collection of buildings in Detroit called "Hitsville U.S.A." is where "all that lovely big, thumping, noshy noise is put together."[128]

Soul in the UK

The TMAS disbanded in early 1966, which reflected a change in Motown's promotional strategy as well as an increased interest in more obscure soul among many British fans. In his "Dear Swinger and Friend" column, Godin wrote,

> I am sorry if this edition is later reaching you than usual (smile), but it is essential that the news I have this month is received by both members and the press at the same time. It has been requested that the Tamla-Motown Appreciation Society disband into separate fan clubs for individual artists under the Tamla-Motown-Gordy-Soul-V. I. P. labels, whilst retaining a Tamla-Motown Fan Club to cover those lesser known TM artists who are not as yet well-known enough to merit the formation of an individual club.[129]

"As of next month, the magazine will undergo a change in both format and title," he continued. "It will in [*sic*] future be 8½″ by 5¼″ in size, and the new title will be RHYTHM & SOUL USA."[130] In the same editorial Godin also announced a new society called Friends of American Rhythm and Blues (FARBS), which was to serve as an umbrella organization for a variety of new fan clubs.

The change in Godin's focus was a direct result of his official break with the Motown corporate office. David Nathan, who worked closely with Godin as a contributing writer for various publications, recalls being in the room when Godin received a telephone call from Esther Gordy Edwards relieving him of his duties as an official British promoter.[131] Godin published only a few issues of *Rhythm & Soul U.S.A.*, which retained the structure and many of the features of *Mary Wells and Motown News* and *Hitsville U.S.A.* After this he redirected his publishing efforts to the seminal British magazine *Blues and Soul*, for which he wrote a regular column. He also opened a record shop and started a record label, both of which were named Soul City.[132]

Changing tastes of British fans paved the way for many American soul musicians to achieve success abroad during the last half of the 1960s. Independents like Atlantic, which had established a British imprint in the fall of 1964, were hot on Motown's tail.[133] Otis Redding scored his first British hit in January 1966 with a version of "My Girl," and a Stax-Volt revue traveled to Europe in the spring of 1967. These changes were evident in the music of the Beatles and Dusty Springfield, once strong links between Motown and Britain. The rise of soul was reflected in the title of the Beatles' album *Rubber Soul*, and Brian Epstein even visited Stax in 1966 to investigate a possible recording session for the Fab Four.[134] Although the Beatles never went through with this plan, Springfield's most critically acclaimed album was made under the Atlantic umbrella at American Studios in Memphis two years later and released in early 1969 as *Dusty in Memphis*.

Motown artists continued to thrive in the UK amid a growing interest in soul during the late 1960s. Later Motown appreciation societies continued for artists like the Supremes and the Four Tops, organizing fan support throughout the decade.[135] Many Motown records appeared on the *Record Retailer* charts in the years immediately following the Tamla-Motown revue, and it was common for more than one of the company's artists to occupy the top sales listings at the same time. Artist visits did not slow down, with television and live performances in 1965 and 1966 by the Four Tops, the Marvelettes, Martha and the Vandellas, and Stevie Wonder. The Four Tops were particularly popular in late 1966 after the release of "Reach Out I'll Be There," which rose to the top of the British charts. The group became active in the UK during this time, performing at the Saville Theater in London and appearing on *The David Frost Programme*.[136] Brian Epstein promoted this visit and an early 1967 Four Tops tour, helping to garner significant attention from the music press.[137] The Four Tops became one of Motown's most popular artists in the UK mainstream after this series of high-profile events.[138]

The Supremes also traveled to the UK multiple times between 1965 and 1968 and were consistently popular on the British charts after the mid-1960s. Diana Ross maintained this popularity after leaving the group, and her singles like "I'm Still Waiting" were more successful in Britain than in the United States. Steve Wonder was also an evergreen Motown artist in the UK, releasing nearly two dozen singles that reached the pop charts in the decade between 1965 and 1975. Other Motown records, such as Marvin Gaye's "I Heard It through the Grapevine," the Miracles' "The Tears of a Clown," Edwin Starr's "War," and a slew of releases by the Jackson 5 and Michael Jackson achieved notable popularity in Britain during the late 1960s and early 1970s. Many of Motown's performers made trips to the UK during this time and some toured regularly.

Motown's past was an important element of the company's British success in the late 1960s. In addition to first-run singles, the EMI Tamla-Motown imprint released several dozen reissues.[139] Several of these records had been released on London American, Fontana, Oriole, or Stateside, predating the start of Tamla-Motown in early 1965. Others had appeared on Tamla-Motown and were simply revived, often after a disappointing initial reception. A number of these releases were quite successful, thrusting classic Motown records back into popular consciousness. The Elgins, who had disbanded in 1967, enjoyed British hits in the early 1970s with "Heaven Must Have Sent You" and "Put Yourself in My Place." In 1968 and 1969 the Isley Brothers appeared on the *Record Retailer* charts in the UK with two records that had found little success two years earlier, "This Old Heart of Mine (Is Weak for You)" and "I Guess I'll Always Love You." "Dancing in the Street" and "The Tracks of My Tears" also reached the top ten of the British charts in 1969. The next year the London Motown office extracted "The Tears of a Clown" from the 1967 Smokey Robinson and the Miracles album *Make It Happen* and released it as a single. The track went to the top of the British charts and inspired a successful single release in the United States.[140] A handful of Jimmy Ruffin tracks also regained popularity in the early 1970s, the most popular of which was "What Becomes of the Brokenhearted."

The British mainstream was not the only important barometer of

Motown's popularity at the time. Beginning in the mid-1960s, a thriving underground dance movement emerged in northern cities like Manchester and Blackpool that favored obscure Motown releases. This scene was populated by British Motown enthusiasts whose subcultural identity drew heavily from music-oriented appreciation societies. Newsletters and magazines similar to *Hitsville U.S.A.* and *Rhythm and Soul U.S.A,* such as Mick Vernon's *R&B Monthly* and Tony Cummings's *Shout* followed this dance-oriented soul music and the "northern" scene closely.[141] Another series of publications edited by John Abbey, which included *Home of the Blues* and its descendant *Blues and Soul,* were also extremely important to this wing of British R&B reception in the late 1960s.[142] Abbey's magazines hosted Godin's new column on the northern scene and contained many important feature articles on Motown artists. This coverage and later magazines catering to the same underground population, such as the 1970s glossy publication *Black Music,* included some of the most in-depth writing about R&B at the time, displaying a deep compassion for African American music at a level not represented in the United States.

During the early 1970s the movement in the North grew into a larger cultural formation that came to be called Northern Soul.[143] Centered on dancing to high-energy music, collecting rare soul recordings, a distinct manner of dress, and the use of drugs to fuel long stretches of physical activity during late hours, Northern Soul was based in clubs such as the Twisted Wheel and the Wigan Casino, both in Manchester, the Blackpool Mecca, and the Golden Torch in Stoke-on-Trent.[144] Dancers often traveled great distances to attend these clubs, which hosted all-night parties, or "all-nighters," during which patrons danced from late one evening until early the next morning.

Motown's most popular music was too mainstream for most Northern Soul aficionados, but the emergence of Tamla-Motown in the UK was widely considered to have spurred the movement's formation. "Motown was my be-all and end-all. It drove my whole life," disc jockey Ian Levine once remarked. "My love of northern soul grew out of my love of Motown."[145] Adherents like Levine resurrected the careers of many marginally successful soul artists by rereleasing their records on British labels or in later compilations and supporting performances in the UK. With the support of Northern Soul clubs, Motown artists like Edwin Starr and Jimmy Ruffin lived in the UK for substantial periods during the 1970s and were much more popular in Britain than at home.

Common elements of Northern Soul tracks were a fast tempo, use of the Motown Beat, repetitive vamps, melismatic vocal technique, and anthemic choruses. Rather than famous records like "Reach Out I'll Be There" and "Stop! In the Name of Love," Motown tracks that entered the Northern Soul canon were often obscure B-sides, unreleased singles, and album tracks, such as the Marvelettes' "I Can't Turn Around" and the Contours' "Just a Little Misunderstanding." "As soon as new releases became popular they were dropped," Mike Ritson and Stuart Russell remember in their book on the scene. "There was no way a chart record would be played at any of the 'In' crowd's haunts."[146] Perhaps the most famous Motown record within Northern Soul culture was Frank Wilson's "Do I Love You (Indeed I Do)," an unreleased single originally planned for Motown's Soul label in 1966 that became the holy grail for many Northern Soul collectors after it first emerged in clubs during the late 1970s.

Northern Soul events and record collecting were closely intertwined, and it was common for dealers to sell records at events. As both collectors and promoters of rare material, disc jockeys were important agents of Northern Soul. Seen as experts, some DJs brazenly advanced their rare finds, while others shielded their records' identifying labels during performances. Record stores also emerged that specialized in hard-to-find American issues of soul music and catered to the interests of Motown enthusiasts. The Soul City shop operated by Godin, David Nathan, and Robert Blackmore was central to the scene.[147] Selectadisc in Nottingham and the Clifton Record Shop in Bristol were other examples of record stores that specialized in soul music at the time. These outlets were cultural centers that supported the reception of soul music in the UK in a number of ways. Soul City and Selectadisc ran record labels and the Clifton Shop distributed a lengthy newsletter called *Groove*, which comprehensively listed Motown releases in Britain and offered a mail-order service.

Godin was a foundational figure in Northern Soul. After Soul City closed, he continued to publish columns in *Blues and Soul* and *Black Music*. He is credited with providing the movement with its name, stemming from his record-store classification system and several prescient *Blues and Soul* columns that profiled the scene in the early 1970s. As an important proponent, Godin helped to bring Northern Soul to the attention of the UK music press during the mid-1970s. This led to a bifurcation in R&B reception. On the one hand, new listeners interested in dancing, in addition to some of the more seasoned proponents of R&B like Godin, were thrilled with the new, enthusiastic following of Motown and other, more obscure R&B in the UK. For many who had campaigned doggedly for British acceptance of pop by African American performers during the 1960s, widespread interest in Northern Soul was the culmination of their hard work.

A 1974 article called "The Strange World of Northern Soul," written by Tony Cummings, exposed another perspective.[148] Cummings wrote that Northern Soul's fanaticism and focus on dancing and obscurity led to a scene that privileged rarity over quality, and his view was shared by many collectors based in and around London. With an obsession for the obscure, the market for Northern Soul favorites caused the value of American soul records to rise tremendously. Considered the most exclusive Northern Soul disc, one copy of Wilson's "Do I Love You (Indeed I Do)" was sold at auction in 2009 for more than £25,000. It is still commonly listed as one of the most valuable records in the world.

Motown around the World

Motown artists and executives navigated a variety of other complex business and cultural exchanges outside of the UK. The company's international scope was apparent in the second *Billboard* "World of Soul," published in the summer of 1968, which was dedicated to R&B reception outside of the United States. This special report included a lengthy article on R&B in the UK and expositions of the soul music environment in France, Scandinavia, Spain, and Czechoslovakia.[149] Motown acts were mentioned prominently in each of these articles, providing a sense that the company's success outside of the United States was noteworthy among its peers. An advertisement published in *Billboard* later that year helped to clarify the breadth of the company's global presence at the time, listing distributors for Motown's records in over two dozen countries around the world (figure 4.5).[150]

In nearby Canada, Motown's records appeared on several small independent labels during the early 1960s. Later singles were circulated on the Tamla-Motown imprint through an agreement with Ampex.[151] A dedicated R&B fan base emerged in larger Canadian cities during the mid-1960s, exemplified by one Toronto-based publication called *Soul*. Issues of this magazine from 1966 and 1967 included features on Stevie Wonder and Jimmy Ruffin.[152] Various domestic versions of Motown songs also appeared in Canada during this period, which were often targeted to the country's French-speaking population.[153] These included a version of "Do You Love Me" by Les Baronets called "Est-ce que tu m'aimes,"

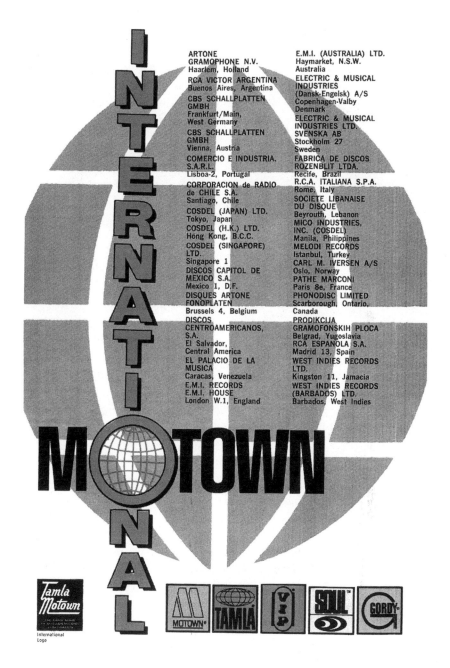

Fig 4.5. An advertisement printed in the December 28, 1968, issue of *Billboard* with contact information for Motown distributors in several dozen countries. (Courtesy of Universal Music Enterprises.)

a French-language recording of "Jimmy Mack" by Les Coquettes, and many others.

Motown's presence was very strong in northern Europe. There was an active Dutch fan club for the Supremes headed by Joop Lamboo.[154] More than a hundred singles and several EPs were released during the mid-1960s in the Netherlands through an arrangement with Artone.[155] The Tamla-Motown label first appeared in Holland and its surrounding provinces later in the decade. These records were sold in high-quality picture sleeves and often contained art and photographs that were not used in American releases. Motown artists also made several notable appearances in Holland. The Supremes visited several times during the mid-1960s and the Four Tops appeared on the Dutch-language television program *Tienerklanken* in 1967 (which was broadcast from Belgium) and performed at a large event called the "Grand Gala du Disque Populaire" in 1968.[156]

In the nearby Scandinavian countries of Norway, Sweden, and Denmark, Motown recordings appeared on Stateside with picture sleeves similar to the company's Dutch releases.[157] The Supremes performed for nearly a week in Stockholm during February 1968, which helped to promote sales in these northern countries. A number of Motown songs were recorded by Scandinavian artists, including Danish recordings of "Mickey's Monkey," a Norwegian version of "Love a Go-Go," and a number of Swedish renditions by Siw Malmkvist.[158] Malmkvist's recordings of "The Happening" ("En hipp häpp happening"), "It's the Same Old Song" ("Samma gamla sång"), and "I Hear a Symphony" ("Jag hör en symfoni") maintained elements of Motown's arrangements, such as the Motown Beat and backing vocal lines, but used Swedish texts, which dramatically altered the lingual quality of these records.[158]

West Germany was also an important outpost. Early Motown records appeared on CBS with special sleeves that announced "Die grössten Hits von Gordy Motown Tamla auf CBS." Versions of "Money," "Shop Around," and "Heat Wave" were released by the Liverbirds, a British all-female band that accompanied themselves with rock-oriented instrumentation and performed in the style of the emerging Beat movement. Several female soloists and girl groups also recorded Supremes songs in German. Maria Martin released a translated version of "Baby Love" in 1964; the French quartet Les Gam's recorded "Where Did Our Love Go" in German ("Wo ist unsere Leibe"); and the Jacobs Sisters interpreted "Stop! In the Name of Love" with the very liberal translation "Was hab' ich dir getan."[159]

The most interesting German-language renditions were by Motown's own artists. Like many American and British record companies hoping to break into the West German market, in early 1965 Motown created several of its own recordings in German. Language coaches came to Detroit to assist with vocal performances and helped to produce four singles, two by the Supremes and one each by the Temptations and Marvin Gaye.[160] Each of these releases had a German version of a Motown hit on one side and a song by the German songwriting team of Fini Busch and Werner Scharfenberger on the other. The Temptations recorded a version of "My Girl" ("Mein Girl"); Marvin Gaye created an interpretation of "How Sweet It Is" called "Wie schön das Ist"; and the Supremes performed a translation of "Where Did Our Love Go" called "Baby, Baby, wo ist unsere Liebe" and a track called "Jonny und Joe," which was an adaptation of "Come See about Me."[161]

Drawing on a long history of black music reception, France was another significant market for Motown during the mid-1960s. Stevie Wonder performed live at the Olympia Theater in Paris in December 1963, and the last stop of the 1965 UK tour also visited this venue.[162] Motown later released a recording of the Motortown Revue concert in Paris, and the Supremes appeared on French television in 1968.[163] French reception of Motown during the 1960s was connected to the country's longtime interest in American jazz and blues. This was evident in a number of fan-oriented publications, such as the bimonthly newsletter of the Rhythm and Blues Club called *Rhythm and Blues Panorama* edited by Serge Tonneau.[164] Dating to 1960, this publication focused mostly on classic jazz and different kinds of folk-oriented blues ("variétés et folklore noir").[165] One 1965 issue of this newsletter focused entirely on Motown, profiling soul-oriented Motown groups and including detailed explanation of the connections between Motown's brand of pop-oriented R&B and blues and jazz, styles that the magazine usually covered. Another important publication was *Soul Bag*, which included many Motown artist profiles during the late 1960s and early 1970s.

The earliest Motown recordings in France were EPs that appeared on Barclay and Columbia. Most had French liner notes that explained how popular the record had been in the United States and, similar to Dutch and Scandinavian releases from the time, their packages used interesting visual design and photography. There were dozens of domestic versions of Motown songs translated into French, more than any other foreign language. Girl groups Les Fizz and Op'4 interpreted Supremes songs; a family band of Madagascan origin called Les Surfs recorded a version of

"You Can't Hurry Love ("C'est grâce à toi"); and a slew of female singers recorded Motown's music in the campy yé-yé style, including Nancy
Holloway and Sylvie Vartan.[166]

Although they were not released at the time, Motown prepared several French-language recordings by the Velvelettes, including versions
of Mary Wells's "You Lost the Sweetest Boy" and the Marvelettes' "As
Long As I Know He's Mine."[167] In 1965 Motown also released a single on
the V. I. P. label in the United States by French singer Richard Anthony
called "I Don't Know What to Do." This track was recorded in London
by British producer Ivor Raymonde, who had worked closely with Dusty
Springfield. It was a rare example of Motown releasing music by an international artist during this period.[168]

Italy was Motown's most important outpost in southern Europe,
where releases appeared on Durium's Marche Estere imprint beginning in 1964 before the Tamla-Motown label was introduced the next
year.[169] As in other important European locales, many Italian versions of
Motown songs were issued during the mid-1960s. Lucio Dalla released an
interpretation of "Every Little Bit Hurts" ("Io al mondo ho solo te"), the
all-female band Le Snobs recorded the Stevie Wonder song "La La La
La La," and several Italian rock bands interpreted Motown songs, drawing heavily from American versions by psychedelic groups like Vanilla
Fudge. The Primitives recorded "Reach Out I'll Be There" ("Gira gira")
and "Standing in the Shadows of Love" ("L'ombra di nessuno") in this
manner, and I Ribelli released a version of "You Keep Me Hanging On"
("Chi mi aiuterà"). Female vocalists were the most common Italian inter-
preters. In contrast with the light and airy French yé-yé style, Italian singers like Rita Pavone and Caterina Caselli performed with heavy and aggressive soul-oriented vocal techniques. Italy was also one of the biggest
targets for Motown's own dubbed-language versions, with about a dozen
singles in Italian performed by Motown artists released between 1967
and 1970.[170] In another instance, Stevie Wonder participated in the 1969
Sanremo Music Festival, performing a song by Vittorio Ferri, Gabriella
Ferri, and Piero Pintucci called "Se tu ragazza mia."[171] (He placed thirty-
eighth in the final voting.)

American troops stationed in Asia made this region especially attractive for international sales.[172] In 1963 Motown worked with Globe
to establish distribution in Japan, Hong Kong, Macao, the Philippines,
and Thailand. Globe's parent company, Cosdel, expanded into Malaysia
in mid-1964.[173] (The Motown vaults hold several interviews with Marvin
Gaye from this period that were recorded for English-speaking listeners in

Hong Kong, Singapore, and Malaysia.) In September 1966 the Supremes toured Japan, Okinawa, Taiwan, Hong Kong, and the Philippines, a trip that was covered by the media in the United States. The Supremes also visited several naval bases during this Far East trip and planned additional appearances in Vietnam before learning that there would not be adequate security for the concerts.[174] Several years later, Stevie Wonder, Martha and the Vandellas, and the Temptations performed in a "Tamla-Motown Festival" tour in Japan.[175]

Another indication of Motown's relationship with the armed forces was the company's participation in the late 1960s syndicated radio show "The In Sound," which was hosted by Harry Harrison and produced by the U.S. Army.[176] The weekly program included a series of five-minute segments, each of which featured a popular record from the time prefaced by an artist interview or fan introduction. Reflecting its sponsor, many of the listeners profiled were members of the military, and the program included advertisements and community service announcements promoting military service. All told, between November 1966 and July 1968 Motown hits were included in about a dozen episodes of the program.[177]

The Tamla-Motown imprint appeared in many other places around the world in the late 1960s. Records were released in Portugal, Argentina, Turkey, Israel, and Pakistan. Covers of Motown songs appeared in Switzerland, Yugoslavia, and Greece.[178] A Spanish-language translation of "Reach Out I'll Be There" ("Es mejor dejarlo como está") was recorded by a half-dozen artists in Spain. Martha Reeves and Stevie Wonder also released numerous Spanish versions of Motown hits during the mid-1960s.

The manner in which Motown exposed international audiences to its music was no accident. The company worked hard to create distribution deals, record foreign-language versions, send artists abroad, and establish international publishing opportunities during the 1960s. Motown's corporate agency had little to do with Jamaican reception, however, which was more of an organic process. Motown released official recordings in Jamaica as early as 1968 through a licensing agreement with Byron Lee's Dynamic Sounds, but official records were not very vital to Jamaican appreciation of Motown.[179] Instead, radio reception from the United States and public broadcasts by sound system men helped to create a large audience for Motown's music. This popularity inspired scores of ska, rocksteady, and reggae recordings of Motown songs.[180]

Like Northern Soul aficionados, Jamaican musicians had a predilection for obscure, soulful Motown tracks. Records made popular by guy groups, especially the Temptations, were the most common subjects of rocksteady and ska versioning. Jamaican "do-overs" from the time were contrafacts of American songs, and Motown music was a popular source for these dialogic pieces. Records like the Gaylads' "Stop Making Love" ("It's the Same Old Song"), Delroy Wilson's "Got to Change Your Ways" ("Beauty Is Only Skin Deep") and the Wailers' "Ska Jerk" ("Shotgun") added new words to the chord progressions and melodies of well-known Motown hits, revealing important connections between textual practices in Jamaica and the long-standing tradition of dialogue within the R&B market of the United States.

Judging from its name alone, International Talent Management might have been a bit hyperbolic when Motown incorporated it in 1960. But it was a fitting label by the end of the decade. Motown's reach had become global and the company's music was a major part of the internationalization of the American music business after the Second World War. Official and unsanctioned, popular and obscure, Motown's music fit into various cultural formations around the world during the last half of the 1960s. Far from the confines of the Hitsville studio on West Grand Boulevard in Detroit, Motown artists, recordings, and songs traveled extensively, creating a new environment for crossover that expanded well beyond the market structure that existed in the United States.

| From Motown to the MoWest

I'm beginning to wonder how much longer we can call ourselves the
"Detroit Sound"? We might have to change our name to the "Detroit
and West Coast Sound." It's either that or start learning how to surf![1]

—Alan Abrams

Television and Film

Motown's management arm arranged many television and film appearances to cross-promote its music during the early 1960s. The company's
work in this area was part of a movement that paralleled the rise of crossover R&B, in which African American musicians were increasingly active in mainstream visual media.[2] Television was on the rise in the late
1950s and both local and network programming featured black artists
with greater regularity.[3] Vocal groups and rock and roll singers appeared
as guests on talk and variety shows, a variety of teen-oriented acts performed on dance-oriented programs like *American Bandstand*, and older
gospel musicians and song stylists like Mahalia Jackson, Sammy Davis
Jr., and Nat "King" Cole acted on television and even hosted their own
programs.

There were similar transformations in film. Early in the century
there had been a market for "race film," but this practice declined after World War II when actors like Jackson and Cole led a new wave of
African Americans who worked in mainstream pictures.[4] Musicians often
branched out into the film industry during this transition. In the teen
market, there was a spate of "jukebox" films featuring popular African
American acts. The 1956 film *The Girl Can't Help It* was a notable example that included performances by Little Richard, Abbey Lincoln, Fats
Domino, and the Platters. A series of films released between 1956 and

1959 starring Alan Freed similarly depicted performances by doo-wop groups, male song stylists, and early rock and roll singers. Other popular black film stars appeared in films targeted to mainstream adult audiences, including people like Lena Horne, Bill "Bojangles" Robinson, Ethel Waters, Eartha Kitt, Ella Fitzgerald, and Cab Calloway. Cole's portrayal of W. C. Handy in the 1958 feature *St. Louis Blues* was an early example of a common formula during the years that followed, in which a currently popular African American musician played the role of an important musical forbearer.

Motown artists entered the fields of television and film during the mid-1960s as part of the youth-oriented market. They performed mostly on variety shows like *Hullabaloo, Shindig!, Shivaree,* and *Hollywood a Go-Go*; national dance shows like *American Bandstand* and *The Lloyd Thaxton Show*; and regional programs like *Shebang!* in Los Angeles, *Swingin' Time* in Windsor, and *Teen Town* in Detroit. Stevie Wonder appeared in *Muscle Beach Party* and *Bikini Beach* in 1964, two "beach party" pictures produced by American International Pictures, which were a series of films that often starred Frankie Avalon and Annette Funicello and depicted a carefree California teenage lifestyle. The Supremes made a similar appearance in *Beach Ball* and their record "The Bikini Machine" was used in the opening credits of the Vincent Price comedy *Dr. Goldfoot and the Bikini Machine.*[5] The Supremes, Marvin Gaye, and the Miracles were later featured in *The T. A. M. I. Show*, a 1965 feature-length documentary that was culled from two October 1964 concerts at the Santa Monica Civic Auditorium.[6]

Motown also established connections with the film industry by releasing soundtracks. The first of these supported *Nothing but a Man*, which starred Abbey Lincoln and Ivan Dixon as an earnest working-class black couple from the South. Early Motown recordings like "Bye Bye Baby," "Fingertips," and "You've Really Got a Hold on Me" were featured throughout the film. It opened at festivals in late 1964, received wider circulation the next year, and Motown released the soundtrack LP in May 1965. In a manner similar to Motown's crossover success in the record business, *Nothing but a Man* received rave reviews in the black press and also achieved a measure of mainstream acceptance.[7]

Visual representation was central to Motown's rise. Motown acts danced on lip-synch oriented programs, gave interviews, and acted on variety shows and in B-movies. In many cases, their fashion also spoke volumes. These performance elements had no "sound," so to speak, but they nevertheless became an important part of the Motown Sound. The company's Artist Development division was crucial in this respect.

Motown artists consistently held themselves with grace and aplomb, broadcasting a distinct form of middle-class blackness to the masses. Many people's first exposure to Motown acts was through television and film, which traveled in ways that live performance could not.

Motown placed greater emphasis on visual media than most record companies of the period. In mid-1968 the company formed a California-based visual production arm called Motown Productions, which created a number of prime-time television specials for Motown artists during the following years.[8] The first of these starred the Supremes and the Temptations and were organized in part by Shelly Berger, who managed both groups.[9] *T. C. B.* (Taking Care of Business) was a televised version of a concert that aired on NBC in December 1968.[10] A variety-hour sequel called *G. I. T.* (Getting It Together) followed a year later.[11] George Schlatter, who was known for his work on *Laugh-In*, produced both of these programs. Motown Productions went on to create many more specials of this type during the next several years, including programs for the Temptations (*The Temptations Show*), Smokey Robinson (*The Smokey Robinson Show*), the Jackson 5 (*Goin' Back to Indiana*), and Diana Ross (*Diana!*). Motown's record division cross-marketed nearly all of these specials by releasing LP soundtracks.[12] In 1970 Motown changed the name of its management arm from International Talent Management to Multi-Media Management Corporation, reflecting the growing role of visual media within this division of the company.[13]

Motown personalities appeared frequently on national programs catering to older youth and adults during the second half of the 1960s, a move into more respectable television time slots that occurred at the same time that many Motown artists began to explore the cabaret market in their live performances. Berry Gordy was a featured guest on *To Tell the Truth* in 1965. The Supremes appeared on Mike Douglas's daytime talk show, the game show *What's My Line* (as the "mystery guest"), and variety shows hosted by celebrities like Sammy Davis Jr. and Dean Martin.[14] In a number of instances, Motown acts performed on variety shows that mixed musical performance and sketch comedy. The Temptations created an odd, psychedelic, military-critique version of "Get Ready" for a 1968 episode of *Laugh In*; Stevie Wonder appeared with Johnny Cash on *The Johnny Cash Show*; and Wonder, the Temptations, the Jackson 5, and the Supremes were on the weekly variety show *Hollywood Palace*.

The most significant prime-time television program for Motown artists was *The Ed Sullivan Show*. Between 1964 and 1971, Motown acts appeared on this program nearly forty times. Stevie Wonder performed

"Fingertips" on *Sullivan* in mid-1963, and later guests included the Temptations, Gladys Knight and the Pips, the Four Tops, Marvin Gaye, Martha and the Vandellas, Smokey Robinson and the Miracles, and the Jackson 5. The Supremes were especially popular on the show, appearing on fourteen episodes between their debut in December 1964 and Diana Ross's departure from the group in 1969.

Motown artists had a long history of recording outside of Detroit, and as Motown's presence in California increased throughout the 1960s the company's musical activities expanded westward. The company had run a dedicated office in Manhattan in the early 1960s, managed first by Berry Gordy's ex-wife Raynoma and later by staff producer Mickey Gentile.[15] Motown producers led more than a hundred sessions in New York during the 1960s with a variety of artists. (The most notable involved several batches of Marvin Gaye's early vocal standards.) Motown artists also recorded in Chicago during the early 1960s. Dozens of sessions in the Motown logs had a Chicago connection, many of which were recorded between 1961 and 1964. The Miracles' "Ain't It Baby," "Everybody's Gotta Pay Some Dues," and "I'll Try Something New" were all moderate hits that originated in Chicago, and many early Motown string parts were also created there, often under the direction of Riley Hampton at the RCA studios on North Lake Shore Drive.

Connections to the film and television industries helped to make Los Angeles Motown's most important outpost very early in the history of the company. Headed by Marc Gordon and Hal Davis, Motown's California-based recording and publishing office opened in 1963 and collaborated with the company's Detroit headquarters to produce hundreds of recordings.[16] Motown's first activity on the West Coast included sessions for records like Little Stevie Wonder's "Castles in the Sand" and Brenda Holloway's "Every Little Bit Hurts." Some records were created completely in California (including backing tracks and overdubs), and others began there as band tracks and were later taken to Detroit (or other locations) for vocal dubbing or mixing. Motown also ran orchestral sessions in California during 1964 and 1965, often arranged by Gene Page. With Motown's salaried backing musicians centered in Detroit and artists like the Supremes spending more time on the West Coast, a lot of California recording work was used to dub vocals over instrumental tracks created in Detroit. Virtually all of Motown's most important artists recorded at least a few tracks in Los Angeles during the mid-1960s. Unlike acts who recorded in New York or Chicago, Motown artists like Holloway and Barbara McNair were based in California and created the

TITLE CHAINED						**Tape Filing Card**		
AUTHORS FRANK WILSON								
PUBLISHER(S) JOBETE								
PRODUCER(S) FRANK WILSON #3 HAL DAVIS #2					#3 *Gline No - 54/70*			
					#1 *Release Record No. 1109*			
ARTIST	SESSION	S SERIES	DM NUMBER	DM NUMBER	DM NUMBER	DM NUMBER	TS
1	PAUL PETERSEN LA		820902	301M08	301M09	304M02	307M06	
	PAUL PETERSEN	3263 ✓	LEAD	307M07	326M12	489S10		
2	BARBARA RANDOLPH *LP*		821003	473M05				
3	MARVIN GAYE	4337	821611	437M02	438M06	442M06	442M13 *LP*	806L
	MARVIN GAYE	4376 ✓	LEAD	456S09	462S11 *PL*			
	MARVIN GAYE	4/22/68 ✓	DEMO					
4	MARVIN GAYE	4/22/68 ✓	LEAD					
	MARVIN GAYE	4503 ✓	VOICES					
	MARVIN GAYE	4514 ✓	VOICES					
5	MARVIN GAYE	4538 ✓	HORNS					
	MARVIN GAYE	6/20/68 ✓	INSTRU					

Fig 5.1. The first of several tape filing cards from the Universal/Motown archive for the song "Chained," which depicts clear documentation of studio work in Los Angeles. (Courtesy of Universal Music Enterprises.)

majority of their music on the West Coast.[17] Although the company's recordkeeping for these sessions wasn't always dutiful, the Supremes probably recorded more material in Los Angeles than any of Motown's Detroit-based groups of the time.

Motown sessions in Los Angeles used local musicians, which has become the source of controversy. Legendary Los Angeles bassist and guitarist Carol Kaye, who was a first-call performer and part of the loose group of session musicians known as the Wrecking Crew, has stated in numerous print and radio interviews that she played on many Motown records of the period, including a lot of well-known hits.[18] Her claims raise a number of issues that stem from Motown's work in California. One surrounds the connection between race and soul music. Kaye maintains that Motown does not acknowledge her performances in order to protect the mystique surrounding the work of James Jamerson and to shield the fact that a white, female musician was responsible for the bass performances on some of the company's most soulful tracks.[19]

Kaye was a vitally important supporting musician in Los Angeles during the 1960s and 1970s, and she faced daily gender discrimination. In this case, however, her revisionist attempts seem to be mostly unfounded.[20] She certainly recorded tracks for Motown, and even played on some well-known songs. Rather than the iconic interpretations that became hit records, however, her performances were mostly limited to versions by other Motown artists and backing tracks used by Motown performers in live television performances.[21]

Individual credit for instrumentation is not really at the heart of this debate. Discussions concerning Motown session players like Kaye and Jamerson are symbolic of a much larger set of contentious issues stemming from Motown's increasing presence in California, including a perceived lack of commitment to its Detroit base and a steadfast commitment to cultural and commercial crossover. Motown's work in California complicated the company's tidy narrative as a homegrown, family-oriented company from the Midwest. The company's Detroit-based employees were increasingly wary of a large-scale move to Los Angeles, fearing that they would lose their jobs. Other Detroiters feared that the company's departure would have an adverse effect on the city's economy. Listeners noticed a change when Motown started targeting older audiences. Television and film appearances were representative of this new direction, and the audible difference of records created for these markets was striking during a period when the soul aesthetic was at its peak.

Caring about Detroit, Moving to California

In early 1967 Motown released a Supremes single called "The Happening." It was an odd track with a square rhythmic groove, an uncharacteristic lyrical style, and a harmonic progression that contrasted with the group's recent work. The record was produced by HDH in Detroit but it didn't sound like the trio's earlier singles. It was a clear example of the Supremes' movement away from styles popular in the R&B market. Accordingly, "The Happening" appeared in two films at the time, reflecting Motown's growing interest in visual media. It was used in the closing credits of a kitschy Anthony Quinn movie called *The Happening*, showing the extent to which Motown catered to film-oriented styles during the late 1960s with its most popular group. The other film was a short, low-budget promotional film called *It's Happening*, which was created for a Detroit-based charity organization called the United Fund.[22] Using footage of the Supremes at their childhood home in Detroit's Brewster-Douglass Housing Projects, *It's Happening* profiled the United Fund making a positive impact on Detroiters. Unlike the Hollywood-produced *The Happening*, *It's Happening* lacked the production value of the Quinn picture and was not distributed widely. It served a reminder of Motown's civic involvement during a period of simultaneous westward expansion, complicating the narrative of the company's move.

Philanthropic work was particularly relevant in Detroit during this period. Like many cities in the urban North with large African American communities that formed as a result of the Great Migration, Detroit showed increasing signs of racial instability during the late 1960s.[23] Issues such as urban renewal, unemployment, and housing problems, stemming from a bifurcation of the black community and white flight, caused poor black residents to lash out, seeking attention and retribution. In July 1967 some of the most devastating riots of the decade, often called "the great rebellion" by those involved, broke out in central Detroit, marking a major turning point in the city's urban decline.[24] The fighting surrounded Motown's buildings on West Grand Boulevard, which were in a neighborhood that was quickly becoming a stereotypical black urban ghetto. The company expanded into a large office building called Motown Center on Woodward Avenue the next year, which relocated a lot of its business activity, but this hardly mitigated the instability created by the city's growing social tensions.

Motown's alliance with the United Fund was only one of the many ways that it worked to revitalize the infrastructure and psyche of Detroit during the years following the riots. The company released a revised version of "The Happening" called "Detroit Is Happening," featuring Detroit Tigers star Willie Horton in a service announcement for summer youth activities. Smokey Robinson recorded a song called "I Care about Detroit" as part of local campaign called "I Care about Detroit Day." Robinson served as chairman of the event and the Miracles performed a free concert.[25] Motown also organized several large-scale benefits in Detroit, including a 1970 tribute event for boxer Joe Louis led by Berry Gordy that featured performances by several Motown acts.[26] Motown's most significant community work came through a community education program called the Loucye Gordy Wakefield Scholarship Fund, which honored the Gordy sister and early Motown vice president whose sudden death had stunned the Motown community. According to its promotional literature, the goal of the foundation was to provide "the youth of the inner city with the incentive and encouragement to develop their potential through education."[27] Most of the fund's scholarship recipients went to Michigan State University, creating a strong link between Motown and the local community.

The Wakefield Fund was known best for a series of charity dinners that started in 1969 called the Sterling Ball, which were organized by Esther Gordy Edwards and held at Berry Gordy's Detroit mansion (figure 5.2). Motown artists attended and performed at these affairs, using the company's star power to attract donors and press coverage. The company released two limited edition LPs to commemorate Sterling Ball evenings. The first was a special printing of *In Loving Memory*, an album of gospel songs recorded by Motown artists that had been released to the public in 1968. The second was called *Sterling Ball 1971*, which was an extremely limited release that included the new song "Let's All Save the Children," performed by Joe Hinton and composed by Ron Miller.[28] These events were national news in the black media. Articles about the Sterling Ball appeared in publications like *Ebony* and *Jet* and a variety of black-oriented newspapers. In 1971 Michigan representative John Conyers even entered into the *Congressional Record* a speech entitled "Berry Gordy, Jr.: Still Paying His Dues," which referred to the Sterling Ball and its mission of helping inner-city high school graduates.[29]

In the midst of this outward commitment to Detroit there were dogged signs that Motown was starting to outgrow its Midwest headquarters. In March 1965 a profile of Motown had been printed in the *Detroit Free Press* magazine, which quoted Berry Gordy discussing his belief in Michigan's workforce and creative talent. "I've always maintained that Detroiters are as smart as anyone in say, Hollywood," Gordy said at the time. "And some of these artists would be waiting on tables somewhere if there hadn't been a place for them in Detroit to recognize their talents."[30] When this quote was reprinted in a June 1968 article in the *Michigan Challenge* it took on a very different meaning.[31] Gordy had become much more interested in working in California during this three-year period. He bought his first home in Los Angeles in the fall of 1968, followed closely by Diana Ross and many others within the Motown organization.[32] He spent a lot of time in Los Angeles after this and promoted Barney Ales to executive vice president and general manager of the Detroit operations.

Gordy's absence from Motown's Detroit headquarters made his Detroit workforce uneasy. It led directly to the departure of HDH and sparked rumors about the company's possible relocation. Motown executives refuted these reports internally and in the press.[33] In April 1970, Ales sent a memo to everyone who worked for the company announcing, "MOTOWN RECORD CORPORATION is not moving to the West Coast."[34] Later that year, articles appeared in both the *Free Press* and *Jet* affirming Motown's resolve to stay in Detroit.[35] A company newsletter from March 1972 echoed this sentiment, explaining a rash of layoffs as a

Fig 5.2. Berry Gordy and an unknown scholarship recipient at a Sterling Ball benefit in 1972. (Courtesy of the E. Azalia Hackley Collection of African Americans in the Performing Arts, Detroit Public Library.)

cost-saving measure connected to the duplication of functions between Los Angeles and Detroit. "There are no plans at present to phase out the Detroit operations," the newsletter claimed, "as many rumors suggest."[36]

Motown's recorded repertoire from the period often reflected an interest in California, which surely provided clues about the move to discerning listeners. The Four Tops released a ballad version of "California Dreamin'" and Marvin Gaye recorded the Ivy Hunter song "I Got to Get to California." The Four Tops' version of "MacArthur Park" cast lead singer Levi Stubbs as the narrator of a story about a neighborhood park in Los Angeles. "California Soul," which was written by Nick Ashford and Valerie Simpson and recorded in a well-known version by Marvin Gaye and Tammi Terrell, depicted a place where melodies ride on the wind, carrying a type of soul that "no matter what you do" is "gonna get a hold on you."[37] Motown also started a new label called MoWest during this period that featured music recorded in Los Angeles. One of its first products, which became extremely popular on the singles charts, was a medley of "What the World Needs Now Is Love" and "Abraham, Martin, and John" recorded by Los Angeles disc jockey Tom Clay.[38]

Motown depicted Detroit as the site of its past in a number of ways, helping to form a narrative in which California was a manifest destiny. A good example of this was *The Motown Story: The First Decade*, a radio documentary that Motown converted into a five-disc boxed set with a lavish full-color booklet, a collection of the company's "golden hits," and spoken recollections of Motown's formation.[39] In the context of Motown's move, *The Motown Story* represented a clear effort to compartmentalize Motown's first decade into a historical period, a time that was quickly coming to a close. With a similar nod to history, Motown executives donated materials to local libraries in the early 1970s. A gift to the E. Azalia Hackley Collection at the Detroit Public Library included recordings, publications, sheet music, and interoffice ephemera.[40] Eastern Michigan University received another large donation. The school awarded Berry Gordy an honorary doctorate and, after a series of negotiations with Esther Gordy Edwards, announced a new "Gordy Motown Record Collection" the next year that included domestic and international Motown releases, print publications, and business materials from Edwards's office (figure 5.3).[41]

It was becoming clear in the press that Motown's future would not be in Detroit. In late 1970 Motown vice president Michael Roshkind told *Rolling Stone* that the "Sunset offices are expanding so fast . . . they'll surpass Detroit operations probably within a year."[42] By June 1972 the *Free Press* reported, "If the present trend continues, there won't be more than a handful of people left tending the local store by the end of the summer—if there are any at all."[43] Barney Ales announced his retirement at this time, which was a strong indication that the Detroit era was coming to a close.[44] A week later Motown officially announced that the company would relocate. Amos Wilder, a new executive vice president, told reporters that Motown was "phasing out immediately its operations in Detroit and establishing worldwide headquarters in Los Angeles."[45]

Sporadic sessions continued for another year at the Hitsville facility on West Grand Boulevard and for a bit longer at Studio B on Davidson Avenue.[46] At Hitsville, Detroit-based performers like Bob Babbitt and Martha Reeves worked on material that never came to fruition and Marvin Gaye recorded lead vocals for several tracks connected to his 1973 duet album with Diana Ross. Blues guitarist Luther Allison recorded two albums, *Bad News Is Coming* and *Luther's Blues*, and Eddie Kendricks and David Ruffin also worked on new music. Norman Whitfield con-

Fig 5.3. Esther Gordy Edwards donating materials to Eastern Michigan University, ca. October 1972; *from left*: Harold E. Sponberg (EMU president), Esther Edwards, and Lonnie Head (EMU director of alumni relations). (Courtesy of Eastern Michigan University Archives, Ypsilanti.)

tinued to work mainly in Detroit, producing large portions of albums by the Undisputed Truth (*Law of the Land* and *Down to Earth*) and the Temptations (*All Directions* and *Masterpiece*) on Davidson Avenue in 1973 and 1974. The last activity at Hitsville was on August 30, 1973, a session that produced a series of unreleased tracks for the obscure group Art and Honey. The final entry in the Detroit studio logs was a Studio B demo recording dated September 13, 1974 by Berry Gordy's nephew Robert Bullock.

Lady Sings the Blues

Longtime Motown acts like Smokey Robinson, Marvin Gaye, and Diana Ross embraced the creative environment of California in different ways. Each of these artists had appeared in television and film during the mid-1960s, which led to further opportunities during and after the company's move. Robinson appeared mostly as a performer on talk shows, variety hours, and awards programs during the early 1970s. He was later involved in the creation of the blaxploitation film *Big Time*. Gaye performed a small role in the television movie *The Ballad of Andy Crocker* and took a larger dramatic part in the feature film *Chrome and Hot Leather*.

Ross's career moved even further into dramatic performance. She appeared in an episode of *Tarzan* in 1968 with the Supremes, performed in comedic sketches on programs like *Hollywood Palace* and *Laugh-In*, worked with Dinah Shore and Lucille Ball on the special *Like Hep*, and had a dramatic guest role in an episode of *Make Room for Granddaddy* with Danny Thomas. More than any other Motown artist, Ross's musical career was subsumed by a move toward spectacle and large-scale entertainment. In early 1970 she left the Supremes in dramatic fashion after a highly anticipated Las Vegas "farewell concert" at the Frontier Hotel. The group's final single as a unit, a version of "Someday We'll Be Together," was released in preparation for the concert and excerpts from the show were compiled onto the double-disc album *Farewell*.[47]

After leaving the Supremes, Ross performed exclusively in cabaret venues, developing an elaborate stage show that focused equally on music and production quality. Her most popular single from the period was an interpretation of the Ashford and Simpson song "Ain't No Mountain High Enough," which dramatized the Gaye and Terrell version by inserting spoken verse sections and creating a long crescendo toward an ecstatic entrance of the final chorus. It became her last notable solo release for nearly three years, a period when she focused on acting and large-scale stage shows.

Not long after Ross's departure from the Supremes, Motown Productions began working to create an original biographical feature film in which she would portray jazz singer Billie Holiday. Berry Gordy had been a fan of Holiday since the 1950s, when he attended her performances at Detroit's Flame Show Bar, and Motown first explored the music of Holiday when the Supremes performed "My Man" on an NBC special hosted by Bob Hope in February 1969.[48] Several months later Ross discussed her attraction to Holiday in a profile published in *Look*, commenting, "I'm trying to find out everything about her. I've never been able to go very deep in my songs, and now I also want to sing about blues and sadness. . . . I'm trying to find out all the *real* psychological reasons Billie Holiday gave up and took to drink and drugs."[49]

The *Los Angeles Times* first reported rumors of a Motown-oriented film about Holiday during the publicity for the *Diana!* television special in the spring of 1971 and shooting for the new Ross vehicle began at the end of the year.[50] The film was called *Lady Sings the Blues*. Motown

Productions partnered with Paramount Pictures to complete the movie and it was by far Motown's biggest California-based project to date. Like many of his other Motown-related projects, Gordy eventually took over many aspects of the film's production. He used Motown staffers Suzanne de Passe and Chris Clark to rewrite the script, assumed the role of producer during filming, and guaranteed the film's financing.[51]

Gordy had crossover goals for *Lady Sings the Blues* that mirrored his success in the music industry, aiming to create a "film with black stars" instead of a "*black* film."[52] The mainstream appeal of Ross was central to the movie's success. Unlike her bit-part work before this, she appeared in nearly every scene of *Lady Sings the Blues* and was the film's driving force. One of the main slogans for the film's publicity was "Diana Ross *is* Billie Holiday," and Ross's visual similarity was highlighted in several promotional stills that used side-by-side photos of Holiday and Ross as Holiday.

The musical element of *Lady Sings the Blues* was a vital part of the film. No original Holiday recordings were used in the picture; instead, Ross performed small bits of songs like "Lover Man" and "All of Me" to help contextualize dramatic scenes, and montages set to musical numbers drifted in and out of the movie's diegetic space. Motown arranger Gil Askey led these recordings and French composer Michel Legrand was commissioned to write a nondiagetic score. Even a scratchy vintage-sounding version of "T'Aint Nobody's Business," which served as an important dramatic marker for the film's opening scenes, was actually a rerecorded performance by Motown performer Blinky Williams. The two songs most commonly associated with Holiday, "Strange Fruit" and "God Bless the Child," received special treatment in the film's narrative arc. "Strange Fruit" was used to accompany an important moment when Holiday witnessed a lynching while touring in the South. "God Bless the Child" appeared during the film's triumphant finale, over which a newspaper headline announced her death.

Motown released an elaborate *Lady Sings the Blues* soundtrack. It featured a large photographic montage and two discs: one with the story depicted through audio sound bites and another that contained Legrand's "Love Theme" and ten complete performances of Ross as Holiday. In an attempt to re-create the look of jazz releases from the 1930s and 1940s, the album's packaging used old-fashioned labels, plain brown record sleeves, and a muted color scheme of brown and gold. A carefully designed logo appeared in the center of the cover, featuring a single hand gripping a microphone adorned with dangling handcuffs.

Ross's more complete interpretations on the soundtrack reveal interesting musical and historical transmutations. Her performance of "Fine and Mellow," for example, incorporates a high-energy big band arrangement that foregrounds her vocals and eschews the sleek, low-down quality of Holiday's interpretations.[53] The music on the soundtrack was arranged mostly for big band in this manner, which didn't account for the many smaller settings in which Holiday performed or the more luscious string arrangements of her Decca recordings from the late 1940s. Accordingly, with no lengthy introductions or extended instrumental solos, there was little sense in the film's music that Holiday had been a collaborative participant in small bands for much of her career.

Despite these differences, much of Ross's vocal work was clearly indebted to historic Holiday performances.[54] Holiday had created a distinct interpretation of "Strange Fruit," for example, by significantly altering the rhythm and melody of the original composition in her well-known 1939 recording on the Commodore label.[55] (This is evident when comparing her performance to the 1939 sheet music.) A later Holiday performance, recorded during the 1945 Jazz at the Philharmonic concerts, offers an even more developed version of the song, using a different key and eliminating a steady rhythmic pulse. Ross conflated these two interpretations in her soundtrack performance, showing careful attention to the spirit of Holiday's performance style while not re-creating any one recording too specifically (example 5.1).[56]

Lady Sings the Blues was popular at the box office, but critical reactions were mixed.[57] Questions concerning biographical accuracy were raised in nearly every review, and several articles focused solely on this aspect of the production.[58] This was mostly due to the main source for the script, the singer's 1956 autobiography written with William Dufty, also called *Lady Sings the Blues*. It was well known at the time that this book contained a lot of fabrication, exaggeration, and factual error.[59] Many reviews praised Ross's performance, however, validating Motown's newest crossover strategy. In the *New York Times*, Vincent Canby cited Ross as the strongest element in an otherwise bad production, asking, "How is it possible for a movie that is otherwise so dreadful to contain such a singularly attractive performance in the title role?"[60] Pauline Kael wrote from a similar perspective in her lengthy *New Yorker* review.[61] The film was well received at a number of high-profile awards ceremonies in 1973. It won several key honors at the Image Awards, hosted annually by the NAACP, including Best Picture, Best Actress for Diana Ross, and Best Actor for Billy Dee Williams. It was also nominated for five Academy Awards, in-

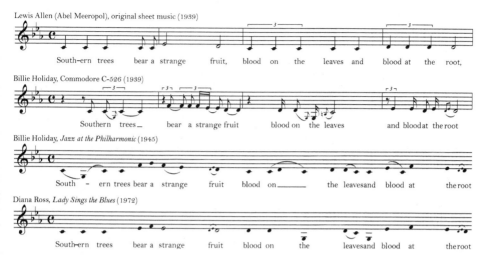

Example 5.1: A comparison of four melodic approaches to the first four measures of
"Strange Fruit," taken from (1) the original 1939 sheet music; (2) Billie Holiday's original
Commodore release (transposed from Bb minor); (3) Billie Holiday's 1945 LP *Jazz at the
Philharmonic* (transposed from Bb minor); and (4) Diana Ross's 1972 LP *Lady Sings the Blues*
(Note: the *Jazz at the Philharmonic* and *Lady Sings the Blues* performances do not conform
to a regular meter; I have aligned these note heads with the metric interpretations of the
sheet music and Holiday's 1939 record.)

cluding Best Actress (Diana Ross) and Best Screenplay (Terence McCloy,
Chris Clark, and Suzanne de Passe), but it did not win in any of these
categories.[62]

As a vehicle for Ross, *Lady Sings the Blues* provided a much-needed
spark to her solo career, inspiring a lot of high-profile print media coverage during the early months of 1973.[63] The industry attention given to
the film, from both traditionally conservative black organizations and
the more mainstream academy, confirmed that Motown's move to Los
Angeles was not in vain and that the company might have a prosperous
future in the film business. As Motown was still settling into its new headquarters, the manner in which *Lady Sings the Blues* incorporated historic
music aligned in interesting ways with the company move. The film conflated Motown's most popular female singer with a jazz legend within
a sympathetic depiction of a historically important African American
musical form, all in the context of a major motion picture. All told, this
helped Motown to situate itself within a larger history of black contributions to popular music while foretelling the company's future expansion.

Trouble Man

Marvin Gaye followed a different path in Los Angeles. His last album created in Detroit was *What's Going On*, which he recorded in two stints in late 1970 and early 1971. It had been an important project for many reasons. Just as Ross's solo work and *Lady Sings the Blues* furthered Motown's move into adult-oriented cabaret crossover, *What's Going On* continued the company's presence in the crossover soul market. The content of *What's Going On* embraced soul in a number of ways. It was a "concept album" that formed a unified musical and textual statement by seamlessly transitioning between tracks, using a logical sequence of keys, and repeating musical and lyrical themes. Similarly, the subject matter of songs like "What's Going On," "Mercy, Mercy Me (The Ecology)," and "Save the Children" dealt with topical themes, which appealed to audiences who valued records that seemed to portray an artist's personal views. Gaye's work as songwriter and producer on the album was novel. Rarely had a Motown artist been given the opportunity to lead so many elements of his own recording. His success helped to loosen the assembly-line model at Motown for artists like Stevie Wonder during the 1970s. Gaye produced *What's Going On* mostly at Hitsville and Studio B, but the final stages of the album's creation occurred during a transitional period when he moved freely between Michigan and California, which created an important regional history for the record. There were two final mixes completed: one in Detroit and the other in Los Angeles. The latter was eventually chosen for release and went on to become one of the most popular albums of 1971.[64]

As he spent more time in Los Angeles, Gaye was commissioned to create the score for a low-budget film called *Trouble Man*. The resulting album was Gaye's next large-scale project, and it became Motown's second important film soundtrack after its official corporate relocation.[65] In contrast to the mainstream appeal of *Lady Sings the Blues*, *Trouble Man* was part of a new "blaxploitation" genre that catered to African American audiences. Orchestral soul was a vital element of the sonic texture and marketing for these films, and well-known R&B stars like Isaac Hayes (*Shaft*), Curtis Mayfield (*Superfly*), James Brown (*Black Caesar*), and Bobby Womack (*Across 110th Street*) all released well-received blaxploitation soundtrack albums during this time.[66] Blaxploitation films were controversial within black communities. Debates in the black press questioned the manner in which they depicted violence, portrayed women, glorified drug use and crime, and furthered negative stereotypes of

African Americans.[67] Nevertheless, Motown embraced this genre as a new segment of the crossover R&B market. The company's artists and executives saw the potential for blaxploitation pictures to provide opportunities for African American film professionals and establish strong black characters in Hollywood.[68]

Gaye's work on *Trouble Man* began in the fall of 1972, and he spent about four weeks on the project.[69] The bulk of the music used in the film was recorded during a single session with a large film band that occurred in late September.[70] Furthering his interest in orchestral composition, Gaye worked with several professional arrangers to prepare music for the ensemble. Ruby Raxon recorded Gaye humming ideas into a tape recorder and transcribed them and Dale Oehler completed arrangements for the band.[71] This film band session was recorded in a large studio using only a few microphones, the orchestra completed most of its cues during the first take, and there were no overdubs. The ensemble finished nearly three hundred separate cues during several sessions that day, ranging from ten-second interludes to lengthy passages of several minutes.

Most of the film band recordings were used to create nondescript thematic material, but there were several experimental segments that especially reflected the blaxploitation genre. One cue included a near-complete interpolation of the hymn "Near the Cross." Another documented a series of small-ensemble African percussion jams that the session engineers called "Wild Rhythm," which reflected the exotic percussion performances featured in many blaxploitation soundtracks.[72] The last thing completed during these sessions was the title song, "Trouble Man," which included the only vocal performances on the film band reels.[73] After Gaye completed his work, he and Oehler had the tapes copied and submitted them to the film studio Twentieth Century Fox.[74] The film's music editors then used Gaye's material as a set of building blocks for what would later become the soundtrack, editing the material heavily to create a composite score.

Gaye used his copy of the tapes in a very different manner. After trips to Chicago and Detroit for live performances, he returned to Los Angeles and constructed a new version of *Trouble Man* for the official soundtrack album.[75] Using the film cues as his starting point, he led a team of Motown engineers directed by Art Stewart to weave together a combination of orchestral material, Motown band sessions, and new recordings. Saxophonist Trevor Lawrence created a running melody throughout most of the album by performing new parts on nearly all of the tracks.[76] Gaye also recorded many overdubs, including lengthy sections of piano and percussive sweeteners like finger snaps, foot stomps, tambourine, and handclaps. He scatted and improvised lead and backing vocals and created various parts using a Moog synthesizer, which he had recently acquired from Stevie Wonder.[77]

Gaye incorporated a variety of different Moog performances into *Trouble Man*. He used the instrument as if he were a serious-minded composer on the track "Deep-In-It," reflecting its history in the electronic music community since the early 1960s. On other tracks, such as "'T' Stands for Trouble," he used it more like a funk musician, highlighting the instrument's melodic capabilities and creating percussive effects to add subtle hits to intensify the strong beats of the groove (example 5.2). "'T' Stands for Trouble" was a typical example of the hybrid nature of *Trouble Man*. It was based on cues originally recorded by the film orchestra but later enhanced with many overdubs.[78] These varied sources made editing a vital part of the album's creative process. This was evident in a track like "'T' Plays It Cool," whose backing tracks were created by cutting and pasting a film band cue to make a loop, over which continuous overdubs were added to generate a lengthy jam-oriented funk track.

Trouble Man premiered in New York on Halloween night in 1972. Its screening was part of a benefit for a new theater group called the Negro Ensemble Company, founded by the film's star, Robert Hooks.[79] The film opened in local theaters the next day and was panned by the few critics who took notice. The *Washington Post* carried one of the only positive reviews of the movie, hailing the plot and Ivan Dixon's direction.[80] Far more common was the tone of Vincent Canby's article in the *New York Times*, which listed it among "The Ten Worst Movies of 1972."[81] Gaye's soundtrack and the title-track single were released in the middle of December and both peaked in popularity during late February 1973, as the film was closing in most theaters nationwide. As with many blaxploitation pictures, reviews of the soundtrack were more positive than assessments of the film. Vince Aletti wrote in *Rolling Stone* that the score was "strong enough to be completely independent" and, in contrast with Canby's movie review in the *Times*, Pittsburgh music critic Greg Mims put Gaye's album on his list of "1973's Top Ten Soul Albums."[82]

At the time, *Lady Sings the Blues* and *Trouble Man* seemed to be diametrically opposed. One was a mainstream breakthrough and the other a niche disappointment. But from a larger historical perspective these projects had a lot in common. They both featured longtime Motown

Example 5.2. The conflation of film band recordings ("basic tracks") and Gaye's later over-dubs in "'T' Stands for Trouble" (1:16-1:27)

artists navigating different areas of the film industry during the period immediately following the company's relocation, and their musical elements provided commentary on Motown's move by using material that juxtaposed elements of high and low culture. *Trouble Man* contrasted elements of funk-oriented blaxploitation with traditional composition, and *Lady Sings the Blues* recounted the music of a talented, drug-abusing jazz singer through the performative lens of a squeaky-clean pop star. Viewed in this context, both *Trouble Man* and *Lady Sings the Blues* grew out of the logistical possibilities of Motown's presence in Los Angeles, which shaded each project with a tinge of conflict related to the company's westward move.

Motown Records in the 1970s

During the 1970s nearly all of the historic independent R&B firms that had emerged in the bullish period after World War II merged with larger corporate conglomerates and stopped releasing new work. There had been no significant Specialty releases since 1960; the Chess family sold its holdings to General Recorded Tape in 1969; King changed hands several times after founder Syd Nathan died in 1968, with no new material released after 1973; Arista purchased the Savoy catalog after the death of figurehead Herman Lubinsky in 1974; and ABC-Dunhill (the company once known as ABC-Paramount) purchased Don Robey's Duke and Peacock labels in the mid-1970s. Many of the newer independent companies that formed during this time were actually aligned with major conglomerates, such as the Philadelphia International outfit run by Kenny Gamble and Leon Huff, which was financed by CBS.[83]

Atlantic remained one of Motown's largest competitors, but only after aligning with a series of big corporations after its executives sold their holdings to Warner Brothers–Seven Arts in 1967. Still under the leadership of Ahmet Ertegun and Jerry Wexler, Atlantic maintained relative autonomy during the decade after selling to Warner, releasing important new music for the R&B market by artists like Aretha Franklin, Wilson Pickett, Roberta Flack, and Donny Hathaway. In a manner that eluded Motown, Atlantic also successfully diversified into heavy rock with groups like Led Zeppelin and the Rolling Stones, acoustic music by Crosby, Stills, and Nash, and progressive rock by groups like Yes and Genesis. Once a fiercely independent company, however, Atlantic became a more ingrained part of the larger Warner group as the 1970s progressed.[84]

As Motown grew, its record division began to emulate the practices of major companies by releasing music on specialty labels and creating distribution agreements.[85] It distributed the Chisa imprint between 1969 and 1971, a label co-founded by South African trumpeter Hugh Masekela that focused on a blend of Afro-pop, soul, and funk-oriented jazz. In another distribution deal, Motown teamed with producer and music executive Mike Curb in 1974 to form Melodyland Records, which later morphed into Hitsville and MC Records. T. G. Sheppard was the most successful act on these imprints, releasing two records that topped the *Billboard* country charts in 1975, "Devil in the Bottle" and "Tryin' to Beat the Morning Home." Motown formed a similar relationship with well-known jazz executive Creed Taylor during this period, distributing his CTI, Kudu, and Salvation records for about two years. During the early

1970s Motown released nearly a hundred singles and albums on a rock-oriented label called Rare Earth.[86] Many of Rare Earth's groups, including a popular band called Rare Earth, explored heavy blues-oriented and progressive rock styles. Run by Motown executive Joe Summers, the Rare Earth imprint was more autonomous that other Motown-owned labels. Many of Rare Earth's groups were from England and other foreign locales, which reflected Motown's increasing international footprint.[87] After the demise of Rare Earth in 1973, Motown continued to released rock music on the Gull, Manticore, and Prodigal labels.

Unlike Atlantic, Motown was still considered an "independent" by the record industry, a status that was largely determined by the manner in which its recordings were distributed.[88] While major conglomerates had the benefit of large, national networks to sell their records, Motown executives still worked within an older, patchwork system of regional distribution firms.[89] This independence allowed for tremendous flexibility in marketing to different regions. It also gave Motown the ability to use opposing firms for different imprints and to establish varied business relationships that were subject to dissolution if either side became dissatisfied. "One of our biggest assets is being a private company," Vice Chairman Michael Roshkind told *Variety* in 1979. "We can move and make a quick decision. Some others can't."[90] As amalgamation increased in the music industry, Motown's older system of distribution was increasingly rare for large companies. The music trades were full of discussion about this change, and Motown was commonly cited as one of the remaining pillars of the independent network in the United States.

Despite its indie status, Motown was a huge operation during the 1970s. The company was awash in distribution deals, the works of a major publishing firm, a television and film arm, and several attempts at moving into Broadway, and it also remained one of the most consistently successful record companies in the music business. In 1973 *Black Enterprise* published its first annual chart of black-owned companies ranked according to annual revenue. Motown appeared at the top of the list and continued to reside in the number-one position for the remainder of the decade.[91]

Motown's most important records during the 1970s continued the crossover R&B approach that had first made the company successful a decade before. Its most popular group at the beginning of the 1970s was a newly signed quintet of brothers from Gary, Indiana, called the Jackson 5. Based on the manner in which Berry Gordy carefully controlled every aspect of their early career, he later called the Jackson 5 "the last big stars to come rolling off my assembly line."[92] The group recorded some early music in Detroit, but all of their hits were created in Los Angeles. Their first three singles, "I Want You Back," "ABC," and "The Love You Save," were written and produced by Berry Gordy, Deke Richards, Fonce Mizell, and Freddie Perren, a four-member team who called themselves The Corporation.

These records had a lot in common. Each was recorded using sixteen tracks and their instrumental backing featured similar conga and handclap parts, extensive backing vocals, and funky rhythm section arrangements. Drawing on lead singer Michael Jackson's young age, the songs were all about youthfulness. Musically, this was conveyed in part by using a prominent major scale moving in stepwise motion as the harmonic driver for the chorus in each of these songs (example 5.3). "I Want You Back" used a descending diatonic scale, "ABC" employed an ascending stepwise pattern, and "The Love You Save" was based on a rising two-measure sequence. This sort of self-dialogue obviously connected to Motown's Detroit-era production strategy, but the Jackson 5's musical style was far from a conventional Motown Sound. Employing repetitive riff-oriented grooves, bongos, fuzz guitar, and crowd noise, the group's upbeat records were more akin to psychedelic soul than the classic Motown Sound of the mid-1960s.

Motown supported the success of the Jackson 5 in a variety of ways, including a number of projects using visual media.[93] After the group's initial popularity, Motown coordinated appearances on television programs like *American Bandstand*, *The Flip Wilson Show*, and *The Ed Sullivan Show* to introduce their newest records. Motown Productions also created several important large-scale vehicles for the group. One was a prime-time variety special called *Goin' Back to Indiana*, which interspersed live footage from a concert held in the group's home town of Gary, Indiana, with skits featuring athletes Elgin Baylor and Rosey Grier and comedians Tom Smothers and Bill Cosby. The animation firm Rankin/Bass Productions also worked with Motown Productions to create nearly two dozen episodes of a cartoon called *Jackson 5ive* in 1971 and 1972. The theme song for the program was a brief medley of Jackson 5 hits, which clearly exhibited the similarities between songs like "I Want You Back," "ABC," and "The Love You Save."

Many of Motown's older acts remained successful during the 1970s, although their records often explored styles associated with more modern forms of crossover R&B. Smokey Robinson wrote and produced many of his solo records during this period. The most famous was *A Quiet Storm*, which was released in 1975 and became the moniker for a

Oh, baby give...

do re mi ...

Stop! The love you save ...

Example 5.3. Stepwise melodic figures used by the Jackson 5 in the bass lines of (a) "I Want You Back" (0:50); (b) "ABC" (0:31); and (c) "The Love You Save" (0:34)

new radio format of sophisticated and relaxed R&B targeted to adults.[94] Marvin Gaye worked in mostly autonomous settings away from Motown's corporate structure at the time, and much of his most popular music incorporated overtly sexual themes. He released a remarkable series of popular albums during the middle of the decade that included *Let's Get It On*, *Live*, *I Want You*, and *Live at the London Palladium*.

Stevie Wonder also remained extremely popular. A lot of his material in the late 1960s continued the soulful orientation of records like "I Was Made to Love Her." These releases incorporated distorted keyboard sounds that emulated the guitar, melismatic vocals, vernacular language, and active drum and bass patterns. After working with producer Hank Cosby and multiple Motown songwriters for several years in the late 1960s, Wonder started to write and produce his own material. The culmination of this activity was the early 1971 record *Where I'm Coming From*. This album took on a spirit that was far removed from the Motown Sound. Many of its tracks highlighted keyboard and multiple-voice textures, and cuts like "Do Yourself a Favor" and "I Wanna Talk to You" used repetitive grooves and stylized spoken vocal parts that were common in the period's most popular funk music.

After favorably renegotiating his Motown contract in 1971, Wonder worked in studio environments that he controlled more closely in New York City and Los Angeles. The first popular single from these sessions was "Superstition," which was a hallmark of his new style. This track was recorded with the help of synthesizer programmers Malcolm Cecil and Robert Margouleff at Electric Lady, a studio built in New York for Jimi

Example 5.4. The main two-measure clavinet and synthesizer figure in Stevie Wonder, "Superstition"

Hendrix. It used an interwoven tapestry of keyboard parts to create a repetitive two-measure figure, establishing a funky dance-oriented texture (example 5.4). Wonder played nearly every track on the record, including drums, a synthesized bass, and two clavinet performances, both of which were copied several times onto the sixteen-track master using different equalization and time delay effects.[95]

Released in the fall of 1972, "Superstition" was one of the most popular singles of year, earning Wonder two Grammy Awards and rising to the top of both the R&B and pop charts. In line with Motown's move into visual media, Wonder performed the song with his band Wonderlove in many contexts on television and film during the period. He appeared on *Soul Train* lip-synching the record and answering questions from the audience, and performed for an hour on the New York public access program *Soul!*.[96] He toured with the Rolling Stones in the United States during the summer of 1972, an infamous set of dates captured in the unreleased film *Cocksucker Blues*; made an appearance at a large benefit staged by John Lennon and Yoko Ono at Madison Square Garden that was later released as a film called *The One to One Concert*; and filmed a lengthy set for the West German television program *Musikladen*. These contexts reflected Wonder's popularity with rock audiences, a significant element of the soul demographic during the time. One of Wonder's best television performances from the time was recorded for the children's program *Sesame Street*. Dozens of kids sat and danced on the studio set during his performance of "Superstition," using shakers and dancing ecstatically to some of the funkiest music of the period.

Echoing Motown's complex history of straddling the pop and soul markets, Wonder's work later in the 1970s vacillated between the heavy, dance-oriented style of "Superstition," middle-of-the-road ballads, and many other styles.[97] Later singles like "Higher Ground," "You Haven't

Done Nothin'," "I Wish," and "Sir Duke" used religious imagery, political statements, remembrances of childhood, and African American historical topics to evoke soul and funk tropes. Other popular Wonder tracks, like "You Are the Sunshine of My Life," were more harmonically active love songs that aligned with MOR pop styles. Containing a vast stylistic mélange, Wonder's albums *Talking Book, Innervisions, Fulfillingness' First Finale,* and *Songs in the Key of Life* were among the most successful and critically lauded R&B records of the 1970s.

Newer styles were widespread in Motown's catalog during the middle of the decade. Motown released at least a dozen iconic disco hits, distributed disco albums on the Ju-Par label, and commissioned a lot of popular extended mixes for the dance market. Eddie Kendricks revived his career in the mid-1970s with dance hits like "Keep on Truckin'" and "Boogie Down," and the Jackson 5 returned to prominence later in the decade with "Dancing Machine." The Miracles had similar success with "Love Machine" and Marvin Gaye with "Got to Give It Up." In addition to reaching mainstream and R&B audiences, many of Motown's disco records topped dance music charts published by *Billboard* and *Record World.*[98]

While Motown's disco records were often written by professional songwriters, performed by studio musicians, and created and manipulated in the recording studio by virtuosic producers and remix engineers, the company's funk music was more often created by large groups of musicians who wrote and performed their own material.[99] The first important act to fit into this larger band-oriented genre at Motown was the Commodores, a group of former students from the historically black Tuskegee Institute who came to Motown in 1972. By the mid-1970s the Commodores were Motown's most popular funk act, releasing records like "Slippery When Wet" and "Brick House." They also released several of the most enduring romantic records of the late 1970s. Saxophonist and vocalist Lionel Richie slowly emerged as the group's balladeer during this time, writing and performing lead vocals on popular singles like "Easy" and "Three Times a Lady." Other funk-oriented Motown acts from the period included Bottom and Company and Switch.

Despite Motown's success during the 1970s, there was little stylistic consistency among the company's releases. The corporate move, the company's changing creative practices, and the dynamic nature of the R&B market led to the decline of some Motown acts and the departure of others. Gladys Knight and the Pips signed to Buddah and Martha Reeves to RCA; Norman Whitfield formed his own company; the Jackson 5 eventually left for Epic; the Supremes disbanded during the late 1970s; and former members of the Temptations David Ruffin and Eddie Kendricks both departed in 1977.[100]

The end of the Motown "assembly line" was a major factor in the diffusion of the Motown Sound. Jobete was still a formidable publishing firm, but Multi-Media Management was far less powerful than its ITMI predecessor. Many Motown records released during the 1970s were recorded outside of the company's facilities, in places like New York, Philadelphia, Muscle Shoals, and Nashville. Perhaps most importantly, the new Sunset Boulevard offices did not have the family atmosphere of the old 2648 West Grand Boulevard headquarters. After using various studios Los Angeles, Motown eventually opened its own recording facility on Romaine Street in West Hollywood, called MoWest.[101] Only a few of the Funk Brothers made the trip to California.[102] In most cases, members of the Crusaders or other Los Angeles session musicians performed on Motown's California sessions.[103]

Motown Productions in the 1970s

In January 1973 Berry Gordy stepped down as president of Motown Records. He assigned this post to sales head Ewart Abner and appointed himself chairman of Motown Industries, a reorganized California-based group that included Motown Records, Jobete Publishing, and Motown Productions.[104] Leaving Abner and others to handle Motown's record division, Gordy focused on visual media for much of the next decade, expanding this area of the company. Drawing on the success of *Lady Sings the Blues*, most of the films and television programs created by Motown Productions featured African American actors and dealt with themes of race and class but were targeted to mainstream viewers. Many of these projects also featured Motown performers and were supported by cross-marketed soundtracks.

The 1975 film *Mahogany* was Gordy's next effort at a full-scale feature. He served as director and the film was produced in part by an important new Motown Productions staffer named Rob Cohen.[105] The film's narrative fit perfectly with Gordy's crossover agenda. It told the story of an African American woman with dreams of becoming a high-end fashion designer, who sought to reconcile her strong ties to a local community organizer with a once-in-a-lifetime opportunity to move to a romantic European city.[106] Diana Ross and Billy Dee Williams costarred in *Mahogany*, continuing the successful on-screen pairing of *Lady Sings the Blues*. The soundtrack featured Ross's popular single "Theme from

Mahogany (Do You Know Where You're Going To)," which also appeared on the album *Diana Ross* the following spring. Written by Michael Masser and Gerry Goffin this orchestra-driven torch-song ballad had origins that were decidedly non-Motown, reflecting Ross's wholesale move into material with little grounding in the R&B market.[107]

Gordy retreated from the director role after *Mahogany*. He worked as producer for his next film, *The Bingo Long Traveling All-Stars and Motor Kings*, which was about an independently run Negro League baseball team and its relationship with the major leagues. This picture continued Motown's class-oriented uplift style. It cast mostly African American actors in leading roles, including Williams, Richard Pryor, and James Earl Jones. Motown Productions worked on two feature films in 1978. *Thank God It's Friday* was made collaboratively with the motion picture arm of Casablanca Records. Starring disco diva Donna Summer, it followed several story lines during a single evening at a Los Angeles disco, focusing on Summer as an aspiring singer who is desperate to get the attention of a star disc jockey. Its most prominent song was Summer's "Last Dance," which was released on Casablanca. The Commodores also appeared during the picture's narrative climax, performing their funk song "Too Hot to Trot." *The Wiz* was Motown's other important film project of the period. Based on the successful stage production that had premiered on Broadway three years earlier, *The Wiz* was an adaptation of *The Wizard of Oz* that depicted modern African American characters in New York City. It starred Diana Ross as Dorothy, Michael Jackson as the scarecrow, and venerable black actors like Lena Horne, Ted Ross, and Nipsey Russell in other supporting roles.[108]

Motown Productions was also active in television throughout the 1970s. In 1976 the company filmed a version of Diana Ross's one-woman show "An Evening with Diana Ross," which was broadcast on NBC the next year. The show itself was a spectacle of costumes, novelty numbers, and torch songs. It had a critically acclaimed two-week run at the Palace Theater on Broadway and then moved to large theaters in Las Vegas, Los Angeles, Chicago, and Boston. Ross was later given a special Tony Award for the Broadway production, and the television special was nominated for four Emmy Awards. At the same time, Motown Productions developed a biographical film for television called *Scott Joplin: King of Ragtime* starring Billy Dee Williams in the title role. There had been a Joplin renaissance brewing for several years, with the release of Joshua Rifkin's album *Piano Rags* (1970), the use of Joplin's music in *The Sting* (1973), and a related single featuring Marvin Hamlisch's performance of "The Entertainer" reaching the upper echelon of the *Billboard* pop charts. (*Bingo Long* had incorporated music associated with New Orleans in a similar manner.) Joplin had a difficult life, and the film's depiction of the pianist and composer echoed the manner in which *Lady Sings the Blues* treated the historical legacy of Billie Holiday. One *Variety* review noted the common "Americana" themes of both *Scott Joplin* and *Bingo Long*, recognizing that their plots both dealt with characters that faced "uphill commercial roadblocks."[109]

A number of Motown's soundtrack records supported productions that were steeped in African American culture. A 1973 release called *Save the Children* contained musical performances taken from a documentary film about the Operation Push Black Expo held the preceding year in Chicago. The soundtrack for *Cooley High* used early Motown tracks from the 1960s to accompany a picture that told the story of a group of African American high school friends in Chicago. New Motown tracks were included in the television film *Norman . . . Is That You?*, which starred Redd Foxx as an old-fashioned black father who discovers his son is gay. Stevie Wonder's expansive two-disc soundtrack for *The Secret Life of Plants* underscored an esoteric documentary that included a choreographed interpretation of his "Black Orchid" by dancer Eartha Robinson and a lengthy segment on the pioneering work of African American botanist George Washington Carver. In the wake of *Trouble Man*, Motown artists released a number of blaxploitation albums during the 1970s. Edwin Starr was featured on the soundtrack for the 1973 film *Hell up in Harlem*, which was written and produced by Motown staffers Freddie Perren and Fonce Mizell; Willie Hutch wrote, produced, and performed on two soundtracks of this type, *The Mack* and *Foxy Brown*; and at the end of the blaxploitation era Smokey Robinson released the soundtrack for *Big Time*, a low-budget film that he helped to write and produce.

The broad reach of Motown Productions was evident in the films and soundtracks it supported that did not feature African American performers or portray Motown's typical brand of black uplift. One made-for-television movie, *Amateur Night at the Dixie Bar and Grill*, told the story of a talent contest at a country bar. The youth-oriented feature *Almost Summer*, which contained songs written and performed by Mike Love of the Beach Boys, was about a group of white high school students from Southern California. Several soundtracks also supported films with little discernible connection to the black community. Phillip Lambro's score for *Murph the Surf* connected stylistically to the blaxploitation style, but it featured all white actors and was a run-of-the-mill caper flick. The 1979 film *Fast Break* included the hit song "With You I'm Born Again" by Billy Preston and Syreeta and starred Gabe Kaplan as a white basketball fan who uses a team of African American players to realize his dream of becoming a successful coach. Motown also released soundtracks for films like *It's My Turn* and *Loving Couples*, which starred white actors and dealt with no overt African American themes.

Motown's large-scale expansion into visual media production was another product of its crossover strategy. Beginning as a typical teen-oriented record company that used film and television to promote its music, Motown's work in these areas became far more adult-oriented during the late 1960s and often courted audiences outside of black demographics. Motown is rarely mentioned in histories of black television and cinema, but its work in these areas was significant.[110] Motown Productions helped to create a new form of visual entertainment that featured black actors but was targeted to mainstream audiences, a strategy that became widespread in film, television, and advertising during the 1980s and 1990s. As with its role in the changing relationship between music markets during the early 1960s, Motown was at forefront of large-scale developments in film and television during this time, expanding the company mission of using African-American artists to reach audiences outside of traditionally black markets.

SIX | The 1980s and Beyond

Crossover in the 1980s

At the beginning of the 1980s Motown was a show-business juggernaut. A decade after moving to California to initiate a visual media arm, it was still the highest-grossing black-owned company in the United States. Its music division released about 450 singles and nearly as many albums during the 1980s and was among the largest independent record companies in the world.[1] There was a lot of stylistic diversity in the Motown catalog at the time. New initiatives were up and running, like the rock label Morocco and a Spanish-language imprint called Motown Latino, and the company released torch-song ballads like "I've Never Been to Me" by Charlene, blues-oriented hits by television star Bruce Willis, and jazz records by Ahmad Jamal, Grover Washington Jr., and Dr. Strut.[2] Despite the departures of longtime artists like Diana Ross and Marvin Gaye, old and new Motown stars alike were very successful during the 1980s and the company's involvement with contemporary styles produced a lot of noteworthy material.

Long-standing artists were still among Motown most popular acts.[3] Smokey Robinson extended his solo style from the 1970s with records like "Cruisin'," "Being with You," "Just to See Her," and "One Heartbeat," all of which used a midtempo Quiet Storm patina that reflected his age and drew upon memories of his past success. The lyrical themes of these records were very appealing to an aging baby boomer audience, in part because they conjured images of 1950s teenage leisure that trafficked in an innocence-based nostalgia that was widespread at the time. Stevie Wonder's albums also sold in great numbers during the 1980s and he appeared on several popular collaborative releases, including a duet with Paul McCartney ("Ebony and Ivory") and a Dionne Warwick single ("That's What Friends Are For"). Wonder's output was remarkably varied. A longtime devotee of technological advances in instrumentation, his records often featured new synthesizers like the Fairlight, Melodian, and E-MU. Stylistically, his releases included reggae-inspired material like "Master Blaster (Jammin')," midtempo standards like "That Girl" and "I Just Called to Say I Love You," and dance-oriented songs like "Part-Time Lover."

There were a handful of important new Motown acts during the early 1980s. A young solo artist named Rockwell, who was actually Berry Gordy's son Kennedy working under an assumed name, had a hit in early 1984 with "Somebody's Watching Me." Other new acts included the nouveau girl group Mary Jane Girls ("In My House") and the funk-oriented Dazz Band ("Let It Whip"). The family act DeBarge became one of the most popular groups to join Motown at the time, releasing a number of sensuous ballads, such as "I Like It," "All This Love," and "Time Will Reveal," which featured the virtuosic lead vocals of Eldra DeBarge. The group had its first significant mainstream success in early 1985 with the upbeat pop record "Rhythm of the Night."

Rick James and Lionel Richie were two of the most successful artists to release music for Motown during this period. Both had been with the company for some time and moved into more prominent roles during the early 1980s. James came out of the soul and funk traditions. His image was risqué and his music often evoked images of sexual exploration and drug use. His 1978 release *Come Get It* and its follow-up, *Bustin' Out of L Seven*, were among the most popular R&B albums of the time, but neither reached the top ten of the *Billboard* pop album charts. The accompanying singles "You and I" and "Mary Jane" were received similarly in the R&B market without much crossover success.[4] The breakthrough album, *Street Songs*, included James's most popular crossover hit, "Super Freak (Part 1)." It was released in 1981 and became one of the most successful albums of the year, remaining at the top of the R&B album charts for five months.

In the lineage of Motown polymaths like Smokey Robinson and Stevie Wonder, James often performed as an instrumentalist, vocalist, songwriter, and producer. He also collaborated with a number of artists to write and produce their music. James was a central figure in the first album released by Teena Marie, *Wild and Peaceful*; he served as the creative guru and leader of Mary Jane Girls, writing and producing all of their records; he wrote and produced the 1985 crossover hit "Party All the Time" for comedian Eddie Murphy; and he worked with longtime Motown artists like Smokey Robinson ("Ebony Eyes") and the Temptations ("Standing on the Top"), inserting a fresh sense of style into their 1980s work.[5]

Richie was Motown's most important crossover artist of the 1980s. While still a member of the Commodores, he had written, produced, and performed the crossover hit "Endless Love," a duet with Diana Ross that became her last Motown single. After leaving the Commodores, he performed many of the creative roles on three full-length albums that were all blockbuster crossover successes: *Lionel Richie, Can't Slow Down*, and *Dancing on the Ceiling*.[6] Richie's music was seemingly everywhere during the mid 1980s. He released twelve consecutive singles during the period that reached the top ten on both the R&B and pop charts, including records like "All Night Long (All Night)," "Hello," and "Say You, Say Me."

Like James, Richie successfully wrote and produced a lot of music for other artists during the 1980s. Before the success of "Endless Love," he had worked with country star Kenny Rogers on the record "Lady," which rose to the top of both the *Billboard* pop and country charts. He later wrote and produced the hit single "Missing You" for Diana Ross after the sudden death of Marvin Gaye.[7] He was integral to the creation of "We Are the World," a song he wrote with Michael Jackson that a group of several dozen of celebrities recorded under the name USA for Africa to benefit a series of highly publicized famine relief efforts.[8] In front of this all-star choir led by producer Quincy Jones, Richie performed the record's opening lines, affirming his star status among the ensemble. "We Are the World" became one of the most popular records of 1985, winning the Grammy Award for both Song of the Year and Record of the Year.

Richie's popularity extended into various forms of visual media in a manner that eluded James. He made prominent music videos and television appearances during the first half of the 1980s and appeared regularly on awards shows. He also signed a major endorsement deal with Pepsi in early 1984, which resulted in a series of high-profile television commercials that featured him performing altered versions of his hits. Drawing on Motown's two-decade history of reaching audiences outside of the United States, Richie was an international celebrity during the mid-1980s. He was the featured artist in the closing ceremony of the 1984 Summer Olympic Games, *Can't Slow Down* was released in two-dozen countries around the world, and his live tours traversed the globe.[9]

Motown Productions also remained active during the 1980s. Suzanne de Passe, who had been one of Berry Gordy's chief assistants throughout the 1970s, was named president of the division in 1981 and worked in this capacity throughout the decade.[10] She helped to create many movies for television, moving away from a focus on more expensive feature films. Many of these projects had little connection to Motown's success as a black-owned record company, including star vehicles for Lynda Carter (*The Last Song*) and Lindsay Wagner (*Callie and Son*), the Ed Asner and Jean Simmons detective drama *A Small Killing*, and a comedy starring John Schneider and Catherine Hicks called *Happy Endings*.[11] Motown Productions also created two episodic television series in 1986 and 1987. The first was a late-night talk show on NBC called *Night Life*, which featured David Brenner as host. It ran for nearly two hundred episodes. The other was *Sidekicks*, a youth-oriented program on ABC that followed the exploits of a young martial arts expert.

The largest Motown visual production of the time was the 1985 feature film *The Last Dragon*. It was set in New York City during the 1980s and told the story of a black martial artist from Harlem named "Bruce" Leroy Green. Several Motown artists were involved. Vanity starred as a singer in the picture and the music video for DeBarge's "Rhythm of the Night" was prominently included in one of the film's dance club scenes. *The Last Dragon* departed significantly from the uplifting style of *Lady Sings the Blues* and *Mahogany*. It featured African American actors and a feel-good plot, but its backdrop of 1970s kung fu films and use of special effects was more youth-oriented.[12] It quickly became the most financially successful Motown-produced feature film to date.

Many of Motown's other television productions were about the company itself, displaying a strong self-commemorative impulse that extended throughout the 1980s and 1990s. The most prominent of these was a 1983 prime-time special called *Motown 25*, which was filmed at a live event in Los Angeles celebrating Motown's silver anniversary. Richard Pryor hosted the show, which included performances by current Motown stars and several well-known acts that had left the company, including Diana Ross (in a reunion with the Supremes), Marvin Gaye, and Michael Jackson. After the success of *Motown 25*, Motown created a number of other prime-time specials that featured its performers in a similarly nostalgic manner, such as *Motown Returns to the Apollo* and *Motown Merry Christmas*.

Motown created two other television series during the period that focused on music. One was a string of cable-television documentaries about Motown artists called *Motown on Showtime*, which mixed new interviews and performances with rare documentary footage. The other, *The Motown Revue*, was a variety show hosted by Smokey Robinson that reflected the company's historical identity. A variety of classic and contemporary Motown artists performed on the program along with a young Arsenio Hall and several other comedians who helped steer the show to the tastes of older viewers. In a manner similar to *Motown 25* and *Motown Returns to the Apollo*, many of the sketches included in *The Motown Revue* focused on Motown itself, such as a recurring segment in which Robinson and several young rappers discussed generational differences in music and culture.

In keeping with its connection to television and film, Motown continued to release soundtracks and other film-oriented music during the 1980s. Lionel Richie's "Say You, Say Me" appeared in *White Nights*.[13] Stevie Wonder contributed the track "Stay Gold" to *The Outsiders* and also wrote, performed, and produced the majority of the soundtrack for *The Woman in Red*.[14] Compilation soundtracks created for *Christine* and *The Flamingo Kid* included collections of innocent, pre-Beatles American pop. Soundtracks for other films, such as *A Fine Mess* and *Get Crazy*, collated a variety of newly recorded songs by contemporary Motown acts and other rock and pop artists.[15] Motown also released the official soundtrack for *The Last Dragon*, which was chock full of new recordings by a variety of its artists.

Motown's most popular soundtrack of the time was released in support of *The Big Chill*. This 1983 film told the story of a group of white college friends from the late 1960s who had gathered together for a funeral fifteen years after graduation.[16] To accompany these thirtysomethings reliving their past, the film used mainstream rock and soul-oriented R&B that had crossed into the pop market during the late 1960s. Motown's official soundtrack did not include much of the rock and southern soul heard in the film. Instead, it featured soul-oriented music by the Temptations, Marvin Gaye, and the Miracles, which helped to revise common notions about Motown's stylistic diversity during its first decade.[17] The film reunited Motown with its core audience from the 1960s, placing Motown at the center of a resurgence of baby boomer nostalgia that was in full swing during the mid-1980s.

The Sale(s)

Motown's independent business model was difficult to maintain. In 1975 it had partnered with A&M, another large independent firm, to create a regional distribution firm in the American Southeast called Together Record Distributing.[18] This arrangement disbanded in 1979 when A&M aligned with the major distributor RCA.[19] By 1982, Chrysalis, Arista, and

Motown were the largest independently distributed record companies in America. Chrysalis moved its distribution to CBS late that year and Arista aligned with RCA not long after. This left Motown as the last of these large firms to use independent distribution. An article in *Variety* from April 1983 summed up the fragile state of the indie network at the time. "Without Motown," a local distributor told journalist Richard Gold, "there would be no independent distribution business."[20]

It became difficult for Motown *not* to align with a major distributor. The Pickwick network, which had released Motown's records on the West Coast and in the Southeast, declined sharply in 1983 after the departures of Chrysalis and Arista. Motown reacted by briefly distributing its own records on the West Coast through Together (without A&M). But this turned out to be a stopgap.[21] Berry Gordy finally capitulated in July 1983, signing a domestic distribution agreement with MCA. This move had various industry-wide implications. For one, it was the death knell for independent distribution, completing a large-scale move into the R&B market by major conglomerates that had begun in the early 1970s.[22] According to industry historian Russell Sanjek, this deal was also the final stage of the six major supply networks—RCA, CBS, MCA, EMI, PolyGram, and WEA—acquiring distribution rights to "virtually all recorded music produced in the United States."[23] It was the financial and symbolic end to the R&B independent record boom that began after World War II, marking a significant change in the business model of black pop.

Gordy continued to own and run Motown for five years with MCA in control of distribution. From a consumer's perspective there was little change in the company's character. Records by people like Lionel Richie, Rick James, Smokey Robinson, and Stevie Wonder maintained widespread appeal during this period. Behind the scenes, however, Motown was faltering. "Whenever you give up the control of your distribution," Gordy wrote in his autobiography, "you give up the control of your destiny."[24] Negotiations with MCA for the sale of company itself continued throughout this time, with Gordy balking at least once after a deal had been arranged. Gordy finally moved forward in June 1988. He sold the record company division of Motown for $61 million to MCA and the investment company Boston Ventures. This deal included artist contracts, record masters, and the Motown brand. Gordy also reduced his other work in the coming years. Suzanne de Passe assumed the leadership of Motown Productions and continued her work in visual entertainment during the 1990s and 2000s. Gordy then sold his most valuable

corporate asset, Jobete Publishing, to EMI in three stages.[25] EMI bought
half of Jobete's publishing rights in 1997 for a reported $132 million;
raised its stake to 80 percent at a cost of an additional $109 million in the
spring of 2003; and purchased Gordy's remaining publishing holdings in
April 2004 for another $80 million.[26]

The Motown record division changed hands several times after this
sale. Boston Ventures bought MCA's stake in Motown during early 1993
and later that year sold the entire company to PolyGram for more than
$300 million; five years later Seagram acquired PolyGram and merged
it with Universal Music; and in 2000 the French conglomerate Vivendi
acquired Seagram. As part of the original sale, Gordy had made provi-
sions to keep Motown under African American leadership, which led
to a number of marquee executives of color running the label in the
coming years. MCA first appointed Jheryl Busby as company president.[27]
He signed important new acts like Queen Latifah, Johnny Gill, and Boyz
II Men, and his success was a major reason for the company's marked
increase in value between Gordy's initial sale and PolyGram's acquisition in 1993. Busby's tenure lasted until 1995, when PolyGram appointed
Andre Harrell as Motown's new chief.[28] After moving Motown's offices to
New York, Harrell led the company for only two years. George Jackson
succeeded Harrell in late 1997. Kedar Massenburg then took the role of
Motown president in late 1998, after the formation of Universal Music,
leading the company until 2004.

Motown's status as a contemporary imprint continued to change after
the turn of the millennium. In 2006, with the newly appointed Sylvia
Rhone as head, Motown's roster merged with the black pop artists on
Universal Records to create a label called Universal Motown, which oper-
ated under the auspices of a larger Universal Motown Republic group.
This group later aligned with Island Def Jam and the Capitol Records
group, both Universal entities. The company then moved back to Los
Angeles in 2014 under the leadership of Ethiopia Habtemariam. Today,
Motown exists in two distinct forms: a catalog imprint that reissues old
material and a front-line label that releases new music by artists like
Erykah Badu, Ne-Yo, and BJ the Chicago Kid.

Motown Remembered

After the sale to MCA Motown's identity became increasingly reliant
on history.[29] The company's "classic" catalog was a valuable asset, and
the various executives who managed it often focused on repackaging

older music. Reissuing material was not an entirely new business move. Motown had often explored historic recordings under Berry Gordy's leadership, creating album-length collections of singles, compiling *The Motown Story*, and later using the Natural Resources imprint as a reissue label.[30] But reissues of older records became a significant growth area in the mid-to-late 1980s, when audio technology evolved to sway listeners' format preferences from vinyl to cassette tape and compact disc (CD).

Motown's back catalog benefited from this movement, which occurred in concert with a wave of 1960s nostalgia. This led to the establishment of a dedicated catalog development division in the early 1990s, which was based in Los Angeles and headed by Candace Bond. Producers Cary Mansfield and Amy Herot curated a lot of historic album reissues through this department, compiling collections of older singles, album tracks, and previously unreleased material from the Motown archives. In 1997, Motown's catalog division was dissolved and subsumed by the larger reissue division of PolyGram Records. After a later merger with MCA, this division was renamed Universal Music Enterprises (UMe). Vice president Harry Weinger led Motown's reissues at PolyGram and UMe, often working closely with corporate tape archivist Andy Skurow.

Most of the artists whose work was being reissued no longer recorded for Motown. Singers like Brenda Holloway, Edwin Starr, Kim Weston, Martha Reeves, and Mary Wells performed on oldies circuits and at Northern Soul events but had no significant recording success after the 1960s. They were representative of a large group of former Motown artists and employees who struggled to maintain relevancy in their post-Motown careers. Great Britain became the most lucrative place for former Motown acts during the late 1980s and early 1990s. Although each of these artists recorded for a variety of small companies, their most prominent new records appeared on labels owned and run by Ian Levine, a DJ who released retro-oriented music for the Northern Soul community. For more than a decade, Levine had worked in the UK as a remix engineer, songwriter, and producer with companies like AVI and Record Shack. He specialized in dance-oriented soul and the post-disco style known widely as Hi-NRG. Seeking to mix the historical prestige of Motown artists with contemporary dance music, Levine formed labels called Nightmare and Motorcity, which released new recordings by artists whose historic work appealed to Northern Soul aficionados.

Levine worked with dozens of former Motown artists and other R&B stars from the 1960s and 1970s. His company released over three hundred extended singles and LPs before it disbanded in the early 1990s.

Most of this music was newly composed, but a few of the records were re-recorded versions of Motown classics, some even by the original artists.[31] Levine's releases often had an uncanny sense of history due to an audible dissonance created through juxtaposing stylized 1980s dance-music production, well-known acts connected to the 1960s, and anachronistic song material created in the present to evoke the past. These records exhibited the continuing importance of rare Motown in England, which for many of Motown's less-remembered acts had grown from an interesting auxiliary market to their central working environment.

Motown's place in the lore of 1960s popular culture was evident in other ways during the 1980s. In 1985 Esther Gordy Edwards created a nonprofit organization called the Motown Historical Museum, which later converted Motown's former offices and recording studio at 2648 West Grand Boulevard into a museum space.[32] From its inception, the Motown Museum was a shrine to the Motown Sound. It presented fans with artifacts, allowed them to walk through the iconic studio and hear the sounds of an exposed reverb chamber, and offered a variety of Motown-branded material for purchase in a well-stocked gift shop. It also hosted parties, conferences, tributes, and exhibitions. The building was declared a historic site by the state of Michigan in 1987 and was significantly renovated during the mid-1990s. Against the backdrop of a declining automobile industry, it quickly became one of Detroit's most popular tourist destinations.

There was an explosion of popular press books in the mid-1980s that focused on Motown's history. Don Waller and J. Randy Taraborrelli wrote company retrospectives with facts and trivia, Sharon Davis provided a comprehensive account of the Motown story from a British vantage point, and Reginald Bartlette compiled an encyclopedic and esoteric volume of Motown's recorded output from the perspective of a record collector.[33] One important Motown study from the time was journalist Nelson George's *Where Did Our Love Go?*[34] Using firsthand accounts from musicians and staffers, George's account challenged Motown's public image as a company that nurtured artists in a supportive, family-oriented environment. Instead, he created a narrative in which Motown consistently betrayed the African American community from which it emerged by discarding artists, hiding the work of background musicians, turning its back on once-helpful concert promoters and radio DJs, and kowtowing to the interests of the mainstream. In a way, George's treatment of Motown and the history depicted by the Motown Museum were similar. They both abridged Motown's story, reducing away important aspects of the company's past to create a tale that resonated with the memories of baby boomers. But their approaches were more obviously at odds, with the museum depicting Motown's history as a laudable extension of the civil rights movement and George questioning the company's authenticity in the face of conflicts surrounding African American identity during the 1980s.

At the same time that Motown was becoming a contested historical phenomenon in the public sphere, a variety of other authors were also starting to write about the company and its music.[35] Gerald Early's 1995 book, *One Nation under a Groove* (which he developed from a lengthy article in the *New Republic*), was a collection of essays that discussed issues of class in 1960s R&B, regional identity in the music business, and black corporate responsibility after World War II.[36] Suzanne Smith's 1999 study of Motown, *Dancing in the Street*, which grew out of her Yale dissertation in the field of American studies, considered the company's work during the 1960s against the backdrop of politics and activism within Detroit's African American community.[37] There were a large number of books about individual Motown acts. David Ritz's biography of Marvin Gaye, *Divided Soul*, was an important benchmark that forged this genre.[38] Patricia Romanowski, J. Randy Taraborrelli, Peter Benjaminson, and Mark Ribowsky all wrote later biographies, sometimes collaborating with Motown artists to develop their own narratives.[39] Some of these books commanded hefty advances and received wide music-industry promotion, such as Diana Ross's *Secrets of a Sparrow*. Similarly, Berry Gordy's memoir, *To Be Loved*, was a big seller. It offered a reasoned account of Gordy's perspective on Motown's history and confirmed publicly for the first time a long personal relationship with Ross.[40] Even the smallest roles at Motown seemed to warrant book-length explication, and dozens of other publications about Motown's history appeared over the years from the perspective of artists, employees, backing musicians, and studio engineers.[41]

Now called de Passe Entertainment, Motown's former video arm furthered this historicization trend by creating a number of television programs during the 1990s and 2000s that celebrated Motown anniversaries.[42] A 1994 broadcast called *Motown 30: What's Goin' On* featured musical performances, dance reviews choreographed by Debbie Allen, testimonials from a wide cast of African American entertainment celebrities, and a series of skits starring Robert Townsend chronicling the emergence of a black presence on television after the 1950s.[43] ABC aired a similar documentary in 1998 narrated by Diana Ross called *Motown 40: The Music Is Forever*, which used stock footage and interviews to chronicle the company's history. In 2004 de Passe produced another variety hour called *Motown 45* hosted by Cedric the Entertainer.

Today Motown celebrations of this type are more newsworthy than the company's new music. There was a rash of attention surrounding Motown's golden anniversary in 2009, for example, which included a spate of Motown 50 reissues from Universal's catalog division, a series of official company-produced iTunes podcasts, a well-documented reunion with Motown alumni and political officials in Detroit, and a Motown exhibit at the Rock and Roll Hall of Fame and Museum in Cleveland. Similarly, Berry Gordy's successful musical adaptation of his autobiography, *Motown: The Musical*, opened to great fanfare in 2013.[44] It condensed Motown's history to a handful of characters and several dozen songs sung by Broadway performers, and audiences loved it. It ran on Broadway for nearly two years and was nominated for several Tony Awards. It also moved to many other North American cities and opened in London's West End in 2016. The success of this production led many fans to take stock of Motown's historical importance one more time, while Berry Gordy and a number of living Motown artists experienced yet another flash of relevance in the public sphere.

motown

During the 2000s there was an interesting legal exchange between Universal Music Group (UMG) and Mattel, the large toy company that makes die-cast Hot Wheels cars. In 2005 Mattel tried to register "Motown Metal" as a trademark for a series of toy cars. UMG protested because it owned the Motown trademark and "Motown Metal" might have confused consumers about the Motown brand. Mattel's lawyers wrote that *Motown* had become both a "generic geographic description" and a "descriptive term for a music style."[45] The U.S. Trademark Trial and Appeal Board eventually denied Mattel's application, but not before hearing arguments about the many instances in which the meaning of *Motown* had lost specificity. The law surrounding this decision is grounded in the concept of trademark dilution, which is also sometimes called "genericide." This the process by which a trademark enters colloquial language and is no longer protected as the property of a company or individual.[46] (Well-known generonyms include aspirin, escalator, and thermos.) Judging from colloquial usage, Mattel's lawyers seemed to have a pretty solid argument. Although Motown is one of the most widely known corporate names in popular music, it has also been used nonspecifically for decades.

In the mid-1960s many Detroit-based record companies—firms like D-Town, Wheelsville, Groovesville, and Groove City—capitalized on Motown's popularity by using similar region-oriented marketing techniques.[47] These companies released a number of hits that were redolent of Motown's style. Deon Jackson's "Love Makes the World Go Round" was extremely similar to the Marvelettes' "Don't Mess with Bill"; the Holidays' "I'll Love You Forever" had an opening figure that replicated a portion of the Four Tops' "Baby I Need Your Loving"; and a number of singles released by J. J. Barnes, including "A Real Humdinger" and "Baby Please Come back Home," closely resembled 1960s Marvin Gaye records. Detroit-based records like Wilson Pickett's "Let Me Be Your Boy" (Correct-Tone), the Reflections' "(Just Like) Romeo and Juliet" (Golden World), and Edwin Starr's "Agent Double-O-Soul" (Ric Tic) all sounded as if they could have been recorded at Motown. In one well-documented example, the Capitols' "Cool Jerk" (Karen) even employed the Funk Brothers in an illicit moonlighting gig, using Motown's actual backing musicians to create the Motown Sound for a different company.[48]

Motown's influence was also evident on a national scale during the first half of the 1960s. From the use of prominent flute in "What Kind of Fool (Do You Think I Am)," released by the Tams on ABC-Paramount in late 1963, to the call-and-response backing vocals, xylophone, and Motown Beat in Betty Everett's "The Shoop Shoop Song," released on Vee-Jay the next year, a lot of popular singles from the time incorporated stylistic elements of the Motown Sound. Recording for Scepter with material written by Burt Bacharach and Hal David, a number of Dionne Warwick's records fell into this category. The 1964 single "Reach Out for Me," for example, included inventive orchestration, prominent backing vocals, and vocal production techniques that were similar to Motown performances by Mary Wells and Brenda Holloway. Other widely known Motown-like hits from the period included Fontella Bass's "Rescue Me," which was produced by Berry Gordy's former partner Billy Davis for the Checker imprint, and Len Barry's "1 2 3" (Decca), which featured Motown Sound attributes like a quarter-note pulse, a prominent bass, a saxophone solo, overt reverb, and Motown-style backing vocals.

Several national releases were also in close dialogue with specific Motown records and groups.[49] The Toys' "A Lover's Concerto" used tambourine emphasized with reverb, baritone saxophone, active bass, and vibes to accompany a girl group vocal texture, inspiring HDH to develop "I Hear a Symphony" for the Supremes.[50] Jackie Lee's "Do the Temptation Walk" opened with a bass figure taken from "My Girl" before describing a new dance attributed to Motown's guy group. The Impressions' single "Can't Satisfy" even took its verse melody from the HDH song "This Old Heart of Mine (Is Weak for You)."[51] From Motown's perspective, the musical similarities between some of these records were so great that it threatened legal action. Notable instances of publishing disputes surrounded songs like "Mashed Potato Time," "1 2 3," and "Can't Satisfy," which were all eventually altered to include Motown writers after they became hits.[52]

The broader "Detroit Sound" created by Motown-like records was one of the many elements that helped to form a genre that I call *motown*.[53] In music, literature, film, and within the music industry itself, motown includes many of Motown's biggest hits, but it also extends far outside the specific corporate and regional borders of Gordy's company. It encompasses music from the 1960s that embraced integration by exhibiting culturally acceptable and nonthreatening forms of African American life from the middle of the twentieth century. A lot of upbeat R&B performed by African Americans might be considered motown, including black pop using the Motown Beat or intricate orchestral arrangements and virtually all black guy and girl groups from this time. Lyrically, motown often depicts youth, nostalgia, and overcoming in the context of teenage-oriented love. There is a strong sense of urbanity and class identity in motown, a lack of nationalism and militancy, and a distinct visual and performative element, which comprises smart 1960s attire and sleek dance steps performed by vocalists with no burden of performing instrumentally.

The motown genre extends far past the music of records from the 1960s. A decade after the emergence of these early instances of motown in the singles market a variety of other entertainment forms began to use biographical and visual motown tropes. Elaine Jesmer's novel *Number One with a Bullet* told the story of a black-run record company from Houston called Finest Records, with many characters who resembled Motown personnel; the film *Sparkle* and the Broadway musical *Dreamgirls* invoked the Supremes; Robert Townsend's film *The Five Heartbeats* depicted a motown Temptations; the John Waters film *Hairspray* used musical and cultural motown references to conjure a 1960s style; and Hollywood features like *You Can't Hurry Love* and *My Girl* took their titles from Motown songs.[54] Ironically, films and musicals that used characters resembling Motown singers and executives often reproduced the *look* of the 1960s with anachronistic musical performances. They viewed this period through a more modern musical lens, evoking soul stereotypes of black vocal production and gospel-oriented content. A good example is the depiction of a fallen Florence Ballard character in both *Sparkle* and *Dreamgirls*. Ballard was unquestionably the Supremes' most soulful singer, but she never displayed the level of virtuosity portrayed by her genericized characters in either of these productions. This is evident most clearly in the commercial R&B hit from *Dreamgirls* "And I Am Telling You I'm Not Going," which was performed by Jennifer Holliday in the 1981 original cast recording and Jennifer Hudson in the popular 2006 film remake.

Today, motown is evoked in a variety of music industry contexts. Commercial radio stations use the term to refer to a style of R&B from the 1960s rather than the specific music of the Motown Record Company. The New York oldies station WCBS once described itself in this manner as "home for Motown, soul, and great rock and roll." Amateur musicians commonly use motown as a genre category to describe their interests to one another in classified ads and online forums. Professional bands also evoke motown to explain their musical character to prospective clients. The literature of the popular band-booking agency Gigmasters, for example, notes that a "live Motown band" might perform the music of "The Jackson 5, Aretha Franklin and much more."[55] At the height of music retail in the 1990s, it was common for brick-and-mortar record stores to create a motown section, within which they included all non-soul R&B from the 1960s. This usage continues today in tagging within media library software like iTunes and Internet streaming services. Plugging the term *Motown* into a service like Pandora, for example, creates a motown playlist that includes music by non-Motown artists like Al Green, the Drifters, and the Chi-Lites.

motown in Advertising

For a company that supported mostly black artists, Motown explored product endorsement remarkably early. The Supremes participated in a number of national and local campaigns during the 1960s, including television advertisements for Arrid deodorant, radio spots and print ads for Coke, and a local supermarket tie-in with Michigan-based Schafer Bakeries, which released a special-edition Supremes white bread.[56] In later years the Four Tops recorded a Pepsi jingle called "Taste That Beats the Others Cold" and the Jackson 5 appeared in commercials for Alpha Bits and Super Sugar Crisp breakfast cereals. Personal spots like these were rare at the time because many corporate sponsors were wary of using black celebrities to promote products targeted to white consumers. Accordingly, print advertisements featuring the Supremes appeared mostly in black-oriented publications like *Ebony* and *Jet* and youth-oriented magazines like *Boy's Life* and *American Girl*.[57]

Far more commercials featured Motown's music during the 1980s, a period when advertisers used African American symbols much more freely to promote products to a mainstream demographic.[58] Some of these spots incorporated segments of original records or altered versions of current hits, such as the music accompanying large-scale campaigns by Pepsi that featured the Jacksons and Lionel Richie.[59] In other instances, advertisements presented Motown songs in mimic versions, spreading knowledge of the company's classic material without using famous performances from the 1960s. This type of advertising was another important factor in Motown's weakening trademark.[60] As the company's most famous songs became part of a ubiquitous television soundscape the Motown brand further diffused into a nonspecific genre of 1960s pop music.[61]

A good example of this occurred in a McDonald's commercial that aired during the national broadcast of *Motown 25* in 1983. The segment focused on the shared elements of history between Motown and McDonald's. It opened in a 1968 setting, the first year of the Big Mac, showing three African American male friends eating at a restaurant while talking about music. The next sequence flashed forward to revisit the men in the same seats fifteen years later, highlighting the continued popularity of both companies during this span. The ad incorporated several visual clues that supported the narrative of changing times in music. Most obviously, the men held 45s during the first segment and LPs in the second, both with visible Motown labels. The commercial's soundtrack also reflected its historical perspective. The music takes on a motown character in its first half, using a bass ostinato and a vocal melody that recalls aspects of "I Can't Help Myself." During a short transition between the two time periods the music also makes two references to "My Girl": a quick vamp featuring a prominent descending fifth (punctuated by a bass voice proclaiming "Big Mac") and backing vocals declaiming "hey, hey, hey" in ascending stepwise motion. In the commercial's second half, its music is more modern, exhibiting sonic changes that help to reinforce a sense of time passing. A new vocalist sings a different melody in a much more melismatic manner, hand claps on the backbeat take on the technological character of a drum machine, and synth pad sounds hover in the upper sonic space of the track.

Many other advertisements used elements of motown during the mid-1980s, with baby boomers as an obvious demographic target.[62] "Ain't No Mountain High Enough" was included in a Lincoln-Mercury campaign, "I Can't Help Myself" appeared in a Duncan Hines advertisement, the Four Tops appeared in a Sun Country wine cooler spot, and Stevie Wonder created a theme song for Kodak using the slogan "You Can Depend on Me." Several motown-oriented campaigns from the period were among the most extensive in the business. A series of Levi's commercials created in the mid-1980s by the British firm of Bartle Bogle Hegarty incorporated songs that had achieved crossover popularity during 1960s to portray the company's 501 jeans as classic, timeless, and "original." Two of the ads featured rerecorded Motown songs.[63] The first was called "Launderette." It depicted an attractive white man in a 1950s setting taking off his clothes and putting them into a washing machine along with a bag of stones in order to achieve a stonewashed look. The soundtrack was a new version of Marvin Gaye's "I Heard It through the Grapevine," which placed the song in a time more than a decade before it actually appeared on the pop charts. The second spot depicted a mid-century solider returning home on a bus and being greeted by a woman who gives him a pair of jeans to wear. It used a soundalike version of "My Girl" in a similarly ahistorical manner.

"I Heard It through the Grapevine" also appeared in a wildly successful series of Claymation advertisements for the "California Raisins" during the 1980s (figure 6.1).[64] The first of these ads depicted a construction worker's Raisins performing "I Heard It through the Grapevine" as a motown group, with a single lead singer and three synchronized backing vocalists. Unlike Marvin Gaye, whose interpretation of "Grapevine" displayed a specific brand of male vulnerability against the backdrop of the soul movement, the California Raisins were hip and cool. There was no sense of lost love or longing in their rendition, which was performed in a mimic version by Buddy Miles. The ad was created by the San Francisco firm of Foote, Cone and Belding and it was extremely effective despite the raisins' strikingly similarity to minstrel caricatures from the nineteenth century.[65] Raisin sales rose dramatically and *Advertising Age* called it the best television commercial of 1986's final quarter.[66] The campaign revitalized the popularity of Gaye's original recording, which was rereleased as a single and reached the top ten in the UK.

A whirlwind of Raisin activity followed. Later commercials used Claymation caricatures of Ray Charles and Michael Jackson performing "I Heard It through the Grapevine" in the style of their best-known records. The Raisins were featured in primetime television specials, a

Fig 6.1. A screen shot of a 1987 California Raisins commercial featuring "I Heard It through the Grapevine"

Saturday morning cartoon series, and an extensive line of merchandise, all while singing "I Heard It through the Grapevine" as their signature song. The Raisins also released several full-length record albums. The first of these, *The California Raisins Sing the Hit Songs*, featured rerecorded music from the Motown catalog ("Grapevine" and "You Can't Hurry Love"), southern soul ("Respect" and "When a Man Loves a Woman"), and 1950s rock and roll ("Heartbreak Hotel" and "La Bamba"). Later releases like *Sweet, Delicious, and Marvelous* and *Meet the Raisins!* included a similar mix of material.

Motown's music appeared regularly in many other television commercials throughout the 1990s and 2000s, altering the connotations of music that once had pointed cultural meaning. Toyota used "Get Ready" to promote its redesigned Camry, Papa John's advertised its "Sweatreat" pizza to the tune of "I Can't Help Myself," ABC announced a new situation comedy about a woman with relationship issues using "I Can't Get Next to You," and Little Debbie sold snack cakes to the accompaniment of "My Girl." A Dockers commercial from 2008 featured Marlena Shaw's non-Motown version of "California Soul" in a depiction of San

Francisco as a cool, upscale city with no visible black residents. In 2009 State Farm featured the Jackson 5 performing "I'll Be There" in a major new campaign. It was part of a joint venture with UMe, in which the two companies "joined together in a unique collaboration expanding outside traditional market models."[67] State Farm promoted its insurance using a stripped-down version of "I'll Be There" supported by images of life-changing catastrophes and triumphs, and UMe used the advertisement to further sales of a remixed "I'll Be There" single on iTunes.[68] An Energizer battery commercial from the same period, called "Band Camp Love," exhibited one of the most divergent uses of Motown material from the time, showing the liberal use of sexually oriented R&B by mainstream advertisers. It depicted a prepubescent white girl on a school bus with a portable music player that would not work because of failing batteries. A boy classmate approached and allowed her to share in the sounds of his own music player, which played Marvin Gaye's "Let's Get It On."

motown in Pop and R&B

Hundreds of Motown covers were released in both the UK and the United States during the 1980s.[69] The magnitude and popularity of these recordings continued Motown's legacy but also helped to weaken the identity of its original records. In many cases, these records aligned with a popular movement of 1960s nostalgia. They coexisted with original recordings for older audiences, but were often the only versions that teenagers knew, supplanting Motown's older recordings as primary texts for a younger generation.

One particularly well-known song was "You Can't Hurry Love." The most popular recording of the time was by Phil Collins.[70] The UK cover sleeve for Collins's single was a visual pastiche of British Tamla-Motown packaging from the 1960s. Similarly, its music video included three different images of Collins laden in various forms of throwback mod attire, performing as each member of a vocal trio (figure 6.2). Collins's version reflected the continued importance of Motown in British popular culture and it rekindled interest in the original Supremes record, which the UK Tamla-Motown office officially reissued at the time. But it also stripped vital elements of race and gender from the original Supremes version, allowing new audiences to learn "You Can't Hurry Love" without experiencing the African American girl group context of the Supremes' performance.

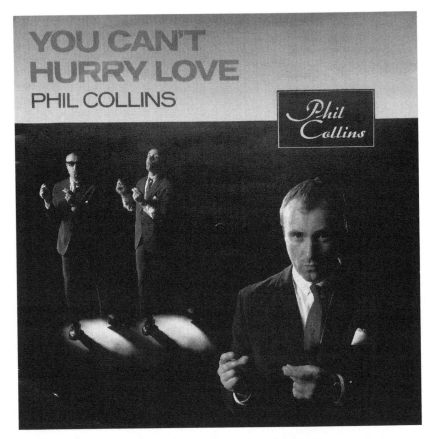

Fig 6.2. The UK picture sleeve of Phil Collins, "You Can't Hurry Love"

Motown was also the dialogic subject of a number of songs. A bass line similar to the ostinato figure used in 1965 Four Tops single "I Can't Help Myself" appeared in two of the biggest hits from the 1980s, Michael Jackson's "Billie Jean" and Madonna's "Like a Virgin." This reference injected both of these singles with a repetitive dance groove that evoked 1960s youthful innocence underneath songs about premarital sex and teen pregnancy, topics that were at the forefront of mainstream culture at the time. The syncopated bass line from "You Can't Hurry Love" was even more widespread, becaming the foundation of a common texture in rock and pop during the late 1970s and early 1980s.[71] Independent rock groups, punk bands, and musicians connected to the British "mod revival" often used this figure, showing the manner in which Motown's international reception translated into a more general stylistic influence.

The Clash's "Hitsville U.K." used it under a text describing an idyllic independent music scene in the United Kingdom; "Town Called Malice" by the Jam incorporated it into a song that recalled the simplicity of childhood; and its use in the Smiths single "This Charming Man" helped to create a sonic palimpsest of the group's androgynous lead singer, Morrissey, and the glamorous Supremes.[72]

A number of other records by UK groups discussed Motown in their lyrics, providing both subtle and obvious instances of historical perspective. In a nod to Northern Soul all-nighters, Spandau Ballet's hit "True" recalled "listening to Marvin" and punctuated this phrase with distinctive background vocals clearly intended to invoke a sense of motown.[73] Billy Bragg's "Levi Stubbs' Tears" used the aural image of Stubbs crying in Four Tops songs to reflect on relationship issues. George Harrison's "Pure Smokey" discussed the importance of Smokey Robinson in British culture. ABC's "When Smokey Sings" was evidence of a continuing relationship between the Hi-NRG movement and Motown; its music used stylized female background singers, a Motown Beat, and an ostinato saxophone part that mostly replicated the bassoon line of "The Tears of a Clown" to invoke the Motown Sound (example 6.1).[74]

In America, Larry John McNally's "The Motown Song" incorporated similar musical and textual allusions. It depicted a nostalgic urban relationship, most likely between an older white couple who had once enjoyed crossover R&B. In the song, a protagonist asks a partner to "bring over some of your old Motown records" so they can "go on the roof and listen to the Miracles echo in the alley down below."[75] Musically, McNally's record evoked a non-frenetic, nostalgic motown by using a midtempo shuffle beat and a distinct background melody in the bridge (example 6.2). This song was rerecorded several years later by British singer Rod Stewart, a former mod and product of the mid-1960s UK blues revival.[76] Stewart's interpretation diverged from McNally's more intimate rendition in a number of ways. It enhanced the role of the motown background vocal passage, which was heard only once on McNally's original record; it featured an actual Motown group—the Temptations—performing these parts; and its animated music video depicted the song as a block party anthem.[77] Versions of "The Motown Song" by McNally and Stewart help to depict common differences between memories of Motown in American and Britain at the time. English listeners often equated Motown with dance culture, while Motown's role in U.S. history was frequently equated with the civil rights movement and changing attitudes toward race during the 1960s.

Example 6.1. The bassoon riff in the Miracles, "The Tears of a Clown" (A) and the saxophone riff in ABC, "When Smokey Sings" (B)

Example 6.2. The Motown-like background vocal part featured in Larry John McNally, "The Motown Song"

Motown's acts also participated in the creation of motown by focusing on historic songs and subjects. Bonnie Pointer had disco hits in the late 1970s with versions of "Heaven Must Have Sent You" and "I Can't Help Myself"; The Jackson 5 recorded "Forever Came Today"; and the Dynamic Superiors revisited "Nowhere to Run." Two acts commonly associated with Motown created extremely popular tributes to Marvin Gaye after his sudden death in 1984. The first was the Diana Ross single "Missing You."[78] Its video used a lengthy montage to remember a number of deceased members of Motown groups, including Florence Ballard of the Supremes and Paul Williams of the Temptations. The second tribute was the Commodores' "Nightshift," which was about Gaye and Jackie Wilson. The video for this record included an uncanny choreographed vocal ensemble performance by the Commodores, which was at odds with their funk background and the performance styles of Gaye and Wilson.

While not as obvious, aspects of motown were also visible and audible in a variety of contemporary R&B records during the 1980s and 1990s. The choreography and vocal arrangements of guy groups like New Edition, Guy, and Tony! Toni! Toné! recalled Motown acts like the Jackson 5, the Temptations, and the Four Tops; En Vogue, TLC, and Destiny's Child drew similarly upon Motown girl groups like the Marvelettes, the Supremes, and the Velvelettes; and the 1991 debut album of the new Motown guy group Boyz II Men, *Cooleyhighharmony*, even took its name from a 1975 film featuring an all-Motown soundtrack.[79]

This Boyz II Men album made numerous references to Motown, providing an interesting example of a contemporary Motown act incorporating aspects of motown into its music. The lyrics of the group's first single, "Motownphilly," refer to Motown by name, and in a striking pair of parenthetical vocal breaks the track's contemporary "New Jack Swing" instrumentation drops out to feature them brandishing group harmonies in a style similar to Motown guy groups from the 1960s. The popular Boyz II Men record "It's So Hard to Say Goodbye to Yesterday" also had Motown roots; Motown artist G. C. Cameron first performed it in the *Cooley High* film that inspired the group's album title.

In the mid-1990s impulses toward historicization within the R&B market led to a style marketed as "neo-soul," which connected in many ways to the motown genre. Neo-soul used iconography, fashion, performance incorporating acoustic and vintage instruments, and textual connections to the past to evoke black pop from the 1960s and 1970s.[80] Singers like D'Angelo, Maxwell, and Erykah Badu were well-known neo-soul singers at the time, and Motown president Kedar Massenburg was one of the leading music executives to support the style. Many of these artists made motown references in their music, and Badu was one of Universal Motown's marquee artists.

One of the most popular neo-soul singles from the late 1990s was Lauryn Hill's single "Doo Wop (That Thing)." This record exemplified neo-soul in a number of ways and connected to motown in a manner typical of this modern style. It opens with Hill asking "remember back on the boogie when cats used to harmonize like," followed by an example of close-voiced vocal harmony in a doo-wop style. The track then launches into a beat-based groove that incorporates elements linked to the past like a driving eighth-note piano part, dense horn lines, an unaffected crisp drumbeat, and stylized backing vocals. The music video for "Doo Wop" uses visual cues to directly invoke motown. Through the use of a split screen, the left side of the picture shows the performance as it might have occurred in 1967, with male background singers in sharp suits performing Temptations-like dances behind Hill, who is dressed like Diana Ross and uses physical movements similar to Cholly Atkins's well-known choreography (figure 6.3). In contrast, the right side of the screen portrays a performance style from 1998, with Hill and the background singers dressed in modern clothing and using contemporary choreography.

Approaches to neo-soul grew more diffuse during the 2000s. Acts like Sharon Jones and the Dap-Kings, Charles Bradley, Kings Go Forth, Mayer Hawthorne, and Raphael Saadiq represented a new generation

Fig 6.3. Screen captures from the music video for Lauryn Hill, "Doo Wop (That Thing)"

of backward-looking soul artists in the United States. They constructed modernist takes on R&B from the 1960s and 1970s by conflating elements of motown, southern soul, Afro-pop, and funk.[81] Saadiq's *The Way I See It* is a particularly illustrative example of an album that contained many motown references. A Motown Beat drove many of its arrangements; several of its songs ("100 Yard Dash" and "Let's Take a Walk") drew on compositional aspects of Gaye's "I Heard It through the Grapevine"; and one track, "Never Give You Up," featured a harmonica solo by Stevie Wonder. Saadiq also incorporated visual elements of motown into his music videos and live performances and was open about these connections during his promotional efforts surrounding the album (figure 6.4).[82]

A contemporaneous form of neo-soul was also extremely popular among artists from the UK. White male vocalists like James Morrison and Jamie Lidell and female singers like Joss Stone, Duffy, and Adele all incorporated motown characteristics into their music and marketing.

Fig 6.4. A screen capture of Raphael Saadiq (*center*) performing his song "Love That Girl" live at the Artist's Den, featuring motown dress and choreography

Amy Winehouse was a particularly well-known British revivalist during this time. Producer Mark Ronson and the Dap-Kings helped to record many of the tracks on her most popular album, *Back to Black*, using old-fashioned recording and arranging techniques.[83] Producer Salaam Remi led another album track, "Tears Dry on Their Own," which had a more direct connection to Motown.[84] Winehouse had originally written it as a ballad, but Remi suggested that she retrofit its melody and lyrics to the chord changes of the Ashford and Simpson song "Ain't No Mountain High Enough." Remi then created a new backing track based on "Ain't No Mountain High Enough," which altered several of the song's structural elements but used the same chord changes and captured the vibe of the 1967 Motown record.[85]

The result was a contrafact that offered a poignant motown-oriented dialogue (example 6.3).[86] Like many couples who had performed duets in both the country and R&B traditions, Marvin Gaye and Tammi Terrell were cast as a perfect pair in "Ain't No Mountain High Enough" and sang about an unflappable, requited love. In contrast, Winehouse's text discussed the difficulty of overcoming a failed relationship.[87] These differing relationship perspectives were especially apparent in the promotional music videos for the two tracks. A historic clip of Gaye and Terrell, filmed at the 1967 International and Universal Exposition in Montreal, shows the two singers playfully lip-synching the record, flirtatiously rib-

Example 6.3. A comparison of vocal melodies in Marvin Gaye and Tammi Terrell, "Ain't No Mountain High Enough" and Amy Winehouse, "Tears Dry on Their Own" (Note: The Winehouse melody is transposed from E major to D major.)

bing each other during their performance. Winehouse's video for "Tears Dry on Their Own" portrays a very different scene, depicting her as a solitary figure while walking through crowds in downtown Los Angeles and sitting alone in a cheap hotel room littered with clothes and empty beer bottles (figure 6.5).

Although he was not necessarily aligned with neo-soul, American singer Robin Thicke also created several dialogic records of this type, showing the widespread use of motown in contemporary R&B. One was a contrafact called "Million Dolla Baby," a track based on Marvin Gaye's "Trouble Man."[88] It retained the chord structure, instrumentation, and many of the instrumental melodies of Gaye's composition but altered its form from a forty-eight-bar structure based on twelve-measure phrases to a large-scale AABA form that used smaller eight-measure units (example 6.4).[89] Thicke and former Motown president Andre Harrell wrote a new melody and set of lyrics for the track, borrowing Gaye's range and falsetto performance style and even quoting him in several instances (example 6.5).[90] Thicke's connection to Gaye continued several years later with his popular single "Blurred Lines," which contained strong stylistic allusions to the 1977 Gaye single "Got to Give It Up." The similarity between these records—mainly in the realm of instrumentation and feel— was weaker than Thicke's earlier contrafact, but "Blurred Lines" was one of the most popular records of 2013 and did not credit Gaye as a songwriter. After a series of lawsuits between the writers of "Blurred Lines" (Thicke, Pharrell, and T. I.) and the Gaye estate, discussions about the relationship between these songs became international news.[91]

There was a lot of controversy surrounding the "Blurred Lines" lawsuit. Thicke's whiteness made it difficult for some listeners to accept his dialogic position, viewing the song through a lens of race-oriented power

Fig 6.5. A comparison of the visual imagery used in videos for Amy Winehouse, "Tears Dry on Their Own" and Marvin Gaye and Tammi Terrell, "Ain't No Mountain High Enough"

and privilege. His popularity plummeted after "Blurred Lines," in part due to a sense that he attempted to unfairly or illegally appropriate Gaye's music. It is apparent, however, that Thicke was operating within a long history of dialogue in the R&B field. From answer songs and covers to quotation and sampling, there is more than a hundred years of recorded evidence that black musicians have incorporated the work of others in a similar manner. In this manner, Thicke's work falls squarely within my consideration of motown alongside the work of Winehouse, Saadiq, UK punk groups, and 1980s musicians like Rod Stewart. Nevertheless, his reception reminds us of the thorny relationship that still exists between R&B and the mainstream and the continuing presence of motown in this negotiated space.

Records by modern artists exhibit a variety of contemporary methods of historicizing R&B. From laudatory and obvious to subtle and clandestine, these works use the past to support a wide range of different musical styles, often altering the meanings of their older subjects. Their collective incorporation of motown is significant. These new records show how artists, audiences, and critics understand motown as a type of vernacular building block on which newer topical themes, visual imagery, and dances can be based. General references like these confirm the ongoing pervasiveness of Motown's legacy within R&B culture—the unshakable presence of music created at 2648 West Grand Boulevard in our understanding of black pop and its roots. These references also further the distance between Motown and motown, slowly stripping away the specific meanings once carefully constructed by Motown's many creative agents. They divorce Diana Ross's movements from the work of the Supremes, help to make compositional elements like the Motown Beat a historical trope, and distance singers like Marvin Gaye and Tammi Terrell from their original works by creating multiple melodic and lyrical interpretations of their iconic songs.

Hearing the Symphony

Crossover was Motown's winning strategy. It wasn't a secret that selling R&B records to audiences outside of black communities was the key to larger success, but Motown's crossover vision was deeper and broader than that of its contemporaries. Motown focused on a wider range of musical styles, sold music in more countries around the world, and operated within a broader set of outlets within the larger entertainment industry. Motown's history is the history of crossover, and viewing this

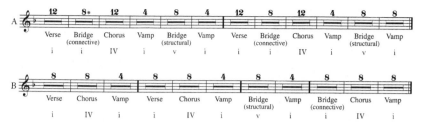

Example 6.4. Formal structures in Marvin Gaye, (A) "Trouble Man"/"Main Theme from *Trouble Man*" and (B) Robin Thicke, "Million Dolla Baby" (*Occurs in the film version, not the single)

Example 6.5. The opening vocal lines in Gaye's "Trouble Man" and Thicke's "Million Dolla Baby"

phenomenon closely helps us to tease out the messy intricacies of breaking down demographic borders in the American entertainment industry. Crossover wasn't just a simple process of "beaming" black music "directly to the white American teenager." Motown's story shows how selling music to multiple audiences allowed voices to move in many different directions and how the dialogue among these voices was extremely varied.

During the 1980s, largely through a continual process of assimilation and weakening identity, both Motown and motown became principal vehicles for remembering the sixties. And they remain so today. In this way, Motown was a triumph for Gordy, Detroit, and Motown's stable of recordists and also for baby boomers, the first generation to make a decisive ideological shift from an American "melting pot" to multiculturalism. Listening to black music was not impossible or unlikely for this generation, and the fact that they grew up with Motown as their soundtrack clearly contributes to the reasons why the company's legacy has persevered so strongly.

Motown's ubiquity is a powerful reminder of the remarkable changes that occurred in the music business during the twentieth century. Once relegated to the black-oriented R&B market, the company's music is now difficult to escape. We hear the Contours at the local coffee shop, the Supremes at the grocery store, and Martha and the Vandellas in the airport. Berry Gordy's Motown has not created new music for decades, but people all over the world still hear Michael Jackson teaching us to spell, Gladys Horton pleading with a letter carrier, and Gladys Knight confessing that she "heard it through the grapevine." And we know these records. The words, melodies, dances, sounds, and iconography of Motown have become part of folk culture.

Pervasiveness is the most significant aspect of Motown's legacy. It provides authoritative evidence of the manner in which African American music became an inextricable part of American culture during the decades after World War II. Once accepted solely through the popularity of their recordings and enjoyability of their performances, Motown artists have since been symbolically recognized by many prestigious cultural institutions that celebrate the heritage of American popular music. Since inducting its first class of honorees in 1987, the Rock and Roll Hall of Fame has honored sixteen Motown inductees, an esteemed group that includes several dozen individuals who worked on the Motown "assembly line" as artists, backing musicians, songwriters, and executives; three Motown artists—Smokey Robinson, Diana Ross, and Stevie Wonder—have been awarded Kennedy Center Honors from the president of the United States; and Wonder was granted the Library of Congress Gershwin Prize for Popular Song in 2008, an award that "recognizes musical achievement in popular culture all over the world."[92]

As the most visible and active Motown artist in contemporary music, Wonder extended his efforts to another important political movement for African American crossover during the mid-2000s: the presidential campaign of Barack Obama. Through media events and live performances, Obama's specific use of Motown's music to support his presidential run—especially Wonder's "Signed, Sealed, Delivered I'm Yours"—recalled similarities between his rise to political power and Motown's efforts to move black musicians into the American cultural mainstream. Wonder's role in this campaign was only one link between Motown and Obama. After his successful win, Suzanne de Passe produced the television special *The Commander-In-Chief Inaugural Ball*, which depicted Barack and Michelle Obama during a series of formal events after his January 2009 inauguration. Unsurprisingly, representatives of latter-day Motown provided both the soundtrack and visual imagery for key elements of Obama's historic presidential run.

Rising from a central site for urban migration in the American North during the late 1950s, Motown's once gargantuan achievement of beaming black music directly to the white American teenager is now a foundational tenet of the popular music business. Music in the direct lineage of R&B from the 1960s and 1970s that features beat-based tracks and melismatic singing dominates the pop charts, and crossover is now unexceptional. After a long history of international reception, the global impact of American R&B is stronger than ever through deep cultural formations in many places outside of the United States, especially Great Britain, while African American actors and media specialists like Tyler Perry and Oprah Winfrey have continued Motown's legacy in visual media by creating mainstream television and film productions that feature black actors in a variety of roles.

When the Supremes first popularized "I Hear a Symphony" in 1965, it may have been odd to hear three black girls from Detroit's Brewster-Douglass Housing Projects singing about one of the most important cultural institutions in the history of Western music. At the time, the symphony orchestra represented the unquestioned pinnacle of musical sophistication. Today our valuation is much different. We no longer assume that the orchestra rests on a higher cultural plane, and various forms of popular music are now widely considered potential conduits for musical ambition and erudition. Motown had a prescient role in this shift, helping to change the place of black-owned businesses within the entertainment field and working to achieve a larger international reception of black pop as an art form with important cultural and musical content. There is no question. The Supremes were hearing a revolution and now, more than half a century later, we all hear the same symphony.

APPENDIX 1 | Selected International Recordings of Motown Songs, 1963–68 (Excluding England)

Country	Motown song	Cover title	Cover artist	Year	Catalog number
Australia	Forever		Lynne Randell	1965	HMV EA 4701
Australia	Mickey's Monkey		Greg Anderson	1967	Kommotion KK 1530
Australia	Mickey's Monkey		Ray Brown and the Whispers	1966	Leedon LL 31,924
Australia	Needle in a Haystack		The Twilights	1966	Columbia DO 4717
Australia	Pride and Joy		Normie Rowe and the Playboys	1966	Sunshine QK 1344
Australia	It's the Same Old Song	The Same Old Song	Ray Brown	1967	Festival FK 1664
Australia	Something about You	Something about You, Baby	The Vibrants	1967	Columbia DO 4761
Australia	S.O.S. (Stop Her on Sight)		The News	1968	Parlophone A 8286
Australia	You'll Never Cherish a Love So True (Until You Lose It)		Johnny O'Keefe	1963	Leedon LK 378
Belgium	Do You Love Me	C'est comme ça dis	Burt Blanca	1963	La Voix De Son Maître EMF 337
Belgium	My Guy	Bye Bye	Jenny Sirena	1964	Decca 23.519
Canada	Back in My Arms Again	La première fois	Les Coquettes	1966	Idéal ID 1946

Country	Motown song	Cover title	Cover artist	Year	Catalog number
Canada	Do You Love Me	Est-ce que tu m'aimes	Les Baronets	1964	Franco F 9347
Canada	The Happening	Le happening	Les Miladys	1967	DSP ID 312
Canada	I Can't Help Myself	Viens plus près mon amour	Pierre Lalonde	1966	Apex 13426
Canada	Jimmy Mack		Les Coquettes	1967	Sabra SA 9801
Canada	Love Is Here and Now You're Gone	L'amour reste	Les Ingénues	1967	Canusa C 315
Canada	Mickey's Monkey		Les Chanceliers	1967	Citation CN 16010
Canada	Mickey's Monkey	Lam di lam	Sophie José	1964	Franco Élite FE 9331
Canada	My Girl	Ma fille	Geralldo	1967	Canusa C 314
Canada	Stop! In the Name of Love	Pense a notre amour	Marthe Fleurant	1965	Choc! C 40
Canada	When the Lovelight Starts Shining through His Eyes	Ne t'en fais pas pour moi	Richard Anthony	1964	Pathé 77.539
Canada	Where Did Our Love Go	Donne-moi ton amour	Les Miladys	1967	DSP 16007
Canada	You Can't Hurry Love	C'est grâce à toi	Les Beatlettes	1967	Première PR 903
Denmark	Mickey's Monkey		The Defenders	1966	Sonet SLPS 1233
France	Baby I Need Your Loving	Car . . . tout le monde a besoin d'amour	Claude François	1967	Philips BE 437.316
France	Baby I Need Your Loving	Tu ne peux pas me faire ça	Thierry Vincent	1965	CBS 6093
France	Baby Love	Baby Love	Annie Philippe	1965	Rivera 231.083
France	Back in My Arms Again	N'hésite pas quand l'mour t'appelle	Katty Line	1965	Barclay 70.880
France	Can I Get a Witness	Un verre de whisky	Monty	1964	Barclay 60482

Country	Motown song	Cover title	Cover artist	Year	Catalog number
France	Come See about Me	Ils sont si gentils	OP'4	1967	Decca 460.995
France	Dancing in the Street	Dans tous les pays	Richard Anthony	1965	Columbia ESRF 1703
France	Do You Love Me	C'est comme ça dis	Jimmy Frey	1963	Fontana 460.884
France	Do You Love Me	Est-ce que tu m'aimes?	Nancy Holloway	1964	Decca 460.830 M
France	Every Little Bit Hurts	Chaque jour, chaque nuit	Jacqueline Boyer	1964	Columbia ESRF 1551
France	Heat Wave	Ça brûle	Fia Karin	1963	Week End WE 8004
France	He Won't Be True (Little Girl Blue)	Il reviendra	Tiny Yong	1964	Disques Salvador 373.280F
France	How Sweet It Is to Be Loved by You	Il serait doux d'être aimé par vous	Herbert Léonard	1967	Mercury 152.091
France	I Can't Help Myself	Garde-moi dans ta poche	Sylvie Vartan	1967	RCA Victor 441.029 S
France	It Should Have Been Me	Cette amitié	Evy	1964	Barclay 700.006
France	It's the Same Old Song	Moi je danse	Sylvie Vartan	1967	RCA Victor 441.029 S
France	It Takes Two	Il faut être deux	Claude François	1967	Philips 437.357
France	I Want to Go Back There Again	Rentrer chez moi	Liliane Saint-Pierre	1968	Disques Flèche CF 001
France	I Was Made to Love Her	Rien rien rien	Claude François	1967	Flèche-Philips 844.800
France	Just as Long as You Need Me	De quel droit peux-tu décider	Nancy Holloway	1964	Decca 154.073
France	La La La La La		Jocelyne	1965	Polydor POL 46153
France	Loving You Is Sweeter Than Ever	N'est-ce pas étrange?	Claude François	1967	Philips BE 437.316
France	Mickey's Monkey	Lam'di'lam'	Jacky Moulière	1963	Disques Salvador 432.993 BE
France	Mickey's Monkey	Mickey's Monkey	Jacques Denjean	1963	Polydor 27076
France	Money (That's What I Want)	Pas de chance	Eddy Mitchell	1964	Barclay 70.646

Country	Motown song	Cover title	Cover artist	Year	Catalog number
France	My Girl	Ma fille	Claude François	1967	Flèche-Philips 844.800
France	My Guy	Bye Bye	Nancy Holloway	1964	Decca 154.073
France	Nowhere to Run	Mon obsession me poursuit	Annie Markan	1965	Mercury 152.047
France	Nowhere to Run	Mon obsession me poursuit	Les Lionceaux	1965	Mercury 152.048
France	Ooo Baby Baby	Toute ma vie	Les Fizz	1966	Encyclopedisc 460 V 727
France	Please Mr. Postman	Monsieur le facteur	Les Kelton	1963	DiscAZ 947
France	Reach Out I'll Be There	J'attendrai	Claude François	1966	Philips BE 437.267
France	Reach Out I'll Be There	J'attendrai	Les Diamants	1966	Trianon ETS 4623
France	Reach Out I'll Be There	J'attendrai	Paul Mauriat	1966	Philips 840.580
France	Shop Around	Si je veux la garder	Cap'tain Michel Group	1965	La Voix De Son Maître EGF 785
France	Stop! In the Name of Love	Stop, tu n'as plus le droit	Les Fizz	1966	Ducretet Thomson 460 V 727
France	Uptight (Everything's Alright)	Les coups	Johnny Hallyday	1966	Philips BE 437.228
France	The Way You Do the Things You Do	Pour revenir chez toi	Harold Nicholas	1964	Diadem JL 2001
France	When the Lovelight Starts Shining through His Eyes	Ne t'en fais pas pour moi	Richard Anthony	1964	Columbia ESRF 1586
France	Where Did Our Love Go	Pourquoi est-il parti	Marianne Mille	1964	RCA Victor 86.076
France	You Beat Me to the Punch	Tu m'as devancée	Arielle	1963	Barclay 70.512 M
France	You Can't Hurry Love	C'est grâce à toi	Les Surfs	1967	Festival FX45 1533
France	You Keep Me Hanging On	Je n'ai pas pu résister	Sylvie Vartan	1967	RCA Victor 441.029 S

Country	Motown song	Cover title	Cover artist	Year	Catalog number
France	You Lost the Sweetest Boy	Ce merveil-leux garçon	Audrey	1963	Disques Salvador 432 998 BE
France	You're a Wonderful One	Le plus bel amour	Nancy Holloway	1964	Decca 154.073
Germany	Baby Love	Baby Love	Maria Martin	1964	Elite Special A 9443
Germany	The Happening	Zweisamkeit	Joy and the Hit Kids	1967	Decca D 19878
Germany	Heat Wave	Heatwave	The Liverbirds	1966	Star Club Records 158 021
Germany	I Hear a Symphony	Wie eine Symphonie	Siw Malmkvist	1969	Metronome MLP 15 333
Germany	Mickey's Monkey		Casey Jones and the Governors	1966	Golden 12 108
Germany	Mickey's Monkey		Lee Curtis and the All-Stars	1965	Star Club Records 158 017
Germany	Mickey's Monkey		The Remo Four	1965	Star Club Records 148 552
Germany	Money (That's What I Want)	Money	The Liverbirds	1965	Star Club Records 148 003
Germany	Money (That's What I Want)	Liebe	The Searchers	1965	Vogue DV 14116
Germany	My Guy	My Boy	Yvonne Carré	1966	Hippo 13 001
Germany	Shop Around		The Liverbirds	1964	Star Club Records 148 508
Germany	Stop! In the Name of Love	Was hab' ich dir getan	Jacob Sisters	1965	CBS 1850
Germany	Where Did Our Love Go	Wo ist unsere Liebe!	Les Gams	1965	Mercury 154 035 MCF
Greece	Reach Out I'll Be There	J'attendrai	Claude François	1966	Philips 3746
Greece	Reach Out I'll Be There	Gira gira	Peppino Di Capri	1966	Melophone 45 M 555
Italy	Baby Love	Baby Love	Carmen Villani	1965	Bluebell BB 03131
Italy	Every Little Bit Hurts	Io al mondo ho solo te	Lucio Dalla	1965	Arc JBAN 4037
Italy	La La La La La	Sha la la la la	Le Snobs	1965	Durium CN A 9172
Italy	Love Is Here and Now You're Gone	Mi mandi via	Elisabetta	1967	Arc AN 4139
Italy	My Guy	Non ti scuso più	Lucia Altieri	1965	Silver Record XP 610
Italy	Reach Out I'll Be There	J'attendrai	Claude François	1966	Philips BE 437.267

Country	Motown song	Cover title	Cover artist	Year	Catalog number
Italy	Reach Out I'll Be There	Gira gira	Rita Pavone	1967	RCA Italiana PM45 3383
Italy	Reach Out I'll Be There	Gira gira	The Primitives	1967	Arc NL 74067
Italy	Standing in the Shadows of Love	L'ombra di nessuno	Caterina Caselli	1967	CGD FG 5033
Italy	Standing in the Shadows of Love	L'ombra di nessuno	The Primitives	1967	Arc NL 74067
Italy	Stop! In the Name of Love	In nome dell'amore	Renata Pacini	1966	Durium CN A 9199
Italy	Where Did Our Love Go	Piano	Anna Maria Izzo	1964	Arc N 4029
Italy	You Keep Me Hanging On	Chi mi aiuterà	I Ribelli	1968	Ricordi SMRP 9052
Italy	You're All I Need to Get By	Dimenticando il mondo	Tihm	1968	Sun SU.A 3005
Mexico	I Hear a Symphony	Escucho una sinfonía	Monica	1966	Columbia LEM 43
Mexico	Twistin' Postman	El cartero	Los Apson	1963	Eco 172
Norway	Love a Go-Go	Love a' gogo	Wenche Myhre	1967	Polydor NH 66794
Portugal	Baby I Need Your Loving	Car . . . tout le monde a besoin d'amour	Claude François	1967	Philips BE 437.316
Portugal	Loving You Is Sweeter Than Ever	N'est-ce pas étrange?	Claude François	1967	Philips BE 437.316
Portugal	Reach Out I'll Be There	J'attendrai	Claude François	1966	Philips BE 437.267
Spain	My Guy	Mi chico	Karina	1964	Hispavox HH 17 290
Spain	My Guy	Non ti scuso più	Lucia Altieri	1964	Marfer MIT 537
Spain	Reach Out I'll Be There	Es mejor de- jarlo como está	Alexandra	1966	Sonoplay SN 20.013
Spain	Reach Out I'll Be There	Es mejor de- jarlo como está	Alex Y Los Findes	1967	Discophon 27.509
Spain	Reach Out I'll Be There	Es mejor de- jarlo como está	Bruno Lomas	1965	Regal SEDL 19.527

Country	Motown song	Cover title	Cover artist	Year	Catalog number
Spain	Reach Out I'll Be There	Es mejor dejarlo como está	Jorge	1967	Philips PE 436.867
Spain	Reach Out I'll Be There	Es mejor dejarlo como está	Los Salvajes	1967	Regal SEDL 19.531
Spain	Reach Out I'll Be There	Extiende tus brazos	Los Stop	1967	Belter 51.792
Spain	Reach Out I'll Be There	Es mejor dejarlo como está	Maruja Garrido	1967	Sonoplay SBP 10.042
Spain	Reach Out I'll Be There	Es mejor dejarlo como está	Vicent	1967	Ekipo 66131 XC
Sweden	Dancing in the Street		Nursery Rhymes	1966	Odeon SD 5994
Sweden	The Happening	En hipp häpp happening	Siw Malmkvist	1967	Metronome J45 754
Sweden	Heat Wave		Nursery Rhymes	1966	Odeon SD 5994
Sweden	I Hear a Symphony	Jag hör en symfoni	Siw Malmkvist	1968	Metronome MLP 15324
Sweden	It's the Same Old Song	Samma gamla sång	Siw Malmkvist	1967	Metronome J45 754
Sweden	Nowhere to Run		Nursery Rhymes	1966	Odeon SD 5990
Sweden	The Tracks of My Tears		Ola and the Janglers	1968	Gazell GMG 1214
Switzerland	Heat Wave	Heatwave	The Ruby Rats	1966	Layola Records L 17 233
Switzerland	Mickey's Monkey		Frankie Farian	1965	Elite Special F 4076
Switzerland	Ruby Soul		The Ruby Rats	1966	Layola Records L 17 233
Yugoslavia	Reach Out I'll Be There	Ja sam tu	Gabi Novak	1968	Jugoton EPY 3943
Yugoslavia	Reach Out I'll Be There	Biću tamo	Nada Knežević	1967	PGP RTB EP 50219

APPENDIX 2 | Selected Recordings of Motown Songs Released in England, 1963–67

Song	Group	Year	Manufacturer number
As Long As I Know He's Mine	Julie Grant	1965	Pye 7N 15884
Baby I Need Your Loving	Sandie Shaw	1965	Pye NPL 18110
Baby I Need Your Loving	The Fourmost	1964	Parlophone R 5194
Beechwood 4-5789	Ian and the Zodiacs	1964	Oriole CB 1849
Bye Bye Baby	Tony Jackson and the Vibrations	1965	Pye 7N 15685
Can I Get a Witness	Dusty Springfield	1964	Philips BE 12564
Can I Get a Witness	The Rolling Stones	1964	Decca LK 4065
Can I Get a Witness	Lulu	1965	Decca LK 4719
Can I Get a Witness	Steve Aldo	1964	Decca F 12041
Dancing in the Street	Petula Clark	1965	Pye NPL 18118
Dancing in the Street	Cilla Black	1965	Parlophone PMC 1243
Dancing in the Street	The Kinks	1965	Pye NPL 18112
Dancing in the Street	The Walker Brothers	1965	Philips BL 7691
Do You Love Me	Brian Poole and the Tremeloes	1963	Decca F 11739
Do You Love Me	Faron's Flamingos	1963	Oriole CB 1834
Do You Love Me	Frank Bacon and the Baconeers	1963	Rocket RKT 002
Do You Love Me	The Dave Clark Five	1963	Columbia DB 7112
Do You Love Me	The Hollies	1964	Parlophone PMC 1220
Every Little Bit Hurts	Cilla Black	1965	Parlophone PMC 1243
Every Little Bit Hurts	Petula Clark	1965	Pye NSPL 18118
Every Little Bit Hurts	The Spencer Davis Group	1965	Fontana TF 530
Forever	Lynne Randell	1965	HMV EA 4701
Heat Wave	Beverley Jones	1964	Parlophone R 5189
Heat Wave	Lulu	1964	Decca DFE 8597
Heat Wave	The Who	1966	Reaction 593 002
Heaven Must Have Sent You	Lulu	1965	Decca LK 4719
Hitch Hike	The Rolling Stones	1965	Decca LK 4733
I Want to Go Back There Again	Truly Smith	1967	Decca F 12645

Song	Group	Year	Manufacturer number
I'll Be Doggone	Billy J. Kramer with the Dakotas	1965	Parlophone R 5362
I'll Be Doggone	The Searchers	1965	Pye NPL 18120
I'll Keep Holding On	The Action	1966	Parlophone R 5410
In My Lonely Room	The Action	1965	Parlophone R 5354
Just Walk in My Shoes	Billie Davis	1966	Piccadilly 7N 35350
A Love Like Yours (Don't Come Knocking Everyday)	Manfred Mann	1965	Ascot ALM 13021
Mickey's Monkey	Doug Sheldon	1963	Decca F.11790
Mickey's Monkey	The Hollies	1965	Parlophone PMC 1261
Money (That's What I Want)	The Beatles	1962	Decca audition
Money (That's What I Want)	Buddy Britten and the Regents	1963	Oriole CB 1827
Money (That's What I Want)	Freddie and the Dreamers	1963	Columbia 33SX 1577
Money (That's What I Want)	King Size Taylor and the Dominoes	1963	Polydor NH 66990
Money (That's What I Want)	The Beatles	1963	Parlophone PMC 1206
Money (That's What I Want)	The Le Roys	1963	Give A Disc LYN 504
Money (That's What I Want)	The Searchers	1963	Pye NEP 24183
Money (That's What I Want)	The Undertakers	1963	Pye 7N 15562
Money (That's What I Want)	Bern Elliott and the Fenmen	1964	Decca F 11770
Money (That's What I Want)	The Rolling Stones	1964	Decca DFE 8560
My 2 Arms—You = Tears	Jan Panter	1965	Oriole CB 1983
My Guy	Helen Shapiro	1964	Columbia 33SX 1661
My Guy	Marilyn Lee	1964	Embassy WB 636
My Smile Is Just a Frown (Turned Upside Down)	Truly Smith	1966	Decca F 12373
Needle in a Haystack	Tawny Reed	1965	Pye 7N 15935
Now I've Got a Witness	The Rolling Stones	1964	Decca LK 4065
The One Who Really Loves You	Jackie Trent	1962	Oriole CB 1749
The One Who Really Loves You	The Mojos	1964	Decca DFE 8591
Please Mr. Postman	Mike Sheridan and the Nightriders	1963	Liverpool Sound LS 902
Please Mr. Postman	The Beatles	1963	Parlophone PMC 1206
Please Mr. Postman	Bern Elliott and the Fenmen	1963	Decca DFE 8561
Please Mr. Postman	Helen Shapiro	1964	Columbia 33SX 1661
Pride and Joy	Georgie Fame	1964	Columbia 33SX 1638
Put Yourself in My Place	Jan Panter	1966	Pye 7N 17097
Shake Sherry Shake	Bern Elliott and the Fenmen	1964	Decca DFE 8561
Shop Around	Bern Elliott and the Fenmen	1964	Decca DFE 8561
Shop Around	Georgie Fame and the Blue Flames	1964	Columbia DB 7193
Shop Around	Helen Shapiro	1964	Columbia DB 7340
Stubborn Kind of Fellow	Lulu	1967	Ace of Clubs ACL 1232
Take Me in Your Arms and Love Me	Lulu	1967	Columbia SX 6201
Take Me in Your Arms and Love Me	Cilla Black	1968	Parlophone PMC 7041
Too Many Fish in the Sea	The Tremeloes	1967	CBS BPG 63138

Song	Group	Year	Manufacturer number
Two Lovers	Louise Cordet	1964	Decca F 11875
The Way You Do the Things You Do	The Trends	1964	PYE 7N 15644
The Way You Do the Things You Do	Adrienne Posta	1965	Decca F 12079
The Way You Do the Things You Do	Elkie Brooks	1965	Decca F 12061
What's Easy for Two Is So Hard for One	Lulu	1964	Decca DFE 8597
When the Lovelight Starts Shining through His Eyes	Beryl Marsden	1964	Decca F 11819
When the Lovelight Starts Shining through His Eyes	Dusty Springfield	1964	Philips BL 7594
When the Lovelight Starts Shining through His Eyes	Lorraine Silver	1966	Pye Records 7N 17055
Where Did Our Love Go	Peter Jay and the Jaywalkers	1964	Piccadilly 7N 35199
You Beat Me to the Punch	Karol Keyes	1964	Fontana TF 517
You Beat Me to the Punch	Tony Jackson and the Vibrations	1964	Pye 7N 15745
You Really Got a Hold on Me	The Beatles	1963	Parlophone PMC 1206
You Really Got a Hold on Me	The Zombies	1965	Decca LK 4679

Notes

Introduction

1. Quoted in Peter Guralnick, *Sweet Soul Music: Rhythm and Blues and the Southern Dream of Freedom* (New York: Back Bay, 1999), 2.

2. David Morse, *Motown and the Arrival of Black Music* (New York: Macmillan, 1971); Peter Benjaminson, *The Story of Motown* (New York: Evergreen, 1979); Don Waller, *The Motown Story* (New York: Scribner, 1985); Nelson George, *Where Did Our Love Go?* (New York: St. Martin's, 1986; Urbana: University of Illinois Press, 2007) (page references are to the 2007 edition); Sharon Davis, *Motown: The History* (Enfield, UK: Guinness, 1988); Gerald Early, *One Nation under a Groove* (New York: Ecco Press, 1995; Ann Arbor: University of Michigan Press, 2004) (page references are to the 2004 edition); Suzanne E. Smith, *Dancing in the Street: Motown and the Cultural Politics of Detroit* (Cambridge MA: Harvard University Press, 1999); Gerald Posner, *Motown: Music, Money, Sex, and Power* (New York: Random House, 2003).

3. Tim Brooks, *Lost Sounds: Blacks and the Birth of the Recording Industry, 1890–1919* (Urbana: University of Illinois Press, 2004).

4. Ibid., 2.

5. David Suisman, *Selling Sounds: The Commercial Revolution in American Music* (Cambridge, MA: Harvard University Press, 2009), 36–41.

6. Karl Hagstrom Miller, *Segregating Sound: Inventing Folk and Pop Music in the Age of Jim Crow* (Durham, NC: Duke University Press, 2010), 187–214.

7. Philip H. Ennis, *The Seventh Stream: The Emergence of Rocknroll in American Popular Music* (Hanover, NH: Wesleyan University Press, 1992); Albin Zak, *I Don't Sound Like Nobody: Remaking Music in 1950s America* (Ann Arbor: University of Michigan Press, 2010); John Broven, *Record Makers and Breakers: Voices of the Independent Rock 'n' Roll Pioneers* (Urbana: University of Illinois Press, 2009).

8. The most comprehensive study of R&B as a market is Brian Ward, *Just My Soul Responding: Rhythm and Blues, Black Consciousness, and Race Relations* (Berkeley: University of California Press, 1998). Early books that consider R&B as a distinct formation include Charlie Gillett, *The Sound of the City: The Rise of Rock and Roll* (New York: Outerbridge and Dienstfrey, 1970); and Arnold Shaw,

Honkers and Shouters: The Golden Years of Rhythm and Blues (New York: Collier, 1978). Studies that consider R&B in the context of soul (or southern soul) include Arnold Shaw, *The World of Soul* (New York: Paperback Library, 1971); Michael Haralambos, *Right On: From Blues to Soul in Black America* (New York: Drake, 1975); Gerri Hirshey, *Nowhere to Run: The Story of Soul Music* (New York: Crown, 1984); and Guralnick, *Sweet Soul Music.*

9. For more on R&B in the context of migration, see Guthrie P. Ramsey, *Race Music: Black Cultures from Bebop to Hip-Hop* (Berkeley: University of California Press, 2003), 149–55.

10. To be sure, Wonder was born and raised in Michigan.

11. For more on gender and R&B, see Jacqueline Warwick, *Girl Groups, Girl Culture: Popular Music and Identity in the 1960s* (New York: Routledge, 2007); Philip Max Gentry, "The Age of Anxiety: Music, Politics, and McCarthyism" (PhD diss., University of California, Los Angeles, 2008), 112–64; Annie J. Randall, *Dusty! Queen of the Postmods* (New York: Oxford University Press, 2009); and Mitchell Morris, *The Persistence of Sentiment: Display and Feeling in Popular Music of the 1970s* (Berkeley: University of California Press, 2014).

12. In academic circles, claims of universal black traits in music often invoke issues of essentialism, which I do not address at length in this book. For an example of these essentialism debates, see Ronald Radano, *Lying Up a Nation: Race and Black Music* (Chicago: University of Chicago Press, 2003); and Guthrie P. Ramsey Jr., "The Pot Liquor Principle: Developing a Black Music Criticism in American Music Studies," *Journal of Black Studies* 35 (November 2004): 210–33.

13. S. Smith, *Dancing in the Street,* 54–93.

14. For more on Motown's class orientation, see Early, *One Nation under a Groove*; Robert Fink, "Goal-Directed Soul?: Analyzing Rhythmic Teleology in African American Popular Music," *Journal of the American Musicological Society* 64 (Spring 2011): 179–238.

15. Wahneema Lubiano, *The House That Race Built: Black Americans, U.S. Terrain* (New York: Pantheon, 1997); Valerie Smith, *Not Just Race, Not Just Gender: Black Feminist Readings* (New York: Routledge, 1998), 63–86; Martin J. Favor, *Authentic Blackness: The Folk in the New Negro Renaissance* (Durham, NC: Duke University Press, 1999).

16. The most productive group of research on record production comes from the Association for the Study of the Art of Record Production, which holds yearly conferences and publishes *Journal on the Art of Record Production.* See also Albin Zak, *The Poetics of Rock: Cutting Tracks, Making Records* (Berkeley: University of California Press, 2001).

17. Richard Taruskin, *The Oxford History of Western Music* (New York: Oxford University Press, 2005), 1:xxvi.

18. Literary theorists often use critical lenses like intertextuality, the anxiety of influence, and signifyin(g) to discuss these types of connections. Even though a number of authors have extended these theories into popular music studies, I don't engage specific critical writings about intertexts in this book.

19. For discussion about the "cover" song, see Reebee Garofalo, "Crossing Over: 1939–1989," in *Split Image: African Americans in the Media,* ed. Jannette L. Dates and William Barlow (Washington, DC: Howard University Press, 1993), 57–128; Gabriel

Solis, "I Did It My Way: Rock and the Logic of Covers," *Popular Music and Society* 33, 297–318; Michael Coyle, "Hijacked Hits and Antic Authenticity: Cover Songs, Race, and Postwar Marketing," in *Rock over the Edge: Transformation in Popular Music Culture*, ed. Roger Beebe, Denise Fulbrook, and Ben Sunders (Durham, NC: Duke University Press, 2002), 133–57; Zak, *I Don't Sound Like Nobody*, 114–15.

20. For more on the manner in which R&B artists used versioning to reinterpret a wide variety of material, see Michael Awkward, *Soul Covers: Rhythm and Blues Remakes and the Struggle for Artistic Identity* (Durham, NC: Duke University Press, 2007).

21. Examples of Cameo releases that "copied" Motown's sound are Candy and the Kisses, "The 81," and Dee Dee Sharp's "Mashed Potato Time." The most popular Chess release of this sort was "Rescue Me" by Fontella Bass, which appeared on the company's Checker imprint.

22. For more on "transatlantic" soul, see Randall, *Dusty!*

23. For a more general discussion of intertextuality within jazz that relates to these looser forms of dialogue, see Ingrid Monson, *Saying Something: Jazz Improvisation and Interaction* (Chicago: University of Chicago Press, 1996), 97–132.

24. Keith Hughes, *Don't Forget the Motor City*, www.dftmc.info

25. This may best be understood through the idea of collective or social memory, which has a large literature in sociology. See Jeffrey K. Olick and Joyce Robbins, "Social Memory Studies: From 'Collective Memory' to the Historical Sociology of Mnemonic Practices," *Annual Review of Sociology* 24 (1998): 105–40; George Lipsitz, *Time Passages: Collective Memory and American Popular Culture* (Minneapolis: University of Minnesota Press, 1990).

26. Most of Motown's business records are not available to researchers. The absence of this material makes it very difficult to write a more complete, informed history of the company.

Chapter One

1. The term *mainstream*, referring generally to the central locus of the music business, was not in regular parlance at this time. It is often attributed to the British jazz critic Stanley Dance, who first used to term during the 1950s to refer to jazz that was neither revivalist nor modern. See Mark Tucker, "Mainstreaming Monk: The Ellington Album," in *Uptown Conversation: The New Jazz Studies*, ed. Robert G. O'Meally, Brent Hayes Edwards, and Farah Jasmine Griffin (New York: Columbia University Press, 2004), 150–65.

2. Brooks, *Lost Sounds*.

3. Miller, *Segregating Sound*, 194.

4. Record sales declined from more than $100 million in 1921 to $6 million in 1933. Russell Sanjek, *Pennies from Heaven: The American Popular Music Business in the Twentieth Century* (New York: Da Capo, 1996), 117–46.

5. Okeh was acquired by Columbia and discontinued releases in the last half of the 1930s, Vocalion stopped production in 1940 after being sold several times, and RCA-Victor's budget Bluebird imprint shifted focus away from black artists during this period.

6. Broven, *Record Makers and Breakers*, 484. This decline was not representative of the entire music industry. The increase in popularity of radio during the 1920s, for example, was linked to the decline of record sales and eventually spurred legal battles between the American Federation of Musicians and record companies over royalties. The growing popularity of radio during the 1930s also led to controversy over blanket performing rights licenses issued by ASCAP and the formation of BMI, which allowed radio stations to pay for individual performances.

7. R. Sanjek, *Pennies from Heaven*, 62–73, 117–46.

8. William Barlow, *Voice Over: The Making of Black Radio* (Philadelphia: Temple University Press, 1999), 91–153.

9. Preston Lauterbach, *The Chitlin' Circuit and the Road to Rock 'n' Roll* (New York: W. W. Norton, 2011).

10. Kerry Segrave, *Jukeboxes: An American Social History* (Jefferson, NC: McFarland, 2002).

11. Joshua Clark Davis, "For the Records: How African American Consumers and Music Retailers Created Commercial Public Space in the 1960s and 1970s South," *Southern Cultures* 17 (Winter 2011): 71–90. The rise of a smaller, higher quality 45 RPM disc further spurred the industry to explore the "tangential" market associated with African Americans during the early 1950s by reducing shipping costs. Jim Dawson and Steve Propes, *45 RPM: The History, Heroes and Villains of a Pop Music Revolution* (San Francisco: Backbeat, 2003).

12. The first "Harlem Hit Parade" chart (October 24, 1942) lists the following shops as the source of its chart data: Rainbow Music Shop, Harvard Radio Shop, Lehman Music Company, Harlem De Luxe Music Store, Ray's Music Shop, and Frank's Melody Music Shop.

13. *Billboard* switched from using sales (February 10, 1945) to coin-operated popularity (February 17, 1945) for chart tabulation. Popular white artists such as Johnny Mercer and the Andrews sisters, who placed well on the sales chart, were not represented on the jukebox chart the following week. *Billboard* reintroduced sales rankings (in addition to jukebox statistics) in May 1948.

14. *Billboard* augmented the name of the country market in the same issue from "Folk" to "Folk (Country & Western)."

15. Ward, *Just My Soul Responding*, 26–29. Mercury formed as a a quasi major in 1945. It opened its own pressing plants competed with the majors in nearly every important area of the business, including pop, classical, country, R&B, and jazz, but used independent distribution.

16. Other prominent companies began in the wake of this first wave, including Bobby Robinson's various labels based in New York City (most prominently Robin, Fury, Fire, and Enjoy) and Chicago-based Vee-Jay Records led by the husband-and-wife team of Vivian Carter and James Bracken.

17. There were a variety of independent companies during this period, ranging from tiny operations that released a handful of recordings to large companies that rivaled the majors in size and power. Ward, *Just My Soul Responding*, 21–29.

18. Jim Cogan and William Clark, *Temples of Sound: Inside the Great Recording Studios* (San Francisco: Chronicle, 2003).

19. Gentry, "Age of Anxiety," 121–22.

20. Ennis, *Seventh Stream*, 173.

21. Jazz had largely split from popular markets after the decline of swing, but when an African American bandleader or vocalist had a popular recording it usually appeared on the R&B charts.

22. Other well-known electric blues artists, all of whom recorded for independent companies, included John Lee Hooker, T-Bone Walker, and Elmore James.

23. B. Lee Cooper and Wayne S. Haney, *Response Recordings: An Answer Song Discography, 1950–1990* (Metuchen, NJ: Scarecrow, 1990).

24. Most of the African American artists whose recordings were simultaneously popular in R&B and pop markets before 1955 were aligned with major labels; others included Blue Lu Barker, the Four Vagabonds, Erskine Hawkins, Buddy Johnson, Nellie Lutcher, the Charioteers, and the 5 Red Caps. (Decca and Capitol were especially adept at navigating this early crossover.) Conversely, a few black vocal groups (like the Deep River Boys and the Four Knights) had hits in the pop market and no success on the *Billboard* race charts.

25. John Bush Jones, *The Songs That Fought the War: Popular Music and the Home Front, 1939–1945* (Waltham, MA: Brandeis University Press, 2006), 2–8.

26. The other recordings were by Count Basie, Jack McVea, "Dusty" Fletcher, and the Three Flames.

27. For a larger discussion of song and record crossover, see Zak, *I Don't Sound Like Nobody*, 114–15. For other studies of R&B and early rock crossover, see Jon Fitzgerald, "Motown Crossover Hits 1963–1966 and the Creative Process," *Popular Music* 14 (January 1995), 1–11; Ian Inglis, "Some Kind of Wonderful: The Creative Legacy of the Brill Building," *American Music* 21 (Summer 2003), 214–35; Garofalo, "Crossing Over"; David Brackett, "The Politics and Practice of 'Crossover' in American Popular Music, 1963 to 1965," *Musical Quarterly* 78 (Winter 1994), 774–97; and David Brackett, "What a Difference a Name Makes: Two Instances of African-American Popular Music," in *The Cultural Study of Music: A Critical Introduction*, ed. Martin Clayton, Trevor Herbert, and Richard Middleton (New York: Routledge, 2003), 238–50.

28. "Oh Babe!" achieved moderate success in the pop market in multiple versions by white artists (Prima, Kay Starr, and the Ames Brothers) but was also popular with R&B audiences in a number of recordings by black artists (Jimmy Preston, Larry Darnell, Roy Milton, and Wynonie Harris [with Lucky Millinder]).

29. "The Hucklebuck" was based on Charlie Parker's "Now's the Time," recorded for Savoy in 1945.

30. Ennis, *Seventh Stream*, 161–92.

31. A firsthand account of Gordy's youth is provided in Berry Gordy, *To Be Loved: The Music, the Magic, the Memories of Motown* (New York: Warner, 1994), 1–30. See also Berry Gordy Sr., *Movin' Up: Pop Gordy Tells His Story* (New York: Harper and Row, 1979). A collection exists at BHL entitled "Gordy Family Papers, 1928–1947," which may shed new light on the role of the family in Detroit's African American community; it is closed to research until 2038 at the request of its unnamed donor.

32. Nicholas Lemann, *The Great Migration and How It Changed America* (New York: Vintage, 1991); James N. Gregory, *The Southern Diaspora: How the Great*

Migrations of Black and White Southerners Transformed America (Chapel Hill: University of North Carolina Press, 2005). A more nuanced account appears in Isabel Wilkerson, *The Warmth of Other Suns: The Epic Story of America's Great Migration* (New York: Random House, 2010). For memories of migration and life in Detroit from 1918 to 1967, see Elaine Latzman Moon, ed., *Untold Tales, Unsung Heroes: An Oral History of Detroit's African American Community, 1918–1967* (Detroit: Wayne State University Press, 1994). For more on the history of Detroit's mass population after the World War II, see Thomas J. Sugrue, *The Origins of the Urban Crisis: Race and Inequality in Postwar Detroit* (Princeton, NJ: Princeton University Press, 1996).

33. "America's Most Amazing Family: The Famous Gordys of Detroit Have What It Takes," *Color*, July 1949, 6–8. The Gordys also owned and ran a grocery, which was named after the late-nineteenth-century African American educator, politician, and businessman Booker T. Washington.

34. Bowling was also a significant sport for the family. Berry Gordy Jr.'s oldest brother, Fuller, became the first African American professional bowler on the Professional Bowling Association tour in 1960.

35. Gordy recalls learning piano as a youngster from his Uncle B. A.; by 1949, the year of the *Color* profile, he was certainly a good amateur pianist. Gordy, *To Be Loved*, 18.

36. Ibid., 59–62. Like many young African American males in the 1950s, Berry Gordy used military severance to support his housing and business ventures; Pops Gordy also borrowed money from a church credit union to help open the store.

37. To be sure, there had been other African American record company owners. A famous early example is the Black Swan imprint, formed in 1921 by Harry Pace, who was a close associate of W. E. B. Du Bois. Other postwar companies owned by African Americans included Class (Leon René), Dootone (Dootsie Williams), and Vee-Jay (Vivian Carter and James Bracken). There were also a number of less successful Detroit R&B labels owned by African Americans; these included Flick and Lu Pine (Robert West), Fortune (Jack and Devora Brown), Great Lakes (Ken Campbell), and JVB (Joseph [von] Battle). Ward, *Just My Soul Responding*, 22.

38. Broven, *Record Makers and Breakers*, 319–40. Roquel Davis should not be confused with Gordy's childhood friend Billy Davis. (Every reference in this book is to the former.)

39. Tarnopol and Wilson quickly distanced Brunswick from Decca and converted it into an R&B-oriented company.

40. Mark Burford, "Sam Cooke as Pop Album Artist: A Reinvention in Three Songs," *Journal of the American Musicological Society* 65 (Spring 2012): 113–78.

41. These were: "To Be Loved," "I'm Wanderin'," "We Have Love," "Lonely Teardrops," "That's Why (I Love You So)," and "I'll Be Satisfied."

42. At the height of Wilson's fame Gordy and Davis used Wilson's popularity to benefit the Gordy family by writing and recording a song called "Let George Do It" for the political campaign of Berry's brother-in-law George H. Edwards, who was an incumbent state representative. S. Smith, *Dancing in the Street*, 77.

43. One exception was an anomalous single by Wade Jones that Gordy and Raynoma released on an imprint called Rayber.

44. This contract is reprinted in Gordy, *To Be Loved*, 108.

45. An early *Billboard* profile of Johnson, printed in this same issue, claims that his favorite artists "range from Doris Day to Chris Connor and Sammy Davis." "Hit Comes to Johnson Via 'Come to Me,'" *Billboard*, April 6, 1959, 6.

46. "See Saw" was written by Davis, Harry Pratt (Fuqua), and Charles Sutton; "Soda Pop" was written by Gordy and Davis; "Don't Be Afraid to Love" was written by Davis, Gordy, and Pratt (Fuqua). (Fuqua used both Harry and Harvey Pratt as pseudonyms.)

47. Harvey Fuqua, interview by Nelson George, date unknown, transcript, NGC.

48. After marrying, Harvey and Gwen drifted further from Berry's activities, forming a new group of imprints that included Harvey, Tri-Phi, H. P. C., and Message. Fuqua was at the center of the creative work released on these labels, collaborating as author on songs with Gwen Gordy and various recording artists and working as producer on many recordings. Several dozen singles were released on the various imprints owned by Fuqua and Gwen Gordy in 1962 and 1963, although few of these reached national audiences. Motown began to distribute Harvey in late 1962 and absorbed the catalogs and the contracts of many artists associated with Harvey and Tri-Phi in the summer of 1963, after Fuqua and Gwen Gordy started to work for Motown. "Tamla-Motown Is Distributing Harvey Label," *Billboard*, October 20, 1962, 8.

49. Harvey Fuqua, interview.

50. *Jobete* was a portmanteau word constructed from the names of Gordy's children, Joy, Berry, and Terry.

51. "Crying Alone" and "Patty Cake" were among a group of early demos recorded in the Gladstone residence. Marv Johnson performed the first and Gwen Murray the second. Copyright information comes from the Library of Congress's Catalog of Copyright Entries for music.

52. "From Boxing to Music," *Michigan Chronicle*, October 10, 1959.

53. Many of Johnson's sides were recorded at United; other recordings completed at this facility included "Got a Job," Bob Kayli's (Robert Gordy) "Everyone Was There" (Carlton, 1958), and Barrett Strong's "You Got What It Takes" (Tamla, 1961). "Lonely Teardrops" may have also been recorded (at least in part) at United Sound. Gordy also worked at Bell Sound in New York to produce other Johnson records as late as 1961.

54. S. Smith, *Dancing in the Street*, 74.

55. The application to incorporate Jobete was submitted to the state of Michigan on June 17, 1959, and registered to Gordy's Gladstone address. Esther Edwards filed a change of address document, using the new West Grand Boulevard address, on September 1, 1959.

56. For the remainder of the book, I will use Motown as the corporate name for Gordy's larger holdings.

57. The application to incorporate ITMI was filed by Esther Gordy Edwards in August 1960; see also "Tamla-Motown Ups Wakefield, Ales to New Responsibility," *Billboard*, July 17, 1961, 45.

58. "National Distrib for Tamla," *Billboard Music Week*, October 23, 1961, 40.

59. Motown introduced the Miracle imprint in early 1961, which changed to

Gordy about a year later. Three other small imprints were also introduced in 1962: Divinity, Workshop, and Mel-O-Dy.

60. The list offered in table 1.1 does not consider singles in the "bubbling under" category, which represented a number of spots just below the top 100. "Come to Me" appeared on both Tamla and United Artists; "Money," appeared on both Tamla and Anna; and "Bad Girl" appeared on both Tamla and Chess.

61. Motown's gospel groups from the period were the Gospel Stars, Rev. Columbus Mann, the Wright Specials, the Golden Harmoneers, the Burnadettes, and Liz Lands. (The Sons of Zion were another Motown gospel group, whose work was recorded but never officially released.) A lot of indies specializing in R&B also released gospel, including Specialty and Peacock. For more on gospel in Detroit, see Horace Clarence Boyer and Lloyd Yearwood, *How Sweet the Sound: The Golden Age of Gospel* (Washington, DC: Elliot and Clark, 1995), 123–34; Nick Salvatore, *Singing in a Strange Land: C. L. Franklin, the Black Church, and the Transformation of America* (New York: Little, Brown, 2005).

62. For more on Motown's interaction in the Great March to Freedom, see S. Smith, *Dancing in the Street*, 21–53, 268–75. Langston Hughes and Margaret Danner also recorded with Motown during this time, but the results of these sessions were not released to the public until 1970. "Poets Sign Reading Pact with Motown," *New York Amsterdam News*, October 26, 1963; S. Smith, *Dancing in the Street*, 94–138.

63. Lars Bjorn and Jim Gallert, *Before Motown: A History of Jazz In Detroit, 1920–60* (Ann Arbor: University of Michigan Press, 2001).

64. Local Banjoist Ford Nix played on Motown sessions in the early 1960s, including a performance on the early Supremes B-side "(The Man With the) Rock and Roll Banjo Band" (1963); Craig Maki and Keith Cady, *Detroit Country Music: Mountaineers, Cowboys, and Rockabillies* (Ann Arbor: University of Michigan Press, 2013), 267–68. Other Detroit labels like Sabre, Fox, and Clix specialized in country, while smaller East Coast outfits like Carlton and Jubilee released country music by Detroit groups. There were several Detroit nightclubs that featured country and rockabilly at the time, including the Red Barn and the Dance Ranch; David A. Carson, *Grit, Noise, and Revolution: The Birth of Detroit Rock 'N' Roll* (Ann Arbor: University of Michigan Press), 17. Detroit-based rockabilly never reached a national audience, but there was popular rock and roll from Detroit at the time, including music by Jack Scott ("My True Love" and "Leroy"), the Royaltones ("Poor Boy"), Johnny and the Hurricanes ("Red River Rock"), and Del Shannon ("Runaway"). See also Terry Gordon, *Rockin' Country Style*, http://rcs-discography.com/rcs/index.html.

65. This was released under the pseudonym Bob Kayli.

66. Verne's release inspired at least three different Motown answers, including "They Rode through the Valley," Popcorn and the Mohawks' "Custer's Last Man," and the Valadiers' "Please Mr. Kennedy."

67. "Motown Pushes out Wall," *Billboard*, January 11, 1964, 32. Motown also released a jazz album called *Modern Innovations on Country and Western Themes*, which was clearly in response to the wildly successful Ray Charles release *Modern Sounds in Country and Western Music. Modern Innovations* had been recorded originally for the Texas-based Duchess imprint. Gordy later purchased the holdings

of Al Klein (including Duchess); most of these records were by African American performers in blues-based styles. For more on the racial implications of Charles performing country music, see Diane Pecknold, "Making Country Modern: The Legacy of *Modern Sounds in Country and Western Music*," in *Hidden in the Mix: The African-American Presence in Country Music*, ed. Diane Pecknold (Durham, NC: Duke University Press, 2013), 82–99.

68. Motown's successful crossover records were also models for other R&B companies and artists. After the popularity of "You Beat Me to the Punch" by Mary Wells, Gene Chandler released a record called "You Threw a Lucky Punch." Similarly, Dee Dee Sharp's recording of "Mashed Potato Time," released on Cameo Records in early 1962, was in dialogue with "Please Mr. Postman." Keith Hughes, "Copies and Cover-Ups," *Yesterday-Today-Forever* 19 (August 1995): 12.

69. There were several other male vocal harmony groups at Motown during this period, such as the Creations, Lee and the Leopards, and the Equadors, whose music was never released.

70. "Eddie Holland," biography, undated (ca. 1959), AAC.

71. Other female singers active during Motown's early years included Mable John and Sherri Taylor, who released records in a heavier style comparable to full-throated vocalists like Etta James and LaVern Baker. The paucity of solo female singers within Motown's catalog was consistent with the larger R&B market, which was dominated by male performers during the 1950s. Much of this changed in 1962, when Kitty Lester ("Love Letters"), Barbara George ("I Know"), Barbara Lynn ("You'll Lose a Good Thing"), Claudine Clark ("Party Lights"), Little Eva ("The Loco-Motion"), and Dee Dee Sharp ("Mashed Potato Time") all released wildly successful singles.

72. J. Warwick, *Girl Groups, Girl Culture*, 15. The most popular girl groups at the time were the Chantels ("Maybe") and the Shirelles ("Will You Love Me Tomorrow"). See also Ward, *Just My Soul Responding*, 150–58. Musicologists often use the term *vocality* to discuss the effect of vocal production. Some examples include Laurie Stras, "Voice of the Beehive: Vocal Technique at the Turn of the 1960s," in *She's So Fine: Reflections on Whiteness, Femininity, Adolescence and Class in 1960s Music*, ed. Laurie Stras (Burlington, VT: Ashgate, 2010), 33–56; Shana Goldin-Perschbacher, "Not with You but of You: 'Unbearable Intimacy' and Jeff Buckley's Transgendered Vocality," in *Oh Boy! Masculinities and Popular Music*, ed. Freya Jarman-Ivens (New York: Routledge, 2007), 213–33.

73. Other Motown records that had a looser sense of double meaning, often in reference to "dancing," were: "Let's Rock," "Yes, No, Maybe So," "Do You Love Me," "It Moves Me," "Hold Me Tight," and "Shake Sherrie." Allusions like these were absent from much of Motown's later work. In one 1964 press release, titled "What's Happened to Show Business," the company made its position on the topic clear by emphatically stating, "a contemporary performer [does] not have to utilize sex as a means of putting across a musical number." [Alan E. Abrams], "What's Happened to Show Business?," Motown press release, undated, AAC.

74. A profile of Esther Gordy Edwards from an internal company newsletter called *The Hitsville Platter* (ca. spring 1963) further illustrated the extent to which Edwards advised the Marvelettes; HAC. See also, "Rock 'n Roll Chaperone," *Afro-*

American, October 14, 1961; Mary Wilson, *Dreamgirl: My Life as a Supreme* (New York: Cooper Square Press, 1999), 137–38. As a child performer, Stevie Wonder needed similar accommodations, although his companion Ted Hull was viewed less as a chaperone and more like a tutor who helped Wonder learn to live as an active performer with a disability. Ted Hull and Paula L. Stahel, *The Wonder Years: My Life and Times with Stevie Wonder* (Tampa, FL: Ted Hull, 2002).

75. This style had a long history of success in the R&B market, with instrumentals by Paul Williams ("The Hucklebuck"), Jimmy Forrest ("Night Train"), Tiny Bradshaw ("Soft"), and Bill Doggett ("Honky Tonk") all popular in the years after the war. The Swinging Tigers and the Twistin' Kings were both aliases for the Motown backing band.

76. Later Detroit sessions led by violinist Gordon Staples used members of the Detroit Symphony Orchestra to perform intricate arrangements created by Motown staffers. Beatriz Staples, telephone interview by author, November 26, 2014.

77. Fink, "Goal-Directed Soul?," 179–87.

78. Ward, *Just My Soul Responding,* 262.

79. George Albert and Frank Hoffman, *The Cash Box Black Contemporary Singles Charts, 1960–1984* (Metuchen, NJ: Scarecrow, 1986), x.

80. Cowriters were listed with Gordy on all nearly of these singles.

81. Despite the popularity of these records, Ballard was more successful as a writer when a version of his 1959 song "The Twist," released by Chubby Checker on Parkway, rose to the top of the charts that year and sparked a national dance craze.

82. "R&B Singles Surge on Hot 100," *Billboard,* June 21, 1961, 1, 43.

83. To be sure, I refer here to the time at which these records rose to the top ten, while table 1.1 lists the records' release dates.

Chapter Two

1. Richard R. Lingeman, "The Big, Happy, Beating Heart of the Detroit Sound," *New York Times,* November 27, 1966.

2. Keith Negus has specifically critiqued "assembly line" analogies in popular music historiography, writing, "Mechanistic models have often been uncritically incorporated into claims that the music business was, like other industries, organized in 'Fordist' terms, utilizing mass production techniques." Keith Negus, *Music Genres and Corporate Cultures* (New York: Routledge, 1999), 17. Negus draws on Scott Lash and John Urry, *Economies of Signs and Space* (London: Sage, 1994).

3. In 1963 Gordy remarked that Motown's staff comprised between fifty and sixty people; Motown 50 Podcast Series, episode 2, "Berry Gordy—A Tour of Hitsville U.S.A., May 1963."

4. These houses, many of which were duplex residences, were located on West Grand Boulevard at 2644/2646 (purchased April 18, 1961); 2648 (August 2, 1959); 2650/2652 (January 3, 1962); 2656 (March 4, 1965); 2657 (January 12, 1966); 2662/2664 (July 11, 1966); 2666/2668 (July 11, 1966); and 2670/2672 (December 6, 1966).

5. ITMI worked with outside firms like General Artists Corporation (GAC) early in the decade, and artists were later aligned with large mainstream companies like William Morris and Creative Management.

6. Gordy described the early purpose of ITMI: "The purpose of ITMI—as we called it—was to act as personal manager to the artists. They did everything from getting them gigs, providing career guidance and negotiating with booking agents to making sure that paid their taxes"; Gordy, *To Be Loved*, 144. Berger compares Motown's management strategy to the Hollywood film studio system of the 1930s and 1940s, which famously enveloped actors and controlled every aspect of their careers; Shelly Berger, telephone interview by author, January 14, 2015.

7. Several of these managers developed long-term relationships with Motown artists. Berger managed the Supremes and the Temptations, for example, and Cox managed the Miracles.

8. "I. M. C. Artists: Assigned Managers, Administrators, Road Managers, and Agencies," Motown internal memorandum, March 30, 1970, EMU. At this time, Berger, Graziano, Wooldridge, and Cox were the personal managers responsible for all of Motown's major acts.

9. Fuqua, interview by Nelson George.

10. Fuqua also worked as a songwriter and producer at Motown during the 1960s.

11. Johnny Allen served as King's assistant and coached vocal performances. Maurice King, interview by Dearborn Hyatt, December 21, 1983, transcript, NGC; Cholly Atkins and Jacqui Malone, *Class Act: The Jazz Life of Choreographer Cholly Atkins* (New York: Columbia University Press, 2001). See also Cholly Atkins, unknown interviewer, unknown date, transcript, NGC. For more about Maxine Powell and the artist development department, see George, *Where Did Our Love Go?*, 87–90; Maxine Powell, interview by Nelson George, December 22, 1983, transcript, NGC.

12. Jobete writers changed affiliation en masse from BMI to ASCAP in 1972. "Jobete Writers Join ASCAP," *Los Angeles Sentinel*, March 23, 1972, B2A.

13. "Catalog: January 1959/March 1967," Jobete Music Company, Inc., EMU.

14. Collections of Jobete sheet music are held at both EMU and HAC. Examples in these archives include arrangements for vocal and piano, jazz combos, and marching bands.

15. "Jobete Expands; Levington Mgr.," *Billboard*, April 20, 1966, 1, 8.

16. Paul Riser, "Motown's Chief Assembly-Line Operator Talks Snakepits, String Arrangements, and R. Kelly," Red Bull Music Academy, http://www.redbullmusicacademy.com/lectures/paul_riser_funk_brothers_gonna_work_it_out.

17. This is an ongoing issue in discussions of the role of the Funk Brothers. See Paul Justman's 2002 film *Standing in the Shadows of Motown*. Arrangers often wrote each section only once and asked the players to repeat these figurations and ornament them. Two rare examples of reprinted band arrangements can be found in Alan Slutsky [Dr. Licks], *Standing in the Shadows of Motown: The Life and Music of Legendary Bassist James Jamerson* (Milwaukee, WI: Hal Leonard, 1989), 33–34.

18. Riser, "Motown's Chief Assembly-Line Operator."

19. Contrary to their current name, the backing band was never officially called the Funk Brothers, instead recording under the name the Soul Brothers for Van Dyke's 1965 release *That Motown Sound.*

20. Motown regularly listed arrangers on albums beginning in the late 1960s. The identities of musicians were unknown to most fans in the United States until their names were listed on album jackets beginning in the summer of 1971. Marvin Gaye's album *What's Going On* is often considered the first album to include the names of the Funk Brothers, but Valerie Simpson's *Exposed,* released about a month earlier, also listed the names of its musicians. For secondary print sources relating to the Funk Brothers, see Jack Ashford, *Motown: A View from the Bottom* (New Romney, UK: Bank House, 2003); Dennis Coffey, *Guitars, Bars, and Motown Superstars* (Ann Arbor: University of Michigan Press, 2004); Slutsky, *Standing in the Shadows.* Slutsky's biography was the source for Justman's *Standing in the Shadows of Motown.* Interviews with Beans Bowles, Bob Babbitt, Choker Campbell, Earl Van Dyke, Johnny Griffith, H. B. Barnum, Mickey Stevenson, and Paul Riser are held in NGC. Union records are held at Detroit's AFM Local 5 and Los Angeles's Local 47.

21. There were many, many other musicians who worked for Motown during the 1960s and 1970s in both Detroit and Los Angeles. Names of various Motown session players can be found on the public web pages associated with the Motown Museum in Detroit and the Motown Alumni Association. The sources for these names come from internal records and recollections of musicians themselves and have been subject to intense public scrutiny from Motown musicians and fans.

22. The Fayettes and the Paulette Singers were also early vocal groups associated with Motown. For more on the Andantes, see Bill Dahl, *Motown: The Golden Years* (Iola, WI: Krause, 2001), 210–13.

23. In 1960 the term *producer* was not common. Instead, record companies used the term *artist and repertoire* (A&R). By the end of the decade, however, *producer* was used commonly to refer to the person who oversaw the recording process. For more on the role of the "producer," see Zak, *Poetics of Rock,* 172–83.

24. Motown studio manager Ralph Terrana, who began to work at Motown in 1969, remembers, "When a producer wanted to go into the studio it was necessary for them to fill out a form that was referred to as 'session notes.' This form would indicate what type of session this was to be, ie [*sic*]: rythym [*sic*], vocal, instrumental over-dub and such. The session notes were turned in to the A&R department for approval. When approved my office would receive the paper work and we would begin the process of setting up the session. If musical instruments were involved we would notify Hank Cosby's arranging department and they would take care of the union paper work and then notify the musicians to be used. The producer generally requested a specific time for the session and we would always try to accomodate [*sic*] that time for them, but in the case of rythym [*sic*] dates they were, as Dennis [Coffey] points out, done at generally the same times. Once we had the time secured the producer was notified of his date and time. If the session was a vocal over-dub the producer would usually notify

his artist but at times we would do this as a courtesy to the producer"; "How Were Motown's Studio Sessions Arranged?," Soulful Detroit Forum (online web forum), http://faac.us/adf/messages/28522/146214.html?1107822773.

25. Gordy discusses this process during the recording of "Come to Me"; Gordy, *To Be Loved*, 109–11.

26. Frances Maclin *I Remember Motown: When We Were All Just Family* (self-published, 2014).

27. A number of singles issued during this time did not credit the producer; Gordy is credited as producer on all other singles issued before this.

28. Other producers to emerge during this time included Andre Williams, George Fowler, and Miss Ray (Raynoma Gordy), who was the first producer other than Berry Gordy to be credited on a Motown-released single, Jimmy Ruffin's "Don't Feel Sorry for Me," released on January 31, 1961. Holland and Bateman were the second, with the Satintones' recording of "I Know How it Feels," released on June 24, 1961. Stevenson also had an illustrious career at Motown as the director of the Artist and Repertoire Department, and he was the driving force behind the formation of the Funk Brothers. (When he left Motown in 1967 Eddie Holland became head of A&R.)

29. Several important records by Whitfield and Strong also included Roger Penzabene as cowriter.

30. Robert Bateman left Motown in 1962 to work with Detroit-based Correc-Tone records and later Double-L in New York. Despite official credits for Holland-Dozer-Holland songs and production, their duties were sometime intermixed. Eddie Holland is audible on session tapes, for example, even though he is not credited as producer.

31. Agreements for shared credit existed between many of Motown's songwriting and production teams, and other informal arrangements were pervasive between songwriters and producers. In his memoir, Stevie Wonder's handler Ted Hull recalls in a compelling manner his foray into writing at Motown and the various people who received credit and royalties for his songs; Hull and Stahel, *Wonder Years*, 155–62.

32. Tracks were divided so that one documented low instruments (i.e., drums and bass) and the other captured high-pitched performances (i.e., guitars, auxiliary percussion, and sometimes piano). McLean worked with Peter Walsh to develop the three-track machine and completed it on his own after Walsh left Motown; Mike McLean, telephone interview by author, March 31, 2015.

33. For more on Mike McLean, see Mike McLean, "The Golden World Story: Studio Appraisal," soulfuldetroit.com, http://soulfuldetroit.com/web07-golden%20world/golden%20world%20story/49-gw-mike-mclean.htm. For more on Russ Terrana and his brother Ralph Terrana, both of whom worked on the technical side of Motown productions, see Ralph Terrana, *Russ Terrana's Motown* (New Romney, UK: Bank House, 2010); Ralph Terrana, *The Road through Motown* (New Romney, UK: Bank House, 2006).

34. According to McLean, there were reverb chambers in three different West Grand Boulevard houses (2644, 2648, and 2652).

35. Instrumental sessions at Motown were delicate due to AFM union regu-

lations that required a singer to be present at recording sessions, a rule that Motown rarely followed.

36. "How Were Motown's Studio Sessions Arranged?" See also Coffey, *Guitars, Bars, and Motown Superstars*.

37. Beatriz Staples, telephone interview.

38. "How Were Motown's Studio Sessions Arranged?"

39. Wingate continued to run Ric Tic (without his studio space) until 1968.

40. Ralph Terrana remembers, "Studio A was the studio used for tracks. It was small and compact and I think that held a lot of the allure. Plus the mystique of all the hits. Producers tend to be somewhat superstitious when recording studios are concerned. . . . Horns and strings were primarily done at Studio B. Extra over-dub rooms had been added to Studio A but they felt to [*sic*] remote to be effective and were rarely used. Mixing was done at both studios until the two mixing rooms in the Donavan Building were completed. At that time all mixing would take place in that building." "How Were Motown's Studio Sessions Arranged?"

41. I refer to "S" tapes as safety reels, but former tape librarian Frances (Heard) Maclin calls them "session clips"; Maclin, *I Remember Motown*.

42. All Detroit activity after this period is well documented, in addition to many sessions in New York, Los Angeles, and Chicago.

43. Maclin, *I Remember Motown*. In late 1969 the studios began to use sixteen-track machines, which offered even more flexibility but corresponded with a period in which Motown's most popular records began to lose their sonic consistency.

44. This is not pictured.

45. One mix, 842S01, was created much later, presumably for the *Motown Story* boxed set.

46. Brian Holland worked in this position for an extended period during the mid-1960s while Brown was in Spain.

47. Gordy, *To Be Loved*, 151.

48. Gordy remembers, "HDH benefited from my policy that, if two records under consideration were equally strong, the release would be given to the producer who had the last hit"; ibid., 223. Many other artists created records in dialogue with their own successful work at the time, especially acts associated with the loose production network in midtown Manhattan surrounding the Brill Building. See also Inglis, "Some Kind of Wonderful," 225.

49. "The One Who Really Loves You" (February 1962), "You Beat Me to the Punch" (July 1962), "Two Lovers" (October 1962), "Laughing Boy" (February 1963), "Your Old Stand By" (April 1963), and "My Guy" (March 1964). "You Beat Me to the Punch" was cowritten with Ronnie White and "Your Old Stand By" was cowritten with Janie Bradford. "What's Easy for Two Is So Hard for One" was released as the B-side of the HDH record "You Lost the Sweetest Boy" but achieved similar success in both the R&B and pop markets.

50. Robinson later explored a different direction with Wells when recording "My Guy" in March 1964, which became her most popular single. The stylistically similar "When I'm Gone" was scheduled as the sequel to "My Guy," but contract negotiations between Wells and Motown stalled after her twenty-first birth-

day later in the year, resulting in her departure from the company. Robinson's work for the Miracles at this time, including "You've Really Got a Hold on Me" (November 1962) and "A Love She Can Count On" (March 1963), did not adhere to this style.

51. The name of this team was sometimes spelled Brian Bert. Bateman contributed to a number of Motown singles between 1959 and 1961, including: The Satintones, "My Beloved" (1959), Eugene Remus, "Hold Me Tight" (1959), Barrett Strong, "Money and Me" (1961), and the Satintones, "A Love That Can Never Be" (1961) and "Angel" (1961). Bateman and Holland also wrote many early songs for the company, sometimes with other contributors, including Henry Lumpkin's "I've Got a Notion" (1961), Little Iva and Her Band's "Continental Strut" (1961), Freddie Gorman's "The Day Will Come" (1961) and "Just for You" (1961), Eddie Holland's "Take a Chance on Me" (1961), and the Valadiers' "Greetings (This Is Uncle Sam)" (1961) and "Take a Chance" (1961). Bateman and Holland wrote and produced four records for the Satintones: "I Know How It Feels" (1961), "My Kind of Love" (1961), "Zing Went the Strings of My Heart" (1961), and "Faded Letter" (1961).

52. There is some debate about the authorship of "Please Mr. Postman." Holland, Bateman, and Gordy are listed as legal authors, but William Garrett and Georgia Dobbins (who was briefly a member of the Marvelettes) also seemed to contribute to the composition of the piece. "Twistin' Postman," written by Brian Holland, Mickey Stevenson, and Robert Bateman, was produced by Brianbert and released on December 6, 1961. "Playboy," written by Brian Holland, Mickey Stevenson, Robert Bateman, and Gladys Horton, was produced by Brianbert and released on April 9, 1962.

53. One of Bateman's first post-Motown productions was a single released in mid-1962 on the Correc-Tone Sonbert subsidiary for the Pyramids called "I'm the Playboy," which was an answer record to his own "Playboy" for the Marvelettes.

54. Brian had released the B-side "Shock" as Briant Holland, written and produced by Berry Gordy, on the Kudo imprint in September 1958. In 1960 and 1961 he also occasionally sang with the Satintones and the Rayber Voices. Eddie first released a single on Mercury called "Little Miss Ruby" in April 1958 (also produced by Gordy), followed by a series of United Artists and Tamla releases; his first release on the Motown label, "Jamie," achieved national success in both the R&B and pop markets in early 1962. He continued to record and release music as a vocalist until mid-1964. Dozier came to Motown as a performer from the Anna Records roster in 1961 after working with the Romeos and the Voice Masters. In 1960 he released "Let's Talk It Over" on Anna Records (as Lamont Anthony) before he moved into writing and production. Although a key member of the HDH team, Eddie Holland also wrote lyrics for a large number of Norman Whitfield's songs in the mid-1960s.

55. Harry Weinger and Allan Slutsky, liner notes, *Standing in the Shadows of Motown: Original Motion Picture Soundtrack* (Deluxe Edition).

56. The Supremes ultimately became Motown's most popular act, but the company had a difficult time finding them a niche. Motown issued eight lackluster singles by the group before "Where Did Our Love Go."

57. In July 1967 the group's official name changed to Diana Ross and the Supremes.

58. Motown press releases written by Alan Abrams called attention to the writing and production of HDH in 1964 and 1965, and their names started to appear in print media alongside artists and Berry Gordy.

59. Ballard never recovered professionally or personally after being released from the Supremes and died penniless in 1976. George's work contains what is perhaps the most revealing information about the politics of personnel changes within the group; *Where Did Our Love Go?*, 79–90. J. Warwick also discusses this departure at length in *Girl Groups, Girl Culture*, 158–60.

60. J. Warwick, *Girl Groups, Girl Culture*, 49.

61. Brian Chin and David Nathan, "Reflections of . . . ," essay included in the Supremes, *The Supremes*, Motown 012 159 075-2 (2000), 21.

62. "Where Did Our Love Go": "Baby, baby, baby don't leave me / ooh, please don't leave me all by myself" (0:05); "Baby Love": "Baby love, my baby love I need you, oh how I need you" (0:04); "Stop! In the Name of Love": "Baby, baby I'm aware of where you go each time you leave my door" (0:19).

63. Lamont Dozier recalls the creation of these vocal backgrounds in "Where Did Our Love Go": "After we cut the track, what few lyrics I had started were finished off by Eddie. There were some vocal harmonies I had worked out for Mary and Florence, but it was a little bit sophisticated. There were some attitudes, because the girls did not like the song, so I just tossed aside the backgrounds I had arranged and I said, 'Listen, let's just do *baby, baby*,' and we did that on the spot, in unison. Sometimes less is more, and in this case, it worked out perfectly. The '*baby, baby*' thing became a signature"; Chin and Nathan, "Reflections," 20 (emphasis in original).

64. Dozier offers an interesting take on HDH's sensitivity to key choice for different singers: "We'd already cut the track of 'Where Did Our Love Go' for the Marvelettes, and it was in the key that Gladys Horton sang. But because the key was lower than what Diana had been doing, it gave a certain low, sultry, kind of sexy sound to her voice that we hadn't known before. It gave a lot of body to her voice. It gave her a sound"; Chin and Nathan, "Reflections," 19.

65. After this, HDH drew evenly between their signature quarter-note feel and a backbeat feel that stressed beats 2 and 4 for their Supremes singles. This "stomping" sound was uncommon in Motown productions before the summer of 1964. Brian Holland and Lamont Dozier had used it as early 1962 in the Stevie Wonder single "Contract on Love," but it did not become common on Motown records until after the success of the Martha and the Vandellas' "Heat Wave" and the Supremes' "Where Did Our Love Go."

66. Covach calls this "simple verse" form. For more on form in rock (and pop) music, see John Covach, "Form In Rock Music: A Primer" in *Engaging Music: Essays in Music Analysis*, ed. Deborah Stein (New York: Oxford University Press, 2005), 65–76.

67. Like many of the Vandellas' singles, "Where Did Our Love Go" and "Baby Love" both employed a saxophone solo performed by Mike Terry in a similar place in the overall song form; a horn-oriented bridge in "Come See about Me" mirrored these saxophone solos.

68. This song is also in C major. The passages in question are: "A Lover's Concerto" (0:10–0:16) and "Stop! In the Name of Love" (0:13–0:20).

69. Michael Long, *Beautiful Monsters: Imagining the Classic in Musical Media* (Berkeley: University of California Press, 2008), 210.

70. A "truck driver" key change refers to a change of key with no preparation, a common occurrence in many pop records. See Walter Everett, "Confessions from Blueberry Hell, or, Pitch Can Be a Sticky Substance," in *Expressions in Pop-Rock Music: A Collection of Critical and Analytical Essays*, ed. Walter Everett (New York: Garland, 2000), 311.

71. "Baby I Need Your Loving" entered the *Billboard* charts on August 15, 1964; "Where Did Our Love Go" on July 11, 1964.

72. "Ask the Lonely" was written and produced by Mickey Stevenson and Ivy Hunter; "Loving You Is Sweeter Than Ever" was written by Ivy Hunter and Stevie Wonder and produced by Hunter. Two later records included covers produced by HDH: "Walk Away Renee" (written by Mike Lookofsky, Bob Calilli, and Tony Sansone and originally recorded by the Left Banke), and "If I Were a Carpenter" (written by Tim Hardin and recorded originally by Bobby Darin).

73. The group's unreleased first album, *Breaking Through*, was scheduled to appear on Workshop Jazz.

74. HDH explored weeping and weakness in many songs for the Four Tops. "Baby I Need Your Loving": "Some say it's a sign of weakness for a man to beg / then weak I'd rather be if it means having you to keep 'cause lately I've been losing sleep"; "Without the One You Love": "People ask why would a grown man cry / I drop my head and I sigh and reply"; "I Can't Help Myself": "Sugar pie honey bunch I'm weaker than a man should be"; "It's the Same Old Song": "A sentimental fool am I to hear a old love song and wanna cry"; "Something about You": "I'm just your puppet on a string and tears sometimes it brings"; "Shake Me, Wake Me": "As the tears stream down my face I can't believe I've been re-placed"; "Standing in the Shadows of Love": "How can you watch me cry after all I've done for you." This was a topic explored elsewhere in the black community. For example, a June 1965 article in *Ebony* asked, "What Kind of Men Cry?" (This issue coincidentally featured the Supremes on its cover.)

75. Stu Hackel, "Brothers in Arms," essay included in the Four Tops, *Fourever*, Motown/Hip-O 314 556 225–2, 2001, 14.

76. The Four Tops has also sang background on the Holland-Dozier B-side "What Goes Up, Must Come Down," released in June 1963. "Baby I Need Your Loving" was the first single released by the Four Tops that resulted from collaboration with HDH.

77. Both songs are in B♭ major with significant sections in A♭ major.

78. In "I Can't Help Myself" Stubbs refers to his "sugar pie honey bunch" and in "It's the Same Old Song" he exclaims, "you're sweet as a honey bee."

79. The sax solo appears in "I Can't Help Myself" at 1:00; in "It's the Same Old Song" it appears at 1:30.

80. Hackel, "Brothers in Arms," 20.

81. "Late one night March in 1965, Brian hunted the Tops down at a Temptations' show at Detroit's 20 Grand Club. He had been playing a test pressing of the music track, he admits, three to four hundred times, hypnotized by

James Jamerson's fleshed-out bass line. . . . They descended on Hitsville at two in the morning. . . . By dawn they had it. . . . The counter-punch of 'It's the Same Old Song,' took a mere two days to get to market."; ibid., 19–20.

82. "Something about You" and "Shake Me, Wake Me (When It's Over)" were the first records in this style.

83. "Reach Out" is set in B♭ major but gravitates toward a temporary center of ♭III during its verse. "Standing in the Shadows of Love" is set in B♭ minor and its chorus progression descends through a minor tetrachord (from B♭ minor to the F dominant). "Bernadette" begins on an E♭ major chord and also incorporates a descending minor tetrachord. Like "Reach Out" and "Standing in the Shadows," the verse of "Bernadette" relies heavily on III and VII (G♭ major and D♭ major).

84. For more on Stevenson, see William "Mickey" Stevenson, *The A&R Man* (self-published, 2015).

85. Stevenson also formed a partnership with Ivy Hunter to produce hits for many acts and teamed with William Weatherspoon to produce the Jimmy Ruffin record "What Becomes of the Brokenhearted."

86. Multitrack recordings provide valuable insight into Motown's recording process. Universal Music has digitized many Motown masters, a preservation process that includes copies of audio and digital scans of original tape boxes, reels, and ephemera. Listening closely to individual tracks for many of Motown's most popular records from the 1960s and 1970s reveals compelling commonalities of instrumentation, timbre, and performance style, which greatly informed my analysis. Between 2003 and 2005, Universal Music and the Singing Machine Company also released eighteen commercial karaoke discs using original recordings that include the ability to separate vocals from backing tracks for 144 recordings. Identifiable styles of this type were not limited to Motown. For writings about sonic and historical consistency at Motown, Stax, and the Brill Building, see Fitzgerald, "Motown Crossover Hits"; Rob Bowman, "Stax: A Musicological Analysis," *Popular Music* 14 (October 1995): 285–320; Inglis, "Some Kind of Wonderful."

87. This was especially true in the UK. See "Shop Window," *New Musical Express*, June 25, 1965, 4; "Potted Pops," *New Musical Express*, August 27, 1965, 4; "Orbison Better, but Not His Best," *New Musical Express*, August 27, 1965, 4. See also Jon Landau, "A Whiter Shade of Black," *Crawdaddy*, October 1967, 34–40. Landau writes, "With regard to rhythm the most important thing is Motown drumming. Up until the time of H-D-H the most common pattern of drumming was for the drummer to hit the snare on the second and fourth beats of every measure. That was changed to the drummer hitting the snare on every beat. . . . It soon became a Motown staple to the point where it would be safe to say that seventy-five percent of the records recorded in a Motown studio since 'Baby Love' have this style of drumming. . . . The Motown beat was to become the key to public identification of the Motown sound." To be sure, critics often used the word *beat* interchangeably with *style* during the mid-1960s, but the above instances referred more specifically to actual rhythmic content. Modern musicians continue use the term *Motown Beat* to describe this texture, which is evident in method books like Ed Friedland, *Bass Grooves: Develop Your Groove and Play Like the Pros in Any Style* (San Francisco: Backbeat, 2004), 66–68. Contemporary academics like Robert

Fink ("Goal-Directed Soul?") have also used this pattern to construct critical arguments about Motown's music.

88. Anthony Jackson cites these characteristics in his discussion of Jamerson's style; Slutsky, *Standing in the Shadows*, 92–95.

89. Bass was nearly always recorded to track 8, an edge track that had the potential to leak in only one direction.

90. Per Elias Drabløs, *The Quest for the Melodic Electric Bass: From Jamerson to Spenner* (Burlington, VT: Ashgate, 2015). Paul McCartney, for example, has often cited Jamerson as a major influence on his bass playing; Slutsky, *Standing in the Shadows*, 102.

91. Peter Doyle has written about reverb and echo in the later-1950s studio work at Sun and Chess, two studios that served as forbearers to Motown's more advanced recording techniques. Peter Doyle, *Echo and Reverb: Fabricating Space in Popular Music Recording, 1900–1960* (Middletown, CT: Wesleyan University Press, 2005).

92. "Mike McLean 4," Soulful Detroit Forum, http://soulfuldetroit.com/archives/1/654.html?1021570291; "Mike McLean 5," Soulful Detroit Forum, http://soulfuldetroit.com/archives/1/672.html?1029867099; Gordy, *To Be Loved*, 126. Olhsson recalls a Fender spring unit, an Echolette, and an Echoplex. See "Artist Spotlight: Bob Olhsson, Audio Mastery, Nashville," http://www.exponentialaudio.com/artists-new/2015/8/19/artist-spotlight-bob-olhsson.

93. It is unclear when this happened, and it certainly could have worked differently among producers or engineers. Effects may have been applied at the temporary reel phase, during the transfer to safety reels, or sometime later, although probably not after the performance had been committed to a safety reel. The absence of temporary reels makes it very difficult to know more about this process.

94. Landau singles out this record in "Whiter Shade of Black." In a recent thread on the Soulful Detroit Forum, Motown fans listed many other "songs that best exemplify the Motown Sound," http://soulfuldetroit.com/showthread.php?10317-Songs-That-Best-Exemplify-quot-The-Motown-Sound-quot-!.

95. Although not used on the final single mix, two separate takes of Levi Stubbs's vocals remain on the master of "Reach Out."

96. As with the term *beat*, it was common during the 1960s to use *sound* to refer to a style. The "Nashville Sound" had been a common descriptor for a style of country music since the late 1950s, and singles reviews in trade magazines like *Billboard* often used terms like "Liverpool Sound" and "Phil Spector Sound" during the middle of the 1960s. For more on genre in popular music, see Negus, *Music Genres*; Simon Frith, *Performing Rites: On the Value of Popular Music* (Cambridge, MA: Harvard University Press, 1996), 75–95; David Brackett, "Questions of Genre in Black Popular Music," *Black Music Research Journal* 25 (Spring–Fall 2005): 73–92; David Brackett, "(In Search of) Musical Meaning: Genres, Categories and Crossover," in *Popular Music Studies*, ed. David Hesmondhalgh and Keith Negus (London: Arnold, 2002), 65–83; and Fabian Holt, *Genre in Popular Music* (Chicago: University of Chicago Press, 2007).

97. References to the Detroit Sound were numerous during 1965, appearing in local Detroit papers, *Billboard*, and magazines like *Newsweek*. "Tamla-Motown

Goes Outside to Get Talent," *Billboard*, September 4, 1965, 10; "Rock and Roll: The Sounds of the Sixties," *Time*, May 21, 1965, 84–88; "No Town Like Motown," *Newsweek*, March 22, 1965, 22. This term also appeared in dozens of press releases, letters, telegrams, and internal notes from this time. Some of these include: Alan Abrams, telegram to S[haron] Prokoff, , March 6, 1965, AAC; [Alan E. Abrams], "More of the 'Detroit Sound' on National Television," Motown press release, March 15, 1965, AAC; Alan Abrams, letter to Frank Judge, March 22, 1965, AAC; and [Alan E. Abrams], "'Detroit Sound' Artists to Climax British Tour with Gala Paris Performance," Motown press release, April 9, 1965, AAC. One handwritten memo in the Alan Abrams Collection dated November 17, 1964, includes a proposal to "get Mayor Cavanaugh of Detroit to issue an official proclamation renaming Detroit as **'Motown'** (or 'Motortown') for the day of December 25, 1964 in honor of Motown/Motortown's significant contribution to Detroit"; Alan Abrams, "Top Priority," internal Motown memorandum, November 17, 1964, AAC; emphasis in original. Abrams also wrote a letter in September 1965 to Barbara Holliday from the *Detroit Free Press* to promote (and show excitement for) *Variety* referring to Detroit as Motown; Alan Abrams, letter to Barbara Holliday, September 13, 1965, AAC.

98. There are three interoffice memos (on "Quicki-Notes") held in the AAC on this topic. Alan Abrams, letter to Ralph Seltzer, March 30, 1965, AAC; Alan Abrams, letter to Ralph Seltzer, May 5, 1965, AAC; Alan Abrams, letter to Ralph Seltzer, May 6, 1965, AAC.

99. The company printed an advertising brochure using this title; "The Motown Sound . . . Acclaimed the World Over, 'The Detroit Sound,'" Motown advertising brochure, ca. 1965, EMU.

100. "The Detroit Sound" had been printed on the back of many record jackets at the beginning of the year, such as the Supremes' *I Hear a Symphony* (February 1966). *The Supremes a' Go-Go* (August 1966) includes "The Motown Sound" in this space, illustrating a change in nomenclature. This later slogan appeared on various LPs until the early 1970s.

101. The white paper and two souvenir tour books from 1966 and 1967, both called "An Evening with the Motown Sound," are held in EMU. Television performances also reflected the term and connected Motown to Detroit. Upon entering the British market in March 1965, Motown artists were featured in an ITV special called *The Sound of Motown*. The June 1965 broadcast of "It's What's Happening Baby" featured Martha and the Vandellas riding in the new 1965 Ford Mustang as it passed through an automobile assembly line. A CBS news special called *Anatomy of Pop* depicted the "Detroit Sound" as "a new export" from Michigan's "Motortown."

102. Thomas Thompson, "Music Streams," *Life*, May 21, 1965, 93–98; "Hear That Big Sound," *Life*, May 21, 1965, 82–92. For commentary on this article, see Bernard Gendron, *Between Montmartre and the Mudd Club: Popular Music and the Avant-Garde* (Chicago: University of Chicago Press, 2002), 175–80.

103. Michaela Williams, "That Motown Sound," *Panorama* (*Chicago Daily News*), September 25, 1965, 6; Lingeman, "The Big, Happy, Beating Heart." Significant planning went into the Williams profile. She visited Detroit and interviewed the Supremes, Berry Gordy, Esther Edwards, and Holland, Dozier, and Holland;

Al Abrams, "Memorandum," August 18, 1965, AAC. See also Alan Abrams, letter to Richard Christiansen, August 19, 1965, AAC; Alan Abrams, letter to Michaela Williams, August 26, 1965, AAC; Alan Abrams, letter to Michaela Williams, September 28, 1965, AAC; and Richard Christiansen, letter to Al Abrams, August 16, 1965, AAC.

104. Both Tamla and Motown were registered as trademarks in 1965 by the Motown Record Corporation, with the first usage of both "in commerce" cited as April 30, 1960. The first claim of "Motown Sound" as a trademark at uspto. gov is August 25, 1966, two days before the publication date of this *Billboard* advertisement. (The claim was filed on August 7, 1967.) The term *Motown* was not common before Gordy started using it in 1960. Gordy was particularly fond of portmanteau wordplay, using the process to construct the name of Motown's major publishing company Jobete (created out of the first two letters of the names of Gordy's three children at the time, Joy, Berry, and Terry) and the early umbrella corporation name Rayber (formed from the first names of he and his wife, Raynoma). Gordy, *To Be Loved*, 103.

105. A review of this performance noted the discrepancy between the age of the audience and the Supremes' material. "The kids, in many instances, have adopted more adult catalogs," wrote one reviewer, "and the elders, who patronize these spots, are ready for what the youngsters have to offer." "Copacabana, N.Y.," *Variety*, August 4, 1965, 60.

106. The decline of middle of the road (MOR) styles from the national pop charts occurred just as Motown emerged in popular markets during the mid-1960s. Keir Keightley, "Long Play: Adult-Oriented Popular Music and the Temporal Logics of the Post-War Sound Recording in the USA," *Media, Culture, and Society* 26 (2004): 375–91.

107. A promotional schedule dated February 11, 1965, lists the Supremes' upcoming live and television engagements; AAC. In a 1966 letter to a *Boston Globe* reporter, Motown publicist Alan Abrams described the gravity of this evolution: "The girls had actually just begun to make their transition from the world of Rock Music one-nighters to the world of plush supper club engagements," Abrams wrote. "Thus, when they began to realize what had suddenly happened to them, they were rather awed by it all. (And somewhat frightened, they now tell me.)" Alan E. Abrams, letter to Bill Buchanan, January 4, 1966, AAC.

108. The Abrams collection helps to shed light on a number of strategies that Motown used to target older audiences. One was to associate Motown artists with acceptable African American forbearers. Stevie Wonder was presented as the next Ray Charles in his album *Tribute to Uncle Ray* (1962). The Four Tops were associated with Eckstine; [Alan E. Abrams], "It's Official! Billy Eckstine Signs with Motown," Motown press release, February 15, 1965, AAC. The Supremes recorded a tribute album to Sam Cooke after his untimely death in December 1964. Marvin Gaye patterned himself after Nat "King" Cole during his early years as a crooner, recording in 1965 the album *A Tribute to the Great Nat King Cole*. Motown even announced to the media that Gaye would fill some of the late singer's outstanding club dates, which turned out to be an erroneous prediction; [Alan E. Abrams], "Marvin Gaye Returns to 20 Grand," Motown press release, February 15, 1965, AAC. Motown also used ceremonies with public officials to court adult audiences. In 1965 the Supremes recorded a radio jingle called "Things Are

Changing" for the President's Committee on Equal Employment Opportunity, and the next year the Temptations recorded a similar spoken radio spot for the Peace Corps; Anthony S. Chen, *The Fifth Freedom: Jobs, Politics, and Civil Rights in the United States, 1941–1972* (Princeton, NJ: Princeton University Press, 2009), 213; [Alan E. Abrams], "Temptations to Record Radio Spot for Domestic Peace Corps," Motown press release, June 21, 1966, AAC. Motown acts performed similar ceremonial acts for local Detroit politicians, with the Supremes performing in a "testimonial banquet" for Detroit mayor Jerome P. Cavanagh in February 1965; [Alan E. Abrams], "Command Performance for Detroit's Supremes," Motown press release, February 18, 1965, AAC. The Detroit Common Council later honored the Supremes for "setting a high moral standard for teenagers"; [Alan E. Abrams], "Detroit Common Council Honors the Supremes," Motown press release, January 28, 1966, AAC.

109. More than twenty versions of "For Once in My Life" were recorded and released on various Motown releases between 1965 and 1971.

110. The changes in Motown's production line are evident in a March 1972 profile of the company's studio complex printed in an internal newsletter. Pat Coleman, "What Motown Is All About: Guardians of the Motown Sound Are with Studio Facilities," *Motown Newsletter: A Monthly Report on Motown Record Corporation.* 1, no. 3 (March 1972): 2, EMU.

111. "Motown A&R Chief and Wife Kim Weston Split Diskery," *Philadelphia Tribune,* January 10, 1967, 11.

112. There was a series of lawsuits surrounding the departure of HDH. First Motown sued HDH for breach of contract; then HDH countersued several Motown entities and personnel. "No Hits for a Year: The Supremes $4 Million Lawsuit; Motown Blames Writers for Supremes' 'Slump,'" *New Journal and Guide,* September 21, 1968; [Alan E. Abrams], "Holland-Dozier-Holland Answers Motown in 22-Million-Dollar Lawsuit," press release, November 15, 1968, AAC; "Composers Sue Motown for 22 Million-Dollars," *Daily Defender,* November 20, 1968. See also NGC, which includes 119 pages of Berry Gordy's testimony from a legal proceeding regarding this case. The legal battle was not settled until January 1972; "Suit against Motown Settled Out of Court," *New Pittsburgh Courier,* January 22, 1972. HDH continued to work as writers and producers after leaving Motown. In May 1969 the trio announced a new partnership with Columbia Records and the formation of the Invictus label. Alan Abrams worked with the company during its early years as a press agent; [Alan E. Abrams], "Invictus/Holland-Dozier-Holland—Capital Tie-In—Precedent Setting Victory for Creative Talent," press release, May 19, 1969, AAC.

113. The Four Tops eventually left Motown for ABC-Dunhill in 1972.

114. "Why Tamla Is Not a Song Factory," *Record Retailer,* February 21, 1970.

Chapter Three

1. For more on the rise of soul music, see Robert W. Stephens, "Soul: A Historical Reconstruction of Continuity and Change in Black Popular Music," *Black Perspective in Music* 12 (Spring 1984): 21–43; Paul Gilroy, *There Ain't*

No Black in the Union Jack: The Cultural Politics of Race and Nation (Chicago: University of Chicago Press, 1991), 171–87; Samuel A. Floyd Jr., *The Power of Black Music: Interpreting Its History from Africa to the United States* (New York: Oxford University Press, 1995), 203–6; Robert Pruter, *Chicago Soul* (Urbana: University of Illinois Press, 1991), xiv; David Brackett, "Soul Music," *Grove Music Online, Oxford Music Online*; Portia K. Maultsby, "Soul," in *African American Music: An Introduction*, ed. Portia K. Maultsby and Mellonee V. Burnim (New York: Routledge, 2006), 271–91; William Van Deburg, *New Day in Babylon: The Black Power Movement and American Culture, 1965–1975* (Chicago: University of Chicago Press, 1992); Jennifer Ryan, "'Can I Get a Witness?': Soul and Salvation in Memphis Music" (PhD diss., University of Pennsylvania, 2008), 76–124. More contemporaneous accounts of the rise of soul include Ulf Hannerz, "The Rhetoric of Soul: Identification in Negro Society," *Race* 9, no. 4 (1968): 453–65; Carl Belz, *The Story of Rock* (New York: Harper Colophon, 1972), 180, 183–88; Shaw, *World of Soul*; Haralambos, *Right On*; Hirshey, *Nowhere to Run*. For an account of soul that focuses more on the metaphysical nature of soul, see Jason Gregory King, "Blue Magic: Stardom, Soul Music and Illumination" (PhD diss., New York University, 2002).

2. Lerone Bennett Jr., "The Soul of Soul," *Ebony*, December 1961, 111–20. In his 1963 book *Blues People*, LeRoi Jones (Amiri Baraka) discusses the rise of the word *soul* as a category expressly for crossover during the late 1950s, placing it in a lineage after *bop* and *cool*; LeRoi Jones, *Blues People: Negro Music in White America* (1963; repr., New York: Perennial, 2002), 216–17; emphasis in original. For more on soul jazz, see John Gennari, *Blowin' Hot and Cool: Jazz and Its Critics* (Chicago: University of Chicago Press, 2006); Mark Anthony Neal, *What the Music Said: Black Popular Music and Black Popular Culture* (New York: Routledge, 1999), 33–36; Ben Sidran, *Black Talk* (New York: Da Capo Press, 1981), 130–37; Scott Saul, *Freedom Is, Freedom Ain't: Jazz and the Making of the Sixties* (Cambridge, MA: Harvard University Press, 2003); Iain Anderson, *This Is Our Music: Free Jazz, the Sixties, and American Culture* (Philadelphia: University of Pennsylvania Press, 2007), 132–34. For more contemporaneous views of soul jazz, see John Tynan, "Funk, Groove, Soul," *Down Beat*, November 24, 1960, 18–19; and J. Gillison, "They Call It 'Soul' Music: 'Down Home' Jazz Feeling Scoring a 'Swinging' Hit with the Public," *Philadelphia Tribune*, May 16, 1961, 5

3. Gennari, *Blowin' Hot and Cool*, 175.

4. Ingrid Monson, *Freedom Sounds: Civil Rights Call Out to Jazz and Africa* (New York: Oxford University Press, 2007), 77.

5. There were two released versions of "Every Beat of My Heart," both by Gladys Knight and the Pips. One appeared on Fury and the other on the tiny HunTom label before being leased by Vee-Jay. The latter was more successful on national pop and R&B charts.

6. Guralnick, *Sweet Soul Music*; Charles L. Hughes, *Country Soul: Making Music and Making Race in the American South* (Chapel Hill: University of North Carolina Press, 2015).

7. There were also a lot of records popular in the R&B market that exemplified the soul style and did not cross freely into the mainstream. A few of these included Tommy Hunt, "I Am a Witness" (Scepter, 1963), Chuck Jackson, "Beg

Me" (Wand, 1964), Don Covay, "Mercy, Mercy" (Rosemart, 1964), and Johnny Nash, "Let's Move and Groove (Together)" (JoDa, 1965).

8. In spite of its common attribution to the Isley Brothers, the first recording of "Twist and Shout," which was written by Phil Medley and Bert Burns, was by a white rock group called the Top Notes. It was released on Atlantic in 1961.

9. "Release Me" had been written in 1946 and mostly associated with the country and western market. Ray Price and Kitty Wells both released popular versions of the song in 1954.

10. Shaw, *World of Soul*, 16.

11. For a later view of *Billboard* changing R&B chart names, see "Billboard Adopts 'R&B' as New Name for Two Charts," *Billboard*, October 27, 1990, 6, 35.

12. "Rudman Joins Billboard's R&B Dept.," *Billboard*, July 25, 1964, 4.

13. "'Soul' Discs Sell," *Cash Box*, May 16, 1964.

14. Bill Gavin, "No Musical Color Line," *Billboard*, April 25, 1964, 46.

15. For contemporaneous debates about the role of blue-eyed soul in the R&B market, see Claude Hall, "R&B Stations Open Airplay to 'Blue-Eyed Soulists,'" *Billboard*, October 9, 1965, 1, 49.

16. "Just for Your Love" was written by Billy Davis, Gwen Gordy, and Berry Gordy.

17. Concert artists Roland Hayes and Paul Robeson regularly performed a song called "Water Boy," and John Lee Hooker, Odetta, and Harry Belafonte performed related pop and blues interpretations.

18. For a larger discussion of this record in the context of Martin Luther King Jr.'s visit to Detroit in June 1963, see S. Smith, *Dancing in the Street*, 35–36.

19. Wonder continued to create records in the mold of "Fingertips" after its success. He released "Workout Stevie, Workout" the following autumn, which recreated many of the musical characteristics of "Fingertips," including prominent offbeat clapping reminiscent of the sanctified church, an extended harmonica solo, and call-and-response with a gospel choir.

20. The phrase "I Gotta Dance to Keep from Crying" is a reworking of "I'm laughin' to keep from cryin'." The latter was the title of a 1952 collection of poetry by Langston Hughes and was also conspicuously printed on the back of the 1960 Harry Belafonte album *Swing Dat Hammer*.

21. Fink, "Goal-Directed Soul?," 179–82.

22. This song was also released in a vocal version by the Darnells.

23. *Life*, May 21, 1965, 93–94. Quoted and discussed in Charles Keil, *Urban Blues* (Chicago: University of Chicago Press, 1991), 94.

24. Keil, *Urban Blues*, 42–43; LeRoi Jones, "Apple Cores," *Down Beat* 32 (March 25, 1965), 34. The quotations in this passage refer to Jones.

25. See also S. Smith, *Dancing in the Street*, 164.

26. Studio band leader Earl Van Dyke created similar soul translations on his album *That Motown Sound*, which was made by overdubbing organ and piano over the existing backing tracks of a number of Motown hits. To be sure, Van Dyke's singles were released on Soul and *That Motown Sound* appeared on the Motown imprint.

27. For a discussion of Al Green's version of this song, see Awkward, *Soul Covers*, 126–27.

28. Bowman cites the use of III, VI, and VII in major (which he labels III, ♭VI, and ♭VII) as markers of the Stax style during last half of the 1960s; Bowman, "Stax," 298.

29. The Elgins' 1966 LP *Darling Baby* also contains interpretations of southern soul records like Percy Sledge's "When a Man Loves a Woman" and Wilson Pickett's "In The Midnight Hour" and "634–5789."

30. "Agent Double-O Soul" was released originally on Ric Tic in 1965.

31. Ed Aaronoff, liner notes, *This Old Heart of Mine* (Tamla 269, 1966).

32. This supplement appeared in the June 24, 1967, issue of *Billboard*. Later installments were published in 1968 (August 17), 1969 (August 16), and 1970 (August 22).

33. Claude Hall, "The Best Ears in the Business," *Billboard*, June 24, 1967, section 2, 14–15.

34. Claude Hall, "Atlantic Helped Pave the Way," *Billboard*, June 24, 1967, section 2, 16–17; "Jim Stewart: The Voice from Soulsville," *Billboard*, June 24, 1967, section 2, 30–31.

35. For a contemporary example of Charles discussing soul, see George E. Pitts, "Ray Charles Explains His 'Soul' Singing," *Pittsburgh Courier*, March 14, 1959.

36. Gerald Early has written about the "peculiar and penetrating gesture" of the Rascals' interest in musical styles associated with African American culture at the same time that Marvin Gaye was interested in becoming a lounge singer; Early, *One Nation under a Groove*, 10–11.

37. "'65 a Vintage Year for Atlantic," *Billboard*, January 1, 1966, 6.

38. C. L. Franklin had released recordings of his sermons on Chess in the 1950s and 1960s, helping him to establish connections within the music business.

39. Franklin's "Respect" was an interpretation of Otis Redding's 1965 single.

40. Remembered as the "King of Soul," Cooke was an important source for soul artists during the second half of the 1960s. For more on this historical revisionism, see Mark Burford, "Sam Cooke," 164–66. Wexler's notes for *I Never Loved a Man the Way I Love You* offer an example of remembering Cooke in this manner during the soul era.

41. Jon Landau, liner notes, Aretha Franklin, *Lady Soul*.

42. "Lady Soul: Singing It Like It Is," *Time*, June 28, 1968, 62–66.

43. For more on return (or reverse) migration, see Stewart E. Tolnay, "The African American 'Great Migration' and Beyond," *Annual Review of Sociology* 29 (2003): 209–32.

44. Revilot owner Don Davis, the well-known Detroit-based record man, led Banks to Stax. Davis also produced many popular singles released for this Memphis-based company between 1968 and 1975.

45. The Falcons' single "I Found a Love" featured a young backing group called the Ohio Untouchables, which was later renamed the Ohio Players.

46. There were many other connections to soul music in Detroit during the mid-1960s. Major companies like MGM recorded artists such as Spyder Turner (who had a hit in 1966 with his rendition of "Stand By Me"), while indies like Revilot, Groovesille, and Ric Tic released Darrell Banks's "Open the Door to Your Heart," the Parliaments' "(I Wanna) Testify," "Baby Please Come Back Home" by J. J. Barnes, and the Fantastic Four's, "The Whole World Is a Stage."

47. "Atlantic to Handle Distribution for Dial," *Billboard*, November 14, 1964. Atlantic was also interested in records created in Detroit. Atlantic distributed the 1962 Lu Pine single "I Found a Love"; "Atlantic-Atco Distrib for Lu Pine, Campus," *Billboard*, January 27, 1962, 5. (Lu Pine released the earliest singles by the Primettes, who later became the Supremes.) Atlantic also worked closely with Detroit label owner Ollie McLaughlin, distributing Deon Jackson's Motown-like single "Love Makes the World Go Round" on the Carla label and the Capitols' "Cool Jerk" on the Karen imprint; "Atco to Handle Jackson's Disc," *Billboard*, January 15, 1966, 18. (The Funk Brothers performed the backing track for "Cool Jerk.")

48. For more on Stax, see Rob Bowman, *Soulsville U.S.A.: The Story of Stax Records* (New York: Schirmer, 2003); Robert Gordon, *Respect Yourself: Stax Records and the Soul Explosion* (New York: Bloomsbury, 2013); Hughes, *Country Soul*, 44–67.

49. "Atlantic to Distribute 'Last Night,'" *Billboard*, May 29, 1961, 5. There were several imprints associated with Stax. The company first used the Satellite label, which Stewart and Axton discontinued in late 1961 in favor of Stax and Volt. Later imprints used by the company included Chalice, Safice, Hip, and Enterprise. For ease of nomenclature, I refer to the company's varied labels using the collective term Stax.

50. Redding's first four singles—"These Arms of Mine," "That's What My Heart Needs," "Pain in My Heart," and "Come To Me"—offer a great example of the manner in which Stax artists used musical self-dialogue that aligned with soul. Each of these songs was a compound meter ballad that used a similar tempo, key signature, and arrangement; the tempos of these performances are about (dotted quarter at) fifty-six to fifty-eight beats per minute; three of the songs are in B♭ major and the other is in F major; and all four records feature organ and piano that dutifully dictate triplets. Records by Stax by artists like Booker T. and the MGs, the Mar-Keys, and Rufus Thomas also exhibit similar aspects of self-dialogue.

51. Hughes, *Country Soul*, 44–79.

52. "Bell to Stax-Volt," *Billboard*, October 9, 1965, 12. Bell was appointed company vice president in mid-1967, which was covered heavily in the African American press: "Al Bell Is First Negro Veep of a Tennessee Disc Firm," *Dallas Post Tribune*, August 12, 1967; "Al Bell Named Veep of Stax-Volt Records," *Birmingham (AL) World*, August 16, 1967; "Al Bell First Negro Veep," *Milwaukee Star*, August 19, 1967.

53. Bowman, *Soulsville U.S.A.*, 61. For instances of Stax advertisements that refer to Memphis, see *Billboard* advertisements for "Last Night": "The Instrumental Hit from Memphis," May 29, 1961, 33; Otis Redding, "Respect" and *Otis Blue/ Otis Redding Sings Soul*: "Otis Redding Has a Smash Single—Otis Redding Has a Smash Album," September 11, 1965, 9; Carla Thomas, "B-A-B-Y": "An Exciting New Star," October 8, 1966, 7; various Stax artists: "New and Fantastic from Stax-Volt," November 26, 1966, 11; and Sam and Dave, "When Something Is Wrong with My Baby" and Booker T. and the MGs, "Hip Hug-Her": "That Great Memphis Sound," March 11, 1967, 9.

54. Memphis-based Hi Records also used the "Memphis Sound" as a slogan. "New from Hi Records," *Billboard,* June 25, 1966, 25.

55. For a study that views the construction of the "Memphis Sound" in opposition to the "Nashville Sound," see Hughes, *Country Soul,* 71.

56. Elton Whisenhunt, "The Memphis Sound: A Southern View," *Billboard,* June 12, 1965, 6.

57. Jim Delehant, "Otis Redding: Soul Survivor," *Hit Parader,* August 1967, quoted in "Whatever Success I Had Was through the Help of the Good Lord," *Rolling Stone,* January 20, 1968, 12–13. See also Jim Delehant, "Steve Cropper," *Hit Parader,* September 1967, 44–45; Jim Delehant, "Steve Cropper, Part 2," *Hit Parader,* October 1967, 42–43. This series continued throughout the year. Later interview subjects included Booker T. Jones, Al Jackson, Duck Dunn, Isaac Hayes and David Porter, and Eddie Floyd.

58. Guralnick writes, "When [Stax] began, neither of it's founders even knew what a record company was, let alone what a rhythm and blues record was supposed to sound like. The austere classicism of Stax did not come about by aesthetic choice but by necessity." *Sweet Soul Music,* 98.

59. Jerry Wexler and David Ritz, *Rhythm and the Blues: A Life in American Music* (New York: St. Martin's, 1993), 172–73.

60. Ward, *Just My Soul Responding,* 264. Ward cites a fascinating depiction of a Stax recording session from several years later led by Don Dixon that appears in Phyl Garland, *The Sound of Soul* (Chicago: Henry Regnery, 1969). Unfortunately, many of the pre-1968 Stax masters were destroyed in a 1979 warehouse fire that housed Atlantic's masters; Bill Holland, "Labels Strive to Rectify Past Archival Problems," *Billboard,* July 12, 1997.

61. S. Smith has written that Motown's use of this "cartographic emblem reinforced the idea that . . . the sound was not from anywhere in America but was deeply tied to a specific locale"; *Dancing in the Street,* 12.

62. Alan E. Abrams, *Hype and Soul: Behind the Scenes at Motown* (Lilleshall, UK: Templestreet, 2011); Alan Abrams, telephone interview by author, May 21, 2008.

63. Motown often associated with politicians and government organizations during Abrams's tenure as press agent. [Abrams], "Command Performance for Detroit's Supremes"; [Alan E. Abrams], "City Honors Berry Gordy," Motown press release, May 27, 1965, AAC.

64. Abrams has said of this project, "The Senator Baker liner notes concept got me the job [at Stax], pure and simple"; Alan Abrams, e-mail message to author, March 27, 2009.

65. [Alan E. Abrams], "U.S. Senate Leaders Unite in Support and Praise of 'The Memphis Sound,'" Stax press release, April 28, 1967, AAC.

66. This presentation occurred on May 25, 1967. Several telegrams and letters concerning the plaque presentation are held in the AAC. (In one letter, dated May 3, 1967, Baker's press assistant Edgar H. Miller Jr. suggested that Stax artists might present him with a plaque but requested that Abrams refrain from calling a large-scale press conference [AAC].) Abrams led other Motown-like press-oriented projects at Stax. In early 1967 he started discussions about a "Stay in School" campaign with the U.S. Department of Labor; Jon Massey, letter to

Al Abrams Associates, March 17, 1967, AAC. Stax eventually recorded a special promotional album called *Stay in School, Don't Be a Dropout*, which was released in a small run of five thousand copies.

67. Don Moore, "Carla and Stax are Synonomous [*sic*]," *Michigan Chronicle*, April 29, 1967.

68. Articles from the Detroit press reflecting many of Abrams's Stax-oriented press releases are held in the AAC.

69. "Our Girls Still Ahead," *Michigan Chronicle*, May 13, 1967, section B, 6; "UAW Begins Talks with General Motors," *Washington Post*, November 28, 1967. See also S. Smith, *Dancing in the Street*, 37–38.

70. Bowman, *Soulsville U.S.A.*, 11. The 1965 Booker T. and MGs single "Bootleg" was a stylistic response to Jr. Walker and the All Stars' "Shotgun"; see Bowman, *Soulsville U.S.A.*, 74. The MGs also recorded a number of Motown covers during the 1960s, including "The One Who Really Loves You," "Get Ready," and "I Hear a Symphony."

71. Ibid., 91.

72. The Otis and Carla single was released in mid-April 1967. A version by the song's author, Lowell Fulsom, had been released several months before; it had peaked in popularity during the middle of February.

73. The Temptations track had been released several months before and was still in heavy rotation on Top 40 radio when "Tramp" was recorded in January 1967.

74. Esther Edwards, "The Role of Youth in a Changing Society," speech delivered at the Annual Workshop for Front People, October 26, 1967, EMU.

75. For more on Whitfield, see Fink, "Goal-Directed Soul?"; Denise Hall, "Norman Whitfield," *Black Music* 3 (1976): 14; Paul Zollo, "The Motown Memories of Norman Whitfield: Legendary Writer of 'War,' 'I Heard It through the Grapevine,' and 'Just My Imagination' Looks Back," in *Calling Out Around the World: A Motown Reader*, ed. Kingsley Abbott (London: Helter Skelter, 2000), 144–48.

76. There have also been popular non-Motown recordings of this song by Credence Clearwater Revival, the Average White Band, Zapp, the Slits, and many others.

77. Quoted in Dahl, *Motown*, 317. This first version was intended for the Isley Brothers on the corporate tape file card; Gaye's version was originally intended for the Temptations.

78. "Gladys Knight and the Pips," promotional booklet, ca. 1967, HAC.

79. Patricia A. Turner, *I Heard It through the Grapevine: Rumor in African-American Culture* (Berkeley: University of California Press, 1999).

80. Bobby Taylor's version follows the Pips arrangement but was recorded down a step (in B♭ Major). The Temptations' version is in C major, but its style is unlike the other four Whitfield-produced versions from the period.

81. This lead sheet is reprinted in Slutsky, *Standing in the Shadows*, 34. It is curious that the sheet includes lyrical incipits, which would have been of little use to session players and may be an indication that it was not actually used for a recording session.

82. Gordy, *To Be Loved*, 275. This is supported by a November 16, 1968, "Top Ten" listing in the *Michigan Chronicle*, which showed Gaye's version at number three despite the fact that was not released officially as a single until two weeks later.

83. At the time, Gaye's "Grapevine" became Motown's best-selling single to date, an ironic twist given the record's history of being rejected by Quality Control.

84. Knight's version places more rhythmic emphasis on the eighth-note subdivision.

85. The organ (with reverb enhancement) faintly supports the electric piano introduction.

86. Unlike Knight's version, the master tapes for Gaye's recording reveal very little electronic gimmickry: A single band track and three overdub sessions (lead vocals, backing vocals, and orchestral instruments) were used to complete the recording, all in complete performances.

87. The group's only charting single from this early period was "(You're My) Dream Come True," which rose to number twenty-two on the R&B chart. Robinson's first hit for the group was "The Way You Do the Things You Do," which was released on January 23, 1964, and peaked at number eleven. Many of these Robinson-produced songs were written with collaborators like Bobby Rogers, Ronnie White, Pete Moore, and Cornelius Grant.

88. Over a period of the next two years the group released four more Robinson-produced singles, none of which charted lower than number four on the *Billboard* R&B charts. (Two of these singles had B-sides that also charted.)

89. For Otis Williams's memories of this change, see Otis Williams and Patricia Romanowski, *Temptations* (New York: Cooper Square Press, 2002), 133–34.

90. For a detailed discussion of the background and musical style of "Cloud Nine," see Fink, "Goal-Directed Soul?"

91. "Cloud Nine" and the Diana Ross and the Supremes' "Love Child" were among Motown's first topical hit songs. For Gordy's recollection of "Cloud Nine," see *To Be Loved*, 276–77. To be sure, "Cloud Nine" retains some key elements of the Motown Sound, including an extremely active bass, a vocal composite featuring heavy call-and-response between Edwards's lead and backing vocals by other members of the group, and a Motown Beat, which starts during the record's conclusive section. Fink claims this rhythmic feature was used as a "tonic rhythm" and reads its appearance late in the record, accompanied by a shift to the major mode, as the culmination of several "large-scale rhythmic 'key-areas'"; Fink, "Goal-Directed Soul?" 203.

92. Five of these records—"Masterpiece," "Zoom," "Smiling Faces Sometimes," "Stop the War Now," and "Papa Was a Rolling Stone"—were longer than twelve minutes! In many cases, extended versions appeared on albums, while singles were edited for radio play. These extended album tracks also exploited the stereo field in ways that Motown productions had not done in the past. (Motown stopped releasing albums in mono in late 1968.)

93. Whitfield had a notable interest in "African culture" during this period. He used a Swahili title for "Ungena Za Ulimwengu (Unite the World)" and

claimed to have informally studied African rhythm: "When we first did a song called 'Cloud Nine' on the Temptations, I started studying African rhythms on my own, and I wanted to know how to make a song have as much impact without using a regular 2/4 or 4/4 backbeat"; Zollo, "Motown Memories," 146.

94. Examples of this are the zenith groove of "Papa Was a Rolling Stone" and the opening measures of "Psychedelic Shack."

95. Records such as "Runaway Child Running Wild" (between 0:24 and 0:36) and "Funky Music Sho Nuff Turns Me On" (from 2:40 to the end) incorporate similar textures using vocables.

96. Whitfield's most popular message song was Edwin Starr's "War."

97. Ironically, psychedelic soul was less popular among rock fans during the late 1960s and early 1970s than more "pure" forms of southern soul or the funk of James Brown and Parliament. Despite brisk sales, many rock critics saw Whitfield's overtures to hippie culture as yet another type of formulaic Motown. Vince Aletti, "Decline of Norman Whitfield," *Rolling Stone*, April 27, 1972, 52.

98. For more on "riff" as a theoretical concept, see Mark Spicer, "British Pop-Rock Music in the Post-Beatles Era: Three Analytical Studies" (PhD diss., Yale University, 2001), 10.

99. It was not out of character for a Motown hit from the mid-1960s to have a harmonically static or repetitive verse (see "Dancing in the Street" and "Ain't Too Proud to Beg"), but earlier songs always exhibited some sort of harmonic change in their chorus or bridge sections. For more on the role of repetition in funk and related styles, see Luis-Manuel Garcia, "On and On: Repetition as Process and Pleasure in Electronic Dance Music," *Music Theory Online* 11, no. 4 (2005) http://www.mtosmt.org/issues/mto.05.11.4/mto.05.11.4.garcia.html; David Brackett, *Interpreting Popular Music* (Berkeley: University of California Press, 1995), 108–56; Robert Walser, "Groove as Niche: Earth, Wind, and Fire," in *This Is Pop: In Search of the Elusive at Experience Music Project*, ed. Eric Weisbard (Cambridge, MA: Harvard University Press, 2004), 266–78.

100. For a diagram of these entrances and exits, see Timothy S. Hughes, "Groove and Flow: Six Analytical Essays on the Music of Stevie Wonder" (PhD diss., University of Washington, 2003), 122.

101. Mitchell Morris also discusses the ambiguity of meter in this record; see *Persistence of Sentiment*, 51–52.

102. Al Calloway, "An Introduction to Soul," in *Smiling through the Apocalypse: "Esquire's" History of the Sixties*, ed. Harold Hayes (New York: McCall, 1970), 708–12.

103. Gayle Wald, *It's Been Beautiful: Soul! and Black Power Television* (Durham, NC: Duke University Press, 2015); Christopher P. Lehman, *A Critical History of Soul Train on Television* (Jefferson, NC: McFarland, 2008).

104. For more on the dissolution of this agreement, see Bowman, *Soulsville U.S.A.*, 108–35.

105. [Alan E. Abrams], "Do Mixed Marriages Work," undated press release, AAC.

106. Bowman, *Soulsville U.S.A.*, 181–83. Bowman cites the infiltration of non-Memphis musicians during this period as an important turning point for the music of Stax; Bowman, "Stax," 286.

107. Early, *One Nation under a Groove*, 87.

108. "Entertainment Writer Blasts Motown Record Corporation," *Pittsburgh New Courier*, September 30, 1967, 9. Ivory had a long history with Motown. He had worked for the company in the early 1960s, before starting his well-known celebrity column "Among the Stars," which was syndicated in various African American newspapers.

109. "Gordy Bares Expansion Plans," *Chicago Defender*, October 30, 1967; "Two Named at Motown in Major Expansion Move," *New York Amsterdam News*, November 4, 1967.

110. Black Forum released eight important spoken word albums. For more on Black Forum, see Pat Thomas, *Listen Whitey: The Sights and Sounds of Black Power, 1965–1975* (Seattle: Fantagraphics, 2012); Charles E. Sykes, "The Black Forum Label: Motown Joins the Revolution," *ARSC Journal* 46 (2015): 1–42. See also S. Smith, *Dancing in the Street*. The company also showed a renewed interested in jazz and gospel during the late 1960s and early 1970s. Jazz albums during the period included Jonah Jones's *Along Came Jonah* (1969) and *A Little Dis, A Little Dat* (1970), Red Jones's *Red Jones Steeerikes Back* (1969), and Joe Harnell's *Moving On* (1969). Gospel compilations included *Shades of Gospel Soul* (1970) and *Rock Gospel: The Key to the Kingdom* (1971).

Chapter Four

1. Michael Pickering, "'A Jet Ornament to Society': Black Music in Nineteenth-Century Britain," in *Black Music in Britain: Essays on the Afro-Asian Contribution to Popular Music*, ed. Paul Oliver (Philadelphia: Open University Press, 1990), 30.

2. Paul Oliver, introduction to Oliver, *Black Music in Britain*, 11.

3. Ibid., 15. See also *Black Music Research Journal* 29, no. 2, 30, no. 1, edited by Howard Rye, which discuss the work of the Southern Syncopated Orchestra.

4. Oliver, introduction, 13.

5. Howard Rye, "Fearsome Means of Discord: Early Encounters with Jazz," in Oliver, *Black Music in Britain*, 55. There was a policy that even exchanges needed to occur when importing musical talent from abroad; in general, the American Federation of Musicians was stricter about these exchanges and was largely responsible for the protracted span when exchanges did not happen. "Jazzers' Importation Gets into Parliament," *Variety*, November 24, 1922, 2; "There'll Always Be an England," *Variety*, February 2, 1946, 33–34; "AFM Ban on Foreign Musicians Causes Pitt Symph. Mex. Headaches," *Variety*, March 19, 1947, 42; "Band Business Speculates on Stand by Petrillo to Bar Foreign Outfits," *Variety*, May 25, 1949, 36; "Heath Asks AFM English-American Exchange of Bands," *Variety*, October 23, 1954, 13; "Petrillo Relaxing Bars on Anglo-U. S. Band Exchange; Heath-Kenton Swap," *Variety*, October 26, 1955, 41–44; "Show Biz's Universal 'Open Door,'" *Variety*, November 9, 1955, 2. See also Martin Cloonan and Matt Brennan, "Alien Invasions: The British Musicians' Union and Foreign Musicians," *Popular Music* 32 (May 2013): 277–95. Conflicts over work permits between the AFM and the British Musician's Union continued into the 1960s. See Michael Roberts, "A Working Class Hero Is Something to

Be: The American Musicians' Union's Attempt to Ban the Beatles," *Popular Music* 29 (2010): 1–16.

6. Roberta Freund Schwartz, *How Britain Got the Blues: The Transmission and Reception of British Blues Style in the United Kingdom* (Burlington, VT: Ashgate, 2007), 34–45.

7. "London Rocks 'n' Rolls as Bill Haley Arrives," *New York Times*, February 6, 1957; Schwartz, *How Britain Got the Blues*, 58–63.

8. There were also notable trips to European countries by other R&B artists during this time. In 1961 Ray Charles performed in Zurich and later appeared at the Antibes Jazz Festival in France. Fats Domino also appeared at this festival in 1962.

9. Less popular papers were *Disc Weekly* and *Mersey Beat* (later *Music Echo*), which combined to form *Disc and Music Echo* in 1966.

10. Roberta Freund Schwartz has traced the history of African-American imports in Britain as far back as the late 1910s; Schwartz, *How Britain Got the Blues*, 5–9. See also the large boxed set *Black Europe: The Sounds and Images of Black People in Europe, Pre-1927*, Bear Family BCD-16095, 2013.

11. Decca in Britain was a different company from Decca in the United States. See Broven, *Record Makers and Breakers*, 395–414; Schwartz, *How Britain Got the Blues*, 29–34. The London imprint, under the auspices of U.S. Decca, also released British music in the United States during this period.

12. Pye and Island were other companies that released imports from the United States; "Pye Records Bringing American R&B, Jazz Series to England," *Billboard*, September 4, 1961.

13. This section was later called "International New Reports."

14. The opening editorial essays in *Cash Box*, presumably written by editor Irv Lichtman, often discussed internationalization: see "The Road to Export Profits Is Paved with Market Research," *Cash Box*, January 5, 1963, 45; "From Abroad," *Cash Box*, January 12, 1963, 3; "The One World Record Market," *Cash Box*, February 1, 1964, 3.

15. For a British-oriented history of Motown, see S. Davis, *Motown*. See also Mike Ritson and Stuart Russell, *The In Crowd: The Story of the Northern and Rare Soul Scene* (London: Bee Cool, 1999), vol. 1. For a complete history of Motown recordings in the UK, see Terry Wilson, *Tamla Motown: The Stories behind the UK Singles* (London: Cherry Red, 2009).

16. Many of Marv Johnson's releases also appeared on British imprints. London released these singles in Australia as well. Although he was officially signed to United Artists, Johnson was the first of Gordy's artists to travel abroad, visiting Australia in May 1960 to perform in a "Big Show" concert in Sydney that was organized by legendary music promoter Lee Gordon; Ainslie Baker, "Listen Here," *Australian Women's Weekly*, August 17, 1960, 39. There was a later Tamla-Motown Appreciation Society in Australia run by Lindsay Farr; Lindsay Farr, telephone interview by author, August 12, 2015.

17. "Please Mr. Postman" also appeared in the Netherlands and Ireland (both on Fontana), Australia (Top Rank International), and Canada (Tamla).

18. "Oriole's Label All-American," *Billboard*, September 15, 1962, 18. See also

John Schroeder, *Sex and Violins: My Affair with Life, Love, and Music* (Brighton, UK: Penn Press, 2009).

19. The major British companies at the time were EMI, Philips, Decca, and Pye.

20. This single was released on October 11, 1963. See "EMI Acquires Tamla-Motown for Britain," *Billboard*, September 28, 1963, 3. A few Stateside singles also appeared in other countries, such as Sweden, Ireland, Portugal, New Zealand, and India.

21. Iain Chambers, *Urban Rhythms: Pop Music and Popular Culture* (New York: St. Martin's, 1985), 1–112.

22. Many British youth also became interested in forms of music associated with the West Indies; Orlando Patterson, "The Dance Invasion," *New Society*, September 15, 1966, 401–3.

23. Dick Hebdige, *Subculture: The Meaning of Style* (New York: Routledge, 2002). See also Stuart Hall and Tony Jefferson, eds., *Resistance through Rituals: Youth Subcultures in Post-War Britain* (London: Hutchinson, 1975); Charles Hamblett and Jane Deverson, *Generation X* (Greenwich, CT: Gold Metal, 1964). For an interesting contemporaneous perspective on these movements in Merseyside, see Colin Fletcher, "Beat and Gangs on Merseyside," *New Society*, February 20, 1964, 11–14.

24. Tony Jefferson has written that the Teds' manner of wearing Savile Row Edwardian suits expressed both their "social reality" and their "social 'aspirations'"; Tony Jefferson, "Cultural Responses of the Teds," in Hall and Jefferson, *Resistance through Rituals*, 81–86.

25. Gilroy, *There Ain't No Black*, 163. See also Anthony Marks, "Young, Gifted and Black: Afro-American and Afro-Caribbean Music in Britain, 1963–88," in Oliver, *Black Music in Britain*, 102; Chambers, *Urban Rhythms*, 24–31.

26. Dick Hebdige, "The Meaning of Mod," in Hall and Jefferson, *Resistance through Rituals*, 87–97.

27. Chambers, *Urban Rhythms*, 69–75. I conducted several interviews and e-mail exchanges with British fans of Motown who listened actively to American music during the period in question but did not associate with a particular subculture or group. These included: Keith Hughes and Eric Charge, interview by author, April 12, 2008, and July 16, 2009; Keith Hughes, e-mail message to author, January 30, 2009; Eric Charge, e-mail message to author, January 31, 2009; David Nathan, interview by author, March 15, 2009; David Bell, telephone interview by author, October 12, 2009; and Alan Curtis, telephone interview by author, October 13, 2009.

28. Chambers, *Urban Rhythms*, 69.

29. Christian O'Connell, *Paul Oliver: Blues, How Do You Do?* (Ann Arbor: University of Michigan Press, 2015).

30. Hebdige, *Subculture*, 46–54.

31. Christine Jacqueline Feldman, *We Are the Mods: A Transnational History of a Youth Subculture* (New York: Peter Lang, 2009).

32. Marks, "Young, Gifted and Black," 104.

33. David Nathan, e-mail message to author, December 9, 2011.

34. Jeremy Reed, *John Stephen: The King of Carnaby Street* (London: Haus, 2010).

35. Peter Burton, *Parallel Lives* (Boston: Alyson, 1985); Gary Pulsifer, "Peter Burton: Writer and Publisher Who Played a Pioneering Role in Gay Journalism," *Guardian*, November 8, 2011.

36. Burton, *Parallel Lives*, 31. Pete Waterman, a member of the British-based 1980s songwriting and production team SAW, has cited similar connections between the Tamla-Motown crowd in the UK and the gay community: "I knew the gay scene very well and knew all the DJs, because it was the old Tamla Motown market, I knew there were potentially 15–20,000 buyers for any record you made in that vein"; quoted in Mark Cunningham, *Good Vibrations: A History of Record Production* (London: Sanctuary, 1996), 313–14.

37. Randall, *Dusty!*

38. Peter Fryer, *Staying Power: The History of Black People in Britain* (London: Pluto Press, 1984).

39. Gilroy, *There Ain't No Black*, 79–85. In addition to R&B, white listeners explored forms such as Trinidadian steel pan music followed by ska, or what was often called Blue Beat after the British record label of the same name. Interest in pan music began after World War I and became especially popular in 1951; see John Cowley, "London Is the Place: Caribbean Music in the Context of Empire: 1900–60," in Oliver, *Black Music in Britain*, 58–76; Thomas Chatburn, "Trinidad All Stars: The Steel Pan Movement in Britain," in Oliver, *Black Music in Britain*, 118–36. For more on the rise of ska and Blue Beat music, see Marks, "Young, Gifted and Black," 105–6.

40. Norman Pannell and Fenner Brockway, *Immigration: What Is the Answer?* (London: Routledge, 1966), 3; Peter Griffiths, *A Question of Colour* (London: Leslie Frewin, 1966), 9; Lord Elton, *The Unarmed Invasion: A Survey of Afro-Asian Immigration* (London: Geoffrey Bles, 1965), 7. Gilroy has outlined several recurring anxieties surrounding immigration in Britain: blacks were more criminal than whites, a new immigrant population was causing housing issues, there were more instances of miscegenation because of this influx, and new black residents showed a general apathy toward venereal diseases. Gilroy, *There Ain't No Black*, 72–113. See also Dilip Hiro, *Black British, White British: A History of Race Relations in Britain* (London: Grafton, 1991).

41. James Maycock, *The Motown Invasion*, BBC Four, originally aired February 20, 2009.

42. Chambers, *Urban Rhythms*, 72. For more on British appropriation of African American music, see Neil A. Wynn, ed., *Cross the Water Blues: African American Music in Europe* (Jackson: University of Mississippi Press, 2007); Randall, *Dusty!*, 42–43.

43. A partial list of rerecorded Motown songs released in the UK between 1963 and 1967 appears in appendix 2.

44. The Beatles version included on *With the Beatles* is perhaps the best-known British cover of "Money." At the time, the recording by Bern Elliot and the Fenmen was only the recording of the song to reach the British singles charts.

45. Modal ambiguity was also present in Richard (Popcorn) Wylie's Motown-based version of the song from 1961.

46. The ascent to scale degree 4 is achieved through a slide in some instances.

The Beatles recorded "Money (That's What I Want)" for their Decca audition on New Year's Day 1962. This "Decca Audition" recording of "Money," incorrectly attributed to the Silver Beetles, was released in 1982 on an album called *The Complete Silver Beetles* and has since been widely available as a bootleg (or unofficial release).

47. *Record Retailer* was the standard industry publication for chart information in the UK during the 1960s. Brian Poole and the Tremeloes was the group that Decca chose to sign instead of the Beatles in early 1962. During the same week that Brian Poole and the Tremeloes' "Do You Love Me" hit the top of the British charts another version of the song recorded by the Dave Clark Five hovered at the bottom of the Top 40. Unlike Poole's recording, Clark's version became popular in the United States; in June 1964 it nearly reached the top ten of the *Billboard* "Hot 100."

48. This pitch rests on scale degree 5 (the tone C in the Contours version and A in the Tremeloes recording).

49. This clip exists only in private collections. At time of writing it is available on YouTube.

50. Frank Gilpin, dir., *The Best of British Swinging UK* (1963; JEF Films, 2004), DVD.

51. "Many people know, and many don't that the original of this was a million-seller in the States just about a year ago," wrote *New Record Mirror* columnist Norman Jopling in late 1963; Norman Jopling, "The Great Unknowns: No. 14—The Contours," *New Record Mirror*, September 28, 1963, 4.

52. Peter Jones, "'I'm No Copyist' Says Brian Poole," *Record Mirror*, November 16, 1963, 12.

53. Reader Sammy Donnachie wrote to *Record Mirror*, "Please stop moaning about British records not being original. Why shouldn't Brian Poole, The Beatles, etc., delve into the past for material, when American stars like Connie Francis, Del Shannon, Peggy March and Johnny Tillotson and so on cover the best of the current British material"; letter to the editor, *Record Mirror*, February 8, 1964, 2.

54. "I Can Dance" begins with the lines, "You said you love me / and I know it's true / so I'm gonna dance girl / all night with you."

55. Jones, "I'm No Copyist," 12.

56. Peter Jones, "Brian Poole Answers His Critics: 'I Can Dance' Is No Copy of 'Do You Love Me,'" *Record Mirror*, December 7, 1963, 6. Just after the British controversy over "I Can Dance," the Contours released their own answer song to "Do You Love Me" called "Can You Do It," which reached the top twenty of the *Cash Box* "Top 50 in R&B Locations" chart. (There was no *Billboard* R&B chart at the time.)

57. Langley Johnson, "'I Was Wrong' Says Brian," *Record Mirror*, February 1, 1964, 7.

58. This recording reached the midrange of the *Record Retailer* chart in late 1964.

59. The group's first two hits, "Hello Little Girl" and "I'm In Love," were both Lennon and McCartney originals. Epstein also managed Cilla Black, Billy J. Kramer, and Tommy Quickly.

60. The Fourmost's live performance of the song was much stiffer than the Four Tops' version. A video of the Four Tops performing "Baby I Need Your Loving" on the Lloyd Thaxton Show in 1966 appears on the Four Tops, *Reach Out: Definitive Performances, 1965–1973*, Hip-O/Motown B-001G9LVB6, 2008, DVD. The Fourmost performed this song live on *Ready Steady Go!* on November 6, 1964. This performance is not available commercially. At time of writing it is available on YouTube.

61. Peter Jones, "'Why We Copied the 4 Tops': Peter Jones Talks to the Fourmost," *Record Mirror*, November 21, 1964, 4; emphasis in original. Martin's role in the recording is not clear. He certainly advised the group and had produced earlier recordings. The physical disc credits Johnny Scott with "accompaniment direction."

62. Mark Lewisohn cites a Beatles performance of "Please Mr. Postman" from March 1962 as the first appearance of Motown material on the BBC; Lewisohn, *All These Years—Tune In: Extended Special Edition* (London: Little, Brown, 2013), 1:1123. The Beatles' versions of "Money," "Please Mr. Postman," and "You Really Got a Hold on Me" were released first in the UK on the album *With the Beatles* on November 2, 1963, and subsequently released in the United States on the LP *The Beatles' Second Album* on April 10, 1964. These three songs were the only Motown pieces performed live by the Beatles; Mark Lewisohn, *The Complete Beatles Chronicle* (London: Hamlyn, 2003), 361–65. Berry Gordy recalls that Beatles manager Brian Epstein asked for a discount rate on the publishing royalty, which may explain the large number of Motown songs on *With the Beatles*; Gordy, *To Be Loved*, 203–5.

63. Lennon mumbles an unclear lyric at the end of the second verse of "Postman," which makes it clear that he learned the words from the Marvelettes record. (This corresponds to the passage at 0:52 in the original Marvelettes recording.)

64. A documentary about this jukebox, directed by Christopher Walker, was broadcast in the UK on the *South Bank Show* and aired in the United States on PBS in 2004 and 2006. This program is not available commercially.

65. After reading an early version of this book, British fan Keith Hughes responded with the following comment: "For me and my school friends, the emergence of the Beatles in 1963 was a hugely transformative experience: we had not been big fans of pop music until then. We wanted to know everything about the Fab Four, and consumed all the newspaper, radio and magazine material avidly. This obsession naturally included their musical tastes. I bought my first two American LPs (*Chuck Berry On Stage* and *The Shirelles' Greatest Hits*) purely on John Lennon's 'recommendation': I had never heard either act before, either on record or live. I knew Lennon was keen on something called 'Tamla Motown,' but despite enquiry at numerous record shops could not get enlightenment. I thought it was probably some kind of dance craze. Eventually, in the fall of 1963, I found an EP titled *The R&B Chartmakers* on a market stall; on the back cover, at the bottom in tiny lettering, were the words 'A Tamla Motown Production.' I had never heard of any of the acts—Martha and the Vandellas, the Miracles, Marvin Gaye and the Marvelettes. I bought the record, took it home and put it on the

record player and the first notes of 'Heat Wave' emerged. I never looked back."
Keith Hughes, e-mail message to author, November 8, 2014.

66. Ray Coleman, "Mary Wells: 'We've Got a Lot to Thank the Beatles For,'"
Melody Maker, June 20, 1964, 7.

67. "Blind Date," *Melody Maker*, December 5, 1964, 11.

68. Lennon's fan club recording was discussed in [Alan E. Abrams], "Motown
Now Number One in U. S. Single Record Sales," Motown press release, January
3, 1966, AAC. See also [Alan E. Abrams], "Beatles Boost Detroit," September 10,
1964, AAC; "'Anatomy of Pop' Analyzes Music," *Chicago Daily Defender*, January
10, 1966, 20; Lee Ivory, "Among the Stars," *Chicago Defender*, February 5, 1966,
national edition, 15. For commentary on the Beatles recording at Motown and
Stax, see Walter Everett, "Detroit and Memphis: The Soul of Revolver," in *Every
Sound There Is: The Beatles "Revolver" and the Transformation of Rock and Roll*, ed.
Russell Reising (Aldershot, UK: Ashgate, 2003), 25–57.

69. [Alan E. Abrams], Motown press release, March 22, 1965, AAC.

70. Motown also initiated a group of tracks during this period for a Supremes
"Around the World" album, which was never completed.

71. All of this occurred on February 7, 1964.

72. Stephen Barnard cites other structural differences that had made radio a
challenging mechanism for promotion in the UK during the period immediately
following World War II, including the lack of available transistors, a difference
in affluence levels among teens, and fewer cars available for youth in British society. Stephen Barnard, *On the Radio: Music Radio in Britain* (Philadelphia: Open
University Press, 1989), 35.

73. Ibid., 33.

74. Also working in radio were "pluggers" like David Most, who promoted
Motown's records to British radio and Jobete's songs to British groups. In a 1972
interview, Most discussed the process of convincing British record producers
and disc jockeys to use Motown records during the mid-1960s, recalling that
"[Motown] was hard to get over to them" because it was perceived largely as
music most appropriate for dance halls. Michael Wale, *Voxpop: Profiles of the Pop
Process* (London: Harrap, 1972), 286. See also Robin Leach, letter to Al Abrams,
October 6, [1965], AAC.

75. Adrienne Lowy, "*Ready Steady Go!* Televisual Pop Style and the Careers
of Dusty Springfield, Cilla Black, Sandie Shaw and Lulu," in *Popular Music and
Television in Britain*, ed. Ian Inglis (Burlington, VT: Ashgate, 2010), 71–84.

76. This publication changed names and added color photos beginning with
the issue dated November 13, 1963.

77. Norman Jopling, "The Great Unknowns," *New Record Mirror*, March 9,
1963, 6; emphasis in original. This series covered several other Tamla-Motown
artists in later installments; see Norman Jopling, "The Great Unknowns—Mary
Wells," *New Record Mirror*, May 4, 1963, 7; Norman Jopling, "Great Unknowns:
No. 7—The Marvelettes," *New Record Mirror*, June 1, 1963, 3; and Jopling, "Great
Unknowns: No. 14—The Contours."

78. Schwartz, *How Britain Got the Blues*, 130–31. For a general history of the live
music environment in the UK after World War II, see Simon Frith, Matt Brennan,

Martin Cloonan, and Emma Webster, eds., *The History of Live Music in Britain*, vol. 1, *1950–1967* (Burlington, VT: Ashgate, 2013).

79. Bob Dawbarn, "Well—What Is R&B?" *Melody Maker*, March 30, 1963, 6. See also "Rhythm Plus Blues Doesn't Mean R&B," *Melody Maker*, January 4, 1964, 8; George Webb, "The Year of Reckoning for Trad," *Melody Maker*, January 11, 1964, 6; "Trad Takes a Beating," *Melody Maker*, January 18, 1964, 8; and Chris Roberts, "To Be: Or Not to R&B," *Melody Maker*, August 29, 1964, 7.

80. Many trad fans did not like these changes, feeing as if R&B musicians were overturning their scene; Chambers, *Urban Rhythms*, 66.

81. Eagle also edited *R&B Scene* and Stevens managed the Sue Records reissue label for Island Records in addition to serving as secretary for the British-based Chuck Berry Appreciation Society. Bill Sykes, *Sit Down! Listen to This! The Roger Eagle Story* (Manchester, UK: Empire, 2012).

82. A wide range of appreciation societies proliferated in Britain at the time on topics ranging from amateur cinema to football. For more on the British Jazz Appreciation Society, see Roberta Freund Schwartz, "Preaching the Gospel of the Blues: Blues Evangelists in Britain," in Wynn, *Cross the Water Blues*, 145–66, esp. 150; and George McKay, *Circular Breathing: The Cultural Politics of Jazz in Britain* (Durham, NC: Duke University Press, 2005), 226–38, esp. 227. For a general discussion of the role of fandom in popular culture, see Joli Jensen, "Fandom as Pathology: The Consequences of Characterization," in *The Adoring Audience: Fan Culture and Popular Media*, ed. Lisa A. Lewis (London: Routledge, 1992), 9–29; John Fiske, "The Cultural Economy of Fandom," in Lewis, *Adoring Audience*, 30–49; and Lawrence Grossberg, "Is There a Fan in the House? The Affective Sensibility of Fandom," in Lewis, *Adoring Audience*, 50–65.

83. Keith Rylatt, *Hitsville! The Birth of Tamla Motown* (Derbyshire: Modus The House of Soul, 2016). Other British fan-based organizations acknowledged in the pages of *Hitsville U.S.A.* included the Dionne Warwick and the Shirelles Fan Club (Gloria Marcantonio, secretary); the Scepter-Wand Appreciation Society (Gloria Marcantonio, secretary); the Nina Simone Appreciation Society (David Nathan, secretary); the James Brown Admiration Society (Alan Curtis, secretary); TCB (Jackie Lee, secretary); the Irma Thomas Fan Club (Bob Nessling, secretary); the Inez and Charlie Foxx Fan Club (Chris Lorimer, secretary); and the Barbara Lynn Fan Club. Other contemporary British publications included *R&B Monthly, R&B Scene, Fame-Goldwax Followers (Soul Survey), R&B Gazette, Soul Beat, Blues Unlimited, Jazzbeat,* and *Blues World.* For more on these publications, see Schwartz, *How Britain Got the Blues*, 169–71; Guralnick, *Sweet Soul Music*, 414; "Britons Launch R&B Gazette," *Billboard*, June 29, 1963, 6.

84. As was customary, Godin referred to himself as secretary. For more on Godin, see Richard Williams, "Dave Godin," *Guardian*, October 16, 2004. Rylatt also considers Clive Stone's leadership role in the TMAS; *Hitsville!*.

85. It is widely accepted that Godin had financial backing from Motown, but the level and timing of this support is not clear.

86. In January 1965 the group's newsletter reported that current membership was over five hundred and that this number was expected to surpass one thousand in a matter of months.

87. Malcolm Harrison, "Report from Liverpool," *Hitsville U.S.A.* 1, no. 6 (June 1965): 116–17.

88. This was published jointly with a group called the Mary Wells Fan Club, also led by Godin, which predated the TMAS. In early 1964 Wells was the most popular Motown artist in the UK, winning best female singer in the *Record Mirror* "R&B Poll" with 1,617 votes (March 25, 1964, 4).

89. Mike Carlyle, letter to the editor, *Hitsville U.S.A.* 1, no. 5 (May 1965): 96. This issue also contains a letter that defends covering American black music. "I'm afraid I have a complaint. Not about the club or the magazine but about your intolerant attitude to 'inferior' British groups and especially the Stones. I realise that one shouldn't try to reform attitudes to agree with one's own, but it strikes me that the attitude you are taking against these poor unfortunates is rather a mean, bigoted one. . . . I am eternally grateful to the Stones because it is through them that my tastes have expanded to T[amla] M[otown]." Mary Russell, letter to the editor, *Hitsville U.S.A.* 1, no. 5 (May 1965): 97.

90. The Rolling Stones released no Motown songs in single form during this period, but they did record several versions as album tracks. One set of examples appears on their first full-length work, a 1964 eponymous LP released in Britain (the American version of this album was called *England's Newest Hitmakers*). This collection includes a version of "Can I Get a Witness" and an answer song entitled "Now I've Got a Witness," an instrumental version of the Motown piece. The group later recorded "Hitch Hike," which was released on both the U.S. and UK versions of *Out of Our Heads* in late 1965.

91. Dave [Godin], "Dear Swinger and Friend," *Mary Wells and Motown News* 1, no. 5 (ca. June 1964): 45–46.

92. Kimasi Lionel John Browne, "'Soul or Nothing': The Formation of Cultural Identity on the British Northern Soul Scene" (PhD diss., University of California, Los Angeles, 2005), 353–54. See also Williams, "Dave Godin." Godin was seven years older than Jagger and was known for his impressive record collection; Rylatt, *Hitsville!*, 17.

93. For more on Godin's activism, see Williams, "Dave Godin." References to Godin's various social causes appear in *Mary Wells and Motown News* 1, no. 4 (ca. June 1964): 38 (Muscular Dystrophy Group); *Hitsville U.S.A.* 1, no. 2 (February 1965): 38 (Muscular Dystrophy Group and Oxfam); and *Hitsville U.S.A.* 1, no. 9 (November 1965): 163 (a guide dog project).

94. This book had been published four years earlier. It received renewed attention at the time because of a film version released in May 1964 in the United States.

95. [Godin], "Dear Swinger and Friend," *Mary Wells and Motown News.*

96. "Editorial," *Hitsville U.S.A. Memorial Edition: Our Mick* (ca. September 1965); emphasis in original.

97. Dave [Godin], "Dear Member," *Mary Wells and Motown News* 1, no. 3 (ca. March 1964): 21. Godin would later report, "About 100 members came to Meet The Supremes. Some from as far as Swansea, Liverpool and Cheltenham"; [Dave Godin], "1964: A Year to Remember," *Hitsville U.S.A.* 1, no. 1 (January 1965): 9–12.

98. [Godin], "1964," 9–12; [Dave Godin], "Recent Visitors," *Hitsville U.S.A.*
1, no. 8 (August 1965): 154–56. Rylatt attributes these photos to Clive Stone.
(Stone's presence in many of the photos means that others were involved in this
documentation.)

99. Bylines of letters printed from Motown executives and artists include
Motown Corporation (*Mary Wells and Motown News* 1, no. 1 [ca. January 1964]: 2);
Berry Gordy Jnr. President Motown Record Corp., Marvin Gaye, Diana [Ross],
and the Miracles Quintet (*Mary Wells and Motown News* 1, no. 4 [ca. May 1964]:
36–37); Berry Gordy Jr. (*Hitsville U.S.A.* 1, no. 3 [ca. March 1965]: 42); and Martha
[Reeves] (*Hitsville U.S.A.* 1, no. 8 [August 1965]: 147). Abrams also mentioned
the TMAS, its publication, and English fascination with Motown in a letter to
Barbara Holliday, July 21, 1965, AAC; and two related letters to John Finlayson,
[*Detroit News*], March 22, 1965, and April 2, 1965, both AAC. In the letter dated
July 21, 1965, he recalls the story of a "young fellow from England and his father"
who came to Detroit to visit the studio, noting that the Hitsville buildings and
their "atmosphere" were "in the stage of becoming "National [*sic*] monuments."

100. This single was circulated in the fall of 1964 and later released as bonus
material on the UK compilation, *A Cellarful of Motown, Vol. 2*.

101. [Dave Godin], "Behind the Scenes at Motown: The Writers," *Hitsville
U.S.A.* 1, no. 1 (January 1965): 15–16; [Dave Godin], "Behind the Scenes at
Motown: The Writers," *Hitsville U.S.A.* 1, no. 2 (February 1965): 26, 33.

102. Motown employee Margaret Phelps was an important source for disco-
graphical material. See also "Complete Tamla-Motown Discography of British
Releases," *Record Mirror*, December 19, 1964, 17.

103. [Godin], "Dear Swinger and Friend," *Hitsville U.S.A.* 1, no. 1 (January
1965): 2.

104. Wonder may have also performed live concerts in northern England during
this visit. "Stevie Wins Hearts of Frenchmen," *New York Amsterdam News*, January
11, 1964, 14. He was also featured in a large Hohner harmonica advertisement
in *Melody Maker* just after this trip abroad; "Hohner Chromatic Harmonicas as
Played by Stevie Wonder" (advertisement), *Melody Maker*, February 1, 1964, 3.

105. For a side-by-side reference that compares U.S. and UK charts, see Dave
McAleer, *Hit Singles: Top 20 Charts from 1954 to the Present Day* (London: Carleton,
2003), which offers a monthly distillation of the most common weekly charts,
using the *Billboard* "Hot 100" as a source for U.S. singles and *New Musical Express*
(1954–63) and *Record Retailer/Music Week* (1964 to the present) as sources for UK
singles.

106. British press coverage of the Supremes' trip includes Ren Grevatt, "Smash-
Hit Supremes Tell Why," *Melody Maker*, September 19, 1964, 7; "Supremes Visit
Here Next Month," *Record Mirror*, September 26, 1964, 6; "Gene Pitney's 72 Days
with the Supremes," *New Musical Express*, October 2, 1964, 14; James Hamilton,
"Supremes Will Not Do Package Shows," *Record Mirror*, October 3, 1964, 6;
"Supremes Click," *New Musical Express*, October 9, 1964, 4; "Supremes Here
for Radio and TV Dates," *Melody Maker*, October 10, 1964, 5; Derek Johnson,
"Pounding Supremes," *New Musical Express*, October 16, 1964, 6; Bob Dawbarn,
"Supremes Suddenly Shoot to Stardom," *Melody Maker*, October 17, 1964, 7; and
Cordell Marks, "Time with the Supremes," *New Musical Express*, October 23,

1964, 3. Representative American coverage includes "Supremes Get Award in London," *Pittsburgh Courier*, October 10, 1964, 17; "Brief Encounter," *Pittsburgh Courier*, October 31, 1964, 17; and "Motown Execs to Europe," *Record World*, October 10, 1964. A photo of the Motown entourage traveling to the UK appears in S. Davis, *Motown*, 37.

107. Bob Dawbarn, "The Detroit Sound Forms a Beach-Head," *Melody Maker*, November 14, 1964, 10. See also "Supremes Make History," *New Musical Express*, November 13, 1964, 3; and "Supremes Supreme!," *Melody Maker*, November 14, 1964, 1 (the wrong date appears on the cover of this issue).

108. [Alan E. Abrams], "Lightening Strikes Thrice," Motown press release, November 23, 1964, AAC.

109. For a more detailed discussion of Motown's visits during this period see Rylatt, *Hitsville!* In some cases Motown acts played before live audiences while taping. Weston performed several live dates and the Miracles performed at Royal Albert Hall in December 1964. Ashford remembers an alternate itinerary with shows in "London, Manchester, Leeds, and a few other places"; Ashford, *Motown*, 60–64. (He seems to mistake the dates of these concerts, placing them a year earlier.) "Top U. S. Stars Storm In—Dates Announced," *Melody Maker*, October 24, 1964, 1.

110. A series of *Melody Maker* articles *published* in early of 1965 shows the continuous attention given to Tamla-Motown from a single publication: "Supremes Top Tamla Tour," *Melody Maker*, January 16, 1965, 5; "Tamla Team for TV," *Melody Maker*, January 23, 1965, 5; "Tamla Steps into Tour with Georgie," *Melody Maker*, March 6, 1965, 4; "Tamla Team Moves in for Tour," *Melody Maker*, March 13, 1965, 5; "TV and Radio Queue Up for Tamla Team," *Melody Maker*, March 20, 1965, 4; "The Girlie Groups," *Melody Maker*, March 20, 1965, 10; and "Tamla Tearaways!" *Melody Maker*, March 20, 1965, 15. On March 5, 1965, several days before the tour's first show, the cover of *New Musical Express* was splashed with a half-page advertisement. Similar reception appeared in *New Musical Express*, including Ian Dove, "A Warning to the Tamla-Motown Visitors from Their Biggest Fan," *New Musical Express*, March 19, 1965, 9; Andy Gray, "The Sound of Motown Plus Georgie Fame—Great!" *New Musical Express*, March 26, 1965, 9.

111. "Tamla-Motown Here in March," *Melody Maker*, December 26, 1964, 4. There had been some mention of a tour before this. Godin discussed a possible British visit in mid-1964. See also, "Yanks Invade! Beatles Favorites Coming Here," *Melody Maker*, April 4, 1964, 1; "Motown Revue Here Next Year," *Record Mirror*, October 17, 1964, 9.

112. Norman Jopling, "America Hits Back with Tamla Motown Attack," *Record Mirror*, March 20, 1965, 6–7; Bob Dawbarn, "Tamla Motown: Not So Much a Pop Sound, More a Way of Life," *Melody Maker*, March 27, 1965, 10. (On the same page as "America Hits Back" there was an advertisement that read, "It's great to be in Britain!" signed "Tamla Motown Recording Artistes Now on Tour.")

113. A photo of Hall and Decca chairman Sir Edward Lewis appeared in *Billboard*, November 30, 1963, 56. Hall is also referenced in Ahmet Ertegun, *What'd I Say: The Atlantic Story, 50 Years of Music* (New York: Welcome Rain, 2001), 176.

114. Tony Hall, "The Tony Hall Column," *Record Mirror*, February 13, 1965, 4.

115. Mick Page, letter to the editor, *Record Mirror*, February 27, 1965, 2; emphasis in original.

116. Dove, "A Warning to the Tamla-Motown Visitors."

117. Mary Wilson recalls that the performers called it the "ghost tour" due to its small audiences; "Motown Invasion," BBC Radio 2, April 5, 2005. See also Randall, *Dusty!*, 51–56. For other evidence of questionable reception outside of London, see Norman Jopling, "The Tamla Fans That Hated Us: The Kinks Talk to RM's Norman Jopling," *Record Mirror*, April 17, 1965, 6.

118. Alan Smith, "Listen! In the Name of the Supremes," *New Musical Express*, April 23, 1965, 12.

119. [Alan E. Abrams], Motown press release, February 15, 1965, AAC. Other American independent labels also worked to create a clearer brand identity in Britain during this period. Atlantic, for example, had established its own British label in the summer of 1964; "Atlantic to Have Its Own Label in Britain," *Record Retailer*, July 16, 1964, 12. In America, Motown's new focus on Britain was discussed in a *Billboard* article during late February 1965, which outlined the company's plan to "become the latest U.S. company to retain its own label identity throughout the world"; "Tamla-Motown Expands Abroad," *Billboard*, February 20, 1965, 9. See also [Alan E. Abrams], Motown press release, March 8, 1965, AAC; [Alan E. Abrams], "Hitsville U.S.A. to Hitsville U.K.," Motown press release, March 23, 1965, AAC; [Alan E. Abrams], telegram to S. Prokoff.

120. "EMI Are to Launch Tamla-Motown Label: Major Promotion Campaign Announced," *Record Retailer*, February 18, 1965, 8; "Biggest Pop Launch Ever for Tamla-Motown," *Record Retailer*, March 11, 1965, 20; "Get This Tamla Motown Sound—On Record" (advertisement), *Record Retailer*, March 18, 1965; "Tamla's Own Label Now," *New Musical Express*, March 19, 1965, 4; "Twelve Million Singles! That's the Tamla Total," *Record Retailer*, April 1, 1965, 16. See also Kingsley Abbott, "Launching the Tamla-Motown Label: Reminiscences with Derek Everett," in Abbott, *Calling Out Around the World*, 62–65.

121. Wilson, *Tamla Motown*, 68–74. The singles released during this launch were the Supremes, "Stop in the Name of Love"; Martha and the Vandellas, "Nowhere to Run"; Smokey Robinson and the Miracles, "Ooo Baby Baby"; the Temptations, "It's Growing"; Stevie Wonder, "Kiss Me Baby"; and Earl Van Dyke, "All for You." (The Temptations was the only one of these groups not featured on the tour.) The albums released at the time were the Supremes, *With Love from Us to You*; Martha and the Vandellas, *Heat Wave*; Various Artists, *A Collection of 16 Tamla Motown Hits*; Marvin Gaye, *How Sweet It Is to Be Loved by You*; and the Miracles, *I Like It Like That*.

122. Wickham later worked closely as manager and songwriter for Dusty Springfield and Labelle. For more on her collaborative efforts with Springfield, see Randall, *Dusty!*

123. One notable substitution was bassist Tony Newton.

124. Gordy discusses this as an important part of the Miracles' show in late 1964; Gordy, *To Be Loved*, 206. Choreography like this was abandoned when Cholly Atkins joined the company later that year.

125. "Wishin' and Hopin'," written by Hal David and Burt Bacharach, was originally released in the United States by Dionne Warwick. "I Can't Hear You," writ-

ten by Gerry Goffin and Carole King, was originally released in the United States by Betty Everett. In the middle of the program Springfield performed a version of the 1963 Mary Wells single "You Lost the Sweetest Boy"; Randall, *Dusty!*, 20–21.

126. Springfield had performed with Motown artists during a ten-day engagement at the Brooklyn Fox Theater September 4–13, 1964. These concerts were promoted by New York disc jockey Murray "the K" Kaufmann, who was well known in the United States as a radio and television host and was famous for his interviews with the Beatles during early 1964. See "Recording Stars Are Big in Brooklyn, N.Y.," *Pittsburgh Courier*, October 3, 1964, 17; Randall, *Dusty!*, 51. A large photograph of the Supremes and Millie from these performances was printed in *Melody Maker*, September 26, 1964, 5.

127. See also Alexandra Marie Apolloni, "Wishin' and Hopin': Femininity, Whiteness, and Voice in 1960s British Pop (PhD diss., University of California Los Angeles, 2013), 74–85.

128. Randall cites *The Sound of Motown* television special as the major launching point for Motown in the UK, writing, "It is surprising how rarely this appearance on *Ready, Steady, Go!* has been compared to the Beatles' 1964 appearance on the *Ed Sullivan Show*. . . . In both cases, lucrative international markets were opened up virtually overnight by exposure on a top-rated television program, and in turn, both engendered transatlantic pop discourse." Randall, *Dusty!*, 54.

129. [Godin], "Dear Swinger and Friend," *Hitsville U.S.A.* 1, no. 12 (February 1966): 231–32.

130. Ibid.

131. For More on Godin's official role at Motown, see Phil Johnson, "Dave Godin," *Independent*, October 20, 2004; Ritson and Russell, *The In Crowd*, 48–53, 60.

132. By 1988 Godin recoiled from any exclusive relationship with Motown as a part of his legacy: "I don't want to be known as Mr. Northern Soul. I don't want to be known as Mr. Deep Soul. . . . I don't want to be known as Mr. Tamla-Motown. I want to be known as Mr. Black American Music fan, lover, and comrade. Because that has been my one mission. I've always tried to take in the broad sweep of postwar black American music"; Browne, "Soul or Nothing," 344.

133. Atlantic had released British records through London American before establishing its own imprint and was also extremely active in other international locations. "Atlantic Israeli and Venezuelan Reps Named by Label," *Billboard*, March 17, 1962, 5; "Atlantic Names Turkish Distrib," *Billboard*, April 28, 1962, 5; "Atlantic Signs Pact with Discos of Peru," *Billboard*, May 5, 1962, 8; "Atlantic Signs with New O'Seas Distrib Firms," *Billboard*, April 20, 1963, 3. See also Steve Traiman, "International Affairs," *Billboard*, January 17, 1991, A-28, A-30.

134. [Abrams], "Motown Now Number One." The Stax visit is discussed in Bowman, *Soulsville U.S.A.*, 96–97.

135. Jim Saphin ran a Supremes club between mid-1966 and early 1969 and published more than two dozen newsletters during this time. Other clubs were established for the Four Tops, Marvin Gaye, Stevie Wonder, Kim Weston, the Temptations, Jimmy Ruffin, and Martha and the Vandellas; Rylatt, *Hitsville!*, 179. Another club active during this period was Motown Ad Astra, run by Sharon Davis. (There were certainly others of which I am not aware.)

136. "Four Tops Score in Great Britain," *New Journal and Guide*, March 18, 1967, 14.

137. Examples of *New Musical Express* coverage included Alan Smith, "NME Chart Woke up Four Tops in Record Time!" *New Musical Express*, October 21, 1966, 15; "Four Tops Tour Set—Here Soon for TV," *New Musical Express*, October 28, 1966, 8; "Four Tops on Frost TV Show," *New Musical Express*, November 4, 1966, 9; "Life Lines of the Four Tops," *New Musical Express*, November 26, 1966, 6; "NME Takes You to Hitsville," *New Musical Express*, December 3, 1966, 4.

138. The Four Tops made several important international trips during the early 1970s, including a 1970 tour of England, Holland, Germany, and France and a visit to Australia. Press releases and photos relating to these performances are held in BGU.

139. For a complete list of UK reissues, see Wilson, *Tamla Motown*, 642–44.

140. John Reid and Adam White's introductory essay to *The Complete Motown Singles, Vol. 10* (1970) ("I'm Here to Change the Records") includes a lengthy recollection of the British release of "The Tears of a Clown."

141. Advertisements for *Motown and Mary Wells News* and a feature on Wells written by Godin appeared in *R&B Monthly* in mid-1964, but for the most part Motown coverage was limited to soul-oriented artists like Jr. Walker, Earl Van Dyke, and the Velvelettes. Cummings's publications morphed over the course of the 1960s, changing names from *Soul* to *Soul Music Monthly* and *Soul Music* and combined with *Soulbeat* and *Fame-Goldwax Followers*. Issue 2 of *Soul Music Monthly* (February 1967) contained profiles of the Miracles and Edwin Starr in addition to a review of a Starr concert. Issue 4 of *Soul Music Monthly* (April 1967) ran a profile and discography of Jr. Walker and the All Stars. Issue 5 of *Soul Music* (February 17, 1968) included a review of Edwin Starr at the Marquee (February 2, 1968). Charlie Gillett wrote extensively for this series of publications, work that later informed his 1970 book *The Sound of the City*. In 1969 Cummings turned over the editorial duties of *Shout* to Clive Richardson, and the publication continued to be an important source of information and community building into the 1970s. See Clive Richardson, *Really Sayin' Something* (New Romney, UK: Bank House, 2010).

142. A prominent Motown feature in *Home of the Blues* was a review of the 1967 Four Tops tour (issue 9, April 1967). *Blues and Soul* included a lot of writing about Motown, including features on the Temptations (issue 2, November 1967), Jr. Walker (issue 3, December 1967), Stevie Wonder (issue 4, January 1968), and Marvin Gaye (issue 7, April 1968). *Blues and Soul* also covered "Tamla-Motown" month in February 1968 (issue 5). See also John Abbey, interview by David Nathan, March 10, 2012, http://www.soulmusic.com/index.asp?S=62&T=65&ART=2423.

143. For more on Northern Soul, see Browne, "Soul or Nothing"; Ady Croasdell, "A Personal History of Northern Soul," *Soul Source*, http://www.soul-source.co.uk/_/words/a-personal-history-of-northern-soul-by-ady-croasdell-r2895; Joanne Hollows and Katie Milestone, "Welcome to Dreamsville: A History and Geography of Northern Soul," in *The Place of Music*, ed. George Revill, Andrew Leyshon, and David Matless (New York: Guilford, 1998), 83–103; Katie Milestone, "Love Factory: The Sites, Practices and Media Relationships of Northern Soul," in *The Clubcultures Reader: Readings in Popular Cultural Studies*,

ed. Steve Redhead, Derek Wynne, and Justin O'Connor (Malden, MA: Blackwell, 1998), 134–49; David Nowell, *Too Darn Soulful: The Story of Northern Soul* (London: Robson, 1999); Dave Rimmer, "Northern Soul and Motown," in Abbott, *Calling Out around the World*, 220–21; Ritson and Russell, *The In Crowd*; Tim Wall, "Out on the Floor: The Politics of Dancing on the Northern Soul Scene," *Popular Music and Society* 25 (October 2006): 431–45; and Andrew Wilson, *Northern Soul: Music, Drugs and Subcultural Identity* (Portland, OR: Willan, 2007), esp. 14–50.

144. Keith Rylatt and Phil Scott, *Central 1179: The Story of Manchester's Twisted Wheel Club* (London: Bee Cool, 2001).

145. Bill Brewster, "Ian Levine: Soul Adventurer," in *The Record Players: DJ Revolutionaries*, ed. Bill Brewster and Frank Broughton (New York: Black Cat, 2010), 81–89.

146. Ritson and Russell, *The In Crowd*, 29.

147. Soul City opened in 1966 in Deptford and later moved to Covent Garden.

148. Tony Cummings, "The Strange World of Northern Soul," *Black Music* (June 1974): 8–9, 38.

149. Ian Dove, "Britain Is Soul Country," *Billboard*, August 17, 1968, section 2 ("The World of Soul"), 47–48; Mike Hennessey, "Gallic Radio, TV Has Soul," *Billboard*, August 17, 1968, section 2 ("The World of Soul"), 50; Espen Eriksen, "Soul in Scandinavia," *Billboard*, August 17, 1968, section 2 ("The World of Soul"), 52; Rafael Reuert, "Spanish Soul on the Rise," *Billboard*, August 17, 1968, section 2 ("The World of Soul"), 54.

150. The genesis of Motown's international sales reach was a 1963 trip to Europe by Berry Gordy, Esther Gordy Edwards, and Barney Ales. See "Motown Crew off to Europe for Big Push," *Billboard*, March 2, 1963, 6; "Motown Record President to Set Up Foreign Deal," *Pittsburgh Courier*, March 9, 1963, 17; "Tamla-Motown Execs Swing across Europe," *Billboard*, March 23, 1963, 28. This trip helped to establish a number of important distribution and publishing deals. See Skip Voogt, "Ngram Distrib Pye and Kapp," *Billboard*, July 20, 1963, 29; "King Brass to Take Road," *Billboard*, October 26, 1963, 49–50; Christian Toersleff, "CBS to Issue Tamla-Motown," *Billboard*, November 2, 1963, 31; "From the Music Capitals of the World: Germany," *Billboard*, November 23, 1963, 36; "From the Music Capitals of the World: Holland," *Billboard*, December 7, 1963, 31; "Music as Written: Rome," *Billboard*, May 16, 1964, 40.

151. Versions of "Shop Around," "Bye Bye Baby," and "Ain't It Baby" appeared on the Reo imprint. Later recordings appeared on London. "Motown Wk. in Canada Is Co-Op Effort," *Billboard*, November 18, 1967, 52.

152. "Stevie's Journey," *Soul* (Toronto), December 1966, 6–7; "Jimmy Ruffin: Just Jimmy," *Soul* (Toronto), May 1967, 3.

153. A list of Motown covers released outside the UK between 1963 and 1968 appears in appendix 1.

154. Copies of a Dutch fan club newsletter written by Lamboo in the late 1960s are held in EMU.

155. EPs were released on Artone's Funckler imprint. The Supremes visited Holland in October 1964, performing at the Koninklijk Theater Carré in Amsterdam. See also "Supremes Repping U.S. at Dutch Pop Festival," *Variety*, September 8, 1965, 52.

156. Another Supremes performance occurred in early October 1965, when they performed at Holland's annual popular song festival in Amsterdam. The group also taped several German television programs during the same visit. [Alan E. Abrams], Motown press release, August 31, 1965, AAC.

157. "From the Music Capitals of the World: Oslo," *Billboard*, July 24, 1965, 21.

158. Henrik Smith-Sivertsen, "How English Became the Language of Pop in Denmark," *Popular Music History* 8, no. 3 (2013): 251–69. By the end of the decade, *Billboard* reported a heightened interest in Motown and Atlantic artists in Denmark due to increased dance club activity and visits from American artists. "From the Music Capitals of the World: Stockholm," *Billboard*, May 20, 1967, 16; "U.S. Labels Spurring Soul Most in Denmark, Norway," *Billboard*, August 30, 1969, 64.

159. Siw Malmkvist was also popular in Germany and recorded a version of "I Hear a Symphony" ("Wie eine Symphonie") for the German market in the late 1960s.

160. A nearly complete set of Motown foreign-language versions is included in Various Artists, *Motown around the World*. For more on Motown's German-language recordings, see "Supremes Brush Up on Deutsch for German Discs," *Variety*, January 27, 1965, 47; A. L. McClain, "Germans Dig the Supremes," *Detroit News*, January 26, 1965, 4; "Documentary to Feature Three Motown Acts," *Billboard*, April 2, 1966, 62.

161. The artists appended new vocals to already existing backing tracks in all of these rerecorded versions. Different people created translations for these songs, including Peter Puma ("Wo ist unsere Liebe"), Kurt Feltz ("Jonny und Joe"), Gunter Loose ("Mein Girl"), and Fini Busch ("Wie schön das ist").

162. "House Review: Olympia Paris," *Variety*, December 25, 1963, 40; Mike Hennessey, "Giant Launching Is Given Tamla-Motown in France," *Billboard*, May 1, 1965, 14. Belgium was another French-language market that Motown artists visited. The Marvelettes appeared on the television show "Face All Public," which was recorded in Belgium in June 1965. [Alan E. Abrams], Motown press release, June 25, 1965, AAC.

163. A recording of the former was released in the United States and the UK as *Motortown Revue in Paris*. In early 1968 the Supremes appeared on television in a number of other European countries, including Italy, Germany, Holland, Spain, and Switzerland.

164. Early issues were titled *R'n'B Panorama*. Tonneau seems to have been based in Brussels, although the club maintained other addresses in Paris, England, and Switzerland.

165. "Le Rhythm and Blues," *R'n'B Panorama* 1 (February 1960), 1.

166. Chris Tinker, "A Singer-Songwriter's View of the French Record Industry: The Case of Léo Ferré," *Popular Music* 21 (2002): 147–57.

167. The French titles for these records included in modern compilations ("Tu perds le plus merveilleux garçon" and "Puisque je sais qu'il est à moi") were established later. Several other French versions reside in the Motown vaults, including a Miracles recording of "Try a Little Tenderness" and Stevie Wonder performing "Castles in the Sand."

168. An advertisement for "I Don't Know What to Do" appeared in *Billboard*,

August 28, 1965, 9. Anthony also released several French-language versions of Motown songs in Canada.

169. "Music as Written: Rome." Later in the decade Motown switched to RCA-Italiana for distribution. "From the Music Capitals of the World: Milan," *Billboard*, November 12, 1966, 54.

170. Motown executives made several well-publicized attempts to increase Italian sales during 1967. See "Tamla-Motown's Sound to Zero in on Italian Market," *Billboard*, March 25, 1967; "RCA Italiana Bows Drive on Italian Tamla Singles," *Billboard*, June 10, 1967, 64, 68; "From the Music Capitals of the World: Milan," *Billboard*, June 17, 1967, 54. "Motown Sound Goes Italiana," *Billboard*, May 6, 1967, 1, 14.

171. "From the Music Capitals of the World: Milan," *Billboard*, December 2, 1967, 72; "San Remo Festival—Boon for Disk Sales," *Billboard*, February 1, 1969, 76.

172. For a discussion of soul music in Vietnam, see Michael J. Kramer, *The Republic of Rock: Music and Citizenship in the Sixties Counterculture* (New York: Oxford University Press, 2013), 183–87.

173. "King Brass to Take Road"; "Cosdel Opens Operations in Singapore," *Billboard*, August 1, 1964, 1. See also "Exports, Imports, Our Marvelettes," *Detroit Free Press*, March 5, 1965, 8B. EMU holds an article from *Radio Weekly* dated March 1, 1965, which includes an English-language Singapore-based record chart and a Motown advertisement from the region sponsored by Cosdel.

174. Wilson, *Dreamgirl*, 190. A 1966 Motown press release publicized the fact that U.S. forces in Vietnam voted the Supremes as their favorite vocal group; [Alan E. Abrams], Motown press release, September 29, 1965, AAC. See also "'Soulists' Not Doing Their Share: Negro Soldier," *Billboard*, February 26, 1966, 8. The Supremes were by far the most internationally active Motown group during the last half of the 1960s. Their music appeared regularly on the *Billboard* "Hits of the World" charts and the group toured abroad, performing live and taping television performances in Sweden, the Netherlands, Germany, Italy, Spain, and France.

175. "KBTR Exclusive: Supremes Far East Tour," *KBRT All American*, September 26, 1966, 3; [Alan E. Abrams], "'Detroit Sound' Leads Pack in Auto Tape Cartridge Sales," Motown press release, June 17, 1966, AAC; "Motown Acts for Overseas," *Billboard*, June 25, 1966, 6. A promotional booklet from the Japan concerts is held in EMU.

176. A photo of Harrison interviewing Robby Taylor for the program appeared in *Billboard*, May 4, 1968, 6.

177. The program was distributed on LP; about a dozen different episodes are held in EMU.

178. "From the Music Capitals of the World: Jerusalem," *Billboard*, June 14, 1969, 79; "CBS Pact with Tamla in Israel," *Billboard*, January 3, 1970, 48–49; "Capitol of Mexico Will Add 2 Labels to Its Catalog in 1968," *Billboard*, January 6, 1968, 37. Several interesting domestic versions also appeared in Spain, including Karina's "Mi chico" ("My Guy") in 1964 and a version of "Reach Out I'll Be There" by the rock band Los Stop ("Extiende tus brazos").

179. Motown's records may have been released earlier in Jamaica (especially

bootlegs), but the earliest evidence I can find is a 1968 release of Stevie Wonder's "Never Had a Dream Come True." For a brief introduction to Jamaican popular styles during this time, see Michael E. Veal, *Dub: Soundscapes and Shattered Songs in Jamaican Reggae* (Middletown, CT: Wesleyan University Press, 2007), 26–36.

180. One slice of this reception, recorded by a single record company, is contained in the Trojan Records *Motor City Reggae* boxed set, which contains fifty versions of Motown songs recorded mostly during the 1970s.

Chapter Five

1. Alan E. Abrams, letter to Joe X. Price (writer for Los Angeles–based *Daily Variety*), August 17, 1965, AAC.

2. Murray Forman, *One Night on TV Is Worth Weeks at the Paramount: Popular Music on Early Television* (Durham, NC: Duke University Press, 2012), 231–72.

3. Herman Gray cites a slow movement during this time away from typecast roles for black actors—like maids, cooks, and farmers—to "more benign and less explicitly stereotypical images of African Americans"; *Watching Race* (Minneapolis: University of Minnesota Press, 1995), 76. See also Donald Bogle, *Primetime Blues: African Americans on Network Television* (New York: Farrar, Straus and Giroux, 2001), 74–77, 83–91; Forman, *One Night on TV*, 263, 270–72.

4. Ed Guerrero, *Framing Blackness: The African American Image in Film* (Philadelphia: Temple University Press, 1993). For a discussion of race film in Chicago, see Davarian L. Baldwin, *Chicago's New Negroes: Modernity, the Great Migration, and Black Urban Life* (Chapel Hill: University of North Carolina Press, 2007), 121–54.

5. "The Bikini Machine" (a.k.a. "Beach Ball"), the record that the Supremes performed in *Beach Ball*, was credited to non-Motown writers Guy Hemric and Jerry Styner. According to corporate records, the Supremes' vocals were the only portion of the record in which Motown participated. For examples of Motown promoting these film appearances, see Alan E. Abrams, letter to Bill Gandell (Exploitation Department, Paramount Pictures), October 28, 1965, AAC; Alan E. Abrams, letter to Bill Gandell, December 20, 1965, AAC.

6. Production records for this film reveal that both Jobete and ITMI took risks to allow Motown acts to appear in the film. Jobete charged Electronovision, the film's production company, $1 for the use of all of its songs and ITMI charged $10,000 for a package deal that included the Supremes, the Miracles, and Marvin Gaye, by far the least expensive fee per act. (By contrast, the Beach Boys were paid $40,000, James Brown received $15,000, and Leslie Gore charged $8,500.) "T.A.M.I. Show Production Documents, 1964–1965," RRF.

7. "'Nothing but a Man': Triumph on a Budget," *Ebony*, August 1965, 198–201; Wyatt Tee Walker, "On Malcolm X: Nothing but a Man," *Negro Digest*, April 1965, 29–32; Brian O'Doherty, "Classic of a Negro Who Stopped Running," *Life*, February 19, 1965, 15; Bosley Crowther, "'Nothing but a Man' and 'Lilith' Presented," *New York Times*, September 21, 1964, 37.

8. California business entity records show that in June 1968 Motown applied for corporate status for Motown Productions, headquartered at 6255 Sunset

Boulevard. For media reception of this corporate development, see Eliot Tiegel, "TV Showcasing Black Artists," *Billboard*, August 24, 1968, 1, 66.

9. Gordy, *To Be Loved*, 228–29; "Motown Expansion in High with B'Way, TV, Movies," *Billboard*, June 11, 1966: 1, 10; Shelly Berger, telephone interview by author, January 14, 2015.

10. For an example of Motown using these television programs to cross-market record sales, see a letter dated March 20, 1970, from sales director Phil Jones to Jim Schwartz of the regional distribution firm Schwartz Brothers. Jones details a contest for the distribution firm that sold the most Supremes and Temptations records surrounding the second airing of *T.C.B.* The winner was to receive a new "wristwatch" television set. "Schwartz Brothers," box 2, folder 72, RRF.

11. Reviews of these specials appeared in mainstream newspapers; George Gent, "An Evening of Specials on N.B.C," *New York Times*, November 13, 1969, 95; Dan Sullivan, "Special for Singers," *New York Times*, December 10, 1968, 95.

12. *The Temptations Show* (featuring Kay Stephens and George Kirby) aired in March 1969, *The Smokey Robinson Show* in 1970, and *Goin' Back to Indiana* in 1971. Selected video footage from these and other Motown television performances can be found in various DVD complications released by Hip-O Records and Reelin' In the Years Productions. "Diana Ross TVer Bows Motown $15 Mil Project," *Billboard*, December 19, 1970, 3.

13. State of Michigan corporate entity applications list the first use of Multi-Media Management Corporation on December 17, 1970. A press release held in BGU uses MMC letterhead to announce Marvin Gaye's "What's Going On," which was released in early 1971.

14. Marvin Gaye also acted in two youth-oriented programs in the mid-1960s: the daytime drama *Never Too Young* and several episodes of the variety show *Malibu U.*

15. Several of Gordy's songs performed by Jackie Wilson were also recorded in New York, including "Reet Petite" (recorded July 12, 1957) and "To Be Loved" (recorded January 8, 1958); dftmc.info.

16. "Motown Opens Coast Office," *Billboard*, November 16, 1963, 48. For a loose timeline of the California office, see Peter Fletcher, "Hal Davis: A History of Gold and Platinum," *Record World*, January 26, 1980, 86.

17. A letter from Brenda Holloway to Berry Gordy citing the difficulties of being based in Los Angeles is reprinted in George, *Where Did Our Love Go?*, 155–57. For more on Holloway in a Los Angeles context, see Kimasi L. Browne, "Brenda Holloway: Los Angeles's Contribution to Motown," in *California Soul*, ed. Jacqueline Cogdell DjeDje and Eddie S. Meadows (Berkeley: University of California Press, 1998), 321–51.

18. Examples of Motown tracks on which Kaye claims to have played include Stevie Wonder's "I Was Made to Love Her"; Diana Ross's "Ain't No Mountain High Enough"; Marvin Gaye and Tammi Terrell's "Ain't Nothing Like the Real Thing"; a number of Supremes recordings ("Love Child," "Baby Love," "Stop! In the Name of Love," "Back in My Arms Again," "You Can't Hurry Love," "My World Is Empty without You," "Reflections," "Love Is Here and Now You're Gone"); and the Four Tops' "I Can't Help Myself" and "Bernadette"; http://www.carolkaye.com/www/library/basshits.htm.

19. In a 2009 radio interview with Bob Edwards, Kaye remarked, "At first they'd hire us and they'd say, 'well, we want to cut demos.' Well, we did hundreds of, quote, demos, you know. And then we realized that some of those tracks had to be the Supremes and the Four Tops, you know. I'm playing on that, um, [plays and sings the main riff from 'I Can't Help Myself']. I'm the second one of nine bass players they used out here. [Edwards: Nine bass players!] Arthur Wright was the first one, I was the second one, and they used other bass players, too"; Carol Kaye, interview on *The Bob Edwards Show*, taped March 9, 2009, aired on XM Radio March 11, 2009, and on National Public Radio March 28, 2009. Allan Slutsky, author of the book *Standing in the Shadows of Motown* (the basis for the feature-length film of the same name), has refuted Kaye's claims; "Who Played 'I Was Made to Love Her'? The Carol Kaye–James Jamerson Enigma" (http://bassland.net/jamerson.html), Slutsky cites research from Motown's corporate archive, signed affidavits, and recollections of several witnesses to discredit Kaye.

20. Led by Hank Cosby, Motown musicians began to file their recording sessions with the Detroit Federation of Musicians (Local 5) in late 1963, and by 1965 Motown work was documented regularly. (This shift corresponded to the company employing Detroit-based union string players.) Motown's sessions in Los Angeles were usually documented by the city's Local 47. Union records for a single date often registered several songs and a large list of musicians, making it challenging to discern which players contributed to individual records. The lists of people who were paid for Detroit-based recording sessions generally included the musicians commonly associated with the Funk Brothers, and Motown bassist James Jamerson appeared on union documentation for a lot of rhythm track sessions. Session logs and multitrack master recordings from Motown's archives, now owned by Universal Music, corroborate this union documentation. The paper logs indicated which sessions were recorded in non-Motown facilities, and the company's tape filing cards also registered outside work. Before 1965, Motown's intricate tape numbering system used a discrete code for tapes recorded in outside sessions. (A three-track tape recorded in the Hitsville studio, for example, might have the number 3S55, while a tape that originated outside of Motown-owned facilities would carry the number 3S55OSS.) Clues within the performances themselves also point to the Detroit origins of many classic tracks on which Kaye claims to have played. These include the use and character of reverb, the manner in which instrumentation was partitioned among the available tape tracks, and the sound of direct-to-board recording for guitars and bass. In Detroit, Motown recorded bass directly to tape, whereas in Los Angeles Kaye regularly performed through an amplifier captured by a microphone. These two techniques created markedly different sounds, which is especially evident when the bass is isolated in a multitrack master. In the case of both "Bernadette" and "I Was Made to Love Her," the two records at the heart of the debate between Kaye and Slutsky, the bass was recorded direct, and thus the sonic evidence points to Jamerson as bassist on these tracks. For more on Kaye's claims, see Jon Erickson, "Carol Kaye: Session Bassist Extraordinaire," *Tape-Op*, http://www.tapeop.com/interviews/45/carol-kaye.

21. Kaye most likely played bass for the following Motown hits: "Love Is Here and Now You're Gone" (the Supremes), "I'm Ready for Love" (Martha

Reeves and the Vandellas), "You've Made Me So Very Happy" (Brenda Holloway), "Someday We'll Be Together" (Diana Ross and the Supremes), and "In and Out of Love" (Diana Ross and the Supremes). In a set of inquiries to archivist Andrew Morris in July 2014 and late 2015, I received a complete set of 1960s Motown-related union-logged sessions from Los Angeles Local 47. I also inquired about Kaye's involvement in Motown sessions, asking for any documentation regarding Los Angeles recordings of "I Was Made to Love Her," "You Can't Hurry Love," and "Bernadette," three of the tracks on which Kaye claims to have performed. Morris was not able to find evidence of Kaye's involvement on these tracks during times commensurate with the release of famous singles. Andrew Morris, e-mail message to author, July 16, 2014. I collaborated with bass scholar Brian F. Wright on some of this research; his future work will surely shed more light on the relationship between Kaye, Jamerson, and Motown.

22. S. Smith, *Dancing in the Street*, 181–89.

23. For more on the Detroit riots, see Dan Georgakas and Marvin Surkin, *Detroit, I Do Mind Dying: A Study in Urban Revolution* (Cambridge, MA: South End Press, 1998); Heather Ann Thompson, *Whose Detroit?: Politics, Labor, and Race in a Modern American City* (Ithaca, NY: Cornell University Press, 2001).

24. Sugrue, *Origins of the Urban Crisis*, 259–71.

25. "Detroit Is Cared About," *Detroit Free Press*, August 12, 1969; Sharon Cassidy, "Enthusiasm Bursts for Smokey Robinson," *Detroit News*, August 14, 1969.

26. A program from this event is held in EMU.

27. The Gordy Foundation, Inc., "The Loucye Gordy Wakefield Scholarship Fund," 1969, pamphlet, EMU.

28. "Bumper Crop Get Gordy Scholarships," *Baltimore Afro-American*, October 3, 1970, 14; "The Sterling Ball Is a Solid Gold Social Event," *Call and Post*, May 8, 1971, 8A; "Politicians and Show World Stars Attend Big Charity Ball in Detroit," *Philadelphia Tribune*, May 8, 1971, 27; Jerry M. Flint, "Scholarship Ball Draws Detroit's Blacks," *New York Times*, April 26, 1971, 45.

29. John Conyers Jr., "Berry Gordy, Jr.: Still Paying His Dues," 92nd Cong., 1st sess., *Congressional Record* 117 (April 19, 1971). There was a similar pronouncement in the United States Senate by Michigan Senator Philip A Hart. See also "1972 Sterling Ball Raises $50,000," *Baltimore Afro-American*, October 7, 1972, 11.

30. Van G. Sauter, "Motown Records, Man, Which Is Big, Really Big," *Detroit* (magazine), March 21, 1965, 14–16.

31. June McKee, "Sound from Motown," *Michigan Challenge*, June 1968, 40–41.

32. Gordy, *To Be Loved*, 278; Diana Ross, *Secrets of a Sparrow: Memoirs* (New York: Villard, 1993), 140.

33. "Ales Reins Motown in General Overhaul," *Variety*, July 30, 1969, 61.

34. Emphasis in original.

35. "Motown Grosses $39 Million; Disc Firm to Remain in Detroit," *Jet*, December 3, 1970, 53; Bill Gray, "In Detroit to Stay: Motown News," *Detroit News*, October 25, 1970.

36. Amos A. Wilder, "Management Explains Reasons for Layoff Activity," *Motown Newsletter: A Monthly Report on Motown Record Corporation* 1, no. 3 (March 1972): 1, EMU.

37. "MacArthur Park" was created in California in 1968 but not released until 1971.

38. To be sure, not all Motown records made in California appeared on the MoWest imprint.

39. A range of press surrounded this release, including Jon Landau, "The Motown Story," *Rolling Stone*, May 13, 1971, 42–44; Vince Aletti, "The Motown Story: The First Decade," *Rolling Stone*, May 13, 1971, 40–42. See also Craig McGregor, "Nothing Like a Shot of Soul to Pep Up Rock," *New York Times*, September 12, 1971, D23.

40. The provenance is not available for this collection. Most of the materials date from the late 1960s and early 1970s. The collection includes a large set of commercial recordings (mostly 45s). During informal conversations, librarians at the Detroit Public Library recalled that this portion of the collection came to the library in the late 1980s or early 1990s, during a period when Motown was cleaning out the Motown Center building on Woodward.

41. Lonny Head, letter to Mildred Smith, August 11, 1972, EMU; Harold E. Sponberg, letter to Esther Edwards [*sic*], August 25, 1972, EMU; Esther G. Edwards, letter to Harold E. Sponberg, September 6, 1972, EMU. EMU officials visited Edwards on October 4, 1972, and made a tentative agreement to donate materials, then Edwards visited EMU in late October to confirm the donation. A. P. Marshall, letter to Harold E. Sponberg, October 5, 1972, EMU; A. P. Marshall, letter to Esther Edwards, November 2, 1972, EMU. EMU announced the donation to the press on November 2, 1972.

42. "Motown Meets Tinseltown," *Rolling Stone*, December 24, 1970, 18. Roshkind himself moved from New York to Los Angeles less than a year later; Michael Roshkind, letter to Al Abrams, October 12, 1971, AAC.

43. Chuck Thurston, "Motown Exiting the City a Little at a Time," *Detroit Free Press*, June 9, 1972, 1B.

44. Motown reported that Ales wanted to devote himself full time to his investment portfolio; Thurston, "Motown Exiting." Ales returned to Motown three years later; "Gordy Shakes up Motown; Abner Exits, Ales Back," *Variety*, September 10, 1975, 71.

45. Rita Griffin, "Motown's New Veep, GM, Tells Firm's Future Plans," *Michigan Chronicle*, June 24, 1972, 1, 4. Many Detroiters felt betrayed by Motown, an attitude that was reflected in the editorial "Cold Good-Bye from Motown," *Detroit Free Press*, June 25, 1972, 2C. Other articles questioned the future of Detroit's session musician community and speculated about Motown's future success. See Chuck Thurston, "Now That Motown Has Gone Mowest Where Will Detroit Musicians Go? Broke Maybe," *Free Press*, June 25, 1972; Bill Gray, "What's Behind Motown Move?," *Detroit News*, June 25, 1972, 1G. (Gray wrote, "Most Motown officials will agree that the company's hottest property currently is the Jackson Five. The brothers consistently have a hit of two on the charts. But what longevity can you expect from the Jackson Five? The lead singer is 12 and probably headed for a voice change.")

46. Motown didn't file official corporate merger forms to finalize the move legally until June 1974.

47. Johnny and Jackey first recorded this song in 1961; it was released on Fuqua's Tri-Phi imprint.

48. A photograph of Gordy and Holiday from this time is reprinted in Gordy, *To Be Loved.*

49. "The Supremes' Diana Ross: 'We Don't Need a Sex Goddess,'" *Look,* September 23, 1969, 72–74; emphasis in original.

50. Robert Hilburn, "Motown Records Spinning Off into Films, TV," *Los Angeles Times,* April 18, 1971, R1. A newspaper article that serves as evidence of this press release is "Diana Ross to Portray Billie Holiday in Film," *Norfolk (VA) New Journal and Guide,* July 3, 1971; Gordy, *To Be Loved,* 311, 315, 320.

51. Ibid., 319–20.

52. Ibid., emphasis in original; Gary Storhoff, "Strange Fruit: *Lady Sings the Blues* as a Crossover Film," *Journal of Popular Film and Television* 30 (Summer 2002): 105. See also James Baldwin, "The Devil Finds Work," in *Collected Essays* (New York: Library of America, 1998), 555. The film *Sounder,* directed by Martin Ritt and starring Cicely Tyson, Paul Winfield, and Kevin Hooks, was also released in the same season and marketed in a similar manner.

53. Holiday had recorded "Fine and Mellow" many times in varying interpretations. Each of these incorporated a sleek, smooth quality that connected to the theme of the lyrics by featuring an obbligato soloist (or set of soloists)—a low saxophone, muted guitar, or trumpet—performing under her vocal line.

54. For Ross's perspective on her research for the role, see Ross, *Secrets of a Sparrow,* 166.

55. Nancy Kovaleff Baker, "Abel Meeropol (a.k.a. Lewis Allan): Political Commentator and Social Conscience," *American Music* 20 (Spring 2002): 25–79. In the context of popular music criticism in 1973, it was known that Holiday had misremembered her authorship of "Strange Fruit"; Ralph J. Gleason, "Perspectives: 'Cover' Versions and Their Origins," *Rolling Stone,* June 7, 1973, 7.

56. Analyses of this song by Lori Burns and Alyssa Woods use a similar method of transcription. Lori Burns, "Feeling the Style: Vocal Gesture and Musical Expression in Billie Holiday, Bessie Smith, and Louis Armstrong," *Music Theory Online* 11 (September 2005), http://mto.societymusictheory.org/issues/mto.05.11.3/mto.05.11.3.burns.html; Lori Burns and Alyssa Woods, "Authenticity, Appropriation, Signification: Tori Amos on Gender, Race, and Violence in Covers of Billie Holiday and Eminem," *Music Theory Online* 10 (June 2004), http://mto.societymusictheory.org/issues/mto.04.10.2/mto.04.10.2.burns_woods.html.

57. *Lady Sings the Blues* was the top-grossing film in the United States for several weeks during October and November 1972.

58. Billy Rowe, "Lady Sings the Blues, but She's Not Billie Holiday," *New York Amsterdam News,* October 28, 1972; Loraine Alterman, "You Can't Beat an Original," *New York Times,* January 7, 1973, AL30. For a range of opinions from the general public on this matter, see "Letters to the Editor," *Ebony,* January 1973, 11A.

59. For a reading of Holiday's biographical construction, see Maya C. Gibson, "Alternate Takes: Billie Holiday at the Intersection of Black Cultural

Studies and Historical Musicology" (PhD diss., University of Wisconsin, Madison, 2008).

60. Vincent Canby, "'Lady Sings the Blues' Stars Diana Ross," *New York Times*, October 19, 1972.

61. Pauline Kael, "The Current Cinema: Pop versus Jazz," *New Yorker*, November 4, 1972, 152.

62. The other nominations were for Art Direction (Carl Anderson and Reg Allen), Scoring Adaptation and Original Score (Gil Askey), and Costume Design (Bob Mackie, Ray Aghayan and Norma Koch). An interesting product of Motown's success with *Lady Sings the Blues* was Suzanne de Passe becoming the first African American female to be nominated in a writing category.

63. For an example of a Ross profile in the wake of *Lady Sings the Blues*, see Michael Thomas, "Diana Ross Goes from Riches to Rags," *Rolling Stone*, February 1, 1973, 28–31.

64. For more on these two mixes, see Marvin Gaye, *What's Going On* (Deluxe Edition).

65. Gertrude Gipson, "Ivan Dixon Directs 'Mr. T,'" *Los Angeles Sentinel*, April 20, 1972, B3A. Gaye was extremely active between the completion of *What's Going On* and his initial work on *Trouble Man*. His single "You're the Man" was released in April, the same week he performed a comeback concert at the Kennedy Center and his hometown of Washington, DC declared a Marvin Gaye Day. Gaye also experimented with several collaborators based in California that summer, including Willie Hutch and the team of Freddie Perren and Fonce Mizell. For examples of these records, see Marvin Gaye, *Let's Get it On* (Deluxe Edition).

66. For a discussion of black masculinity and *Shaft*, see M. Morris, *Persistence of Sentiment*, 48–51.

67. There were critiques of this new genre by black leaders. Examples include "CORE Supports Fight of Black Exploitation," *Los Angeles Sentinel*, August 17, 1972, B7; Celeste Durant, "CORE Moves to Pre-edit Black Films," *Los Angeles Times*, September 20, 1972, A24; and Vernon E. Jordan Jr., "How Hollywood Degrades Blacks," *New York Amsterdam News*, October 14, 1972, D1 (printed contemporaneously in the *Chicago Defender*, *Philadelphia Tribune*, and *Baltimore Afro-American*). For examples that consider the topic from both sides, see Chester Higgins, "'Shaft' Spotlights Newest Black Stars," *Jet*, July 8, 1971, 54–58; Chester Higgins, "Black Films: Boom or Bust?" *Jet*, June 8, 1972, 52–59; and William Earl Berry, "How 'Super Fly' Is Changing the Behavior of Blacks," *Jet*, December 28, 1972, 54–58. For more on blaxploitation in general, see Guerrero, *Framing Blackness*, 69–111.

68. This perspective was apparent in more subtle ways in the press. For example, there was a series of articles about *Trouble Man* director Ivan Dixon casting an African American billiards professional in the film; "Pro Pool Player Gets Motion Picture Break," *Philadelphia Tribune*, July 8, 1972, 18. The film also employed the first black film operator used in a major Hollywood picture; "Major Film Company Hires First Black Camera Operator," *Philadelphia Tribune*, July 11, 1972, 19. See also "Stars of 'Super Fly' Draws Raving Fans and Defends Movie," *Atlanta Daily World*, September 28, 1972, 3.

69. Unless otherwise specified, all original research on *Trouble Man* was con-

ducted by the author from corporate archival materials held by Universal Music, including digitized reels of multitrack recordings, digital reproductions of the original tapes and boxes, and session logs.

70. Dale Oehler, telephone interview by Harry Weinger, February 8, 2006.

71. Robert O. Ragland, Jack Hayes and Leo Shuken, and J. J. Johnson also did arranging work for this album.

72. On the tape box these cues were labeled "Wild Bongo Trills."

73. Presumably, Gaye and his team faced pressure from the film producers to complete this crucial element of the soundtrack. Oehler remembers, "[The film studio] hired Marvin because they wanted the single, but they also wanted the score for the same amount of money"; Oehler, telephone interview. This popular single version includes an edit, while a longer, unedited version appears during the opening credits of the film.

74. To hear the film cues as they appear in the movie, see Gaye's *Trouble Man* (40th Anniversary Expanded Edition).

75. Gaye traveled to Chicago to perform in the 1972 Operation PUSH Expo at the Chicago Amphitheater. He was a featured performer on the program and his song "Save the Children" was used the next year as the title of a documentary about the event. He also performed in Detroit at the second Sterling Ball benefit.

76. It is unlikely that Lawrence performed the saxophone solo on the "Trouble Man" single. The master tapes reveal that this performance was recorded with the film band, not in an overdub session.

77. David Ritz, *Divided Soul: The Life of Marvin Gaye* (New York: McGraw Hill, 1985; New York Da Capo, 1991; New York: Da Capo, 2003), 159.

78. In example 5.2, tracks have been combined, separated, and reordered in order to illustrate the creative process. The original order and contents of tracks are: (1) piano and electric piano, (2) kick drum, (3) Moog rhythm, (4) bongo, (5) various other percussion, (6) bass, (7) drums left, (8) drums right, (9) combined rhythm and wah-wah guitars, (10) brass, (11) guitar overdub/handclaps/box percussion, (12) vocals, (13) winds, (14) tambourine, (15) saxophone solo, (16) melodic Moog.

79. The opening was covered widely in the black press. Representative coverage included, "'Trouble Man' Opens in N.Y. November 1," *Atlanta Daily World*, November 2, 1972, 6; "'Trouble Man' Premieres at the Roosevelt Theater," *Chicago Daily Defender*, November 7, 1972, 10; "'Trouble Man' Premiere Aids Negro Ensemble Co.," *Norfolk (VA) New Journal and Guide*, November 11, 1972, 14.

80. Gary Arnold, "A Cool Hero in 'Trouble,'" *Washington Post, Times Herald*, November 18, 1972, C7. See also Kevin Thomas, "Black 'Trouble Man' Lives by Own Rules," *Los Angeles Times*, November 29, 1972, D23.

81. Canby was one of the critics who had praised Ross several months earlier for her portrayal of Holiday. One of the reasons he was disappointed in *Trouble Man* was the fact that, "so many good people were involved in it"; "The Ten Worst Movies of 1972," *New York Times*, January 7, 1972. For other poor reviews, see James P. Murray, "'Trouble Man': A Shameful Imitation of Original 'Shaft,'" *New York Amsterdam News*, November 4, 1972, D6; Larry G. Coleman, "The Trouble with 'Trouble Man,'" *New Pittsburgh Courier*, November 25, 1972, 17.

82. Vince Aletti, "Trouble Man," *Rolling Stone*, March 1, 1973, 63; Greg Mims, "1973's Top Ten Soul Albums," *New Pittsburgh Courier*, December 22, 1973, 19.

83. For more on the initiation of PIR, see John A. Jackson, *A House on Fire: The Rise and Fall of Philadelphia Soul* (New York: Oxford, 2004), 97–99. A well-known artifact of the large-scale amalgamation of the R&B market was a white paper written in 1971 called "A Study of the Soul Music Environment," often called simply the "Harvard Report." CBS Records commissioned the study from researchers at the Harvard Business School to understand better the relationship between the mostly independent R&B market and the mainstream. By all accounts, this report suggested *against* acquiring any of the large R&B independents of the time, such as Stax and Motown, and instead recommended that larger conglomerations like the Columbia Records Group start black-oriented divisions to compete with independents. According to David Sanjek, the initial announcement of an agreement between Columbia and Gamble and Huff predated the Harvard Report. For more on the Harvard Report, see Nelson George, *The Death of Rhythm and Blues* (New York: Penguin, 2004), 135–38; David Sanjek, "Tell Me Something I Don't Already Know: The Harvard Report on Soul Music Revisited," in *Rhythm and Business: The Political Economy of Black Music*, ed. Norman Kelley (New York: Akashic, 2002), 59–76.

84. Atlantic is now part of the Warner Records Group, which is one of the three major music companies based in the United States, along with Universal and Sony.

85. Eliot Tiegel, "Soul Label? Motown Becoming Much More," *Billboard*, February 8, 1975, 3, 45.

86. "Fete Blasts Off Rare Earth—Motown's New Hip Label," *Billboard*, August 30, 1969, 78.

87. A lot of these Rare Earth records were licensed from UK sources. There was also other evidence of Motown's alignment with British popular music. In 1970 the company set up a London office run by John Marshall; "Motown Setting up Offices in England," *Variety*, May 20, 1970, 47. Motown also released British singer Kiki Dee's *Great Expectations* LP in June 1970, with album art that featured the Union Jack. The next year Elton John wrote the liner notes for the Supremes' *Touch* LP.

88. For more on Motown's ongoing relationship with a regional distributor, see "Schwartz Brothers, Incorporated Records," box 2, folders 72–76, box 3, folders 1–7, RRF.

89. Promotion, returns, and manufacturing were among the many differences between independent and "branch" (or major) distribution at the time. Motown worked with a variety of regional distributors during its time as an independently distributed company. In some instances Motown contracted the services of a well-established regional firm. In other cases the company had more of a financial interest, starting subsidiary branches called "Hitsville."

90. "Motown's Distrib. Stays Indie; 1979 Looks Like Biggest Year," *Variety*, April 4, 1979, 106.

91. "The Nation's Top 100 Top Black Businesses," *Black Enterprise*, June 1973; "Black Businesses Grow," *New Pittsburgh Courier*, May 24, 1980, 24.

92. Gordy, *To Be Loved*, 288.

93. Motown's commitment to the Jackson 5 was evident in the use of an out-

side promotion firm (Rogers, Cowan, and Brenner) to promote the group's first singles. Many of these press releases are held at BGU. Motown also made licensing deals to sell youth-oriented Jackson 5 merchandise like lunch boxes and breakfast cereal, and group members appeared in various cross-promotional advertisements for these products.

94. For more on Quiet Storm as a genre, see Neal, *What the Music Said*, 126–29.

95. The two guest performers on "Superstition" were Steve Madaio (trumpet) and Trevor Lawrence (saxophone); Lawrence also performed with Marvin Gaye on *Trouble Man*.

96. Wald, *It's Been Beautiful.*

97. A press release dated March 16, 1970, claims that Wonder had "broadened his range and style to include haunting, melodic sounds that soar 'beyond soul.'" "Stevie says the melodic tunes are coming back," the statement continues, "tunes with melodies that stick with you." Junius Griffin, "'Stevie Wonder . . . The Man' Headlines Copacabana Show March 19–April 1," BGU.

98. Motown dance hits included "Forever Came Today" by the Jackson 5, "Love Hangover" and "The Boss" by Diana Ross, "Got to Give It Up" by Marvin Gaye, and "Don't Leave Me This Way" and "Any Way You Like It" by Thelma Houston.

99. Popular funk groups like the Ohio Players, Kool and the Gang, and Parliament worked in this manner, often performing elaborate stage shows with outlandish costumes and sets.

100. Several performers and writers who had loudly departed during the 1960s and 1970s realigned with the company in a quieter fashion at a later time. Brian and Eddie Holland, without their longtime partner Lamont Dozier, wrote and produced several tracks for Michael Jackson and the Supremes in 1975 and 1976. The Temptations signed to Atlantic in 1976 and came back to Motown four years later. The Four Tops left Motown in 1972 to record for ABC-Dunhill, signed to Casablanca in 1981, and returned to Motown in 1983.

101. Motown used various studios in Los Angeles in the late 1960s and early 1970s, including Crystal, the Sound Factory, and Wally Heider. The MoWest studio had been called Poppy before it was purchased and renovated by Motown. The name change appears in union documents in February 1971, although this facility seemed to be small at the time and Motown continued to use other studios after this date.

102. James Jamerson, Robert White, and Eddie "Bongo" Brown were three of the main instrumentalists who moved to California.

103. Jamerson was released from his exclusive Motown contract in a terse, one-sentence letter in June 1973, a year after the official announcement that the Detroit operations were closing down.

104. "Gordy Expands Motown Industries," *Variety*, January 10, 1973, 51.

105. Mary Murphy, "Motown Firms Film Commitment," *Los Angeles Times*, September 3, 1975, 14.

106. Mitchell Morris describes the plot as having "powerful nostalgia for the interior stability of a pre-civil rights past"; *Persistence of Sentiment*, 84.

107. Ibid., 85.

108. Motown released an extensive two-disc soundtrack for the film collaboratively with MCA. To be sure, Jackson had departed Motown for Epic in 1976.

109. Mack, "Scott Joplin (Color)," *Variety*, February 9, 1977, 22.
110. Large-scale studies of blackness in television and film that give scant mention to the contributions of Motown include Guerrero, *Framing Blackness*; Bogle, *Primetime Blues*; Gray, *Watching Race*; Alan Nadel, *Television in Black-and-White America: Race and National Identity* (Lawrence: University Press of Kansas, 2005); Manthia Diawara, ed., *Black American Cinema* (New York: Routledge, 2003); and J. Fred MacDonald, *Blacks and White TV: Afro-Americans in Television since 1948* (Chicago: Nelson Hall, 1983).

Chapter Six

1. Motown held the top spot on the annual "BE 100" published by *Black Enterprise* until 1984, when Johnson Publishing overtook the number-one position.
2. Motown ended its Soul imprint in mid-1978.
3. Other acts once associated with Motown were also popular during this time. The Four Tops had a top-ten hit on Casablanca with "When She Was My Girl," Gaye's first single for CBS was the wildly popular "Sexual Healing," and Gladys Knight and the Pips had crossover success with "Love Overboard."
4. Motown press materials often pitched James as a rock musician. One James biography by Motown's publicity department ca. 1982 began with the question, "Is America ever going to accept an unadulterated rock star, that just happens to be black?"; "Biography of Rick James," Motown press release, ca. 1982, BGU.
5. "Party All the Time" was released on Columbia.
6. Richie's material was consistently coproduced by James Anthony Carmichael, who once wrote for the Mirwood label and worked on Motown-like records like Jackie Lee's "Do the Temptation Walk."
7. The other popular tribute single to Gaye at the time was "Nightshift" by the Commodores, their most popular single without Richie.
8. Other Motown-related performers in the ensemble included Diana Ross, Stevie Wonder, Smokey Robinson, and various members of the Jackson family.
9. Sharon Davis, *Lionel Richie: Hello* (Oakville, CT: Equinox, 2009), 111.
10. Morrie Gelman, "Motown Productions Reorganized; De Passe Heads Film-TV Division," *Variety*, February 4, 1981, 30. De Passe had been head of the company's creative division since 1972, overseeing A&R, studio operations, business affairs, and graphics.
11. *Happy Endings* included three songs: "Happy Endings" (written by William Goldstein and Molly-Ann Leikin and performed by Syreeta), "Rainbows" (written by Ken Hirsch and Ron Miller and performed by featured actress Catherine Hicks), and "I'll Never Fall in Love Again" (written by Burt Bacharach and Hal David and performed by Syreeta).
12. For more on African American reception of kung fu films, see Sundiata Keita Cha-Jua, "Black Audiences, Blaxploitation and Kung Fu Films, and Challenges to White Celluloid Masculinity," in *China Forever: The Shaw Brothers and Diasporic Cinema*, ed. Poshek Fu (Urbana: University of Illinois Press, 2008), 199–223.

13. "Say You, Say Me" did not appear on the soundtrack to *White Nights* released on Atlantic.

14. Wonder performed two duets with Dionne Warwick on the soundtrack, and Warwick performed one song as a solo artist. Wonder produced the record and performed instrumental parts on every track.

15. *Get Crazy* was released on the new imprint Morocco, which was a portmanteau word derived from the name "MOtown ROCk COmpany."

16. Craig Werner, *A Change is Gonna Come: Music, Race and the Soul of America* (Ann Arbor: University of Michigan Press, 2006), 22–26.

17. The popularity of this soundtrack inspired a second Motown release called *More Songs from the Big Chill,* which included another set of tracks featured in the film.

18. "Motown and A&M Form Joint Distrib," *Variety,* January 15, 1975, 75.

19. "A&M Ties with RCA for Distrib, Pressing in U.S.," *Variety,* January 17, 1979, 73. Motown signed a licensing agreement in late 1981 with RCA for British distribution while remaining committed to independent distribution in the United States.

20. Richard Gold, "Motown Not Seeking Distribution Deal with Major, Says Lasker; Indie Wholesalers Hang Tough," *Variety,* April 6, 1983, 69.

21. "Motown Dumps Pickwick Distrib to Launch It's Own Coast Branch; Pickwick Cedes Southeast to M.S.," *Variety,* April 13, 1983, 71; "Motown Distribbing 14 Labels on Coast," *Variety,* May 18, 1983, 63.

22. "MCA 'Official' Motown Distributor; Overseas Licensees Standing Firm," *Variety,* July 6, 1983.

23. R. Sanjek, *Pennies from Heaven,* 609.

24. Gordy, *To Be Loved,* 389. For a general discussion of the Motown sale from Gordy's perspective, see pages 382–98.

25. Jobete also housed artist-based publishers like Stone Diamond and Black Bull, which had been created during the early 1970s.

26. For another overview of the Motown sale, see Posner, *Motown,* 320–32.

27. Dennis Hevesi, "Jheryl Busby, 59, Reviver of the Motown Label, Dies," *New York Times,* November 8, 2008, A22.

28. Adam Sandler, "Motown Topper Harrell Hopes to Revive Label," *Variety,* October 9, 1995, 21–22.

29. During its post-Gordy years, Motown's roster included Brian McKnight, Erykah Badu, Akon, India.Arie, Ne-Yo, and Boyz II Men. Stevie Wonder was the only pre-sale Motown artist who remained. Several of the company's singles, such as Boyz II Men's "End of the Road" and "I'll Make Love to You," were among the most popular releases of the decade, displaying the resilience of Motown as a contemporary, crossover-oriented R&B imprint within a larger corporate structure.

30. The Motown Sales Department called LPs that contained reissued singles "oldies but goodies albums." See memorandum from Ron Newman (national sales director, album and tape cartridges), May 12, 1967, "Schwartz Brothers," box 2, folder 72, RRF.

31. Some rerecorded singles by original artists on Motorcity include the Elgins, "Heaven Must Have Sent You"; Kim Weston, "Helpless"; Levi Stubbs, "I Can't

Help Myself"; Kim Weston and Frankie Gaye, "It Takes Two"; the Undisputed Truth, "Law of the Land"; the Miracles, "Love Machine"; and the Velvelettes, "Needle in a Haystack." Only two Motorcity singles achieved mainstream popularity in the UK: Francis Nero's recording of "Footsteps Following Me" and Chuck Jackson's "All Over the World."

32. "Hitsville Is Converted into Motown Museum," *Variety*, December 9, 1987, 72; J. R. Reynolds, "An Expanded Motown Museum Reopens; IAAAM Confab Just around the Corner," *Billboard*, May 27, 1995, 22.

33. Waller, *Motown Story*; J. Randy Taraborrelli, *Motown: Hot Wax, City Cool, and Solid Gold* (New York: Doubleday, 1986); S. Davis, *Motown*; Reginald J. Bartlette, *Off the Record: Motown by Master Number, 1959–1989*, vol. 1 (Ann Arbor, MI: Popular Culture, 1991).

34. George, *Where Did Our Love Go?*

35. Other books to focus on larger histories of Motown include Dahl, *Motown*; Posner, *Motown*.

36. Gerald Early, "One Nation under a Groove," *New Republic*, July 15 and 22, 1991, 30–41; Early, *One Nation under a Groove*.

37. S. Smith, *Dancing in the Street*.

38. Ritz, *Divided Soul*.

39. Smokey Robinson and David Ritz, *Smokey: Inside My Life* (New York: McGraw Hill, 1989); Williams and Romanowski, *Temptations*; Martha Reeves and Mark Bego, *Dancing in the Street: Confessions of a Motown Diva* (New York: Hyperion, 1994). Wilson published two books: Mary Wilson, *Dreamgirl (New York: St. Martin's, 1986)*; and Mary Wilson and Patricia Romanowski, *Supreme Faith: Someday We'll Be Together* (New York: HarperCollins, 1990). These were combined into a single volume with additional material in 1999, Mary Wilson, *Dreamgirl and Supreme Faith: My Life as a Supreme* (New York: Cooper Square Press, 1999). See also J. Randy Taraborrelli, *Call Her Miss Ross: The Unauthorized Biography of Diana Ross* (New York: Birch Lane, 1989). Taraborrelli's work was later edited, updated, and reprinted as J. Randy Taraborrelli, *Diana Ross: An Unauthorized Biography* (New York: Citadel, 2007).

40. Ross, *Secrets of a Sparrow*; Gordy, *To Be Loved*.

41. Books published since the mid-2000s include Peter Benjaminson, *The Lost Supreme: The Life of Dreamgirl Florence Ballard* (Chicago: Lawrence Hill, 2008); Peter Benjaminson, *Mary Wells: The Tumultuous Life of Motown's First Superstar* (Chicago: Chicago Review, 2012); Mark Ribowsky, *The Supremes: A Saga of Motown Dreams, Success, and Beyond* (New York: Da Capo, 2009); Mark Ribowsky, *Signed, Sealed, and Delivered: The Soulful Journey of Stevie Wonder* (Hoboken, NJ: John Wiley and Sons, 2010); Mark Ribowsky, *Ain't Too Proud to Beg: The Troubling Lives and Enduring Soul of the Temptations* (Hoboken, NJ: John Wiley and Sons, 2010); Rick James and David Ritz, *Glow: The Autobiography of Rick James* (New York: Atria, 2014); Terrana, *The Road through Motown*; Ralph Terrana, *Russ Terrana's Motown*; and Coffey, *Guitars, Bars, and Motown Superstars*.

42. To be sure, de Passe Entertainment produced a lot of other material during this period, including the highly rated miniseries *Lonesome Dove*.

43. Steve Hochman, "A 'Motown' History Lesson," *Los Angeles Times*, October 24, 1990.

44. Motown had made many attempts to launch Broadway musicals since the mid-1960s. Its only successful production was *Pippin*, which opened in October 1972 and ran for nearly five years. (Motown and Jobete financed the show and acted as publisher for the score.) The company also released a *Guys and Dolls* soundtrack in 1976 with an all-black Broadway cast. Other musicals planned over the years included a production called *Cotillion* (with music by Smokey Robinson and Willie Hutch) and the Stephen Schwartz musical *The Baker's Wife.* "Motown Begins Empire-Building," *Variety,* November 28, 1973, 5; Eliot Tiegel, "Baker's Wife Undergoing Surgery; Motown Owns LP," *Billboard,* June 26, 1976, 6.

45. U.S. Trademark and Patent Office, Trademark Trial and Appeal Board, *UMG Recordings, Inc. vs. Mattel, Inc.,* filed November 10, 2005, mailed September 30, 2011. Mattel filed a suit after the decision to overturn the ruling, and the parties settled about a year later.

46. For more on branding and the concept of genericide, see Robert E. Moore, "From Genericide to Viral Marketing: On 'Brand,'" *Language and Communication* 23 (July–October 2003): 331–57. For more on cultural genericide from the perspective of linguistics, see Ronald R. Butters and Jennifer Westerhaus, "Linguistic Change in One's Own Words: How Trademarks Become 'Generic,'" in *Studies in the History of the English Language II: Unfolding Conversations,* ed. Anne Curzan and Kimberly Emmons (New York: Mouton de Gruyter, 2004), 111–23. For a discussion of the international history of trademark dilution, see Tony Martino, *Trademark Dilution* (New York: Oxford University Press, 1996). See also Shoshana Stern, "Is Genericide a Matter of Fact or of Merit?," March 26, 2008, *Boston College Intellectual Property & Technology Forum,* http://bciptf.org/wp-content/uploads/2011/07/20-IS-GENERICIDE-A-MATTER-OF-FACT-OR-OF-MERIT.pdf; Shawn M. Clankie, "Brand Name Use in Creative Writing: Genericide or Language Right?" in *Perspectives on Plagiarism and Intellectual Property in a Postmodern World,* ed. Lise Buranen and Alice M. Roy (Albany: State University of New York Press, 1999), 253–63.

47. Keith Rylatt, *Groovesville U.S.A.: The Detroit Soul and R&B Index* (Worthing, UK: Stuart Russell, 2010). There were a lot of other independent R&B companies active in Detroit during the mid-1960s with connections to Motown. Ed Wingate and Joanne Jackson (Bratton) ran the Golden World, Ric Tic, and Wingate labels, which were Gordy's biggest in-town competition. Gordy bought the majority of the couple's assets in late 1966, but the Wingates continued to operate the Wingate and Ric Tic imprints for the next two years. See "Motown Buys Golden World," *Billboard,* September 10, 1966, 10; "Motown Expands," *Variety,* September 7, 1966, 43. Don Davis formed Thelma and Ge Ge with Hazel Coleman and later teamed with LeBaron Taylor to release recordings on the Revilot and Solid Hit imprints. (Coleman was Berry Gordy's former mother-in-law; Thelma, the label's namesake, was his first wife.) Detroit was such a hot market in 1966 that *Billboard* named it one of the best places in the country to "break a record." "Detroit and L.A. Sales 'Happening Places,'" *Billboard,* July 2, 1966, 1.

48. The Funk Brothers discuss this openly in the documentary *Standing in the Shadows of Motown.*

49. Several threads on the Soulful Detroit "Motown Forum" have discussed non-Motown music that incorporated the Motown Sound, including "Sounds

Like Motown but Wasn't," http://soulfuldetroit.com/showthread.php?10433-Sounds-like-Motown-but-wasn-t.

50. The Supremes also recorded "A Lover's Concerto" for their 1966 album *I Hear a Symphony*.

51. Current credits for this song on the BMI database list the Motown writers instead of Mayfield.

52. This could have been the result of Jobete buying the rights to these songs but it was more likely due to acquiescence. Any lawsuits in these cases settled out of court, which left few publicly accessible records.

53. For the remainder of the book, I will consistently use *Motown* (capitalized) in reference to the specific company and *motown* (lowercase) as a more general term.

54. Elaine Jesmer, *Number One with a Bullet* (New York: Farrar, Straus, and Giroux, 1974). Connections between this book and Motown were discussed at the time in the popular press. For an example, see Robert B. Frederick, "Music-Records: Drugs, Brutal Sex, Chicanery Part of Jesmer's Black Disk Novel," *Variety*, May 22, 1974, 68. Motown once threatened to sue the production company of *Sparkle* due to similarities between the film's story and the history of the Supremes; Charles Barnes, "'Sparkle' Faces Suit by Motown," *Philadelphia Tribune*, April 10, 1976, 1, 2. In the mid-2000s a new film version of *Dreamgirls* starring Beyoncé and a remake of *Sparkle* featuring Jordin Sparks also created connections between these singers and the Supremes, much like Diana Ross had with her depiction of Billie Holiday in *Lady Sings the Blues*. (The *Sparkle* remake changed its setting from New York in the 1950s to Detroit in the mid-1960s, connecting more obviously to Motown.)

55. "Motown Band," http://www.gigmasters.com/services/Motown-Band.

56. Timothy D. Taylor, *The Sounds of Capitalism: Music, Advertising, and the Conquest of Culture* (Chicago: University of Chicago Press, 2012), 151.

57. "Coke to Aim at Ethnic Groups," *Billboard*, October 15, 1966, 1, 10; "Boss! 'Things Go Better with Coke,'" *Chicago Defender*, February 22, 1966, 28. For some advertisements from this campaign, see "The Supremes Make It All Look So Easy" (advertisement), *Ebony* (February 1967), 25; "The Supremes Make It All Look So Easy" (advertisement), *Jet*, February 9, 1967, 29; "Diana Ross and the Supremes: Where Do They Go from Here?" (advertisement), *Ebony* (March 1968), 13. The *Boy's Life* advertisement appeared on the back cover of the February 1967 issue. The *American Girl* advertisement appeared on the back cover of the June 1968 issue. Cereal commercials featuring the Jackson 5 followed suit, airing during network cartoon programming on Saturday mornings.

58. Kennell Jackson, "The Shadow of Texts: Will Black Music and Singers Sell Everything on Television?," in *Black Cultural Traffic: Crossroads in Global Performance and Popular Culture*, ed. Harry J. Elam Jr. and Kennell Jackson (Ann Arbor: University of Michigan Press, 2005), 88–107. As Nicholas Cook writes on his work dealing with music in advertising, "Viewers rarely hear the music [in commercials] as such; they are rarely aware of it as an entity in itself"; Cook, *Analysing Musical Media* (Oxford: Clarendon Press, 1998), 20. See also Joyce Kurpiers, "Reality by Design: Advertising Image, Music and Sound Design in the Production of Culture" (PhD diss., Duke University, 2009); David Huron,

"Music in Advertising: An Analytic Paradigm," *Musical Quarterly* 73 (1989): 557–74; Bethany Klein, *As Heard on TV: Popular Music in Advertising* (Burlington, VT: Ashgate, 2009).

59. Joanna Love, "From Cautionary Chart-Topper to Friendly Beverage Anthem: Michael Jackson's 'Billie Jean' and Pepsi's 'Choice of a New Generation' Television Campaign," *Journal of the Society for American Music* 9 (2015): 178–203.

60. For another perspective on brand weakening, see Ronald Rodman, "Advertising Music: Strategies of Imbuement in Television Advertising Music," in *Sound and Music in Film and Visual Media*, ed. Graeme Harper, Ruth Doughty, and Jochen Eisentraut (New York: Continuum, 2009), 617–32.

61. See Michael Schudson's essay "Advertising as Capitalist Realism," which is quoted in Robert Fink, *Repeating Ourselves: American Minimal Music as Cultural Practice* (Berkeley: University of California Press, 2005), 74. See also Anahid Kassabian, *Ubiquitous Listening: Affect, Attention, and Distributed Subjectivity* (Berkeley: University of California Press, 2013), xi.

62. Taylor, *Sounds of Capitalism*, 165–75.

63. Other commercials from this campaign featured original versions of "When a Man Loves a Woman," by Percy Sledge; "Stand by Me," by Ben E. King; and "Wonderful World," by Sam Cooke.

64. A video exploring this advertising phenomenon ("Grown from the Grapevine: Race, Motown and the California Raisins") was produced by Manan Desai, Rob Crozier, Brad Norman, and Michael Walle for the conference "Growing Up Motown: Stevie Wonder, Michael Jackson and the Making of Motown," sponsored by the University of Michigan Center for Afro-American and African Studies.

65. For a literary reading of the Raisins as minstrelsy, see Ben Slote, "'The Goophered Grapevine' and Hearing Raisins Sing," *American Literary History* 6 (Winter 1994): 684–94.

66. Julie Liesse Erickson, "Hip Raisins Top List of Quarter's Best Ads," *Advertising Age*, January 19, 1987, 40.

67. Universal Music Enterprises and State Farm, "Universal Music Enterprises and State Farm Join in Unique Effort to Promote Popular TV Commercial and the Song "I'll Be There,'" press release, June 18, 2009, http://ume.edgeboss.net/download/ume/motown/statefarm.pdf.

68. The cross-marketing was extensive: "From a link on the State Farm homepage (statefarm.com), viewers may stream the 90-second high-definition version of the commercial also accessible on YouTube. In addition, a buy button on statefarm.com will click through to the 'I'll Be There' Minus Mix (a stripped down/acoustic version of the song) on iTunes. In turn, UMe will place the 60-second version of the commercial on its ilovethatsong.com and classic.motown.com Web sites; alert visitors to the Motown Facebook page of its availability; send e-mail blasts to all Motown.com subscribers with the commercial embedded; and conduct a search campaign tagging the commercial and song with a link to statefarm.com. The emotionally touching 'I'll Be There' commercial, which shows people helping, encouraging and supporting others, was prominently aired during the blockbuster 'American Idol' finale and will continue to be seen on broadcast television through the fall." Universal Music Enterprises and State Farm,

"Universal Music Enterprises and State Farm Join." Michael Jackson died a week after this press release was issued and State Farm stopped airing the commercial for a short period. Harry Weinger, telephone interview by author, May 25, 2010.

69. A number of Motown songs performed by white artists appeared prominently on the *Billboard* pop charts in the mid-1970s, including the Carpenters, "Please Mr. Postman"; Linda Ronstadt, "Heat Wave"; the Doobie Brothers, "Take Me in Your Arms"; James Taylor, "How Sweet It Is (To Be Loved by You)"; and Captain and Tennille, "Shop Around." There were many other popular Motown covers during the 1970s and 1980s. Many of these came after the arrival of Lester Sill as the president of Jobete in 1985, a legendary music publisher who helped to spur new uses of Motown's song catalog. These included the Beat, "Tears of a Clown"; the Flying Lizards, "Money (That's What I Want)"; Roger Troutman, "I Heard It through the Grapevine"; Soft Cell "Tainted Love"/"Where Did Our Love Go?"; Sister Sledge, "My Guy"; Mickey Gilley, "You Really Got a Hold on Me"; Van Halen, "Dancing in the Street"; David Bowie and Mick Jagger, "Dancing in the Street"; Bruce Springsteen, "War"; Kim Wilde, "You Keep Me Hangin' On"; Cyndi Lauper, "What's Going On"; Suavé, "My Girl"; and Mariah Carey, "I'll Be There."

70. D. L. Byron and the Stray Cats recorded other versions. In 2010 Collins also released the album *Going Back*, which included many other rerecordings of Motown songs.

71. Fitzgerald discusses this rhythmic motif as an essential aspect of the Motown Sound. Fitzgerald, "Motown Crossover Hits." See also Jon Fitzgerald, "Black Pop Songwriting 1963–1966: An Analysis of U.S. Top Forty Hits by Cooke, Mayfield, Stevenson, Robinson, and Holland-Dozier-Holland," *Black Music Research Journal* 27 (Fall 2007): 97–140.

72. Many other contemporaneous tracks incorporated this trope, such as Iggy Pop's "Lust for Life" and Elvis Costello's "Love for Tender."

73. This passage occurs in the song's second verse. It was reprinted on the single's picture sleeve. A number of pop songs mention Gaye. In addition to songs released after his death (discussed below), two modern examples are "Marvin Gaye" (Charlie Puth) and "Marvin Gaye and Chardonnay" (Big Sean).

74. The music video for "When Smokey Sings" includes many references to Northern Soul culture, demonstrating the manner in which Motown's music was still associated with this cultural formation during the late 1980s.

75. McNally's version of the song was released on his 1986 album *Fade to Black* and the soundtrack to the film *Quicksilver*. The track appears only minimally in the film (15:20–17:05) during a narrative section when a prominent African American character played by Laurence Fishburne appears for the first time.

76. Stewart released many R&B covers as singles in his career, including "(I Know) I'm Losing You" in 1971, two versions of "Twistin' the Night Away" (in 1972 and 1987), and "This Old Heart of Mine" in 1976. In the late 1980s Stewart also recorded several duets with prominent R&B performers, including another version of "This Old Heart of Mine" (with Ronald Isley) and a rendition of "It Takes Two" (with Tina Turner).

77. The Temptations' lineup had changed many times since the group's inception in the early 1960s. The only two original members were Otis Williams and

Melvin Franklin. Adding to a sense of generalization, this recording uses the Temptations to sing about the Miracles, freely interchanging one Motown vocal group for another.

78. RCA released this single after Ross's departure from Motown. It was written and coproduced by Lionel Richie.

79. Anecdotes cite a local Boston promoter using the name New Edition as a response to the Jackson 5; accordingly, there were many similarities between New Edition's first single, "Candy Girl," and the Jackson 5's "ABC." En Vogue incorporated a segment from "Who's Lovin' You" into the single "Hold On" and TLC released a track called "Ain't 2 Proud 2 Beg" on their first album.

80. Kedar Massenburg worked directly with both D'Angelo and Erykah Badu to promote neo-soul heavily before and after he became president of Motown.

81. Mayer Hawthorne's records provide a good example of the manner in which this form of retro-soul incorporated motown. He was a white singer born in 1979 who promoted his Michigan roots, dressed in sleek suits and horn-rimmed glasses, and used classic R&B instrumentation in his recordings. One of his early tracks was called "I Wish It Would Rain," taking its title from a popular Temptations song, and he used the "You Can't Hurry Love" trope as the musical foundation for another track, "Your Easy Lovin' Ain't Pleasin' Nothin.'" Other Hawthorne recordings begin with drum fills found commonly in Motown, use motown harmonic progressions, feature stylized backing vocals, and incorporate the Motown Beat. Rob Hoerburger, "Can a Nerd Have Soul?," *New York Times Magazine*, November 14, 2010, 40.

82. Critics commonly discussed connections between Saadiq's work and Motown. See Nate Chinen, "Multiple Visions of Soul Music's Past and Future," *New York Times*, August 29, 2008; Drew Tewksbury, "Raphael Saadiq at the Wiltern: A Perfect-Pitch Frontman," *LA Weekly*, November 23, 2009. Saadiq spoke about his indebtedness to Motown's music during the promotional period surrounding the release of *The Way I See It*; he also cooperated in an official "Motown 50 Podcast" called "Motown Built to Last" (episode 16, http://classic.motown.com/news.aspx?bid=78; page no longer available), and spoke at New York University on December 7, 2009, as part of a celebration of Motown's fiftieth anniversary.

83. For more on the Dap-Kings, see Saki Knafo, "Soul Reviver," *New York Times Magazine*, December 7, 2008, 38–43. Critics often cited Motown in reviews of this record. For examples, see Sasha Frere-Jones, "Amy's Circus: The Strange Power of Junkie Retro Soul," *New Yorker*, March 3, 2008, 76–78; Christian John Wikane, "Amy Winehouse: *Back to Black*," *PopMatters*, March 12, 2007, http://www.popmatters.com/pm/review/11293/amy-winehouse-back-to-black; Jon Pareles, "Amy Winehouse: 'Back to Black,'" *New York Times*, March 12, 2007, E4; and Christian Hoard, "Amy Winehouse," *Rolling Stone*, February 22, 2007, 76.

84. "Tears Dry on Their Own" was released as the fourth single from *Back to Black* in the United Kingdom in August 2007.

85. Remi's track uses slightly different instrumentation, changes the opening key from D major to E major, eliminates the modulation in the bridge, and adds two four-bar verse cycles after the first chorus section. (The original record abbreviates the second verse from four to two verse cycles, which accelerates the entrance of the second chorus; Remi's rerecording simply makes the structure of

the second verse-chorus complex parallel to the first.) Salaam Remi, telephone interview by author, May 26, 2010.

86. References to motown were widespread in hip-hop music during the 1990s and 2000s. Among countless references to Motown artists, Marvin Gaye was a particular subject of interest for rap lyricists. Ice Cube mentioned Gaye in "Bop Gun" and 2Pac created two lyrical passages that invoked Gaye, one in "Keep Ya Head Up" and the other on the track "Thugz Mansion," a collaboration with Nas. Hip-hop producers also sampled Motown tracks. Two important rap hits that incorporated significant elements of Motown records were "O. P. P.," by Naughty by Nature (which used "ABC"), and "I'll Be There for You," by Method Man and Mary J. Blige (which used "You're All I Need to Get By"). See also Fergie's version of the Temptations' "Get Ready," titled "Here I Come."

87. Wikane notes how "Tears Dry on Their Own" "recasts the spirit of its instantly recognizable source material. . . . Here, the song is an ode to Winehouse's independence, even though her heart is broken. In contrast to Marvin Gaye's soaring vocal, Winehouse flips the melody in the verses so that it descends rather than ascends. . . . The way she spits out the syllables of *inevitable* conveys a forced admission that she might be better off without her man"; Wikane, "Amy Winehouse"; emphasis in original.

88. This track appeared on Thicke's 2009 album *Sex Therapy*.

89. The rerecording was made explicit at the time on Thicke's website: "'Million Dollar Baby' completes this trilogy of more troubled songs, using, appropriately enough, the music bed from Marvin Gaye's 'Trouble Man' (played by Robin's band, not sampled). With Jazmine Sullivan singing background, Thicke sings about needing Lady Luck to get his life back on track"; http://www.robin-thicke.com/bio, accessed May 26, 2010 (this biography has since changed).

90. Thicke was open about these connections in the press surrounding the release of *Sex Therapy*, noting that the album title overtly aligned with "the history of Marvin Gaye." Robin Thicke, interview aired on Fox 5 (Atlanta), January 22, 2010 (*Good Day Atlanta*). On the subject of ethnic crossover, Thicke showed a willingness to poke fun at himself by participating in the parody "White in America—The Children," *Daily Show with Jon Stewart*, produced by Ian Berger, edited by Mark Paone, aired May 7, 2009, http://www.thedailyshow.com/watch/thu-may-7-2009/white-in-america—the-children.

91. Ben Sisario, "In Dispute over a Song, Marvin Gaye's Family Files a Countersuit," *New York Times*, October 31, 2013, B2; Ben Sisario and Noah Smith, "'Blurred Lines' Infringed on Marvin Gaye Copyright, Jury Rules," *New York Times*, March 10, 2015, B1.

92. These inductees include: Benny Benjamin (2003), the Four Tops (1990), Marvin Gaye (1987), Berry Gordy (1988), Holland-Dozier-Holland (1990), the Isley Brothers (1992), the Jackson 5 (1997), Michael Jackson (2001), James Jamerson (2000), Gladys Knight and the Pips (1996), Martha and the Vandellas (1995), Smokey Robinson (1987), the Supremes (1988), the Temptations (1989), Stevie Wonder (1989), and the Miracles (2012). Library of Congress, "Paul Simon to be Awarded First Annual Gershwin Prize for Popular Song by Library of Congress," press release, March 1, 2007, http://www.loc.gov/today/pr/2007/07–010.html.

Bibliography

AAC   Alan E. Abrams Collection, Bentley Historical Library, University of Michigan

BGU   Music Library and Sound Recordings Archives, Bowling Green State University, Bowling Green, OH

BHL   Bentley Historical Library, University of Michigan, Ann Arbor

BL   British Library, London, UK

EMU   Gordy Motown Audio Collection, Eastern Michigan University, Ypsilanti

HAC   Motown Collection, E. Azalia Hackley Collection, Detroit Public Library

NGC   Nelson George Collection, Archives of African-American Music and Culture, Indiana University, Bloomington

RRF   Rock and Roll Hall of Fame, Library and Archives, Cleveland

UME   Universal Music Enterprises Corporate Archive, New York

I. Interviews and Personal Communication

Abrams, Alan. Telephone interview by author. May 21, 2008.
Abrams, Alan. E-mail message to author. March 27, 2009.
Atkins, Cholly. Interview by unknown person. Date unknown. Transcript. NGC.
Bell, David. Telephone interview by author. October 12, 2009.
Berger, Shelly. Telephone interview by author. January 14, 2015.
Charge, Eric. E-mail message to author. January 31, 2009.
Curtis, Alan. Telephone interview by author. October 13, 2009.
Farr, Lindsay. Telephone interview by author. August 12, 2015.
Fuqua, Harvey. Interview by Nelson George. Date unknown. Transcript. NGC.
Hughes, Keith. E-mail message to author. January 30, 2009.
Hughes, Keith. E-mail message to author. November 8, 2014.
Hughes, Keith, and Eric Charge. Interview by author. April 12, 2008.
Hughes, Keith, and Eric Charge. Interview by author. July 16, 2009.
King, Maurice. Interview by Dearborn Hyatt. December 21, 1983. Transcript. NGC.

McLean, Mike. Telephone interview by author. March 31, 2015.

Morris, Andrew. E-mail message to author. July 16, 2014.

Nathan, David. Interview by author. March 15, 2009.

Nathan, David. E-mail message to author, December 9, 2011.

Oehler, Dale. Telephone interview by Harry Weinger. February 8, 2006.

Powell, Maxine. Interview by Nelson George. December 22, 1983. Transcript. NGC.

Remi, Salaam. Telephone interview by author. May 26, 2010.

Staples, Beatriz. Telephone interview by author. November 26, 2014.

Weinger, Harry. Telephone interview by author. May 25, 2010.

II. Unpublished Material and Press Releases

[Abrams, Alan E.]. "Beatles Boost Detroit." Motown press release, September 10, 1964. AAC.

[Abrams, Alan E.]. "City Honors Berry Gordy." Motown press release, May 27, 1965. AAC.

[Abrams, Alan E.]. "Command Performance for Detroit's Supremes." Motown press release, February 18, 1965. AAC.

[Abrams, Alan E.]. "Detroit Common Council Honors the Supremes." Motown press release, January 28, 1966. AAC.

[Abrams, Alan E.]. "'Detroit Sound' Artists to Climax British Tour with Gala Paris Performance." Motown press release, April 9, 1965. AAC.

[Abrams, Alan E.]. "'Detroit Sound' Leads Pack in Auto Tape Cartridge Sales." Motown press release, June 17, 1966. AAC.

[Abrams, Alan E.]. "Do Mixed Marriages Work." Stax press release, undated. AAC.

[Abrams, Alan E.]. "Hitsville U.S.A. to Hitsville U.K." Motown press release, March 23, 1965. AAC.

[Abrams, Alan E.]. "Holland-Dozier-Holland Answers Motown in 22-Million-Dollar Lawsuit." Press release, November 15, 1968. AAC.

[Abrams, Alan E.]. "Invictus/Holland-Dozier-Holland—Capital Tie-In—Precedent Setting Victory for Creative Talent." Press release, May 19, 1969. AAC.

[Abrams, Alan E.]. "It's Official! Billy Eckstine Signs with Motown." Motown press release, February 15, 1965. AAC.

Abrams, Alan E. Letter to Barbara Holliday. July 21, 1965. AAC.

Abrams, Alan E. Letter to Bill Buchanan. January 4, 1966. AAC.

Abrams, Alan E. Letter to Bill Gandell. October 28, 1965. AAC.

Abrams, Alan E. Letter to Bill Gandell. December 20, 1965. AAC.

Abrams, Alan E. Letter to Frank Judge. March 22, 1965. AAC.

Abrams, Alan E. Letter to Joe X. Price. August 17, 1965. AAC.

Abrams, Alan E. Letter to John Finlayson. March 22, 1965. AAC.

Abrams, Alan E. Letter to John Finlayson. April 2, 1965. AAC.

Abrams, Alan E. Letter to Michaela Williams. August 26, 1965. AAC.

Abrams, Alan E. Letter to Michaela Williams. September 28, 1965. AAC.

Abrams, Alan E. Letter to Ralph Seltzer. March 30, 1965. AAC.

Abrams, Alan E. Letter to Ralph Seltzer. May 5, 1965. AAC.

Abrams, Alan E. Letter to Ralph Seltzer. May 6, 1965. AAC.

Abrams, Alan E. Letter to Richard Christiansen. August 19, 1965. AAC.

[Abrams, Alan E.]. "Lightening Strikes Thrice." Motown press release, November 23, 1964. AAC.

[Abrams, Alan E.]. "Marvin Gaye Returns to 20 Grand." Motown press release, February 15, 1965. AAC.

Abrams, Alan E. Memorandum. August 18, 1965. AAC.

[Abrams, Alan E.]. "More of the 'Detroit Sound' on National Television." Motown press release, March 15, 1965. AAC.

[Abrams, Alan E.]. "Motown Now Number One in U.S. Single Record Sales." Motown press release, January 3, 1966. AAC

[Abrams, Alan E.]. Motown press release, February 15, 1965. AAC.

[Abrams, Alan E.]. Motown press release, March 8, 1965. AAC.

[Abrams, Alan E.]. Motown press release, March 22, 1965. AAC.

[Abrams, Alan E.]. Motown press release, June 25, 1965. AAC.

[Abrams, Alan E.]. Motown press release, August 31, 1965. AAC.

[Abrams, Alan E.]. Motown press release, September 29, 1965. AAC.

[Abrams, Alan E.]. "T.A.M.I. Show Production Documents, 1964–1965." RRF.

Abrams, Alan E. Telegram to S. Prokoff. March 6, 1965. AAC.

[Abrams, Alan E.]. "Temptations to Record Radio Spot for Domestic Peace Corps." Motown press release, June 21, 1966. AAC.

Abrams, Alan E. "Top Priority." Internal Motown memorandum. November 17, 1964. AAC.

[Abrams, Alan E.]. "U.S. Senate Leaders Unite in Support and Praise of 'The Memphis Sound.'" Stax press release, April 28, 1967. AAC.

[Abrams, Alan E.]. "What's Happened to Show Business?" Motown press release, undated. AAC.

"Biography of Rick James." Motown press release, ca. 1982. BGU.

"Catalog: January 1959/March 1967." Jobete Music Company, Inc. EMU.

Christiansen, Richard. Letter to Al Abrams. August 16, 1965, AAC. "Eddie Holland." Biography, undated (ca. 1959). AAC.

Edwards, Esther G. Letter to Harold E. Sponberg. September 6, 1972. EMU.

Edwards, Esther. "The Role of Youth In a Changing Society." Speech delivered at the Annual Workshop for Front People, October 26, 1967. EMU.

"An Evening with the Motown Sound." Motortown Revue tour booklet, undated (ca. 1966), EMU.

"An Evening with the Motown Sound." Motortown Revue tour booklet, undated (ca. 1967). EMU.

"Gladys Knight and the Pips." Promotional booklet (ca. 1967). HAC.

Gordy Foundation, Inc. "The Loucye Gordy Wakefield Scholarship Fund." Pamphlet, 1969. EMU.

Griffin, Junius. "'Stevie Wonder . . . The Man' Headlines Copacabana Show March 19–April 1." Motown press release, March 16, 1970. BGU.

Head, Lonny. Letter to Mildred Smith. August 11, 1972. EMU.

"I. M. C. Artists: Assigned Managers, Administrators, Road Managers, and Agencies." March 30, 1970. EMU.

Leach, Robin. Letter to Al Abrams. October 6, [1965]. AAC.

Marshall, A. P. Letter to Esther Edwards. November 2, 1972. EMU.

Marshall, A. P. Letter to Harold E. Sponberg. October 5, 1972. EMU.

Massey, Jon. Letter to Al Abrams Associates. March 17, 1967. AAC.

Miller, Edgar H. Letter to Mr. Al Abrams. May 3, 1967. AAC.

"The Motown Sound . . . Acclaimed the World Over, 'The Detroit Sound.'" Motown advertising brochure. ca. 1965. EMU.

Roshkind, Michael. Letter to Al Abrams. October 12, 1971. AAC.

"Schwartz Brothers Collection." RRF.

Sponberg, Harold E. Letter to Ester Edwards [sic]. August 25, 1972. EMU.

Supremes promotional schedule. February 11, 1965. AAC.

U.S. Trademark and Patent Office, Trademark Trial and Appeal Board. *UMG Recordings, Inc. vs. Mattel, Inc.* Filed November 10, 2005, mailed September 30, 2011.

III. Newsletter Articles

Carlyle, Mike. Letter to the editor. *Hitsville U.S.A.* 1, no. 5 (May 1965): 96.

Coleman, Pat. "What Motown Is All About: Guardians of the Motown Sound Are with Studio Facilities." *Motown Newsletter: A Monthly Report on Motown Record Corporation* 1, no. 3 (March 1972): 2.

"Editorial." *Hitsville U.S.A. Memorial Edition: Our Mick* (ca. September 1965).

Gaye, Marvin. Letter to the editor. *Mary Wells and Motown News* 1, no. 4 (ca. May 1964): 36–37.

[Godin, Dave]. "Behind the Scenes at Motown: The Writers." *Hitsville U.S.A.* 1, no. 1 (January 1965): 15–16.

[Godin, Dave]. "Behind the Scenes at Motown: The Writers." *Hitsville U.S.A.* 1, no. 2 (February 1965): 26, 33.

[Godin], Dave. "Dear Member." *Mary Wells and Motown News* 1, no. 3 (ca. March 1964): 21.

[Godin], Dave. "Dear Swinger and Friend." *Hitsville U.S.A.* 1, no. 12 (February 1966): 231–32.

[Godin], Dave. "Dear Swinger and Friend." *Mary Wells and Motown News* 1, no. 5 (ca. June 1964): 45–46.

[Godin, Dave]. "1964: A Year to Remember." *Hitsville U.S.A.* 1, no. 1 (January 1965): 9–12.

[Godin, Dave]. "Recent Visitors." *Hitsville U.S.A.* 1, no. 8 (August 1965): 154–56.

Gordy, Berry, Jr. Letter to the editor. *Hitsville U.S.A.* 1, no. 3 (ca. March 1965): 42.

Gordy, Berry, Jr. Letter to the editor. *Mary Wells and Motown News* 1, no. 4 (ca. May 1964): 36.

Harrison, Malcolm. "Report from Liverpool." *Hitsville U.S.A.* 1, no. 6 (June 1965): 116–17.

"Jimmy Ruffin: Just Jimmy." *Soul* (Toronto), May 1967, 3.

Miracles Quintet. Letter to the editor. *Mary Wells and Motown News* 1, no. 4 (ca. May 1964): 36–37.

[Reeves], Martha. Letter to the editor. *Hitsville U.S.A.* 1, no. 8 (August 1965): 147.

"Le Rhythm and Blues." *R'n'B Panorama* 1 (February 1960): 1.

Russell, Mary. Letter to the editor. *Hitsville U.S.A.* 1, no. 5 (May 1965), 97.

"Stevie's Journey." *Soul* (Toronto), December 1966, 6–7.

Wilder, Amos A. "Management Explains Reasons for Layoff Activity." *Motown Newsletter: A Monthly Report on Motown Record Corporation* 1, no. 3 (March 1972): 1. EMU.

IV. Contemporary Press

"A&M Ties with RCA for Distrib, Pressing in U.S." *Variety*, January 17, 1979, 73.

"AFM Ban on Foreign Musicians Causes Pitt Symph. Mex. Headaches." *Variety*, March 19, 1947, 42.

"Al Bell First Negro Veep." *Milwaukee Star*, August 19, 1967.

"Al Bell Is First Negro Veep of a Tennessee Disc Firm." *Dallas Post Tribune*, August 12, 1967.

"Al Bell Named Veep of Stax-Volt Records." *Birmingham (AL) World*, August 16, 1967.

"Ales Reins Motown in General Overhaul." *Variety*, July 30, 1969, 61.

Aletti, Vince. "Decline of Norman Whitfield." *Rolling Stone*, April 27, 1972, 52.

Aletti, Vince. "The Motown Story: The First Decade." *Rolling Stone*, May 13, 1971, 40–42.

Aletti, Vince. "Trouble Man." *Rolling Stone*, March 1, 1973, 63.

Alterman, Loraine. "You Can't Beat an Original." *New York Times*, January 7, 1973, AL30.

"America's Most Amazing Family: The Famous Gordys of Detroit Have What It Takes." *Color*, July 1949, 6–8.

"'Anatomy of Pop' Analyzes Music." *Chicago Daily Defender*, January 10, 1966, 20.

Arnold, Gary. "A Cool Hero in 'Trouble.'" *Washington Post, Times Herald*, November 18, 1972, C7.

"Atco to Handle Jackson's Disc." *Billboard*, January 15, 1966, 18.

"Atlantic-Atco Distrib for Lu Pine, Campus." *Billboard*, January 27, 1962, 5.

"Atlantic Israeli and Venezuelan Reps Named by Label." *Billboard*, March 17, 1962, 5.

"Atlantic Names Turkish Distrib." *Billboard*, April 28, 1962, 5.

"Atlantic Signs Pact with Discos of Peru." *Billboard*, May 5, 1962, 8.

"Atlantic Signs with New O'Seas Distrib Firms." *Billboard*, April 20, 1963, 3.

"Atlantic to Distribute 'Last Night.'" *Billboard*, May 29, 1961, 5.

"Atlantic to Handle Distribution for Dial." *Billboard*, November 14, 1964, 4.

"Atlantic to Have Its Own Label in Britain." *Record Retailer*, July 16, 1964, 12.

Baker, Ainslie. "Listen Here." *Australian Women's Weekly*, August 17, 1960, 39.

"Band Business Speculates on Stand by Petrillo to Bar Foreign Outfits." *Variety*, May 25, 1949, 36.

Barnes, Charles. "'Sparkle' Faces Suit by Motown." *Philadelphia Tribune*, April 10, 1976, 1, 2.

"Bell To Stax-Volt." *Billboard*, October 9, 1965, 12.

Bennett, Lerone, Jr. "The Soul of Soul." *Ebony*, December 1961, 111–20.

Berry, William Earl. "How 'Super Fly' Is Changing the Behavior of Blacks." *Jet*, December 28, 1972, 54–58.

"Biggest Pop Launch Ever for Tamla-Motown." *Record Retailer*, March 11, 1965, 20.

"Billboard Adopts 'R&B' as New Name for Two Charts." *Billboard*, October 27, 1990, 6, 35.

"Black Businesses Grow." *New Pittsburgh Courier*, May 24, 1980, 24.

"Blind Date." *Melody Maker*, December 5, 1964, 11.

"Boss! 'Things Go Better with Coke.'" *Chicago Defender*, February 22, 1966, 28.

"Brief Encounter." *Pittsburgh Courier*, October 31, 1964, 17.

"Britons Launch R&B Gazette." *Billboard*, June 29, 1963, 6.

"Bumper Crop Get Gordy Scholarships." *Baltimore Afro-American*, October 3, 1970, 14.

Calloway, Al. "An Introduction to Soul." In *Smiling through the Apocalypse: "Esquire's" History of the Sixties*, edited by Harold Hayes, 708–12. New York: McCall, 1970.

Canby, Vincent. "'Lady Sings the Blues' Stars Diana Ross." *New York Times*, October 19, 1972.

Canby, Vincent. "The Ten Worst Movies of 1972." *New York Times*, January 7, 1972.

"Capitol of Mexico Will Add 2 Labels to Its Catalog in 1968." *Billboard*, January 6, 1968, 37.

Cassidy, Sharon. "Enthusiasm Bursts for Smokey Robinson." *Detroit News*, August 14, 1969.

"CBS Pact with Tamla in Israel." *Billboard*, January 3, 1970, 48–49.

Chinen, Nate. "Multiple Visions of Soul Music's Past and Future." *New York Times*, August 29, 2008.

"Coke to Aim at Ethnic Groups." *Billboard*, October 15, 1966, 1, 10.

"Cold Good-Bye from Motown." *Detroit Free Press*, June 25, 1972, 2C.

Coleman, Larry G. "The Trouble with 'Trouble Man.'" *New Pittsburgh Courier*, November 25, 1972, 17.

Coleman, Ray. "Mary Wells: 'We've Got a Lot to Thank the Beatles For.'" *Melody Maker*, June 20, 1964, 7.

"Complete Tamla-Motown Discography of British Releases." *Record Mirror*, December 19, 1964, 17.

"Composers Sue Motown for 22 Million-Dollars." *Daily Defender*, November 20, 1968.

Conyers, John, Jr. "Berry Gordy, Jr.: Still Paying His Dues." 92nd Cong., 1st sess., *Congressional Record* 117 (April 19, 1971).

"Copacabana, N.Y." *Variety*, August 4, 1965, 60.

"CORE Supports Fight of Black Exploitation." *Los Angeles Sentinel*, August 17, 1972, B7.

"Cosdel Opens Operations in Singapore." *Billboard*, August 1, 1964, 1.

Crowther, Bosley. "'Nothing but a Man' and 'Lilith' Presented." *New York Times*, September 21, 1964, 37.

Cummings, Tony. "The Strange World of Northern Soul." *Black Music*, June 1974, 8–9, 38.

Dawbarn, Bob. "The Detroit Sound Forms a Beach-Head." *Melody Maker*, November 14, 1964, 10.

Dawbarn, Bob. "Supremes Suddenly Shoot to Stardom." *Melody Maker*, October 17, 1964, 7.

Dawbarn, Bob. "Tamla Motown: Not So Much a Pop Sound, More a Way of Life." *Melody Maker*, March 27, 1965, 10.

Dawbarn, Bob. "Well—What Is R & B?" *Melody Maker*, March 30, 1963, 6.

Delehant, Jim. "Otis Redding: Soul Survivor." *Hit Parader*, August 1967.

Delehant, Jim. "Steve Cropper." *Hit Parader*, September 1967, 44–45.

Delehant, Jim. "Steve Cropper, Part 2." *Hit Parader*, October 1967, 42–43.

"Detroit and L.A. Sales 'Happening Places.'" *Billboard*, July 2, 1966, 1.

"Detroit Is Cared About." *Detroit Free Press*, August 12, 1969.

"Diana Ross and the Supremes: Where Do They Go from Here?" (advertisement). *Ebony*, March 1968, 13.

"Diana Ross to Portray Billie Holiday in Film." *Norfolk, VA New Journal and Guide*, July 3, 1971.

"Diana Ross TVer Bows Motown $15 Mil Project." *Billboard*, December 19, 1970, 3.

"Documentary to Feature Three Motown Acts." *Billboard*, April 2, 1966, 62.

Donnachie, Sammy. Letter to the editor. *Record Mirror*, February 8, 1964, 2.

Dove, Ian. "Britain Is Soul Country." *Billboard*, August 17, 1968, section 2 ("The World of Soul"), 47–48.

Dove, Ian. "A Warning to the Tamla-Motown Visitors from Their Biggest Fan!" *New Musical Express*, March 19, 1965, 9. Reprinted in *Hitsville U.S.A.* 1, no. 4 (April 1965): 79.

Durant, Celeste. "CORE Moves to Pre-edit Black Films." *Los Angeles Times*, September 20, 1972, A24.

"EMI Acquires Tamla-Motown for Britain." *Billboard*, September 28, 1963, 3.

"EMI Are to Launch Tamla-Motown Label: Major Promotion Campaign Announced." *Record Retailer*, February 18, 1965, 8.

"Entertainment Writer Blasts Motown Record Corporation." *Pittsburgh New Courier*, September 30, 1967, 9.

Eriksen, Espen. "Soul in Scandinavia." *Billboard*, August 17, 1968, section 2 ("The World of Soul"), 52.

"An Exciting New Star" (advertisement). *Billboard*, October 8, 1966, 7.

"Exports, Imports, Our Marvelettes." *Detroit Free Press*, March 5, 1965, 8B.

"Fete Blasts Off Rare Earth—Motown's New Hip Label." *Billboard*, August 30, 1969, 78.

Fletcher, Colin. "Beat and Gangs on Merseyside." *New Society*, February 20, 1964, 11–14.

Fletcher, Peter. "Hal Davis: A History of Gold and Platinum." *Record World*, January 26, 1980, 86.

Flint, Jerry M. "Scholarship Ball Draws Detroit's Blacks." *New York Times*, April 26, 1971, 45.

"Four Tops on Frost TV Show." *New Musical Express*, November 4, 1966, 9.

"Four Tops Score in Great Britain," *New Journal and Guide*, March 18, 1967, 14.

"Four Tops Tour Set—Here Soon for TV." *New Musical Express*, October 28, 1966, 8.

Frederick, Robert B. "Music-Records: Drugs, Brutal Sex, Chicanery Part of Jesmer's Black Disk Novel." *Variety*, May 22, 1974, 68.

Frere-Jones, Sasha. "Amy's Circus: The Strange Power of Junkie Retro Soul." *New Yorker*, March 3, 2008, 76–78.

"From Abroad." *Cash Box*, January 12, 1963, 3.

"From Boxing to Music." *Michigan Chronicle*, October 10, 1959.

"From the Music Capitals of the World: Germany." *Billboard*, November 23, 1963, 36.

"From the Music Capitals of the World: Holland." *Billboard*, December 7, 1963, 31.

"From the Music Capitals of the World: Jerusalem." *Billboard*, June 14, 1969, 79.

"From the Music Capitals of the World: Milan." *Billboard*, November 12, 1966, 54.

"From the Music Capitals of the World: Milan." *Billboard*, June 17, 1967, 54.

"From the Music Capitals of the World: Milan." *Billboard*, December 2, 1967, 72.

"From the Music Capitals of the World: Oslo." *Billboard*, July 24, 1965, 21.

"From the Music Capitals of the World: Stockholm." *Billboard*, May 20, 1967, 16.

Gavin, Bill. "No Musical Color Line." *Billboard*, April 25, 1964, 46.

Gelman, Morrie. "Motown Productions Reorganized; De Passe Heads Film-TV Division." *Variety*, February 4, 1981, 30.

"Gene Pitney's 72 Days with the Supremes." *New Musical Express*, October 2, 1964, 14.

Gent, George. "An Evening of Specials on N.B.C." *New York Times*, November 13, 1969, 95.

"Get this Tamla Motown Sound—On Record" (advertisement). *Record Retailer*, March 18, 1965.

Gillison, J. "They Call It 'Soul' Music: 'Down Home' Jazz Feeling Scoring a 'Swinging' Hit with the Public." *Philadelphia Tribune*, May 16, 1961, 5.

Gipson, Gertrude. "Ivan Dixon Directs 'Mr. T.'" *Los Angeles Sentinel*, April 20, 1972, B3A.

"The Girlie Groups." *Melody Maker*, March 20, 1965, 10.

Gleason, Ralph J. "Perspectives: 'Cover' Versions and Their Origins." *Rolling Stone*, June 7, 1973, 7.

Gold, Richard. "Motown Not Seeking Distribution Deal with Major, Says Lasker; Indie Wholesalers Hang Tough." *Variety*, April 6, 1983, 69.

"Gordy Bares Expansion Plans." *Chicago Defender*, October 30, 1967.

"Gordy Expands Motown Industries." *Variety*, January 10, 1973, 51.

"Gordy Shakes up Motown; Abner Exits, Ales Back." *Variety*, September 10, 1975, 71.

Gray, Andy. "The Sound of Motown Plus Georgie Fame—Great!" *New Musical Express*, March 26, 1965, 9.

Gray, Bill. "In Detroit to Stay: Motown News." *Detroit News*, October 25, 1970.

Gray, Bill. "What's Behind Motown Move?" *Detroit News*, June 25, 1972, 1G.

Grevatt, Ren. "Smash-Hit Supremes Tell Why." *Melody Maker*, September 19, 1964, 7.

Griffin, Rita. "Motown's New Veep, GM, Tells Firm's Future Plans." *Michigan Chronicle*, June 24, 1972, 1, 4.

Hall, Claude. "Atlantic Helped Pave the Way." *Billboard*, June 24, 1967, section 2 ("The World of Soul"), 16–17.

Hall, Claude. "The Best Ears in the Business." *Billboard*, June 24, 1967, section 2 ("The World of Soul"), 14–15.

Hall, Claude. "R&B Stations Open Airplay to 'Blue-Eyed Soulists.'" *Billboard*, October 9, 1965, 1, 49.

Hall, Tony. "The Tony Hall Column." *Record Mirror*, February 13, 1965, 4.

Hamilton, James. "Supremes Will Not Do Package Shows." *Record Mirror*, October 3, 1964, 6.

Hartford, Margaret. "The Detroit-Liverpool Sound." *Los Angeles Times*, March 19, 1965, D12.

"Hear That Big Sound." *Life*, May 21, 1965, 82–92.

"Heath Asks AFM English-American Exchange of Bands." *Variety*, October 23, 1954, 13.

Hennessey, Mike. "Gallic Radio, TV Has Soul." *Billboard*, August 17, 1968, section 2 ("The World of Soul"), 50.

Hennessey, Mike. "Giant Launching Is Given Tamla-Motown in France." *Billboard*, May 1, 1965, 14.

Hevesi, Dennis. "Jheryl Busby, 59, Reviver of the Motown Label, Dies." *New York Times*, November 8, 2008, A22.

Higgins, Chester. "'Shaft' Spotlights Newest Black Stars." *Jet*, July 8, 1971, 54–58.

Higgins, Chester. "Black Films: Boom or Bust?" *Jet*, June 8, 1972, 52–59.

Hilburn, Robert. "Motown Records Spinning Off into Films, TV." *Los Angeles Times*, April 18, 1971, R1.

"Hit Comes to Johnson Via 'Come to Me.'" *Billboard*, April 6, 1959, 6.

"Hitsville Is Converted into Motown Museum." *Variety*, December 9, 1987, 72.

Hoard, Christian. "Amy Winehouse." *Rolling Stone*, February 22, 2007, 76.

Hochman, Steve. "A 'Motown' History Lesson." *Los Angeles Times*, October 24, 1990.

Hoerburger, Rob. "Can a Nerd Have Soul?" *New York Times Magazine*, November 14, 2010, 40.

"Hohner Chromatic Harmonicas as Played by Stevie Wonder" (advertisement). *Melody Maker*, February 1, 1964, 3.

Holland, Bill. "Labels Strive to Rectify Past Archival Problems." *Billboard*, July 12, 1997.

"House Review: Olympia Paris." *Variety*, December 25, 1963, 40.

"I Don't Know What to Do" (advertisement). *Billboard*, August 28, 1965, 9.

"The Instrumental Hit from Memphis" (advertisement). *Billboard*, May 29, 1961, 33.

Ivory, Lee. "Among the Stars." *Chicago Defender*, February 5, 1966, national edition, 15.

"Jazzers' Importation Gets into Parliament." *Variety*, November 24, 1922, 2.

"Jim Stewart: The Voice from Soulsville." *Billboard*, Section 2, June 24, 1967, section 2, 30–31.

"Jobete Expands; Levington Mgr." *Billboard*, April 20, 1966, 1, 8.

"Jobete Writers Join ASCAP." *Los Angeles Sentinel*, March 23, 1972, B2A.

Johnson, Derek. "Pounding Supremes." *New Musical Express*, October 16, 1964, 6.

Johnson, Langley. "'I Was Wrong' Says Brian." *Record Mirror*, February 1, 1964, 7.

Jones, LeRoi. "Apple Cores." *Down Beat* 32 (March 25, 1965): 34.

Jones, Peter. "Brian Poole Answers His Critics: 'I Can Dance' Is No Copy of 'Do You Love Me.'" *Record Mirror*, December 7, 1963, 6.

Jones, Peter. "'I'm No Copyist' Says Brian Poole." *Record Mirror*, November 16, 1963, 12.

Jones, Peter. "'Why We Copied the 4 Tops': Peter Jones Talks to the Fourmost." *Record Mirror*, November 21, 1964, 4.

Jopling, Norman. "America Hits Back with Tamla Motown Attack." *Record Mirror*, March 20, 1965, 6–7.

Jopling, Norman. "The Great Unknowns." *New Record Mirror*, March 9, 1963, 6.

Jopling, Norman. "The Great Unknowns—Mary Wells." *New Record Mirror*, May 4, 1963, 7.

Jopling, Norman. "The Great Unknowns: No. 7—The Marvelettes." *New Record Mirror*, June 1, 1963, 3.

Jopling, Norman. "The Great Unknowns: No. 14—The Contours." *New Record Mirror*, September 28, 1963, 4.

Jopling, Norman. "The Tamla Fans That Hated Us: The Kinks Talk to RM's Norman Jopling." *Record Mirror*, April 17, 1965, 6.

Jordan, Vernon E., Jr. "How Hollywood Degrades Blacks." *New York Amsterdam News*, October 14, 1972, D1.

Kael, Pauline. "The Current Cinema: Pop versus Jazz." *New Yorker*, November 4, 1972, 152.

"KBTR Exclusive: Supremes Far East Tour." *KBRT All American*, September 26, 1966, 3.

"King Brass to Take Road." *Billboard*, October 26, 1963, 49–50.

Knafo, Saki. "Soul Reviver." *New York Times Magazine*, December 7, 2008, 38–43.

"Lady Soul: Singing It Like It Is." *Time*, June 28, 1968, 62–66.

Landau, Jon. "The Motown Story." *Rolling Stone*, May 13, 1971, 42–44.

Landau, Jon. "A Whiter Shade of Black." *Crawdaddy*, October 1967, 34–40.

"Letters to the Editor." *Ebony*, January 1973, 11A.

"Life Lines of the Four Tops." *New Musical Express*, November 26, 1966, 6.

Lingeman, Richard R. "The Big, Happy, Beating Heart of the Detroit Sound." *New York Times*, November 27, 1966.

"London Rocks 'n' Rolls as Bill Haley Arrives." *New York Times*, February 6, 1957.

Mack. "Scott Joplin (Color)." *Variety*, February 9, 1977, 22.

"The Magnificent Puts Soul Behind His Work." *Billboard*, May 23, 1964, 14, 39.

"Major Film Company Hires First Black Camera Operator." *Philadelphia Tribune*, July 11, 1972, 19.

Marks, Cordell. "Time with the Supremes." *New Musical Express*, October 23, 1964, 3.

"MCA 'Official' Motown Distributor; Overseas Licensees Standing Firm." *Variety*, July 6, 1983.

McClain, A. L. "Germans Dig the Supremes." *Detroit News*, January 26, 1965, 4.

McGregor, Craig. "Nothing Like a Shot of Soul to Pep Up Rock." *New York Times*, September 12, 1971, D23.

McKee, June. "Sound from Motown." *Michigan Challenge*, June 1968, 40–41.

Mims, Greg. "1973's Top Ten Soul Albums." *New Pittsburgh Courier*, December 22, 1973, 19.

Moore, Don. "Carla and Stax are Synonomous [*sic*]." *Michigan Chronicle*, April 29, 1967.

"Motown A&R Chief and Wife Kim Weston Split Diskery." *Philadelphia Tribune*, January 10, 1967, 11.

"Motown Acts for Overseas." *Billboard*, June 25, 1966, 6.

"Motown and A&M Form Joint Distrib." *Variety*, January 15, 1975, 75.

"Motown Begins Empire-Building." *Variety*, November 28, 1973, 5.

"Motown Buys Golden World." *Billboard*, September 10, 1966, 10.

"Motown Crew off to Europe for Big Push." *Billboard*, March 2, 1963, 6.

"Motown Distribbing 14 Labels on Coast." *Variety*, May 18, 1983, 63.

"Motown Dumps Pickwick Distrib to Launch It's Own Coast Branch; Pickwick Cedes Southeast to M.S." *Variety*, April 13, 1983, 71.

"Motown Execs to Europe." *Record World*, October 10, 1964.

"Motown Expands." *Variety*, September 7, 1966, 43.

"Motown Expansion in High with B'Way, TV, Movies." *Billboard*, June 11, 1966, 1, 10.

"Motown Grosses $39 Million; Disc Firm to Remain in Detroit." *Jet*, December 3, 1970, 53.

"Motown Meets Tinseltown." *Rolling Stone*, December 24, 1970, 18.

"Motown Opens Coast Office." *Billboard*, November 16, 1963, 48.

"Motown Pushes out Wall." *Billboard*, January 11, 1964, 32.

"Motown Record President to Set Up Foreign Deal." *Pittsburgh Courier*, March 9, 1963, 17.

"Motown Revue Here Next Year." *Record Mirror*, October 17, 1964, 9.

"Motown's Distrib. Stays Indie; 1979 Looks Like Biggest Year." *Variety*, April 4, 1979, 106.

"Motown Setting up Offices in England." *Variety*, May 20, 1970, 47.

"The Motown Sound" (advertisement). *Billboard*, August 27, 1966, LV25.

"Motown Sound Goes Italiana." *Billboard*, May 6, 1967, 1, 14.

"Motown Wk. in Canada Is Co-Op Effort." *Billboard*, November 18, 1967, 52.

Murphy, Mary. "Motown Firms Film Commitment." *Los Angeles Times*, September 3, 1975, 14.

Murray, James P. "'Trouble Man': A Shameful Imitation of Original 'Shaft.'" *New York Amsterdam News*, November 4, 1972, D6.

"Music as Written: Rome." *Billboard*, May 16, 1964, 40.

"National Distrib for Tamla." *Billboard Music Week*, October 23, 1961, 40.

"The Nation's Top 100 Top Black Businesses." *Black Enterprise*, June 1973.

"New and Fantastic from Stax-Volt" (advertisement). *Billboard*, November 26, 1966, 11.

"New from Hi Records." *Billboard*, June 25, 1966, 25.

"1972 Sterling Ball Raises $50,000." *Baltimore Afro-American*, October 7, 1972, 11.

"NME Takes You to Hitsville." *New Musical Express*, December 3, 1966, 4.

"No Hits for a Year: The Supremes $4 Million Lawsuit; Motown Blames Writers for Supremes' 'Slump.'" *New Journal and Guide*, September 21, 1968.

"'Nothing but a Man': Triumph on a Budget." *Ebony*, August 1965, 198–201.

"No Town Like Motown." *Newsweek*, March 22, 1965, 22.

O'Doherty, Brian. "Classic of a Negro Who Stopped Running." *Life*, February 19, 1965, 15.

"The One World Record Market." *Cash Box*, February 1, 1964, 3.

"Orbison Better, but Not His Best." *New Musical Express*, August 27, 1965, 4.

"Oriole's Label All-American." *Billboard*, September 15, 1962, 18.

"Otis Redding Has a Smash Single—Otis Redding Has a Smash Album" (advertisement). *Billboard*, September 11, 1965, 9.

"Our Girls Still Ahead." *Michigan Chronicle*, May 13, 1967, section B, 6.

Page, Mick. Letter to the editor. *Record Mirror*, February 27, 1965, 2.

Pareles, Jon. "Amy Winehouse: 'Back to Black.'" *New York Times*, March 12, 2007, E4.

Patterson, Orlando. "The Dance Invasion." *New Society*, September 15, 1966, 401–3.

"Petrillo Relaxing Bars on Anglo-U.S. Band Exchange; Heath-Kenton Swap." *Variety*, October 26, 1955, 41–44.

Pitts, George E. "Ray Charles Explains His 'Soul' Singing." *Pittsburgh Courier*, March 14, 1959.

"Poets Sign Reading Pact with Motown." *New York Amsterdam News*, October 26, 1963.

"Politicians and Show World Stars Attend Big Charity Ball in Detroit." *Philadelphia Tribune*, May 8, 1971, 27.

"Potted Pops." *New Musical Express*, August 27, 1965, 4.

"Pro Pool Player Gets Motion Picture Break." *Philadelphia Tribune*, July 8, 1972, 18.

"Pye Records Bringing American R&B, Jazz Series to England." *Billboard*, September 4, 1961.

"R&B Poll." *Record Mirror*, March 25, 1964, 4.

"R&B Singles Surge on Hot 100." *Billboard*, June 21, 1961, 1, 43.

"RCA Italiana Bows Drive on Italian Tamla Singles." *Billboard*, June 10, 1967, 64, 68.

"Recording Stars Are Big in Brooklyn, N.Y." *Pittsburgh Courier*, October 3, 1964, 17.

Reuert, Rafael. "Spanish Soul on the Rise." *Billboard*, August 17, 1968, section 2 ("The World of Soul"), 54.

Reynolds, J. R. "An Expanded Motown Museum Reopens; IAAAM Confab Just around the Corner." *Billboard*, May 27, 1995, 22.

"Rhythm Plus Blues Doesn't Mean R & B." *Melody Maker*, January 4, 1964, 8.

"The Road to Export Profits Is Paved with Market Research." *Cash Box*, January 5, 1963, 45.

Roberts, Chris. "To Be: Or Not to R & B." *Melody Maker*, August 29, 1964, 7.

"Rock and Roll: The Sounds of the Sixties." *Time*, May 21, 1965, 84–88.

"Rock 'n' Roll Chaperone." *Afro-American*, October 14, 1961.

Rowe, Billy. "Lady Sings the Blues, but She's Not Billie Holiday." *New York Amsterdam News*, October 28, 1972.

"Rudman Joins Billboard's R&B Dept." *Billboard*, July 25, 1964, 4.

Sandler, Adam. "Motown Topper Harrell Hopes to Revive Label." *Variety*, October 9, 1995, 21–22.

"San Remo Festival—Boon for Disk Sales." *Billboard*, February 1, 1969, 76.

Sauter, Van G. "Motown Records, Man, Which Is Big, Really Big." *Detroit* (magazine), March 21, 1965, 14–16.

"Shop Window." *New Musical Express*, June 25, 1965, 4.

"Show Biz's Universal 'Open Door.'" *Variety*, November 9, 1955, 2.

Sisario, Ben. "In Dispute over a Song, Marvin Gaye's Family Files a Countersuit." *New York Times*, October 31, 2013, B2.

Sisario, Ben, and Noah Smith. "'Blurred Lines' Infringed on Marvin Gaye Copyright, Jury Rules." *New York Times*, March 10, 2015, B1.

"'65 a Vintage Year for Atlantic." *Billboard*, January 1, 1966, 6.

Smith, Alan. "Listen! In the Name of the Supremes." *New Musical Express*, April 23, 1965, 12.

Smith, Alan. "NME Chart Woke up Four Tops in Record Time!" *New Musical Express*, October 21, 1966, 15.

"'Soul' Discs Sell." *Cash Box*, May 16, 1964.

"'Soulists' Not Doing Their Share: Negro Soldier." *Billboard*, February 26, 1966, 8.

"Stars of 'Super Fly' Draws Raving Fans and Defends Movie." *Atlanta Daily World*, September 28, 1972, 3.

"The Sterling Ball Is a Solid Gold Social Event." *Call and Post*, May 8, 1971, 8A.

"Stevie Wins Hearts of Frenchmen." *New York Amsterdam News*, January 11, 1964, 14.

"Suit against Motown Settled Out of Court." *New Pittsburgh Courier*, January 22, 1972.

Sullivan, Dan. "Special for Singers." *New York Times*, December 10, 1968, 95.

"Supremes Brush Up on Deutsch for German Discs." *Variety*, January 27, 1965, 47.

"Supremes Click." *New Musical Express*, October 9, 1964, 4.

"The Supremes' Diana Ross: 'We Don't Need a Sex Goddess.'" *Look*, September 23, 1969, 72–74.

"Supremes Get Award in London." *Pittsburgh Courier*, October 10, 1964, 17.

"Supremes Here for Radio and TV Dates." *Melody Maker*, October 10, 1964, 5.

"Supremes Make History." *New Musical Express*, November 13, 1964, 3.

"The Supremes Make It All Look So Easy" (advertisement). *Ebony*, February 1967, 25.

"The Supremes Make It All Look So Easy" (advertisement). *Jet*, February 9, 1967, 29.

"Supremes Repping U.S. at Dutch Pop Festival." *Variety*, September 8, 1965, 52.

"Supremes Supreme!" *Melody Maker*, November 14, 1964, 1.

"Supremes Top Tamla Tour." *Melody Maker*, January 16, 1965, 5.

"Supremes Visit Here Next Month." *Record Mirror*, September 26, 1964, 6.

"Tamla-Motown Execs Swing across Europe." *Billboard*, March 23, 1963, 28.

"Tamla-Motown Expands Abroad." *Billboard*, February 20, 1965, 9.

"Tamla-Motown Goes Outside to Get Talent." *Billboard*, September 4, 1965, 10.

"Tamla-Motown Here in March." *Melody Maker*, December 26, 1964, 4.

"Tamla-Motown Is Distributing Harvey Label." *Billboard*, October 20, 1962, 8.

"Tamla-Motown's Sound to Zero in on Italian Market." *Billboard*, March 25, 1967.

"Tamla-Motown Ups Wakefield, Ales to New Responsibility." *Billboard*, July 17, 1961, 45.

"Tamla's Own Label Now." *New Musical Express*, March 19, 1965, 4.

"Tamla Steps into Tour with Georgie." *Melody Maker*, March 6, 1965, 4.

"Tamla Team for TV." *Melody Maker*, January 23, 1965, 5.

"Tamla Team Moves in for Tour." *Melody Maker*, March 13, 1965, 5.

"Tamla Tearaways!" *Melody Maker*, March 20, 1965, 15.

Teigel, Eliot. "Soul Label? Motown Becoming Much More." *Billboard*, February 8, 1975, 3, 45.

Tewksbury, Drew. "Raphael Saadiq at the Wiltern: A Perfect-Pitch Frontman." *LA Weekly*, November 23, 2009.

"That Great Memphis Sound" (advertisement). *Billboard*, March 11, 1967, 9.

"There'll Always Be an England." *Variety*, February 2, 1946, 33–34.

Thomas, Kevin. "Black 'Trouble Man' Lives by Own Rules." *Los Angeles Times*, November 29, 1972, D23.

Thomas, Michael. "Diana Ross Goes from Riches to Rags." *Rolling Stone*, February 1, 1973, 28–31.

Thompson, Thomas. "Music Streams." *Life*, May 21, 1965, 93–98.

Thurston, Chuck. "Motown Exiting the City a Little at a Time." *Detroit Free Press*, June 9, 1972, 1B.

Thurston, Chuck. "Now That Motown Has Gone Mowest Where Will Detroit Musicians Go? Broke Maybe." *Free Press*, June 25, 1972.

Tiegel, Eliot. "Baker's Wife Undergoing Surgery; Motown Owns LP." *Billboard*, June 26, 1976, 6.

Tiegel, Eliot. "TV Showcasing Black Artists." *Billboard*, August 24, 1968, 1, 66.

Toersleff, Christian. "CBS to Issue Tamla-Motown." *Billboard*, November 2, 1963, 31.

"Top U.S. Stars Storm In—Dates Announced." *Melody Maker*, October 24, 1964, 1.

"Trad Takes a Beating." *Melody Maker*, January 18, 1964, 8.

Traiman, Steve. "International Affairs." *Billboard*, January 17, 1991, A-28, A-30.

"'Trouble Man' Opens in N.Y. November 1." *Atlanta Daily World*, November 2, 1972, 6.

"'Trouble Man' Premiere Aids Negro Ensemble Co." *Norfolk (VA) New Journal and Guide*, November 11, 1972, 14.

"'Trouble Man' Premieres at the Roosevelt Theater." *Chicago Daily Defender*, November 7, 1972, 10.

"TV and Radio Queue Up for Tamla Team." *Melody Maker*, March 20, 1965, 4.

"Twelve Million Singles! That's the Tamla Total." *Record Retailer*, April 1, 1965, 16.

"Two Named at Motown in Major Expansion Move." *New York Amsterdam News*, November 4, 1967.

Tynan, John. "Funk, Groove, Soul." *Down Beat*, November 24, 1960, 18–19.

"UAW Begins Talks with General Motors." *Washington Post*, November 28, 1967.

"U.S. Labels Spurring Soul Most in Demark, Norway." *Billboard*, August 30, 1969, 64.

Voogt, Skip. "Ngram Distrib Pye and Kapp." *Billboard*, July 20, 1963, 29.

Walker, Wyatt Tee. "On Malcolm X: Nothing but a Man." *Negro Digest*, April 1965, 29–32.

Webb, George. "The Year of Reckoning for Trad." *Melody Maker*, January 11, 1964, 6.

"What Kind of Men Cry?" *Ebony*, June 1965, 47–56.

"Whatever Success I Had Was through the Help of the Good Lord." *Rolling Stone*, January 20, 1968, 12–13.

Whisenhunt, Elton. "The Memphis Sound: A Southern View." *Billboard*, June 12, 1965, 6.

"Why Tamla Is Not a Song Factory." *Record Retailer*, February 21, 1970.

Williams, Michaela. "That Motown Sound." *Panorama* (*Chicago Daily News*), September 25, 1965, 6.

"Yanks Invade! Beatles Favorites Coming Here." *Melody Maker*, April 4, 1964, 1.

V. Books, Articles, and Dissertations

Abbott, Kingsley. "Launching the Tamla-Motown Label: Reminiscences with Derek Everett." In *Calling Out around the World: A Motown Reader*, edited by Kingsley Abbott, 62–65. London: Helter Skelter, 2001.

Abrams, Alan E. *Hype and Soul: Behind the Scenes at Motown*. Lilleshall, UK: Templestreet, 2011.

Albert, George, and Frank Hoffman. *The Cash Box Black Contemporary Singles Charts, 1960–1984*. Metuchen, NJ: Scarecrow, 1986.

Anderson, Iain. *This Is Our Music: Free Jazz, the Sixties, and American Culture*. Philadelphia: University of Pennsylvania Press, 2007.

Apolloni, Alexandra Marie. "Wishin' and Hopin': Femininity, Whiteness, and Voice in 1960s British Pop." PhD diss., University of California, Los Angeles, 2013.

Ashford, Jack. *Motown: A View from the Bottom*. New Romney, UK: Bank House, 2003.

Atkins, Cholly, and Jacqui Malone. *Class Act: The Jazz Life of Choreographer Cholly Atkins*. New York: Columbia University Press, 2001.

Awkward, Michael. *Soul Covers: Rhythm and Blues Remakes and the Struggle for Artistic Identity*. Durham, NC: Duke University Press, 2007.

Baldwin, Davarian L. *Chicago's New Negroes: Modernity, the Great Migration, and Black Urban Life*. Chapel Hill: University of North Carolina Press, 2007.

Baldwin, James. "The Devil Finds Work." In *Collected Essays*. New York: Library of America, 1998.

Baker, Nancy Kovaleff. "Abel Meeropol (a.k.a. Lewis Allan): Political Commentator and Social Conscience." *American Music* 20 (Spring 2002): 25–79.

Barlow, William. *Voice Over: The Making of Black Radio*. Philadelphia: Temple University Press, 1999.

Barnard, Stephen. *On the Radio: Music Radio in Britain*. Philadelphia: Open University Press, 1989.

Bartlette, Reginald J. *Off the Record: Motown by Master Number, 1959–1989*. Vol. 1. Ann Arbor, MI: Popular Culture, 1991.

Belz, Carl. *The Story of Rock*. New York: Harper Colophon, 1972.

Benjaminson, Peter. *The Lost Supreme: The Life of Dreamgirl Florence Ballard*. Chicago: Lawrence Hill, 2008.

Benjaminson, Peter. *Mary Wells: The Tumultuous Life of Motown's First Superstar*. Chicago: Chicago Review, 2012.

Benjaminson, Peter. *The Story of Motown*. New York: Evergreen, 1979.

Bjorn, Lars, and Jim Gallert. *Before Motown: A History of Jazz in Detroit, 1920–60*. Ann Arbor: University of Michigan Press, 2001.

Bogle, Donald. *Primetime Blues: African Americans on Network Television*. New York: Farrar, Straus and Giroux, 2001.

Bowman, Rob. *Soulsville U.S.A.: The Story of Stax Records.* New York: Schirmer, 2003.

Bowman, Rob. "Stax: A Musicological Analysis." *Popular Music* 14 (October 1995): 285–320.

Boyer, Horace Clarence, and Lloyd Yearwood. *How Sweet the Sound: The Golden Age of Gospel.* Washington, DC: Elliot and Clark, 1995.

Brackett, David. "(In Search of) Musical Meaning: Genres, Categories and Crossover." In *Popular Music Studies*, edited by David Hesmondhalgh and Keith Negus, 65–83. London: Arnold, 2002.

Brackett, David. *Interpreting Popular Music.* Berkeley: University of California Press, 1995.

Brackett, David. "The Politics and Practice of 'Crossover' in American Popular Music, 1963 to 1965." *Musical Quarterly* 78 (Winter 1994): 774–97.

Brackett, David. "Questions of Genre in Black Popular Music." *Black Music Research Journal* 25 (Spring–Fall 2005): 73–92.

Brackett, David. "Soul Music." *Grove Music Online, Oxford Music Online.*

Brackett, David. "What a Difference a Name Makes: Two Instances of African-American Popular Music." In *The Cultural Study of Music: A Critical Introduction*, edited by Martin Clayton, Trevor Herbert, and Richard Middleton, 238–50. New York: Routledge, 2003.

Brewster, Bill. "Ian Levine: Soul Adventurer." In *The Record Players: DJ Revolutionaries*, edited by Bill Brewster and Frank Broughton, 80–89. New York: Black Cat, 2010.

Brooks, Tim. *Lost Sounds: Blacks and the Birth of the Recording Industry, 1890–1919.* Urbana: University of Illinois Press, 2004.

Broven, John. *Record Makers and Breakers: Voices of the Independent Rock 'n' Roll Pioneers.* Urbana: University of Illinois Press, 2009.

Browne, Kimasi L. "Brenda Holloway: Los Angeles's Contribution to Motown." In *California Soul*, edited by Jacqueline Cogdell DjeDje and Eddie S. Meadows, 321–51. Berkeley: University of California Press, 1998.

Browne, Kimasi Lionel John. "'Soul or Nothing': The Formation of Cultural Identity on the British Northern Soul Scene." PhD diss., University of California, Los Angeles, 2005.

Burford, Mark. "Sam Cooke as Pop Album Artist: A Reinvention in Three Songs." *Journal of the American Musicological Society* 65 (Spring 2012): 113–78.

Burns, Lori. "Feeling the Style: Vocal Gesture and Musical Expression in Billie Holiday, Bessie Smith, and Louis Armstrong." *Music Theory Online* 11 (September 2005). http://mto.societymusictheory.org/issues/mto.05.11.3/mto.05.11.3.burns.html.

Burns, Lori, and Alyssa Woods. "Authenticity, Appropriation, Signification: Tori Amos on Gender, Race, and Violence in Covers of Billie Holiday and Eminem." *Music Theory Online* 10 (June 2004). http://mto.societymusictheory.org/issues/mto.04.10.2/mto.04.10.2.burns_woods.html.

Burton, Peter. *Parallel Lives.* Boston: Alyson, 1985.

Butters, Ronald R., and Jennifer Westerhaus. "Linguistic Change in One's Own Words: How Trademarks Become 'Generic.'" In *Studies in the History of the English Language II: Unfolding Conversations*, edited by Anne Curzan and Kimberly Emmons, 111–23. New York: Mouton de Gruyter, 2004.

Carson, David A. *Grit, Noise, and Revolution: The Birth of Detroit Rock 'N' Roll.* Ann Arbor: University of Michigan Press, 2005.

Cha-Jua, Sundiata Keita. "Black Audiences, Blaxploitation and Kung Fu Films, and Challenges to White Celluloid Masculinity." In *China Forever: The Shaw Brothers and Diasporic Cinema*, edited by Poshek Fu, 199–223. Urbana: University of Illinois Press, 2008.

Chambers, Iain. *Urban Rhythms: Pop Music and Popular Culture.* New York: St. Martin's, 1985.

Chatburn, Thomas. "Trinidad All Stars: The Steel Pan Movement in Britain." In *Black Music in Britain: Essays on the Afro-Asian Contribution to Popular Music*, edited by Paul Oliver, 118–36. Philadelphia: Open University Press, 1990.

Chen, Anthony S. *The Fifth Freedom: Jobs, Politics, and Civil Rights in the United States, 1941–1972.* Princeton, NJ: Princeton University Press, 2009.

Chin, Brian, and David Nathan. "Reflections of . . ." Essay included in the Supremes, *The Supremes.* Motown 012 159 075-2, 2000.

Clankie, Shawn M. "Brand Name Use in Creative Writing: Genericide or Language Right?" In *Perspectives on Plagiarism and Intellectual Property in a Postmodern World*, edited by Lise Buranen and Alice M. Roy, 253–63. Albany: State University of New York Press, 1999.

Cloonan, Martin, and Matt Brennan. "Alien Invasions: The British Musicians' Union and Foreign Musicians." *Popular Music* 32 (May 2013): 277–95.

Coffey, Dennis. *Guitars, Bars, and Motown Superstars.* Ann Arbor: University of Michigan Press, 2004.

Cogan, Jim, and William Clark. *Temples of Sound: Inside the Great Recording Studios.* San Francisco: Chronicle, 2003.

Cook, Nicholas. *Analysing Musical Media.* Oxford: Clarendon Press, 1998.

Cooper, B. Lee, and Wayne S. Haney. *Response Recordings: An Answer Song Discography, 1950–1990.* Metuchen, NJ: Scarecrow, 1990.

Covach, John. "Form in Rock Music: A Primer." In *Engaging Music: Essays in Music Analysis*, edited by Deborah Stein, 65–76. New York: Oxford University Press, 2005.

Cowley, John. "London Is the Place: Caribbean Music in the Context of Empire: 1900–60." In *Black Music in Britain: Essays on the Afro-Asian Contribution to Popular Music*, edited by Paul Oliver, 58–76. Philadelphia: Open University Press, 1990.

Coyle, Michael. "Hijacked Hits and Antic Authenticity: Cover Songs, Race, and Postwar Marketing." In *Rock over the Edge: Transformation in Popular Music Culture*, edited by Roger Beebe, Denise Fulbrook, and Ben Sunders, 133–57. Durham, NC: Duke University Press, 2002.

Cunningham, Mark. *Good Vibrations: A History of Record Production.* London: Sanctuary, 1996.

Dahl, Bill. *Motown: The Golden Years.* Iola, WI: Krause, 2001.

Davis, Joshua Clark. "For the Records: How African American Consumers and Music Retailers Created Commercial Public Space in the 1960s and 1970s South." *Southern Cultures* 17 (Winter 2011): 71–90.

Davis, Sharon. *Lionel Richie: Hello.* Oakville, CT: Equinox, 2009.

Davis, Sharon. *Motown: The History.* Enfield, UK: Guinness, 1988.

Dawson, Jim, and Steve Propes. *45 RPM: The History, Heroes and Villains of a Pop Music Revolution.* San Francisco: Backbeat, 2003.

Diawara, Manthia, ed. *Black American Cinema*. New York: Routledge, 2003.

Doyle, Peter. *Echo and Reverb: Fabricating Space in Popular Music Recording, 1900–1960*. Middletown, CT: Wesleyan University Press, 2005.

Drabløs, Per Elias. *The Quest for the Melodic Electric Bass: From Jamerson to Spenner*. Burlington, VT: Ashgate, 2015.

Early, Gerald. "One Nation under a Groove." *New Republic*, July 15 and 22, 1991, 30–41.

Early, Gerald. *One Nation under a Groove*. New York: Ecco Press, 1995; Ann Arbor: University of Michigan Press, 2004. Page references are to the 2004 edition.

Elton, Lord [Godfrey]. *The Unarmed Invasion: A Survey of Afro-Asian Immigration*. London: Geoffrey Bles, 1965.

Ennis, Philip H. *The Seventh Stream: The Emergence of Rocknroll in American Popular Music*. Hanover, NH: Wesleyan University Press, 1992.

Erickson, Julie Liesse. "Hip Raisins Top List of Quarter's Best Ads." *Advertising Age*, January 19, 1987, 40.

Ertegun, Ahmet. *What'd I Say: The Atlantic Story, 50 Years of Music*. New York: Welcome Rain, 2001.

Everett, Walter. "Confessions from Blueberry Hell, or, Pitch Can Be a Sticky Substance." In *Expressions in Pop-Rock Music: A Collection of Critical and Analytical Essays*, edited by Walter Everett, 269–345. New York: Garland, 2000.

Everett, Walter. "Detroit and Memphis: The Soul of Revolver." In *Every Sound There Is: The Beatles "Revolver" and the Transformation of Rock and Roll*, edited by Russell Reising, 25–57. Aldershot, UK: Ashgate, 2003.

Favor, Martin J. *Authentic Blackness: The Folk in the New Negro Renaissance*. Durham, NC: Duke University Press, 1999.

Feldman, Christine Jacqueline. *We Are the Mods: A Transnational History of a Youth Subculture*. New York: Peter Lang, 2009.

Fink, Robert. "Goal-Directed Soul? Analyzing Rhythmic Teleology in African American Popular Music." *Journal of the American Musicological Society* 64 (Spring 2011): 179–238.

Fink, Robert. *Repeating Ourselves: American Minimal Music as Cultural Practice*. Berkeley: University of California Press, 2005.

Fiske, John. "The Cultural Economy of Fandom." In *The Adoring Audience: Fan Culture and Popular Media*, edited by Lisa A. Lewis, 30–49. London: Routledge, 1992.

Fitzgerald, Jon. "Black Pop Songwriting 1963–1966: An Analysis of U.S. Top Forty Hits by Cooke, Mayfield, Stevenson, Robinson, and Holland-Dozier-Holland." *Black Music Research Journal* 27 (Fall 2007): 97–140.

Fitzgerald, Jon. "Motown Crossover Hits 1963–1966 and the Creative Process." *Popular Music* 14 (January 1995): 1–11.

Floyd, Samuel A., Jr. *The Power of Black Music: Interpreting Its History from Africa to the United States*. New York: Oxford University Press, 1995.

Forman, Murray. *One Night on TV Is Worth Weeks at the Paramount: Popular Music on Early Television*. Durham, NC: Duke University Press, 2012.

Friedland, Ed. *Bass Grooves: Develop Your Groove and Play Like the Pros in Any Style*. San Francisco: Backbeat, 2004.

Frith, Simon. *Performing Rites: On the Value of Popular Music.* Cambridge, MA: Harvard University Press, 1996.

Frith, Simon, Matt Brennan, Martin Cloonan, and Emma Webster, eds. *The History of Live Music in Britain. Vol. 1, 1950–1967.* Burlington, VT: Ashgate, 2013.

Fryer, Peter. *Staying Power: The History of Black People in Britain.* London: Pluto Press, 1984.

Garcia, Luis-Manuel. "On and On: Repetition as Process and Pleasure in Electronic Dance Music." *Music Theory Online* 11, no. 4 (2005). http://www.mtosmt.org/issues/mto.05.11.4/mto.05.11.4.garcia.html.

Garland, Phyl. *The Sound of Soul.* Chicago: Henry Regnery, 1969.

Garofalo, Reebee. "Crossing Over: 1939–1989." In *Split Image: African Americans in the Media,* edited by Jannette L. Dates and William Barlow, 57–128. Washington, DC: Howard University Press, 1993.

Gendron, Bernard. *Between Montmartre and the Mudd Club: Popular Music and the Avant-Garde.* Chicago: University of Chicago Press, 2002.

Gennari, John. *Blowin' Hot and Cool: Jazz and Its Critics.* Chicago: University of Chicago Press, 2006.

Gentry, Philip Max. "The Age of Anxiety: Music, Politics, and McCarthyism." PhD diss., University of California, Los Angeles, 2008.

Georgakas, Dan, and Marvin Surkin. *Detroit, I Do Mind Dying: A Study in Urban Revolution.* Cambridge, MA: South End Press, 1998.

George, Nelson. *The Death of Rhythm and Blues.* New York: Penguin, 2004.

George, Nelson. *Where Did Our Love Go?* New York: St. Martin's, 1986; Urbana: University of Illinois Press, 2007. Page references are to the 2007 edition.

Gibson, Maya C. "Alternate Takes: Billie Holiday at the Intersection of Black Cultural Studies and Historical Musicology." PhD diss., University of Wisconsin, Madison, 2008.

Gillett, Charlie. *The Sound of the City: The Rise of Rock and Roll.* New York: Outerbridge and Dienstfrey, 1970.

Gilroy, Paul. *There Ain't No Black in the Union Jack: The Cultural Politics of Race and Nation.* Chicago: University of Chicago Press, 1991.

Goldin-Perschbacher, Shana. "Not with You but of You: 'Unbearable Intimacy' and Jeff Buckley's Transgendered Vocality." In *Oh Boy! Masculinities and Popular Music,* edited by Freya Jarman-Ivens, 213–33. New York: Routledge, 2007.

Gordon, Robert. *Respect Yourself: Stax Records and the Soul Explosion.* New York: Bloomsbury, 2013.

Gordy, Berry, Sr. *Movin' Up: Pop Gordy Tells His Story.* New York: Harper and Row, 1979.

Gordy, Berry. *To Be Loved: The Music, the Magic, the Memories of Motown.* New York: Warner, 1994.

Gray, Herman. *Watching Race.* Minneapolis: University of Minnesota Press, 1995.

Gregory, James N. *The Southern Diaspora: How the Great Migrations of Black and White Southerners Transformed America.* Chapel Hill: University of North Carolina Press, 2005.

Griffiths, Peter. *A Question of Colour.* London: Leslie Frewin, 1966.

Grossberg, Lawrence. "Is There a Fan in the House? The Affective Sensibility of

Fandom." In *The Adoring Audience: Fan Culture and Popular Media*, edited by Lisa A. Lewis, 50–65. London: Routledge, 1992.

Guerrero, Ed. *Framing Blackness: The African American Image in Film*. Philadelphia: Temple University Press, 1993.

Guralnick, Peter. *Sweet Soul Music: Rhythm and Blues and the Southern Dream of Freedom*. New York: Back Bay, 1999.

Hackel, Stu. "Brothers in Arms." Essay included in the Four Tops, *Fourever*. Motown/Hip-O 314 556 225-2, 2001.

Hall, Denise, "Norman Whitfield." *Black Music* 3 (1976): 14.

Hall, Stuart, and Tony Jefferson, eds. *Resistance through Rituals: Youth Subcultures in Post-War Britain*. London: Hutchinson, 1975.

Hamblett, Charles, and Jane Deverson. *Generation X*. Greenwich, CT: Gold Metal, 1964.

Hannerz, Ulf. "The Rhetoric of Soul: Identification in Negro Society." *Race and Class* 9, no. 4 (1968): 453–65.

Haralambos, Michael. *Right On: From Blues to Soul in Black America*. New York: Drake, 1975.

Hebdige, Dick. "The Meaning of Mod." In *Resistance through Rituals*, edited by Stuart Hall and Tony Jefferson, 87–97. London: Hutchinson, 1975.

Hebdige, Dick. *Subculture: The Meaning of Style*. New York: Routledge, 2002.

Hiro, Dilip. *Black British, White British: A History of Race Relations in Britain*. London: Grafton, 1991.

Hirshey, Gerri. *Nowhere to Run: The Story of Soul Music*. New York: Crown, 1984.

Hollows, Joanne, and Katie Milestone. "Welcome to Dreamsville: A History and Geography of Northern Soul." In *The Place of Music*, edited by George Revill, Andrew Leyshon, and David Matless, 83–103. New York: Guilford, 1998.

Holt, Fabian. *Genre in Popular Music*. Chicago: University of Chicago Press, 2007.

Hughes, Charles L. *Country Soul: Making Music and Making Race in the American South*. Chapel Hill: University of North Carolina Press, 2015.

Hughes, Keith. "Copies and Cover-Ups." *Yesterday-Today-Forever* 19 (August 1995): 12.

Hughes, Timothy S. "Groove and Flow: Six Analytical Essays on the Music of Stevie Wonder." PhD diss., University of Washington, 2003.

Hull, Ted, and Paula L. Stahel. *The Wonder Years: My Life and Times with Stevie Wonder*. Tampa, FL: Ted Hull, 2002.

Huron, David. "Music in Advertising: An Analytic Paradigm." *Musical Quarterly* 73 (1989): 557–74.

Inglis, Ian. "Some Kind of Wonderful: The Creative Legacy of the Brill Building." *American Music* 21 (Summer 2003): 214–35.

Jackson, John A. *A House on Fire: The Rise and Fall of Philadelphia Soul*. New York: Oxford, 2004.

Jackson, Kennell. "The Shadow of Texts: Will Black Music and Singers Sell Everything on Television?" In *Black Cultural Traffic: Crossroads in Global Performance and Popular Culture*, edited by Harry J Elam Jr. and Kennell Jackson, 88–107. Ann Arbor: University of Michigan Press, 2005.

James, Rick, and David Ritz. *Glow: The Autobiography of Rick James*. New York: Atria, 2014.

Jefferson, Tony. "Cultural Responses of the Teds." In *Resistance through Rituals*, edited by Stuart Hall and Tony Jefferson, 81–86. London: Hutchinson, 1975.

Jensen, Joli. "Fandom as Pathology: The Consequences of Characterization." In *The Adoring Audience: Fan Culture and Popular Media*, edited by Lisa A. Lewis, 9–29. London: Routledge, 1992.

Jesmer, Elaine. *Number One with a Bullet*. New York: Farrar, Straus, and Giroux, 1974.

Johnson, Phil. "Dave Godin." *Independent*, October 20, 2004.

Jones, John Bush. *The Songs That Fought the War: Popular Music and the Home Front, 1939–1945*. Waltham, MA: Brandeis University Press, 2006.

Jones, LeRoi [Imamu Amiri Baraka]. *Blues People: Negro Music in White America*. 1963. Reprint, New York: Perennial, 2002.

Kassabian, Anahid. *Ubiquitous Listening: Affect, Attention, and Distributed Subjectivity*. Berkeley: University of California Press, 2013.

Keightley, Keir. "Long Play: Adult-Oriented Popular Music and the Temporal Logics of the Post-War Sound Recording in the USA." *Media, Culture, and Society* 26 (2004): 375–91.

Keil, Charles. *Urban Blues*. Chicago: University of Chicago Press, 1991.

King, Jason Gregory. "Blue Magic: Stardom, Soul Music and Illumination." PhD diss., New York University, 2002.

Klein, Bethany. *As Heard on TV: Popular Music in Advertising*. Burlington, VT: Ashgate, 2009.

Kramer, Michael J. *The Republic of Rock: Music and Citizenship in the Sixties Counterculture*. New York: Oxford University Press, 2013.

Kurpiers, Joyce. "Reality by Design: Advertising Image, Music and Sound Design in the Production of Culture." PhD diss., Duke University, 2009.

Lash, Scott, and John Urry. *Economies of Signs and Space*. London: Sage, 1994.

Lauterbach, Preston. *The Chitlin' Circuit and the Road to Rock 'n' Roll*. New York: W. W. Norton, 2011.

Lehman, Christopher P. *A Critical History of Soul Train on Television*. Jefferson, NC: McFarland, 2008.

Lemann, Nicholas. *The Great Migration and How It Changed America*. New York: Vintage, 1991.

Lewisohn, Mark. *All These Years—Tune In: Extended Special Edition*. London: Little, Brown, 2013.

Lewisohn, Mark. *The Complete Beatles Chronicle*. London: Hamlyn, 2003.

Lipsitz, George. *Time Passages: Collective Memory and American Popular Culture*. Minneapolis: University of Minnesota Press, 1990.

Long, Michael. *Beautiful Monsters: Imagining the Classic in Musical Media*. Berkeley: University of California Press, 2008.

Love, Joanna. "From Cautionary Chart-Topper to Friendly Beverage Anthem: Michael Jackson's 'Billie Jean' and Pepsi's 'Choice of a New Generation' Television Campaign." *Journal of the Society for American Music* 9 (2015): 178–203.

Lowy, Adrienne. "*Ready Steady Go!* Televisual Pop Style and the Careers of Dusty Springfield, Cilla Black, Sandie Shaw and Lulu." In *Popular Music and Television in Britain*, edited by Ian Inglis, 71–84. Burlington, VT: Ashgate, 2010.

Lubiano, Wahneema. *The House That Race Built: Black Americans, U. S. Terrain.* New York: Pantheon, 1997.

MacDonald, J. Fred. *Blacks and White TV: Afro-Americans in Television since 1948.* Chicago: Nelson Hall, 1983.

Maclin, Frances. *I Remember Motown: When We Were All Just Family.* Self-published, 2014.

Maki, Craig, and Keith Cady. *Detroit Country Music: Mountaineers, Cowboys, and Rockabillies.* Ann Arbor: University of Michigan Press, 2013.

Marks, Anthony. "Young, Gifted and Black: Afro-American and Afro-Caribbean Music in Britain 1963–88." In *Black Music in Britain: Essays on the Afro-Asian Contribution to Popular Music,* edited by Paul Oliver, 102-117. Philadelphia: Open University Press, 1990.

Martino, Tony. *Trademark Dilution.* New York: Oxford University Press, 1996.

Maultsby, Portia K. "Soul." In *African American Music: An Introduction,* edited by Portia K. Maultsby and Mellonee V. Burnim, 271–91. New York: Routledge, 2006.

McAleer, Dave. *Hit Singles: Top 20 Charts from 1954 to the Present Day.* London: Carleton, 2003.

McKay, George. *Circular Breathing: The Cultural Politics of Jazz in Britain.* Durham, NC: Duke University Press, 2005.

Milestone, Katie. "Love Factory: The Sites, Practices and Media Relationships of Northern Soul." In *The Clubcultures Reader: Readings in Popular Cultural Studies,* edited by Steve Redhead, Derek Wynne, and Justin O'Connor, 134–49. Malden, MA: Blackwell, 1998.

Miller, Karl Hagstrom. *Segregating Sound: Inventing Folk and Pop Music in the Age of Jim Crow.* Durham, NC: Duke University Press, 2010.

Monson, Ingrid. *Freedom Sounds: Civil Rights Call Out to Jazz and Africa.* New York: Oxford University Press, 2007.

Monson, Ingrid. *Saying Something: Jazz Improvisation and Interaction.* Chicago: University of Chicago Press, 1996.

Moore, Robert E. "From Genericide to Viral Marketing: On 'Brand.'" *Language and Communication* 23 (July–October 2003): 331–57.

Morris, Mitchell. *The Persistence of Sentiment: Display and Feeling in Popular Music of the 1970s.* Berkeley: University of California Press, 2014.

Morse, David. *Motown and the Arrival of Black Music.* New York: Macmillan, 1971.

Nadel, Alan. *Television in Black-and-White America: Race and National Identity.* Lawrence: University Press of Kansas, 2005.

Neal, Mark Anthony. *What the Music Said: Black Popular Music and Black Popular Culture.* New York: Routledge, 1999.

Negus, Keith. *Music Genres and Corporate Cultures.* New York: Routledge, 1999.

Nowell, David. *Too Darn Soulful: The Story of Northern Soul.* London: Robson, 1999.

Olick, Jeffrey K., and Joyce Robbins. "Social Memory Studies: From 'Collective Memory' to the Historical Sociology of Mnemonic Practices." *Annual Review of Sociology* 24 (1998): 105–40.

Oliver, Paul. Introduction to *Black Music in Britain: Essay on the Afro-Asian Contribution to Popular Music,* edited by Paul Oliver, 2–15. Philadelphia: Open University Press, 1990.

O'Connell, Christian. *Paul Oliver: Blues, How Do You Do?* Ann Arbor: University of Michigan Press, 2015.

Pannell, Norman, and Fenner Brockway. *Immigration: What Is the Answer?* London: Routledge, 1966.

Pecknold, Diane. "Making Country Modern: The Legacy of *Modern Sounds in Country and Western Music.*" In *Hidden in the Mix: The African-American Presence in Country Music*, edited by Diane Pecknold, 82–99. Durham, NC: Duke University Press, 2013.

Pickering, Michael. "'A Jet Ornament to Society': Black Music in Nineteenth-Century Britain." In *Black Music in Britain: Essays on the Afro-Asian Contribution to Popular Music*, edited by Paul Oliver, 16–33. Philadelphia: Open University Press, 1990.

Posner, Gerald. *Motown: Music, Money, Sex, and Power.* New York: Random House, 2003.

Pruter, Robert. *Chicago Soul.* Urbana: University of Illinois Press, 1991.

Pulsifer, Gary. "Peter Burton: Writer and Publisher Who Played a Pioneering Role in Gay Journalism." *Guardian*, November 8, 2011.

Radano, Ronald. *Lying Up a Nation: Race and Black Music.* Chicago: University of Chicago Press, 2003.

Ramsey, Guthrie P. *Race Music: Black Cultures from Bebop to Hip-Hop.* Berkeley: University of California Press, 2003.

Ramsey, Guthrie P., Jr. "The Pot Liquor Principle: Developing a Black Music Criticism in American Music Studies." *Journal of Black Studies* 35 (November 2004): 210–33.

Randall, Annie J. *Dusty! Queen of the Postmods.* New York: Oxford University Press, 2009.

Reed, Jeremy. *John Stephen: The King of Carnaby Street.* London: Haus, 2010.

Reeves, Martha and Mark Bego. *Dancing in the Street: Confessions of a Motown Diva.* New York: Hyperion, 1994.

Ribowsky, Mark. *Ain't Too Proud to Beg: The Troubling Lives and Enduring Soul of the Temptations.* Hoboken, NJ: John Wiley and Sons, 2010.

Ribowsky, Mark. *Signed, Sealed, and Delivered: The Soulful Journey of Stevie Wonder.* Hoboken, NJ: John Wiley and Sons, 2010.

Ribowsky, Mark. *The Supremes: A Saga of Motown Dreams, Success, and Beyond.* New York: Da Capo, 2009.

Richardson, Clive. *Really Sayin' Something.* New Romney, UK: Bank House, 2010.

Rimmer, Dave. "Northern Soul and Motown." In *Calling Out around the World: A Motown Reader*, edited by Kingsley Abbott, 220–21. London: Helter Skelter, 2001.

Ritson, Mike, and Stuart Russell. *The In Crowd: The Story of the Northern and Rare Soul Scene.* Vol. 1. London: Bee Cool, 1999.

Ritz, David. *Divided Soul: The Life of Marvin Gaye.* New York: McGraw Hill, 1985; New York Da Capo, 1991; New York: Da Capo, 2003.

Roberts, Michael. "A Working Class Hero Is Something to Be: The American Musicians' Union's Attempt to Ban the Beatles." *Popular Music* 29 (2010): 1–16.

Robinson, Smokey, and David Ritz. *Smokey: Inside My Life.* New York: McGraw Hill, 1989.

Rodman, Ronald. "Advertising Music: Strategies of Imbuement in Television Advertising Music." In *Sound and Music in Film and Visual Media*, edited by Graeme Harper, Ruth Doughty, and Jochen Eisentraut, 617–32. New York: Continuum, 2009.

Ross, Diana. *Secrets of a Sparrow: Memoirs.* New York: Villard, 1993.

Ryan, Jennifer. "'Can I Get a Witness?': Soul and Salvation in Memphis Music." PhD diss., University of Pennsylvania, 2008.

Rye, Howard. "Fearsome Means of Discord: Early Encounters with Jazz." In *Black Music in Britain: Essays on the Afro-Asian Contribution to Popular Music*, edited by Paul Oliver, 45–57. Philadelphia: Open University Press, 1990.

Rylatt, Keith. *Groovesville U.S.A.: The Detroit Soul and R&B Index.* Stuart Russell, 2010.

Rylatt, Keith. *Hitsville! The Birth of Tamla Motown.* Derbyshire: Modus the House of Soul, 2016.

Rylatt, Keith, and Phil Scott. *Central 1179: The Story of Manchester's Twisted Wheel Club.* London: Bee Cool, 2001.

Salvatore, Nick. *Singing in a Strange Land: C. L. Franklin, the Black Church, and the Transformation of America.* New York: Little, Brown, 2005.

Sanjek, David. "Tell Me Something I Don't Already Know: The Harvard Report on Soul Music Revisited." In *Rhythm and Business: The Political Economy of Black Music*, edited by Norman Kelley, 59–76. New York: Akashic, 2002.

Sanjek, Russell. *Pennies from Heaven: The American Popular Music Business in the Twentieth Century.* New York: Da Capo, 1996.

Saul, Scott. *Freedom Is, Freedom Ain't: Jazz and the Making of the Sixties.* Cambridge, MA: Harvard University Press, 2003.

Schroeder, John. *Sex and Violins: My Affair with Life, Love, and Music.* Brighton, UK: Penn Press, 2009.

Schwartz, Roberta Freund. *How Britain Got the Blues: The Transmission and Reception of British Blues Style in the United Kingdom.* Burlington, VT: Ashgate, 2007.

Schwartz, Roberta Freund. "Preaching the Gospel of the Blues: Blues Evangelists in Britain." In *Cross the Water Blues: African American Music in Europe*, edited by Neil A. Wynn, 145–66. Jackson: University of Mississippi Press, 2007.

Segrave, Kerry. *Jukeboxes: An American Social History.* Jefferson, NC: McFarland, 2002.

Shaw, Arnold. *Honkers and Shouters: The Golden Years of Rhythm and Blues.* New York: Collier, 1978.

Shaw, Arnold. *The World of Soul.* New York: Paperback Library, 1971.

Sidran, Ben. *Black Talk.* New York: Da Capo Press, 1981.

Slote, Ben. "'The Goophered Grapevine' and Hearing Raisins Sing." *American Literary History* 6 (Winter 1994): 684–94.

Slutsky, Alan [Dr. Licks]. *Standing in the Shadows of Motown: The Life and Music of Legendary Bassist James Jamerson.* Milwaukee, WI: Hal Leonard, 1989.

Smith, Suzanne E. *Dancing in the Street: Motown and the Cultural Politics of Detroit.* Cambridge, MA: Harvard University Press, 1999.

Smith, Valerie. *Not Just Race, Not Just Gender: Black Feminist Readings.* New York: Routledge, 1998.

Smith-Sivertsen, Henrik. "How English Became the Language of Pop in Denmark." *Popular Music History* 8, no. 3 (2013): 251–69.

Solis, Gabriel. "I Did It My Way: Rock and the Logic of Covers." *Popular Music and Society* 33 (July 2010): 297–318.

Spicer, Mark. "British Pop-Rock Music in the Post-Beatles Era: Three Analytical Studies." PhD diss., Yale University, 2001.

Stephens, Robert W. "Soul: A Historical Reconstruction of Continuity and Change in Black Popular Music." *Black Perspective in Music* 12 (Spring 1984): 21–43.

Stevenson, William. "Mickey." *The A&R Man.* Self-published, 2015.

Storhoff, Gary. "Strange Fruit: *Lady Sings the Blues* as a Crossover Film." *Journal of Popular Film and Television* 30 (Summer 2002): 105–13.

Stras, Laurie. "Voice of the Beehive: Vocal Technique at the Turn of the 1960s." In *She's So Fine: Reflections on Whiteness, Femininity, Adolescence and Class in 1960s Music*, edited by Laurie Stras, 33–56. Burlington, VT: Ashgate, 2010.

Sugrue, Thomas J. *The Origins of the Urban Crisis: Race and Inequality in Postwar Detroit.* Princeton, NJ: Princeton University Press, 1996.

Suisman, David. *Selling Sounds: The Commercial Revolution in American Music.* Cambridge, MA: Harvard University Press, 2009.

Sykes, Bill. *Sit Down! Listen to This! The Roger Eagle Story.* Manchester, UK: Empire, 2012.

Sykes, Charles E. "The Black Forum Label: Motown Joins the Revolution." *ARSC Journal* 46 (2015): 1–42.

Taraborrelli, J. Randy. *Call Her Miss Ross: The Unauthorized Biography of Diana Ross.* New York: Birch Lane, 1989.

Taraborrelli, J. Randy. *Diana Ross: An Unauthorized Biography.* New York: Citadel, 2007.

Taraborrelli, J. Randy. *Motown: Hot Wax, City Cool, and Solid Gold.* New York: Doubleday, 1986.

Taruskin, Richard. *The Oxford History of Western Music.* New York: Oxford University Press, 2005.

Taylor, Timothy D. *The Sounds of Capitalism: Music, Advertising, and the Conquest of Culture.* Chicago: University of Chicago Press, 2012.

Terrana, Ralph. *The Road through Motown.* New Romney, UK: Bank House, 2006.

Terrana, Ralph. *Russ Terrana's Motown.* New Romney, UK: Bank House, 2010.

Thomas, Pat. *Listen Whitey: The Sights and Sounds of Black Power, 1965–1975.* Seattle: Fantagraphics, 2012.

Thompson, Heather Ann. *Whose Detroit?: Politics, Labor, and Race in a Modern American City.* Ithaca, NY: Cornell University Press, 2001.

Tinker, Chris. "A Singer-Songwriter's View of the French Record Industry: The Case of Léo Ferré." *Popular Music* 21 (2002): 147–57.

Tolnay, Stewart E. "The African American 'Great Migration' and Beyond." *Annual Review of Sociology* 29 (2003): 209–32.

Tucker, Mark. "Mainstreaming Monk: The Ellington Album." In *Uptown Conversation: The New Jazz Studies*, edited by Robert G. O'Meally, Brent Hayes Edwards, and Farah Jasmine Griffin, 150–65. New York: Columbia University Press, 2004.

Turner, Patricia A. *I Heard It through the Grapevine: Rumor in African-American Culture.* Berkeley: University of California Press, 1999.

Van DeBurg, William. *New Day in Babylon: The Black Power Movement and American Culture, 1965–1975.* Chicago: University of Chicago Press, 1992.

Veal, Michael E. *Dub: Soundscapes and Shattered Songs in Jamaican Reggae.* Middletown, CT: Wesleyan University Press, 2007.

Wald, Gayle. *It's Been Beautiful: Soul! and Black Power Television.* Durham, NC: Duke University Press, 2015.

Wale, Michael. *Voxpop: Profiles of the Pop Process.* London: Harrap, 1972.

Wall, Tim. "Out on the Floor: The Politics of Dancing on the Northern Soul Scene." *Popular Music and Society* 25 (October 2006): 431–45.

Waller, Don. *The Motown Story.* New York: Scribner, 1985.

Walser, Robert. "Groove as Niche: Earth, Wind, and Fire." In *This Is Pop: In Search of the Elusive at Experience Music Project,* edited by Eric Weisbard, 266–78. Cambridge, MA: Harvard University Press, 2004.

Ward, Brian. *Just My Soul Responding: Rhythm and Blues, Black Consciousness, and Race Relations.* Berkeley: University of California Press, 1998.

Warwick, Jacqueline. *Girl Groups, Girl Culture: Popular Music and Identity in the 1960s.* New York: Routledge, 2007.

Werner, Craig. *A Change is Gonna Come: Music, Race and the Soul of America.* Ann Arbor: University of Michigan Press, 2006.

Wexler, Jerry, and David Ritz. *Rhythm and the Blues: A Life in American Music.* New York: St. Martin's, 1993.

Wilkerson, Isabel. *The Warmth of Other Suns: The Epic Story of America's Great Migration.* New York: Random House, 2010.

Williams, Otis, and Patricia Romanowski. *Temptations.* New York: Cooper Square Press, 2002.

Williams, Richard. "Dave Godin." *Guardian,* October 16, 2004.

Wilson, Andrew. *Northern Soul: Music, Drugs and Subcultural Identity.* Portland, OR: Willan, 2007.

Wilson, Mary. *Dreamgirl: My Life as a Supreme.* New York: St. Martin's, 1986.

Wilson, Mary. *Dreamgirl and Supreme Faith: My Life as a Supreme.* New York: Cooper Square Press, 1999.

Wilson, Mary, and Patricia Romanowski. *Supreme Faith: Someday We'll Be Together.* New York: HarperCollins, 1990.

Wilson, Terry. *Tamla Motown: The Stories behind the UK Singles.* London: Cherry Red, 2009.

Wynn, Neil A., ed. *Cross the Water Blues: African American Music in Europe.* Jackson: University of Mississippi Press, 2007.

Zak, Albin. *I Don't Sound Like Nobody: Remaking Music in 1950s America.* Ann Arbor: University of Michigan Press, 2010.

Zak, Albin. *The Poetics of Rock: Cutting Tracks, Making Records.* Berkeley: University of California Press, 2001.

Zollo, Paul. "The Motown Memories of Norman Whitfield: Legendary Writer of 'War,' 'I Heard It through the Grapevine,' and 'Just My Imagination' Looks Back." In *Calling Out around the World: A Motown Reader,* edited by Kingsley Abbott, 144–48. London: Helter Skelter, 2000.

VI. Domestic Recordings

Abbey Tavern Singers. *We're Off to Dublin in the Green.* VIP 402 (1966).

Alexander, Arthur. "Detroit City." Dot 14737 (1965).

Allison, Luther. *Bad News Is Coming.* Gordy 964L (1972).

Allison, Luther. *Luther's Blues.* Gordy 967V1 (1973).

Ames Brothers. "Oh Babe!" Coral 9–60327 (1950).

Ames Brothers. "Rag Mop." Coral 9–60140 (1950).

Anthony, Lamont. "Let's Talk It Over." Anna 1125 (1960).

Anthony, Richard. "I Don't Know What to Do." VIP 25022 (1965).

Armstrong, Louis, and His Orchestra. "I Wonder." Decca 18652 (1945).

August, Joe "Mr. Google Eyes." Acc. by Billy Ford and His Musical V-8's. "No Wine, No Women." Okeh 6820 (1949).

Baker, LaVern. "It's So Fine." Atlantic 2001 (1958).

Baker, LaVern. "Jim Dandy." Atlantic 1116 (1956).

Baker, LaVern. "Jim Dandy Got Married." Atlantic 1136 (1957).

Baker, LaVern. "Soul on Fire." Atlantic 1004 (1953).

Ballard, Hank, and the Midnighters. "Finger Poppin' Time." King 4341 (1960).

Ballard, Hank, and the Midnighters. "Let's Go, Let's Go, Let's Go." King 5400 (1960).

Banks, Darrell. "Open the Door to Your Heart." Revilot 201 (1966).

Barnes, J. J. "Baby Please Come Back Home." Groovesville 1006 (1967).

Barnes, J. J. "A Real Humdinger." Ric-Tic 110 (1966).

Barry, Len. "1 2 3." Decca 31827 (1965).

Bartholomew, Dave. "My Ding-a-Ling." King 4544 (1952).

Basie, Count, and His Orchestra. "Open the Door, Richard!" RCA Victor 20–2127 (1947).

Bass, Fontella. "Rescue Me" b/w "The Soul of a Man." Checker 1120 (1965).

Beatles. *The Beatles Second Album.* Capitol 2080 (1964).

Beatles. "I Want to Hold Your Hand." Capitol 5112 (1963).

Beatles. "Money (That's What I Want)." Unreleased Decca audition (1962).

Belafonte, Harry. *Swing Dat Hammer.* RCA Victor LSP 2194 (1960).

Ben, LaBrenda. "The Chaperone." Gordy 7009 (1962).

Benton, Brook. "Endlessly." Mercury 71443 (1959).

Benton, Brook. "It's Just a Matter of Time." 71394 Mercury (1959).

Big Sean. *Finally Famous.* G.O.O.D. 15831 (2011).

Bland, Billy. "Let the Little Girl Dance." Old Town 1076 (1960).

Bobbettes. "Mr. Lee." Atlantic 1144 (1957).

Booker T and the MGs. "Boot-Leg." Stax 169 (1965).

Booker T and the MGs. "Green Onions." Stax 127 (1960).

Booker T and the MGs. *Green Onions.* Stax 701 (1962).

Booker T and the MGs. "Hip Hug-Her." Stax 211 (1967).

Booker T and the MGs. *Hip Hug-Her.* Stax 717 (1967).

Booker T and the MGs. *Soul Men.* Stax 725 (1967).

Bowie, David, and Mick Jagger. "Dancing in the Street." EMI America B-8288 (1985).

Boyd, Eddie, and His Chess Men. "Tortured Soul." Chess 1552 (1953).

Boyz II Men. *Cooleyhighharmony*. Motown MOTD-6320 (1991).

Boyz II Men. "The End of the Road." Motown 374632178–7 (1992).

Boyz II Men. "I'll Make Love to You." Motown 374632257–7 (1994).

Boyz II Men. "Sympin" b/w "It's So Hard to Say Goodbye to Yesterday." Motown 374632168–7 (1992).

Bradshaw, Tiny. "Soft." King 4577 (1952).

Brenston, Jackie, and His Delta Cats. "Rocket 88." Chess 1458 (1951).

Brown, James. *Black Caesar (Original Soundtrack)*. Polydor PD-6014 (1973).

Brown, James, and the Famous Flames. "Cold Sweat, Part 1." King 6110 (1967).

Brown, Roy, and His Mighty Men. "Boogie at Midnight." Deluxe 3300 (1949).

Brown, Roy, and His Mighty Men. "Rockin' at Midnight." Deluxe 3212 (1949).

Brown, Roy, with Bob Ogden and Orchestra. "Good Rocking Tonight." Deluxe 1093 (1947).

Burnett, Frances. "How I Miss You So." Coral 9–62127 (1959).

Butler, Jerry, and the Impressions. "For Your Precious Love." Falcon 1013 (1958).

California Raisins. *The California Raisins Sing the Hit Songs*. Priority SL-9706 (1987).

California Raisins. "I Heard It through the Grapevine." Priority LS-9717 (1987).

California Raisins. *Meet the Raisins!* Atlantic 81917 (1988).

California Raisins. *Sweet, Delicious, and Marvelous*. Priority SL-9755 (1988).

Campbell, Choker. *Hits of the Sixties*. Motown MT-620 (1965).

Candy and the Kisses, "The 81." Cameo 336 (1964).

Capitols. "Cool Jerk." Karen 1524 (1966).

Captain and Tennille. "Shop Around." A&M 1817 (1976).

Carey, Mariah. "I'll Be There." Columbia 38–74330 (1992).

Carpenters. "Please Mr. Postman." A&M 1646 (1974).

Cash, Alvin, and the Crawlers. "Twine Time." Mar-V-Lus 6002 (1964).

Celebration. *Almost Summer: Music from the Original Motion Picture Score*. MCA MCF-2840 (1978).

Chandler, Gene. "Duke of Earl." Vee-Jay 416 (1961).

Chandler, Gene. "Soul Hootenanny, Pt. I." Constellation 114 (1964).

Chandler, Gene. "You Threw a Lucky Punch." Vee-Jay 468 (1962).

Chantels. "Maybe." End 1005 (1957).

Charlene. "I've Never Been to Me." Motown 1611MF (1982).

Charles, Jimmy, and the Revelletts. "A Million to One." Promo 1002 (1960).

Charles, Ray. "Georgia on My Mind." ABC-Paramount 10135 (1960).

Charles, Ray. "Hallelujah, I Love Her So." Atlantic 1096 (1956).

Charles, Ray. *Modern Sounds in Country and Western Music*. ABC-Paramount ABC-410 (1962).

Charles, Ray, and His Band. "A Fool for You" b/w "This Little Girl of Mine." Atlantic 1063 (1955).

Charles, Ray, and His Band. "I've Got a Woman." Atlantic 1050 (1955).

Charlie Parker's Ree Boppers. "Billies Bounce" b/w "Now's the Time." Savoy 573 (1945).

Checker, Chubby. "The Twist." Parkway 811 (1960).

Clark, Chris. *Soul Sounds*. Motown MT-664 (1966).

Clarke, Claudine. "Party Lights." Chancellor 1113 (1962).

Clay, Tom. "Tom Clay's 'What the World Needs Now Is Love'/'Abraham, Martin, and John.'" MoWest 5002F (1971).

Commodores. "Brick House." Motown 1425F (1977).

Commodores. "Easy." Motown 1418F (1977).

Commodores. "Machine Gun." Motown 1307F (1974).

Commodores. "Nightshift." Motown 1773MF (1984).

Commodores. "Three Times a Lady." Motown 1443F (1978).

Commodores. "Too Hot Ta Trot." Motown 1432F (1977).

Contours. "Can You Do It." Gordy 7029 (1964).

Contours. "Do You Love Me." Gordy 7005 (1962).

Contours. *Do You Love Me.* Gordy 901 (1962).

Contours. "First I Look at the Purse." Gordy 7044 (1965).

Contours. "Just a Little Misunderstanding." Gordy 7052 (1966).

Contours. "Shake Sherrie." Gordy 7012 (1962)

Contours. "Whole Lotta Woman" b/w "Come On and Be Mine." Motown 1008 (1961).

Cooke, Sam. "Chain Gang." RCA Victor 47–7783 (1960).

Cooke, Sam. "Shake" b/w "A Change Is Gonna Come." RCA 8486 (1964).

Cooke, Sam. "Wonderful World." Keen 82112 (1960).

Cosby, Bill. "Little Ole Man (Uptight-Everything's Alright)." Warner Brothers 7072 (1967).

Costello, Elvis, and the Attractions. *Get Happy!!* Columbia JC-36347 (1980).

Covay, Don, and the Goodtimers. "Mercy, Mercy." Rosemart 801 (1964).

Creations. "This Is Our Night" b/w "You're My Inspiration." Mel-O-Dy 101 (1962).

Crystals. "Da Doo Ron Ron (When He Walked Me Home)." Phillies 112 (1963).

Crystals. "He's a Rebel." Phillies 106 (1962).

Culley, Frank "Floorshow," and His Band. "Cole Slaw." Atlantic 874 (1949).

Curtis, King, and the Noble Knights. "Soul Twist." Enjoy 1000 (1962).

Dalton Boys. "I've Been Cheated." V.I.P. 25025 (1965).

Darnell, Larry. "Oh Babe!" Regal 3298 (1950).

Darnells. "Too Hurt to Cry, Too Much in Love to Say Goodbye" b/w "Come on Home." Gordy 7024 (1963).

Dazz Band. "Let It Whip." 1609MF (1982).

Dean, Debbie. "Don't Let Him Shop Around." Motown 1007 (1961).

Dean, Jimmy. "Big Bad John." Columbia 42175 (1961).

DeBarge. "All This Love." Gordy 1660GF (1983).

DeBarge. "I Like It." Gordy 1645GF (1983).

DeBarge. "Rhythm of the Night." Gordy 1770GF (1985).

DeBarge. "Time Will Reveal." Gordy 1705GF (1983).

Dee, Kiki. *Great Expectations.* Tamla TS-303 (1970).

DeSanto, Sugar Pie. "Soulful Dress." Checker 1082 (1964).

Dionne and Friends. "That's What Friends Are For." Arista 9422 (1985).

Dixie Drifter. "Soul Heaven." Roulette 4641 (1965).

Doggett, Bill. "Honky Tonk (Part 1)." King 4950 (1956).

Domino, Fats. "Walking to New Orleans." Imperial 5675 (1960).

Dominoes. "Sixty Minute Man." Federal 12022 (1951).

Doobie Brothers. "Take Me in Your Arms." Warner Brother 8092 (1975).

Dorsey, Jimmy, and His Original "Dorseyland" Jazz Band. "Rag Mop." Columbia 38710 (1950).

Dorsey, Lee. "Ya Ya." Fury 1053 (1961).

Dorsey, Tommy, and His Orchestra. "The Huckle-Buck." RCA Victor 20–3427 (1949).

Drifters. "Save the Last Dance for Me." Atlantic 2071 (1960).

Drifters. "There Goes My Baby." Atlantic 2025 (1959).

Dynamic Superiors. "Nowhere to Run (Part 1)." Motown 1419F (1977).

Eckstine, Billy. *My Way*. Motown M-646 (1966).

Elgins. *Darling Baby*. V.I.P. 400 (1966).

Elgins. "Heaven Must Have Sent You." V.I.P. 25037 (1966).

En Vogue. "Hold On." Atlantic 7–87984 (1990).

Evans, Warren. "I Wonder." National 9003 (1944).

Everett, Betty. "I Can't Hear You." Vee-Jay 599 (1964).

Everett, Betty. "The Shoop Shoop Song (It's in His Kiss)." Vee-Jay 585 (1964).

Falcons. "Just for Your Love." Anna 1110 (1960).

Falcons. "You're So Fine." Unart 2013 (1959).

Falcons and Band (Ohio Untouchables). "I Found a Love." Lu Pine 1003 (1962).

Fantastic Four. "The Whole World Is a Stage." Ric-Tic 122 (1967).

Fergie. *The Dutchess*. A&M 7490 (2006).

Flanagan, Ralph, and His Orchestra. "Rag Mop." RCA Victor 20–3688 (1950).

Fletcher, "Dusty," with Jimmy Jones and His Band. "Open the Door, Richard!—Part 1." National 4012.

Forrest, Jimmy. "Night Train." United 110 (1952).

Four Tops. "Ain't That Love." Columbia 41755 (1960).

Four Tops. "Ain't That Love." Columbia 43356 (1965).

Four Tops. "Ask the Lonely." Motown 1073 (1965).

Four Tops. "Baby I Need Your Loving." Motown 1062 (1964).

Four Tops. "Bernadette." Motown 1104 (1967).

Four Tops. "I Can't Help Myself." Motown 1076 (1965).

Four Tops. "If I Were a Carpenter." Motown 1124 (1968).

Four Tops. "It's the Same Old Song." Motown 1081 (1965).

Four Tops. "Loving You Is Sweeter Than Ever." Motown 1096 (1966).

Four Tops. "MacArthur Park (Part II)." Motown 1189 (1971).

Four Tops. "Reach Out I'll Be There." Motown 1098 (1966).

Four Tops. "Shake Me, Wake Me (When It's Over)." Motown 1090 (1966).

Four Tops. "Something about You." Motown 1084 (1965).

Four Tops. "Standing in the Shadows of Love." Motown 1102 (1966).

Four Tops. "Walk Away Renee." Motown 1119 (1968).

Four Tops. "When She Was My Girl." Casablanca NB-2338 (1981).

Four Tops. "Without the One You Love (Life's Not Worthwhile)." Motown 1069 (1964).

Foxx, Inez. "Mockingbird." Symbol 919 (1964).

Franklin, Aretha. "Baby I Love You." Atlantic 2427 (1967).

Franklin, Aretha. "Chain of Fools." Atlantic 2464 (1967).

Franklin, Aretha. *I Never Loved a Man the Way I Love You*. Atlantic SD-8139 (1967).

Franklin, Aretha. *Lady Soul.* Atlantic SD-8176 (1968).

Franklin, Aretha. "A Natural Woman (You Make Me Feel Like)." Atlantic 2441 (1967).

Franklin, Aretha. "Respect." Atlantic 2403 (1967).

Franklin, Aretha. "Today I Sing the Blues." Columbia 41793 (1960).

Franklin, Aretha. "Won't Be Long." Columbia 41923 (1960).

Fulsom, Lowell. "Tramp." Kent 456 (1967).

Fuqua, Harvey. "Twelve Months of the Year" b/w "Don't Be Afraid to Love." Chess 1725 (1959).

Gant, Cecil. "I Wonder." Gilt-Edge 500 (1944).

Gaye, Marvin. "Ain't That Peculiar." Tamla 54122 (1965).

Gaye, Marvin. "Can I Get a Witness." Tamla 54087 (1963).

Gaye, Marvin. "Got to Give It Up (Pt. 1)." Tamla 54280F (1977).

Gaye, Marvin. *Hello Broadway.* Tamla TM-259 (1964).

Gaye, Marvin. "Hitch Hike." Tamla 54075 (1962).

Gaye, Marvin. "How Can I Forget." Tamla 54190 (1969).

Gaye, Marvin. "How Sweet It Is to Be Loved by You." 54107 (1964).

Gaye, Marvin. "I Heard It through the Grapevine." Tamla 54176 (1968).

Gaye, Marvin. "I'll Be Doggone." Tamla 54112 (1965).

Gaye, Marvin. *In The Groove.* Tamla TS-285 (1968).

Gaye, Marvin. "I Want You." Tamla 54264F (1976).

Gaye, Marvin. *I Want You.* Tamla T6–342S1 (1976).

Gaye, Marvin. *Let's Get It On* (Deluxe Edition). Motown 440–014–757–2 (2001).

Gaye, Marvin. "Let's Get It On." Tamla 54234 (1973).

Gaye, Marvin. "Let Your Conscience Be Your Guide." Tamla 54041 (1961).

Gaye, Marvin. *Marvin Gaye Live.* Tamla TS-333S1 (1974).

Gaye, Marvin. *Marvin Gaye Live at the London Palladium.* Tamla T7–352R2 (1977).

Gay, Marvin. "Masquerade (Is Over)" b/w "Witchcraft." Tamla [promotional] (1961).

Gaye, Marvin. *M. P. G.* Tamla TS-292 (1969).

Gaye, Marvin. "Mr. Sandman." Tamla 54055 (1962).

Gaye, Marvin. "One More Heartache." Tamla 54129 (1966).

Gaye, Marvin. "Pride and Joy." Tamla 54079 (1963).

Gaye, Marvin. "Sexual Healing." Columbia 38–03302 (1982).

Gaye, Marvin. *The Soulful Moods of Marvin Gaye.* Tamla TM-221 (1961).

Gaye, Marvin. "Stubborn Kind of Fellow." Tamla 54068 (1962).

Gaye, Marvin. *That Stubborn Kinda Fellow.* Tamla TM-239 (1962).

Gaye, Marvin. *A Tribute to the Great Nat King Cole.* Tamla TS-261 (1965).

Gaye, Marvin. "Trouble Man." Tamla 54228 (1972).

Gaye, Marvin. *Trouble Man.* Tamla T-322L (1972).

Gaye, Marvin. *Trouble Man* (40th Anniversary Expanded Edition). Hip-O Select B0017676 (2012).

Gaye, Marvin. "What's Going On." Tamla 54201 (1971).

Gaye, Marvin. *What's Going On.* Tamla TS-310 (1971).

Gaye, Marvin. *What's Going On* (Deluxe Edition). Motown 440013304 (2001).

Gaye, Marvin. "Your Unchanging Love." Tamla 54153 (1967).

Gaye, Marvin, and Tammi Terrell. "Ain't No Mountain High Enough." Motown 54149 (1967).

Gaye, Marvin, and Tammi Terrell. "Ain't Nothing Like the Real Thing." Tamla 54163 (1968).

Gaye, Marvin, and Tammi Terrell. "The Onion Song" b/w "California Soul." Tamla 54192 (1970).

Gaye, Marvin, and Tammi Terrell. "You're All I Need to Get By." Tamla 54169 (1968).

Gentry, Bobbie. "Ode to Billie Joe." Capitol 5950 (1967).

George, Barbara. "I Know (You Don't Love Me No More)." A. F. O. 302 (1961).

Gilley, Mickey. "You've Really Got a Hold On Me." Epic 04269 (1983).

Gorman Freddie. "The Day Will Come" b/w "Just for You." Miracle 11 (1961).

Green, Al. *Call Me.* HI XSHL-32077 (1973).

Greer, Paula. *Introducing Miss Paula Greer.* Workshop Jazz 203 (1963).

Goldstein, William. *Music from the Original Motion Picture Soundtrack "Bingo Long Traveling All Stars and Motor Kings."* MCA 2094 (1976).

Gospel Stars. *Shades of Gospel Soul.* Motown 701 (1970).

Haines, Connie. "For Once in My Life." Motown Unreleased 1965 (iTunes 2015).

Hamlisch, Marvin. "The Entertainer." MCA 40174 (1974).

Hampton, Lionel, and His Orchestra. "The Huckle-Buck." Decca 24652 (1949).

Hampton, Lionel, and His Orchestra. "Rag Mop." Decca 24855 (1950).

Harnell, Joe. *Moving On.* Motown S-698 (1969).

Harris, Wynonie. "Drinkin' Wine, Spo-Dee-O-Dee." King 4292 (1949).

Harris, Wynonie. "Good Rockin' Tonight." King 4210 (1948).

Harris, Wynonie, with Lucky Millinder and His Orchestra. "Oh Babe!" King 4418 (1950).

Hawkins, Erskine, and His Orchestra. "Bewildered" b/w "Corn Bread." RCA Victor 3326 (1949).

Hawkins, Erskine, and His Orchestra. "Caldonia." Victor 1659 (1945).

Hawthorne, Mayer. "Maybe So, Maybe No" b/w "I Wish It Would Rain." Stones Throw 2212 (2009).

Hawthorne, Mayer. *A Strange Arrangement.* Stones Throw 2219 (2009).

Hayes, Isaac. *Hot Buttered Soul.* Enterprise ENS-1001 (1969).

Hayes, Isaac. *Shaft.* Enterprise ENS-2–5002 (1971).

Headliners. "We Call It Fun." V. I. P. 25026 (1965).

Heard, Oma. "Lifetime Man." V. I. P. 25008 (1964).

Heidelberg Quintette. "By the Beautiful Sea." Victor 17560 (1914).

Herman, Woody, and His Orchestra. "Caldonia." Columbia 36789 (1945).

Hill, Lauryn. "Doo Wop (That Thing)." Ruffhouse 38–78868-ZSS (1998).

Holden, Ron. "Love You So." Donna 1315 (1959).

Holiday, Billie. "Strange Fruit" b/w "Fine and Mellow." Commodore 526 (1939).

Holiday, Billie. "These Foolish Things (Remind Me of You)" b/w "Strange Fruit." Verve 10181 (1959).

Holidays. "I'll Love You Forever." Golden World 36 (1966).

Holliday, Jennifer. "And I Am Telling You I'm Not Going." Geffen 29983 (1982).

Holland, Bryant. "(Where's the Joy) In Nature Boy" b/w "Shock." Kudo 667 (1959).

Holland, Eddie. "It Moves Me." Tamla 102 (1959).

Holland, Eddie. "Jamie" b/w "Take a Chance on Me." Motown 1021 (1961).

Holland, Eddie. "Little Miss Ruby." Mercury 71290 (1958).

Holland-Dozier. "What Goes Up, Music Come Down" b/w "Come on Home." Motown 1045 (1963).

Holloway, Brenda. "Every Little Bit Hurts." Tamla 54094 (1964).

Holloway, Brenda. "You've Made Me So Very Happy." Tamla 54155 (1967).

Hornets. "Give Me a Kiss." V. I. P. 25004 (1964).

Horton, Willie. "Detroit Is Happening." Motown M-1900 [promotional] (1967).

Houston, Thelma. *Any Way You Like It.* Tamla T6-345S1 (1976).

Howard, Eddy, and His Orchestra. "Rag Mop." Mercury 5371 (1950).

Hughes, Jimmy. "Steal Away." Fame 6401 (1964).

Hunt, Tommy. "I Am a Witness." Scepter 1261 (1963).

Hutch, Willie. *Foxy Brown.* Motown M6-811S1 (1974).

Hutch, Willie. *The Mack.* Motown M-766L (1973).

Ice Cube. "Bop Gun (One Nation)." Priority PVL-53161 (1994).

Impressions. "Can't Satisfy." ABC 10831 (1966).

Impressions. "It's All Right." ABC-Paramount 10487 (1963).

Impressions. "Keep On Pushing." ABC-Paramount 10554 (1964).

Impressions. "Woman's Got Soul." ABC-Paramount 10647 (1965).

Isley Brothers. *Soul on the Rocks.* Tamla TS-275 (1967).

Isley Brothers. *This Old Heart of Mine.* Tamla T-269 (1966)

Isley Brothers. "Twist and Shout." Wand 124 (1962).

Jackson, Chuck. "Beg Me." Wand 154 (1964).

Jackson, Deon. "Love Makes the World Go Round." Carla 2526 (1965).

Jackson 5. "ABC." Motown 1163 (1970).

Jackson 5. "Dancing Machine." Motown 1286 (1974).

Jackson 5. "Forever Came Today." Motown 1365F (1975).

Jackson 5. *Goin' Back to Indiana.* Motown 742L (1971).

Jackson 5. "I'll Be There." Motown 1171 (1970).

Jackson 5. "I Want You Back." Motown 1157 (1969).

Jackson 5. "The Love You Save." Motown 1166 (1970).

Jackson, Mahalia. "Move On up a Little Higher." Apollo 164 (1947).

Jackson, Michael. "Billie Jean." Epic 34-03509 (1982).

Jackson, Moose. "Big Ten-Inch Record." King 4580 (1952).

James, Etta. "All I Could Do Was Cry." Argo 5359 (1960).

James, Etta, and "The Peaches." "The Wallflower." Modern 947 (1955).

James, Rick. *Bustin' Out of L Seven.* Gordy G7-984R1 (1979).

James, Rick. *Come Get It.* Gordy G7-981R1 (1978).

James, Rick. "Mary Jane." Gordy 7162F (1978).

James, Rick. *Street Songs.* Gordy G8-1002M1 (1981).

James, Rick. "Super Freak." Gordy 7205F (1981).

James, Rick. "You and I." Gordy 7156F (1978).

James, Rick, featuring Smokey Robinson. "Ebony Eyes." Gordy 1714F (1983).

John, Mable. "No Love." Tamla 54040 (1961).

Johnny and the Hurricanes. "Red River Rock." Warwick 509 (1959).

Johnson, Marv. "Come to Me." Tamla 101 (1959).

Johnson, Marv. "Come to Me." United Artists 160 (1959).

Johnson, Marv. "You Got What It Takes." United Artists 185 (1961).

Jones, Jimmy. "Good Timin'." Cub 9067 (1960).

Jones, Jimmy. "Handy Man." Cub 9049 (1959).

Jones, Joe. " You Talk Too Much." Ric 972 (1960).

Jones, Jonah. *Along Came Jonah.* Motown S-683 (1968).

Jones, Jonah. *A Little Dis, a Little Dat.* Motown MS-690 (1970).

Jones, Red. *Red Jones Steeerikes Back.* Motown MS-691 (1969).

Jordan, Lewis, and His Tympany Five. "Caldonia." Decca 8670 (1945).

Jordan, Lewis, and His Tympany Five. "Cole Slaw." Decca 24633 (1949).

Jordan, Lewis, and His Tympany Five. "G. I. Jive" b/w "Is You Is or Is You Ain't (Ma' Baby)." Decca 8659 (1944).

Jordan, Lewis, and His Tympany Five. "Honeysuckle Rose." Decca 7675 (1939)

Jordan, Lewis, and His Tympany Five. "Keep A-Knockin'." Decca 7609 (1939).

Jordan, Lewis, and His Tympany Five. "Open the Door Richard!" Decca 23841 (1947).

Kayli, Bob. "Everyone Was There." Carlton 482 (1958).

Kayli, Bob. "Small Sad Sam." Tamla 54051 (1961).

Kendricks, Eddie. "Boogie Down." Tamla 54243 (1973).

Kendricks, Eddie. "Keep on Truckin'." Tamla 54238 (1973).

King, B. B. "Story from My Heart and Soul." RPM 374 (1952).

King, Ben E. "Spanish Harlem." Atco 6185 (1960).

King, Ben E. "Stand by Me." Atco 6194 (1961).

King, Rev. Martin Luther. *The Great March on Washington.* Gordy 908 (1963).

King, Rev. Martin Luther. *The Great March to Freedom.* Gordy 906 (1963).

Knight, Gladys, and the Pips. "Every Beat of My Heart." Vee-Jay 386 (1961).

Knight, Gladys, and the Pips. "Every Beat of My Heart." Fury 1050 (1961).

Knight, Gladys, and the Pips. *Everybody Needs Love.* Soul SS-706 (1967).

Knight, Gladys, and the Pips. "I Heard It through the Grapevine" Soul 35039 (1967).

Knight, Gladys, and the Pips. "I Wish It Would Rain." Soul 35047 (1968).

Knight, Gladys, and the Pips. "Love Overboard." MCA 53210 (1987).

Lambro, Phillip. *Murph the Surf.* Motown M6–839 S1 (1975).

Lauper, Cyndi. "What's Going On." Portrait 37–06970 (1986).

Lee, Jackie. "The Shotgun and the Duck" b/w "Do the Temptation Walk." Mirwood 5510 (1966).

Lester, Ketty. "Love Letters." Era 3068 (1962).

Leverett, Chico. "Solid Sender" b/w "I'll Never Love Again." Tamla 54024 (1959).

Lewis, Ramsey. "The 'In' Crowd." Argo 5506 (1965).

Liggins, Jimmy, and His Drops of Joy. "Cadillac Boogie." Specialty 521 (1947).

Liggins, Joe, and His Honeydrippers. "Rag Mop." Specialty 350 (1950).

Little Eva. "The Loco-Motion." Dimension 1000 (1962).

Little Iva and Her Band. "Continental Strut." Miracle 2 (1961).

Little Otis. "I Out-Duked the Duke." Tamla 54058 (1962).

Long, Shorty. "Devil with the Blue Dress." Soul 35001 (1964).

Long, Shorty. "Function at the Junction." Soul 35021 (1966).

Long, Shorty. "Night Fo' Last." Soul 35040 (1968).

Lumpkin, Henry. "I've Got a Notion" b/w "We Really Love Each Other." Motown 1005 (1960).

Lumpkin, Henry. "Mo Jo Hannah." Motown 1029 (1962).

Lynn, Barbara. "You'll Lose a Good Thing." Jamie 1220 (1962).

Madonna. "Like a Virgin." Sire 7–29210 (1984).

Marie, Teena. *Wild and Peaceful.* Gordy G7–986R1 (1979).

Mar-Keys. *The Great Memphis Sound.* Stax SD-707 (1966).

Mar-Keys. "Last Night." Stax 107 (1960).

Martha and the Vandellas. "Come and Get These Memories." Gordy 7014 (1963).

Martha and the Vandellas. "Dancing in the Street." Gordy 7033 (1964).

Martha and the Vandellas. "Heat Wave." Gordy 7022 (1963).

Martha and the Vandellas. "I'm Ready for Love." Gordy 7056 (1966).

Martha and the Vandellas. "Live Wire." Gordy 7027 (1964).

Martha and the Vandellas. "Nowhere to Run." Gordy 7039 (1965).

Martha and the Vandellas. "Quicksand." Gordy 7025 (1963).

Martha and the Vandellas. "Wild One." Gordy 7036 (1964).

Marvelettes. "Beechwood 4–5789" b/w "Someday, Someway." Tamla 54065 (1962).

Marvelettes. "Don't Mess with Bill." Tamla 54126 (1965).

Marvelettes. *The Marvelettes.* Tamla T-274 (1967).

Marvelettes. "Playboy." Tamla 54060 (1962).

Marvelettes. "Please Mr. Postman." Tamla 54046 (1961).

Marvelettes. "Strange I Know." Tamla 54072 (1962).

Marvelettes. "Twistin' Postman." Tamla 54054 (1961).

Mary Jane Girls. "In My House." Gordy 1741GF (1985).

Massner, Michael. *The Original Soundtrack of Mahogany.* Motown M6–858S1 (1974).

Mayer, Nathaniel, and the Fabulous Twilights. "Village of Love." Fortune 449 (1962).

Mayfield, Curtis. *Superfly.* Curtom CRS-8014 (1972).

McCartney, Paul. "Ebony and Ivory." Columbia 18–02860 (1982).

McCullers, Mickey. "Same Old Story." Tamla 54064 (1962).

McGhee, "Stick," and His Buddies. "Drinkin' Wine Spo-Dee-O-Dee." Atlantic 873 (1949).

McNally, Larry John. "The Motown Song." Atco 7–99536 (1986).

McVea, Jack, and His All Stars. "Open the Door Richard!" Black and White 792 (1946).

Method Man and Mary J. Blige. "I'll Be There for You." Def Jam 422–851–879 (1995).

Midnighters. "Annie Had a Baby." Federal 12195 (1955).

Midnighters. "Annie's Aunt Fannie." Federal 12200 (1954).

Midnighters. "Work with Me Annie." Federal 12169 (1954).

Milburn, Amos. *Return of the Blues Boss.* Motown MT-608 (1963).

Milburn, Amos, and His Aladdin Chickenshackers. "One Scotch, One Bourbon, One Beer." Aladdin 3197 (1953).

Milton, Roy, and His Solid Senders. "Christmas Time Blues" b/w "Oh Babe." Specialty 381 (1950).

Milton, Roy, and His Solid Senders. "The Huckle-Buck." Specialty 328 (1949).

Mimms, Garnet, and the Enchanters. "Cry Baby." United Artists 629 (1963).

Miracles. "Ain't It Baby." Tamla 54036 (1961).

Miracles. "All I Want (Is You)" b/w "I Need a Change." Chess 1768 (1960).

Miracles. "Bad Girl." Chess 1734 (1959).

Miracles. "Bad Girl." Tamla G1 (1959).

Miracles. "Broken Hearted" b/w "Mighty Good Lovin'." Tamla 54044 (1961).

Miracles. "Everybody's Gotta Pay Some Dues." Tamla 54048 (1961).

Miracles. "Got a Job." End 1016 (1958).

Miracles. "I Gotta Dance to Keep from Crying." Tamla 54098 (1963).

Miracles. "I'll Try Something New." Tamla 54059 (1962).

Miracles. "Love Machine." Tamla 54262 (1975).

Miracles. "A Love She Can Count On." Tamla 54078 (1963).

Miracles. "Ooo Baby Baby." Tamla 54113 (1965).

Miracles. "Shop Around." Tamla 54034 (1960).

Miracles. "The Tracks of My Tears." Tamla 54118 (1965).

Miracles. "Way over There." Tamla 54028 (1960).

Miracles. "What's So Good about Good-By." Tamla 54053 (1961).

Miracles. "You've Really Got a Hold on Me." Tamla 54073 (1962).

Mongo Santamaria Band. "Watermelon Man." Battle 45909 (1963).

Moonglows. "In the Middle of the Night" b/w "Soda Pop." Chess 1689 (1958).

Moonglows. "See Saw." Chess 1629 (1956).

Moonglows. "Sincerely." Chess 1581 (1954).

Morgan, Lee. "The Sidewinder." Blue Note 911 (1964).

Murphy, Eddie. "Party All the Time." Columbia 38–05609 (1985).

Naughty by Nature. "O. P. P." Tommy Boy 512–7 (1991).

Nash, Johnny. "Let's Move and Groove (Together)." JoDa 102 (1965).

New Edition. "Candy Girl." Street Wise 1108 (1983).

Oddis, Ray. "Randy, the Newspaper Boy." V. I. P. 25012 (1964).

Otis and Carla. "Tramp." Stax 216 (1967).

Parker, Sonny. "She Sets My Soul on Fire." Peacock 1620 (1952).

Parliaments. "(I Wanna) Testify." Revilot 207 (1967).

Phillips, Esther. "Release Me." Lenox 5555 (1962).

Pickett, Wilson. "Funky Broadway." Atlantic 2430 (1967).

Pickett, Wilson. "In the Midnight Hour." Atlantic 2289 (1965).

Pickett, Wilson. "It's Too Late." Double L 717 (1963).

Pickett, Wilson. "Let Me Be Your Boy." Correct-Tone 501 (1962).

Pointer, Bonnie. "Heaven Must Have Sent You." Motown 1459F (1979).

Pointer, Bonnie. "I Can't Help Myself (Sugar Pie, Honey Bunch)." Motown 1478F (1979).

Pop, Iggy. *Lust for Life*. RCA Victor AFL1–2488 (1977).

Popcorn and the Mohawks. "Custer's Last Man." Motown 1002 (1960).

Preston, Billy, and Syreeta. *Music from the Motion Picture "Fast Break."* Motown M7–915R (1979).

Preston, Billy, and Syreeta. "With You I'm Born Again." Motown 1477F (1979).

Preston, Jimmy. "Oh Babe!" Derby 748 (1950).

Price, Ray. "Release Me." Columbia 21214 (1954).

Prima, Louis, and Keely Smith. "Oh Babe!" Robin Hood 101 (1950).

Puth, Charlie. *Nine Track Mind*. Atlantic 551934 (2016).

Pyramids. "I'm the Playboy." Cub 9112 (1962).

Pyramids. "I'm the Playboy." Sonbert 82661 (1962).

Rare Earth. "(I Know) I'm Losing You." Rare Earth 5017 (1970).

Redding, Otis. "Come to Me." Volt 116 (1964).

Redding, Otis. *Otis Blue/Otis Redding Sings Soul.* Volt 412 (1965).

Redding, Otis. "Pain in My Heart." Volt 112 (1963).

Redding, Otis. "Respect." Volt 128 (1965).

Redding, Otis. "That's What My Heart Needs." Volt 109 (1963).

Redding, Otis. "These Arms of Mine." Volt 103 (1962).

Redding, Otis, and Carla Thomas. *King and Queen.* Stax S-716 (1967).

Reeves, Martha, and the Vandellas. "Honey Chile." Gordy 7067 (1967).

Reflections. "(Just Like) Romeo and Juliet." Golden World 9 (1964).

Remus, Eugene. "You Never Miss a Good Thing" b/w "Gotta Have Your Lovin'." Motown 1001 (1959).

Remus, Eugene. "You Never Miss a Good Thing" b/w "Hold Me Tight." Motown 1001 (1959).

Richie, Lionel. "All Night Long (All Night)." Motown 1698MF (1983).

Richie, Lionel. *Can't Slow Down.* Motown 6059ML (1983).

Richie, Lionel. *Dancing on the Ceiling.* Motown 6158ML (1985).

Richie, Lionel. "Hello." Motown 1722MF (1984).

Richie, Lionel. *Lionel Richie.* Motown 6007ML (1982).

Richie, Lionel. "Say You, Say Me." 1819MF (1985).

Riftkin, Joshua. *Piano Rags.* Nonesuch H-71248 (1970).

Righteous Brothers. "Unchained Melody." Phillies 129 (1965).

Righteous Brothers. "You've Lost That Lovin' Feelin'." Phillies 124 (1964).

Robinson, Smokey. "Being with You." Tamla 54321F (1981).

Robinson, Smokey. *Big Time.* Tamla TS-355S1 (1977).

Robinson, Smokey. "Cruisin'." Tamla 54306F (1979).

Robinson, Smokey. "Just to See Her." Motown 1877MF (1987).

Robinson, Smokey. "One Heartbeat." Motown 1897MF (1987).

Robinson, Smokey. *A Quiet Storm.* Tamla T6-337S1 (1975).

Robinson, Smokey, and the Miracles. "I Care about Detroit." [No Label] 13090 (1968).

Robinson, Smokey, and the Miracles. *Special Occasion.* Tamla TS-290 (1968).

Robinson, Smokey, and the Miracles. "The Tears of a Clown." Tamla 54199 (1970).

Rockwell. "Somebody's Watching Me." Motown 1702MF (1983).

Roger. "I Heard It through the Grapevine." Warner Brothers 49786 (1981).

Rogers, Kenny. "Lady." Liberty UA-X1380-Y (1980).

Ron and Bill. "It" b/w "Don't Say Bye-Bye." Tamla 54025 (1959).

Ron and Bill. "It" b/w "Don't Say Bye-Bye." Argo 5350 (1959).

Ronettes. "Be My Baby." Phillies 116 (1963).

Ronstadt, Linda. "Heat Wave." Asylum 54282 (1975).

Ross, Diana. "Ain't No Mountain High Enough." Motown 1169 (1970).

Ross, Diana. "The Boss." Motown 1462F (1979).

Ross, Diana. *Diana!* Motown 719 (1971).

Ross, Diana. *An Evening with Diana Ross.* Motown M7-877R2 (1977).

Ross, Diana. *Lady Sings the Blues.* Motown M-758D (1972).

Ross, Diana. "Love Hangover." Motown 1392F (1976).

Ross, Diana. "Missing You." RCA 13966 (1984).

Ross, Diana. "Theme from *Mahogany* (Do You Know Where You're Going To)." Motown 1377F (1975).

Ross, Diana, and Lionel Richie. "Endless Love." Motown 1519F (1981).

Ross, Diana, and the Supremes. *Diana Ross and the Supremes Sing and Perform Funny Girl.* Motown MS-672 (1968).

Ross, Diana, and the Supremes. *Farewell.* Motown MS2–708 (1970).

Ross, Diana, and the Supremes. "I'm Livin' in Shame." Motown 1139 (1969).

Ross, Diana, and the Supremes. "In and Out of Love." Motown 1116 (1967).

Ross, Diana, and the Supremes. *Join the Temptations.* Motown MS-679 (1968).

Ross, Diana, and the Supremes. "Love Child." Motown 1135 (1968).

Ross, Diana, and the Supremes. "Someday We'll Be Together." Motown 1156 (1969).

Ross, Diana, and the Supremes and the Temptations. *On Broadway.* Motown S-699 (1969).

Ross, Diana, and the Supremes and the Temptations. *Together.* Motown MS-692 (1969).

Ross, Diana, and the Supremes with the Temptations. *TCB.* MS-682 (1968).

Royaltones. "Poor Boy." Jubilee 5338 (1958).

Ruffin, Jimmy. "Don't Feel Sorry for Me." Miracle 1 (1962).

Ruffin, Jimmy. "What Becomes of the Brokenhearted." Soul 35022 (1966).

Saadiq, Raphael. *The Way I See It.* Columbia 88697–08585 (2008).

Sam and Dave. "Hold On! I'm a Comin'." Stax 189 (1966).

Sam and Dave. "Soul Man." Stax 231 (1967).

Sam and Dave. "When Something Is Wrong with My Baby." Stax 210 (1967).

Satintones. "Angel" b/w "A Love That Can Never Be." Motown 1006 (1961).

Satintones. "Going to the Hop" b/w "Motor City." Tamla 54026 (1959).

Satintones. "I Know How It Feels" b/w "My Kind of Love." (1961).

Satintones. "My Beloved." Motown 1000 (1959).

Satintones. "Tomorrow and Always." Motown 1006 (1961).

Satintones, "Zing Went the Strings of My Heart" b/w "Faded Letter." Motown 1020 (1961).

Sausage, Doc and His Mad Lads. "Rag Mop." Regal 3251 (1950).

Scott, Jack. "My True Love" b/w "Leroy." Carlton 462 (1958).

Shannon, Del. "Runaway." Big Top 3067 (1961).

Sharon, Ralph. *Modern Innovations on Country and Western Themes.* Gordy 903 (1963).

Sharp, Dee Dee. "Mashed Potato Time." Cameo 212 (1962).

Sheppard, T. G. "Devil in the Bottle." Melodyland 6002F (1974).

Sheppard, T. G. "Tryin' to Beat the Morning Home." Melodyland 6006F (1975).

Shirelles. "Will You Love Me Tomorrow." Scepter 1211 (1960).

Silhouettes. "Get a Job." Ember 1029 (1957).

Simpson, Valerie. *Exposed.* Tamla S-311 (1971).

Sinatra, Frank. "The Huckle Buck." Columbia 38486 (1949).

Singer, Hal, Sextette. "Beef Stew." Savoy 686 (1949).

Singer, Hal, Sextette. "Corn Bread." Savoy 671 (1948).

Sledge, Percy. "When a Man Loves a Woman." Atlantic 2326 (1966).

Sledge, Sister. "My Guy." Cotillion 4700 (1982).

Small, Millie. "My Boy Lollipop." Smash 1893 (1964).

Smith, Mamie, and Her Jazz Hounds. "Crazy Blues." Okeh 4169 (1920).

Soul, Jimmy. "If You Wanna Be Happy." S. P. Q. R. 3305 (1962).

Soul Survivors. "Expressway to Your Heart." Crimson 1010 (1967).

Springfield, Dusty. *Dusty in Memphis*. Atlantic SD-8214 (1969).

Springsteen, Bruce, and the E Street Band. "War." Columbia 38–06432 (1986).

Starlighters. "Rag Mop." Capitol 844 (1950).

Starr, Edwin. "Agent Double-O-Soul." Ric-Tic 103 (1965).

Starr, Edwin. *Hell Up in Harlem*. M-802V1 (1974).

Starr, Edwin. *Soul Master*. Gordy GS-931 (1968).

Starr, Edwin. "War." Gordy 7107 (1970).

Starr, Kay. "Oh, Babe." Capitol 1278 (1950).

Stray Cats. "Rock This Town" b/w "You Can't Hurry Love." EMI America 8132 (1982).

Strong, Barrett. "Let's Rock." Tamla 54021 (1959).

Strong, Barrett. "Money and Me." Tamla 54035 (1961).

Strong, Barrett. "Money (That's What I Want)." Tamla 54027 (1959).

Strong, Barrett. "Money (That's What I Want)." Anna 1111 (1960).

Strong, Barrett. "Yes, No, Maybe So" b/w "You Knows What to Do." Anna 1116 (1960).

Strong, Barrett. "Yes, No, Maybe So" b/w "You Knows What to Do." Tamla 54029 (1960).

Suavé. "My Girl." Capitol 44124 (1988).

Summer, Donna. "Last Dance." Casablanca 926 (1978).

Supremes. *At the Copa*. Motown M-636 (1965).

Supremes. "Baby Love." Motown 1066 (1964).

Supremes. "Back in My Arms Again." Motown 1075 (1965).

Supremes. "The Bikini Machine" (aka "Beach Ball"). American International 6514 (1965).

Supremes. *A Bit of Liverpool*. Motown MS-623 (1964).

Supremes. "A Breath Taking Guy" b/w "(The Man with the) Rock and Roll Banjo Band." Motown 1044 (1963).

Supremes. "Buttered Popcorn" b/w "Who's Loving You." Tamla 54045 (1961).

Supremes. "Come See about Me." Motown 1068 (1964).

Supremes. "The Happening." Motown 1107 (1967).

Supremes. "I Hear a Symphony." Motown 1083 (1965).

Supremes. *I Hear a Symphony*. Motown S-643 (1966).

Supremes. "Let Me Go the Right Way." Motown 1034 (1962).

Supremes. "Love Is Here and Now You're Gone." Motown 1103 (1967).

Supremes. "Love Is Like an Itching in My Heart." Motown 1094 (1966).

Supremes. "My World Is Empty without You." Motown 1089 (1965).

Supremes. "Nothing but Heartaches." Motown 1080 (1965).

Supremes. "Reflections." Motown 1111 (1967).

Supremes. "Stop! In the Name of Love." Motown 1074 (1965).

Supremes. *Supremes Sing Country, Western and Pop*. Motown MS-625 (1965).

Supremes. *Supremes Sing Holland, Dozier, Holland*. Motown M-650 (1966).

Supremes. *Supremes Sing Rodgers and Hart.* MS-659 (1967).

Supremes. "Things Are Changing." Advertising Council [promotional] SL4M-3114 (1966).

Supremes. *Touch.* Motown M-737 (1971).

Supremes. *We Remember Sam Cooke.* Motown MT-629 (1965).

Supremes. "Where Did Our Love Go." Motown 1060 (1964).

Supremes. "You Can't Hurry Love." Motown 1097 (1966).

Supremes. "You Keep Me Hangin' On." Motown 1101 (1966).

Supremes. "Your Heart Belongs to Me." Motown 1027 (1962).

Swinging Tigers. "Snake Walk." Tamla 54024 (1959).

Sykes, Roosevelt. "I Wonder." Bluebird 721 (1945).

Tams. "What Kind of Fool (Do You Think I Am)." ABC-Paramount 10502 (1963).

Taylor, Bobby, and the Vancouvers. *Bobby Taylor and the Vancouvers.* Gordy GLPS-930 (1968).

Taylor, James. "How Sweet It Is (To Be Loved by You)." Warner Brothers 8109 (1975).

Temptations. "Ain't Too Proud to Beg." Gordy 7054 (1966).

Temptations. *All Directions.* Gordy G-962L (1972).

Temptations. "Ball of Confusion (That's What the World Is Today)." Gordy 7099 (1970).

Temptations. "Check Yourself" b/w "Your Wonderful Love." Miracle 12 (1961).

Temptations. "Cloud Nine." Gordy 7081 (1968).

Temptations. *Cloud Nine.* Gordy GS-939 (1969).

Temptations. "Don't Let the Joneses Get You Down." Gordy 786 (1969).

Temptations. "Farewell My Love" b/w "May I Have This Dance." Gordy 7020 (1963).

Temptations. "Dream Come True" b/w "Isn't She Pretty." Gordy 7001 (1962).

Temptations. "Get Ready." Gordy 7049 (1966).

Temptations. "Girl (Why You Wanna Make Me Blue)." Gordy 7035 (1964).

Temptations. "Gonna Give Her All the Love I Got." Gordy 7072 (1968).

Temptations. "Heavenly" b/w "Zoom." Gordy 7135F (1974).

Temptations. "I Can't Get Next to You." Gordy 7093 (1969).

Temptations. "(I Know) I'm Losing You." Gordy 7057 (1966).

Temptations. *In a Mellow Mood.* Gordy S-924 (1967).

Temptations. "I Wish It Would Rain." Gordy 7068 (1967).

Temptations. "Let Your Hair Down" b/w "Ain't No Justice." Gordy 7133F (1973).

Temptations. "Masterpiece." Gordy 7126F (1973).

Temptations. *Masterpiece.* Gordy G-765L (1973).

Temptations. "Mother Nature" b/w "Funky Music Sho Nuff Turns Me On." Gordy 7119F (1972).

Temptations. "My Baby" b/w "Don't Look Back." Gordy 7047 (1965).

Temptations. "My Girl." Gordy 7038 (1964).

Temptations. *1990.* Gordy G-966V1 (1973).

Temptations. "Papa Was a Rollin' Stone." Gordy 7121F (1972).

Temptations. "Paradise" b/w "Slow Down Heart." Gordy 7010 (1962).

Temptations. "Plastic Man" b/w "Hurry Tomorrow." Gordy 7129F (1973).

Temptations. "Psychedelic Shack." Gordy 7069 (1969).

Temptations. *Psychedelic Shack.* Gordy GS-947 (1970).

Temptations. *Puzzle People.* Gordy S-949 (1969)

Temptations. "Runaway Child, Running Wild." Gordy 7084 (1969).

Temptations. *Sky's the Limit.* Gordy GLPS-957 (1971).

Temptations. *Solid Rock.* Gordy G-961L (1971).

Temptations. "Standing on Top." Gordy 1616GF (1982).

Temptations. "Superstar (Remember How You Got Where You Are)." Gordy 7111F (1971).

Temptations. "Take a Look Around." Gordy 7115F (1972).

Temptations. *The Temptations Show.* Gordy S-933 (1969).

Temptations. "Ungena Za Ulimwengu (Unite the World)" b/w "Hum Along and Dance." Gordy 7102 (1970).

Temptations. "The Way You Do the Things You Do." Gordy 7028 (1964).

Temptations. *With a Lot 'O Soul.* Gordy S-922 (1967).

Temptations. "(You're My) Dream Come True." Gordy 7001 (1962).

Temptations. "You've Got My Soul on Fire." Gordy 7136F (1974).

Tex, Joe. "Hold What You've Got." Dial 4001 (1964).

Tharpe, Sister Rosetta. "Silent Night (Christmas Hymn)." Decca 48119 (1949).

Tharpe, Sister Rosetta. "Strange Things Happening Every Day." Decca 48009 (1946).

Tharpe, Sister Rosetta, and Marie Knight. "Up above My Head, I Hear Music in the Air." Decca 48090 (1949).

Thicke, Robin. *Blurred Lines.* Star Trak 18679 (2013).

Thicke, Robin. *Sex Therapy: The Experience.* Star Trak 1375802 (2009).

Thomas, Carla. "B-A-B-Y." Stax 195 (1966).

Thomas, Carla, and Rufus Thomas. "Cause I Love You." Satellite 102 (1960).

Thomas, Rufus. "Walking the Dog." Stax 140 (1963).

Three Flames. "Open the Door, Richard." Columbia 37268 (1947).

TLC. *Oooooooohhh . . . On the TLC Tip.* LaFace 73008–26003 (1992).

Top Notes. "Twist and Shout." Atlantic 2115 (1961).

Toys. "A Lover's Concerto." DynoVoice 209 (1965).

Tucker, Sophie. "Some of These Days." Edison Amberol 4M-691 (1911).

Turner, Spyder. "Stand by Me." M-G-M 13617 (1966).

Twistin' Kings. "Congo." Motown 1023 (1961).

Twistin' Kings. *Twistin' the World Around.* Motown MLP-601 (1961).

2Pac. "Keep Ya Head Up." Interscope 95972 (1993).

2Pac. "Thugz Mansion." Interscope 10878 (2002).

Underdogs. "Love Gone Bad." V. I. P. 25040 (1967).

Undisputed Truth. *Down to Earth.* Gordy G6–968S1 (1974).

Undisputed Truth. "Papa Was a Rollin' Stone." Gordy 7117F (1972).

Undisputed Truth. *Undisputed Truth.* (1971). Gordy GS-955L (1971).

USA for Africa. "We Are the World." Columbia 4839 (1985).

Valadiers. "Greetings (This Is Uncle Sam)" b/w "Take a Chance." Miracle 6 (1961).

Valadiers. "Please Mr. Kennedy." Tamla 54052 (1962).

Van Dyke, Earl, and the Soul Brothers. "I Can't Help Myself" b/w "How Sweet It Is." Soul 35014 (1965).

Van Dyke, Earl, and the Soul Brothers. *That Motown Sound.* Motown M-631 (1965).

Van Halen. "Dancing in the Street." Warner Brothers 29986 (1982).

Various Artists. *Black Europe: The Sounds and Images of Black People in Europe, Pre-1927.* Bear Family BCD-16095 (2013).

Various Artists. *The Complete Motown Singles. Vol. 1, 1959–1961.* Hip-O Select/Motown. B0003631–02 (2005).

Various Artists. *The Complete Motown Singles. Vol. 2, 1962.* Hip-O Select/Motown B0004402–02 (2005).

Various Artists. *The Complete Motown Singles. Vol. 3, 1963.* Hip-O Select/Motown B0005352–02 (2005).

Various Artists. *The Complete Motown Singles. Vol. 4, 1964.* Hip-O Select/Motown B0005946–02 (2006).

Various Artists. *The Complete Motown Singles. Vol. 5, 1965.* Hip-O Select/Motown B0006775–02 (2006).

Various Artists. *The Complete Motown Singles. Vol. 6, 1966.* Hip-O Select/Motown B0007872–02 (2006).

Various Artists. *The Complete Motown Singles. Vol. 7, 1967.* Hip-O Select/Motown B0008993–02 (2007).

Various Artists. *The Complete Motown Singles. Vol. 8, 1968.* Hip-O Select/Motown B0009708–02 (2007).

Various Artists. *The Complete Motown Singles. Vol. 9, 1969.* Hip-O Select/Motown B0010270–02 (2008).

Various Artists. *The Complete Motown Singles. Vol. 10, 1970.* Hip-O Select/Motown B0011056–02 (2008).

Various Artists. *The Complete Motown Singles. Vol. 11a, 1971.* Hip-O Select/Motown B0011579–02 (2008).

Various Artists. *The Complete Motown Singles. Vol. 11b, 1971.* Hip-O Select/Motown B0012227–02 (2009).

Various Artists. *The Complete Motown Singles. Vol. 12a, 1972.* Hip-O Select/Motown B0012935–02 (2013).

Various Artists. *The Complete Motown Singles. Vol. 12b, 1972.* Hip-O Select/Motown B0019213–02 (2013).

Various Artists. *Cooley High.* Motown M7–840R2 (1975).

Various Artists. *Guys and Dolls: Original Cast Album.* Motown M6–876S1 (1976).

Various Artists. *In Loving Memory.* Motown MT-642 (1968).

Various Artists. *Motor City Reggae.* Trojan TJETD 309 (2006).

Various Artists. *Motortown Revue in Paris.* Tamla TM-264 (1965).

Various Artists. *Motown around the World.* Hop-O-Select B0013187–02 (2010).

Various Artists. *Motown Sings Motown Treasures.* Hip-O Select B0003619–02 (2005).

Various Artists. *The Motown Story: The First Decade.* Motown 727–731 (1971).

Various Artists. *Music from the Original Motion Picture: "Loving Couples."* Motown M8–949M1 (1980).

Various Artists. *Music from the Original Motion Picture Soundtrack: "The Big Chill."* Motown 6062ML (1983).

Various Artists. *Music from the Original Motion Picture Soundtrack: "A Fine Mess."* Motown 6180ML (1986).

Various Artists. *Music from the Original Motion Picture Soundtrack: "It's My Turn."* Motown M8–947M1 (1980).

Various Artists. *Nothing but a Man.* Motown MT-630 (1965).

Various Artists. *Original Motion Picture Soundtrack: "Christine."* Motown 6086ML (1983).

Various Artists. *Original Motion Picture Soundtrack: "The Flamingo Kid."* Motown 6131ML (1984).

Various Artists. *Original Motion Picture Soundtrack: "Get Crazy."* Morocco 6065CL (1983).

Various Artists. *Original Motion Picture Soundtrack: Standing in the Shadows of Motown* (Deluxe Edition). Hip-O 440-066-365 (2004).

Various Artists. *Original Motion Picture Soundtrack: "White Nights."* Atlantic 81273 (1985).

Various Artists. *Original Motion Picture Soundtrack: "The Wiz."* MCA MCA2–14000 (1978).

Various Artists. *Original Motion Picture Soundtrack of "Thank God It's Friday."* Casablanca NBLP-7099 (1978).

Various Artists. *"Pippin": Original Cast Recording.* Motown M-760L (1972).

Various Artists. *"Quicksilver": Original Motion Picture Soundtrack.* Atlantic 81631 (1986).

Various Artists. *Save the Children.* Motown M-800R2 (1973).

Various Artists. *Souvenir Album: 1971 Sterling Ball Benefit.* Motown M-739 (1971).

Various Artists. *Stay in School, Don't Be a Dropout.* Stax A-11 (1967).

Verne, Larry. "Mr. Custer." Era 3042 (1960).

Walker, Jr., and the All Stars. "Do the Boomerang." Soul 35012 (1965).

Walker, Jr., and the All Stars. "(I'm a) Road Runner." Soul 35015 (1965).

Walker, Jr., and the All Stars. *Road Runner.* Soul SS-703 (1966).

Walker, Jr., and the All Stars. "Shake and Fingerpop." Soul 35013 (1965).

Walker, Jr., and the All Stars. "Shotgun." Soul 30558 (1965).

Walker, Jr., and the All Stars. *Shotgun.* Soul SS-701 (1965).

Walker, Jr., and the All Stars. *Soul Session.* Soul SS-702 (1966).

Ward, Billy, and His Dominoes. "Rags to Riches." King 1280 (1953).

Ward, Billy, and His Dominoes. "You Can't Keep a Good Man Down." Federal 12139 (1953).

Ward, Singin' Sammy. "Big Joe Moe." Tamla 54057 (1962).

Ward, Singin' Sammy. "Who's the Fool." Tamla 54030 (1961).

Warwick, Dionne. "Reach out for Me." Scepter 1285 (1964).

Warwick, Dionne. "This Empty Place" b/w "Wishin' and Hopin'." Scepter 1247 (1963).

Washington, Dinah. "Long John Blues." Mercury 8148 (1949).

Wells, Kitty. "Release Me." Decca 29023 (1954).

Wells, Mary. "Bye Bye Baby." Motown 1003 (1960).

Wells, Mary. "I Don't Want to Take a Chance." Motown 1011 (1961).

Wells, Mary. "Laughing Boy." Motown 1039 (1963).

Wells, Mary. "My Guy." Motown 1056 (1964).

Wells, Mary. "The One Who Really Loves You." Motown 1024 (1962).

Wells, Mary. "Strange Love." Motown 1016 (1961).

Wells, Mary. "Two Lovers." Motown 1035 (1962).

Wells, Mary. "You Beat Me to the Punch." Motown 1032 (1962).

Wells, Mary. "You Lost the Sweetest Boy" b/w "What's Easy for Two Is So Hard for One." Motown 1048 (1963).

Wells, Mary. "Your Old Stand By." Motown 1042 (1963).

Wilde, Kim. "You Keep Me Hangin' On." MCA 53024 (1987).

Williams, Andre. "Bacon Fat." Fortune 831 (1956).

Williams, Maurice, and the Zodiacs. "Stay." Herald 552 (1960).

Williams, Paul. "The Huckle-Buck." Savoy 683 (1949).

Willis, Chuck. "C. C. Rider." Atlantic 130 (1957).

Willis, Chuck. "What Am I Living For." Atlantic 1179 (1958).

Wills, Johnnie Lee. "Rag Mop." Bullet 696 (1949).

Wilson, Frank. "Do I Love You (Indeed I Do)." Soul 35019 (1965).

Wilson, Jackie. "I'll Be Satisfied." Brunswick 55136 (1958).

Wilson, Jackie. "I'm Wanderin'." Brunswick 55070 (1958).

Wilson, Jackie. "Let George Do It." [promotional] (1958).

Wilson, Jackie. "Lonely Teardrops." Brunswick 55015 (1958).

Wilson, Jackie. "Night" b/w "Doggin' Around." Brunswick 55166 (1960).

Wilson, Jackie. "Reet Petite (The Finest Girl You Ever Want to Meet)." Brunswick 55024 (1958).

Wilson, Jackie. "That's Why (I Love You So)." Brunswick 55121 (1959).

Wilson, Jackie. "To Be Loved." Brunswick 55052 (1958).

Wilson, Jackie. "We Have Love." Brunswick 55086 (1958).

Wilson, Jackie. "(Your Love Keeps Lifting Me) Higher and Higher." Brunswick 55336 (1967).

Winehouse, Amy. *Back to Black*. Universal Republic B0008428–02 (2006).

Womack, Bobby. *Across 110th Street*. United Artists UAS-5225 (1972).

Wonder, Little Stevie. "Castles in the Sand." Tamla 54090 (1964).

Wonder, Little Stevie. "Contract on Love." Tamla 54074 (1962).

Wonder, Little Stevie. "Fingertips." Tamla 54080 (1963).

Wonder, Little Stevie. "I Call It Pretty Music but the Old People Call It the Blues." Tamla 54061 (1961).

Wonder, Little Stevie. *The Jazz Soul of Little Stevie*. Tamla TM-233.

Wonder, Little Stevie. "Little Water Boy." Tamla 54070 (1962).

Wonder, Little Stevie. *Tribute to Uncle Ray*. Tamla TM-232 (1963).

Wonder, Little Stevie. *The 12 Year Old Genius*. Tamla TM-240 (1963).

Wonder, Little Stevie. "Workout Stevie, Workout." Tamla 54086 (1963).

Wonder, Stevie. "For Once in My Life." Tamla 54174 (1968).

Wonder, Stevie. *Fulfillingness' First Finale*. Tamla 332 (1974).

Wonder, Stevie. "Happy Street." Tamla 54103 (1964).

Wonder, Stevie. "Hey Harmonica Man." Tamla 54096 (1964).

Wonder, Stevie. "Higher Ground." Tamla 54235 (1973).

Wonder, Stevie. "High Heel Sneakers" b/w "Funny How Time Slips Away." Tamla 54119 (1965).

Wonder, Stevie. "High Heel Sneakers" b/w "Music Talk." Tamla 54119 (1965).

Wonder, Stevie. "I Just Called to Say I Love You." Motown 1745MF (1984).

Wonder, Stevie. *Innervisions.* Tamla T-326L (1973).

Wonder, Stevie. "I Was Made to Love Her." Tamla 54151 (1967).

Wonder, Stevie. "I Wish." Tamla 54274 (1976).

Wonder, Stevie. *Journey through the Secret Life of Plants.* Tamla T13–371C2 (1979).

Wonder, Stevie. "Kiss Me Baby." Tamla 54114 (1965).

Wonder, Stevie. "Master Blaster (Jammin')." Tamla 54317 (1980).

Wonder, Stevie. "Nothing's Too Good for My Baby." Tamla 54130 (1966).

Wonder, Stevie. "Part-Time Lover." Tamla 1808TF (1985).

Wonder, Stevie. *Selections from the Original Motion Picture Soundtrack " The Woman In Red."* Motown 6108ML (1984).

Wonder, Stevie. "Signed, Sealed, Delivered I'm Yours." Tamla 54196 (1970).

Wonder, Stevie. "Sir Duke." Tamla 54281F (1977).

Wonder, Stevie. *Songs in the Key of Life.* Tamla T13–340C2 (1976).

Wonder. Stevie. "Superstition." Tamla 54226F (1972).

Wonder, Stevie. *Talking Book.* Tamla T-319L (1972).

Wonder, Stevie. "That Girl." Tamla 1602TF (1981).

Wonder, Stevie. "Uptight (Everything's Alright)." Tamla 54124 (1965).

Wonder, Stevie. "You Are the Sunshine of My Life." Tamla 54232F (1973).

Wonder, Stevie." You Haven't Done Nothin'." Tamla 54252 (1974).

Woods, Mickey. "Poor Sam Jones" b/w "They Rode through the Valley." Tamla 54039 (1961).

Wylie, Richard and His Band. "Money (That's What I Want)." Motown 1009 (1961).

Young Rascals. "Good Lovin.'" Atlantic 2321 (1966).

VII. International Recordings (Not Included in Appendix 1)

ABC. "When Smokey Sings." Neutron 111 (1987). UK.

Beat. "Tears of a Clown." 2 Tone 6 (1979). UK.

Beatles. *Rubber Soul.* Parlophone PMC-1267 (1965). UK.

Beatles. *With the Beatles.* Parlophone PMC-1206 (1963). UK.

Bragg, Billy. "Levi Stubbs' Tears." Go! 12 (1986). UK.

Clash. "Hitsville U.K." CBS 9480 (1981). UK.

Collins, Phil. "You Can't Hurry Love." Virgin 531 (1982). UK.

Contours. "Just a Little Misunderstanding." Tamla Motown 723 (1970). UK.

Elgins. "Heaven Must Have Sent You." Tamla Motown 771 (1971). UK.

Elgins. "Heaven Must Have Sent You." Nightmare MARE 92 (1989). UK.

Elgins. "Put Yourself in My Place." Tamla Motown 787 (1971). UK.

Flying Lizards. "Money." Virgin 276 (1979). UK.

Fourmost. "Hello Little Girl." Parlophone 5056 (1963). UK.

Fourmost. "I'm in Love." Parlophone 5078 (1963). UK.

Four Tops. "Reach Out I'll Be There." Tamla Motown 579 (1966). UK.

Gaye, Frankie, and Kim Weston. "It Takes Two." Nightmare 110 (1989). UK.

Gaye, Marvin. *How Sweet It Is to Be Loved by You.* Tamla Motown TML-11004 (1965). UK.

Gaye, Marvin. "I Heard It through the Grapevine." Tamla Motown 40701 (1986). UK.

Gaye, Marvin. "Sympatica" b/w "Wie schön das ist (How Sweet It Is)." CBS 1841 (1965). Germany.

Harrison, George. "True Love" b/w "Pure Smokey." Dark Horse 16896 (1977). UK.

Holland, Eddie. "Jamie." Fontana 387 (1962). UK.

Isley Brothers. "I Guess I'll Always Love You." Tamla Motown 683 (1969). UK.

Isley Brothers. "This Old Heart of Mine (Is Weak for You)." Tamla-Motown 555 (1966). UK.

Jackson, Chuck. "All over the World." Debut 3119 (1991). UK.

Jam. "Town Called Malice." Polydor 400 (1982). UK.

Johnson, Marv. "Come to Me." London 1522 (1959). Australia.

Johnson, Marv. "Come to Me." London 8856 (1959). UK.

Marly, Bob, and the Wailers. "Ska-Jerk." Studio 1 [no cat. no.] (1965). Jamaica.

Martha and the Vandellas. "Dancing in the Street." Stateside 345 (1964). UK.

Martha and the Vandellas. "Heat Wave." Stateside 228 (1963). UK.

Martha and the Vandellas. *Heat Wave*. Tamla-Motown TML-11005 (1964). UK.

Martha and the Vandellas. "Nowhere to Run" Tamla-Motown 502 (1965). UK.

Marvelettes. *The Marvelettes*. Tamla-Motown STML-11052. UK.

Marvelettes. "Please Mr. Postman." Fontana 355 (1961). Ireland.

Marvelettes. "Please Mr. Postman." Fontana 267–185 (1961). Netherlands.

Marvelettes. "Please Mr. Postman." Fontana 355 (1961). UK.

Marvelettes. "Please Mr. Postman." Tamla 7003 (1961). Canada.

Marvelettes. "Please Mr. Postman." Top Rank 182 (1962). Australia.

Marvelettes. "Twistin' Postman." Fontana 386 (1962). UK.

Miracles, "Ain't It Baby." London-American 9366 (1961). UK.

Miracles. "Ain't It Baby." Reo 8566 (1961). Canada.

Miracles. *I Like It Like That*. Tamla-Motown TML-11003 (1964). UK.

Miracles. "Love Machine." Motorcity 52 (1990). UK.

Miracles. "Ooo Baby Baby." Tamla-Motown 503 (1965). UK.

Miracles. "Shop Around." Reo 8352 (1960). Canada.

Miracles. "Shop Around." London 20–381 (1961). Germany.

Miracles. "Shop Around." London-American 9276 (1961). UK.

Miracles. "Tracks of My Tears." Tamla-Motown 745 (1970). UK.

Miracles. "What's So Good about Good Bye." Fontana 384 (1962). UK.

Miracles. "You Really Got a Hold on Me." Oriole-American 1795 (1963). UK.

Motorcity All-Stars. "I Can't Help Myself." Motorcity 6 (1989).

Nero, Francis. "Footsteps Following Me." Motorcity 24 (1990). UK.

Poole, Brian, and the Tremeloes. "I Can Dance." Decca 11771 (1963). UK.

Redding, Otis. "My Girl." Atlantic 4050 (1965). UK.

Robinson, Smokey, and the Miracles. "The Tears of a Clown." Tamla-Motown 745 (1970). UK.

Ross, Diana. "I'm Still Waiting." Tamla-Motown 781 (1971). UK.

Ruffin, Jimmy. "What Becomes of the Brokenhearted." Tamla-Motown 577 (1966). UK.

Ruffin, Jimmy. "What Becomes of the Brokenhearted." Tamla-Motown 911 (1974). UK.

Seaton, H., and the Gaylads. "Stop Making Love." Coxsone 47 (1966). Jamaica.

Smiths. "This Charming Man." Rough Trade 136 (1983). UK.

Soft Cell. "Tainted Love/Where Did Our Love Go." Some Bizarre Label 212 (1981). UK.

Spandau Ballet. "True." Reformation 1 (1983).

Starr, Edwin. "War." Tamla-Motown 754 (1970). UK.

Stewart, Rod. *Every Picture Tells a Story.* Mercury 6336–548 (1971). UK.

Stewart, Rod. "The Motown Song." Warner Brothers 0030 (1991). UK.

Stewart, Rod. *Sing It Again Rod!* Mercury 6499–484 (1972). UK.

Stewart, Rod. "This Old Heart of Mine." Riva 1 (1975). UK.

Stewart, Rod. "Twisting the Night Away." Geffen RODS 1 (1987). UK.

Stewart, Rod, and Ronald Isley. "This Old Heart of Mine." Warner Brothers 2686 (1989). UK.

Stewart, Rod, and Tina Turner. "It Takes Two." Warner Brothers ROD 1 (1990). UK.

Strong, Barrett. "Money (That's What I Want)." London-American 9088 (1960). UK.

Supremes. "Baby, Baby, wo is unsere Liebe." CBS 1719 (1965). Germany.

Supremes. "Baby Love." Stateside 350 (1964). UK.

Supremes. "Jonny und Joe." CBS 1839 (1965). Germany.

Supremes. "Stop! In the Name of Love." Tamla-Motown 501 (1965). UK.

Supremes. "Where Did Our Love Go." Stateside 327 (1964). UK.

Supremes. *With Love (From Us to You).* Tamla Motown TML-11002 (1965). UK.

Temptations. "It's Growing." Tamla-Motown 504 (1965). UK.

Temptations. "Mein Girl." CBS 1840 (1965). Germany.

Undisputed Truth. "Law of the Land." Motorcity 53 (1991).

Van Dyke, Earl, and the Soul Brothers. "All for You." Tamla-Motown 506 (1965). UK.

Various Artists. *A Cellarfull of Motown,* Vol. 2. Universal 982-929-7 (2005). UK.

Various Artists. *A Collection of 16 Tamla Big Hits.* Tamla-Motown TML-11001 (1965). UK.

Various Artists. "Greetings to Tamla Motown Appreciation Society." [promotional] (1965). UK.

Various Artists. *R&B Chartmakers.* Stateside SE-1009 (1963). UK.

Velvelettes. "Needle in a Haystack." Nightmare 28 (1987). UK.

Wells, Mary. "Bye Bye Baby." Reo 8540 (1961). Canada.

Wells, Mary. "My Guy." Stateside 288 (1964). UK.

Weston, Kim. "Helpless." Nightmare 55 (1988). UK.

Wilson, Delroy. "You Got to Change Your Ways." Coxsone [no cat. no.]. Jamaica.

Wilson, Delroy. "You Got to Change Your Ways." Island 3033 (1967). UK.

Wonder, Stevie. "Kiss Me Baby." Tamla-Motown 505 (1965). UK.

Wonder, Stevie. "Never Had a Dream Come True." Tamla-Motown 54191 (1970). Jamaica.

Wonder, Stevie. "Se tu ragazza mi." Tamla-Motown 8043 (1968). Italy.

VIII. Podcasts, Radio, and Online Resources

Abbey, John. Interview by David Nathan. March 10, 2012. http://www.soulmusic. com/index.asp?S=62&T=65&ART=2423.

"Artist Spotlight: Bob Olhsson, Audio Mastery, Nashville." http://www.exponentialaudio.com/artists-new/2015/8/19/artist-spotlight-bob-olhsson.

Croasdell, Ady. "A Personal History of Northern Soul." April 18, 2014. *Soul Source*, http://www.soul-source.co.uk/_/words/a-personal-history-of-northern-soul-by-ady-croasdell-r2895.

Desai, Manan, Rob Crozier, Brad Norman, and Michael Walle. "Grown from the Grapevine: Race, Motown and the California Raisins." https://www.youtube. com/watch?v=Dd1TohCK5nk.

Erickson, Jon. "Carol Kaye: Session Bassist Extraordinaire." *Tape-Op*, http://www. tapeop.com/interviews/45/carol-kaye.

Gordon, Terry. *Rockin' Country Style*. http://rcs-discography.com/rcs/index. html.

"How Were Motown's Studio Sessions Arranged?" Soulful Detroit Forum. http:// faac.us/adf/messages/28522/146214.html?1107822773.

Hughes, Keith. *Don't Forget the Motor City*. www.dftmc.info.

Kaye, Carol. "Electric Bass Hits." http://www.carolkaye.com/www/library/ basshits.htm.

Kaye, Carol. Interview on *The Bob Edwards Show*. Taped March 9, 2009, aired on XM Radio March 11, 2009, and on National Public Radio March 28, 2009.

Library of Congress. "Paul Simon to be Awarded First Annual Gershwin Prize for Popular Song by Library of Congress." Press release. March 1, 2007. http:// www.loc.gov/today/pr/2007/07-010.html.

Maycock, James. *The Motown Invasion*. BBC Four. Originally aired February 20, 2009.

McLean, Mike. "The Golden World Story: Studio Appraisal." Soulfuldetroit.com. http://soulfuldetroit.com/web07-golden%20world/golden%20world%20 story/49-gw-mike-mclean.htm.

"Mike McLean 4." Soulful Detroit Forum. http://soulfuldetroit.com/archives/1/654.html?1021570291.

"Mike McLean 5." Soulful Detroit Forum. http://soulfuldetroit.com/archives/1/672.html?1029867099.

Motown 50 Podcast Series. Episode 2. "Berry Gordy—A Tour of Hitsville U.S.A., May 1963." http://classic.motown.com/2009/01/09/motown-50-podcast-series. Accessed November 20, 2013. (Page no longer available.)

Motown 50 Podcast Series. Episode 16. "Motown Built to Last." http://classic. motown.com/news.aspx?bid=78 (Page no longer available.)

"Motown Invasion." BBC Radio 2. April 5, 2005.

Riser, Paul. "Motown's Chief Assembly-Line Operator Talks Snakepits, String Arrangements, and R. Kelly," Red Bull Music Academy. http://www.redbullmusicacademy.com/lectures/paul_riser_funk_brothers_gonna_work_it_out.

Slutsky, Allan. "Who Played 'I Was Made to Love Her'? The Carol Kaye–James Jamerson Enigma." http://bassland.net/jamerson.html.

"Songs That Best Exemplify 'The Motown Sound.'" Soulful Detroit Forum.

http://soulfuldetroit.com/showthread.php?10317-Songs-That-Best-Exemplify-quot-The-Motown-Sound-quot-!.

"Sounds Like Motown but Wasn't." Soulful Detroit Forum. http://soulfuldetroit.com/showthread.php?10433-Sounds-like-Motown-but-wasn-t.

Stern, Shoshana. "Is Genericide a Matter of Fact or of Merit?" March 26, 2008. *Boston College Intellectual Property & Technology Forum.* http://bciptf.org/wp-content/uploads/2011/07/20-IS-GENERICIDE-A-MATTER-OF-FACT-OR-OF-MERIT.pdf.

Universal Music Enterprises and State Farm. "Universal Music Enterprises and State Farm Join in Unique Effort to Promote Popular TV Commercial and the Song 'I'll Be There.'" Press release. June 18, 2009. http://ume.edgeboss.net/download/ume/motown/statefarm.pdf.

"White in America—The Children." *Daily Show with Jon Stewart.* Produced by Ian Berger, edited by Mark Paone. Aired May 7, 2009. http://www.thedailyshow.com/watch/thu-may-7-2009/white-in-america—the-children.

Wikane, Christian John. "Amy Winehouse: *Back to Black.*" *PopMatters.* March 11, 2007. http://www.popmatters.com/pm/review/11293/amy-winehouse-back-to-black.

IX. Selected Film and Television Releases

Badham, John, dir. *The Bingo Long Traveling All-Stars & Motor Kings.* Universal City, CA: Universal Studios, 2001. DVD.

Binder, Steve, dir. *T.A.M.I. Show,* collector's ed. Los Angeles, CA: Shout! Factory, 2009. DVD.

The California Raisins Collection. Hen's Tooth Video, 1990. DVD.

Campus, Michael, dir. *The Mack.* Los Angeles, CA: New Line Home Entertainment, 2002. DVD.

Condon, Bill, dir. *Dreamgirls.* Sam O'Steen, dir. *Sparkle.* Double feature. Burbank, CA: Warner Home Video, 2013. DVD.

Dixon, Ivan, dir. *Trouble Man.* Beverly Hills, CA: Twentieth Century Fox Home Entertainment, 2005. DVD.

Furie, Sidney J., dir. *Lady Sings the Blues,* special collector's ed. Hollywood, CA: Paramount Pictures, 2005. DVD.

Justman, Paul, dir. *Standing in the Shadows of Motown.* Santa Monica, CA: Artisan Home Entertainment, 2003. DVD.

Kagan, Jeremy Paul, dir. *Scott Joplin.* Universal City, CA: Universal Studios, 2000. Videocassette (VHS), 96 min.

Kasdan, Lawrence, dir. *The Big Chill.* Culver City, CA. Columbia Tristar Home Entertainment, 1998.

Klane, Robert, dir. *Thank God It's Friday.* Culver City, CA: Sony Pictures Home Entertainment, 2006. DVD.

Lumet, Sidney, dir. *The Wiz.* Universal City, CA: Universal Studios Home Entertainment, 2010.

Mahogany. Hollywood, CA: Paramount Pictures, 2005. DVD.

Marvin Gaye: The Real Thing In Performance 1964–1981. Santa Monica, CA: Universal Music Enterprises, 2006. DVD.

Motown Gold: From The Ed Sullivan Show. Santa Monica, CA: Universal Music Enterprises, 2011. DVD.

Motown: The DVD: Definitive Performances. Toronto, Ontario: Universal Music Canada, 2009. DVD.

Parks, Gordon, dir. *Shaft.* Burbank, CA: Warner Home Video, 2000. DVD.

Parks, Gordon, dir. *Superfly.* Burbank, CA: Warner Home Video, 2004. DVD.

Roemer, Michael, dir. *Nothing But a Man*, 40th anniversary special ed. New York, NY: New Video Group. 2004. DVD.

Schultz, Michael, dir. *Berry Gordy's the Last Dragon.* Culver City, CA: Sony Pictures Home Entertainment, 2005. DVD.

Schultz, Michael, dir. *Cooley High.* Santa Monica, CA: MGM Home Entertainment, 2001. DVD.

Sears, Fred F., dir. *Rock Around the Clock.* Culver City, CA: Sony Pictures Home Entertainment, 2006. DVD.

Smokey Robinson and the Miracles: Definitive Performances 1963–1987. Santa Monica, CA: Universal Music Enterprises, 2006. DVD.

The Supremes Reflections: The Definitive Performances 1964–1969. Santa Monica, CA: Universal Music Enterprises, 2006. DVD.

The Temptations: Get Ready: Definitive Performances 1965–1972. Santa Monica, CA: Universal Music Enterprises, 2006. DVD.

Townsend, Robert, dir. *The Five Heartbeats.* Beverly Hills, CA: Twentieth Century Fox Home Entertainment, 2013. DVD.

Index

Page numbers in italics indicate figures.